Preachers, Pastors and Ambassadors

Puritan Wisdom for Today's Church

St Antholin Lectures
2001-2010

The Latimer Trust

Preachers, Pastors, and Ambassadors: Puritan Wisdom for Today's Church edited by Lee Gatiss © The Latimer Trust and St Antholin's Lectureship Charity, October 2011

ISBN 978-1-906327-02-6

Published by The Latimer Trust, October 2011

Cover photograph: © dundanim – fotolia.com
Scripture quotations marked (NIV) are from THE HOLY BIBLE, NEW INTERNATIONAL VERSION®, NIV® Copyright © 1973, 1978, 1984, 2011 by Biblica, Inc.™ Used by permission. All rights reserved worldwide.

The Latimer Trust (formerly Latimer House, Oxford) is a conservative Evangelical research organisation within the Church of England, whose main aim is to promote the history and theology of Anglicanism as understood by those in the Reformed tradition. Interested readers are welcome to consult its website for further details of its many activities.

The Latimer Trust
PO Box 26685, London N14 4XQ UK
Registered Charity: 1084337
Company Number: 4104465
Web: www.latimertrust.org
E-mail: administrator@latimertrust.org

Views expressed in works published by The Latimer Trust are those of the authors and do not necessarily represent the official position of The Latimer Trust.

Contents

Acknowledgements 1

Foreword.. 2

The Grand Nursery of Puritanism: St. Antholin's as a Strategic Centre for Gospel Ministry
by Lee Gatiss 3

Word and Spirit: The Puritan-Quaker Debate
by Peter Adam...49

Ussher on Bishops: A Reforming Ecclesiology
by Wallace Benn...97

Strangers to Correction: Christian Discipline and the English Reformation
by Peter Ackroyd..123

"Decalogue" Dod and his Seventeenth Century Bestseller
by David Field..149

A Puritan Theology of Preaching
by Chad B Van Dixhoorn..205

'To Bring Men to Heaven by Preaching': John Donne's Evangelistic Sermons
by Peter Adam.. 261

1807-2007: John Newton and the Twenty-first Century
by Tony Baker..293

From Life's First Cry: John Owen on Infant Baptism and Infant Salvation
by Lee Gatiss...325

Evangelical Mission and Anglican Church Order: Charles Simeon Reconsidered
by Andrew Atherstone..367

Re-establishing the Christian Faith – and the Public Theology Deficit
by David Holloway..397

St. Antholin's Lectureship Charity Lectures...................... 427

ST. ANTHOLIN, FROM WATLING STREET

Acknowledgements

In this volume we have collected together the revived, annual St. Antholin's Lectures for 2001-2010. They unpack various aspects of Puritan theology, but particularly on *the word* (e.g. Chad van Dixhoorn on the Puritan theology of preaching and Peter Adam on Donne's evangelistic sermons), *the sacraments* (e.g. John Owen's doctrine of infant baptism), and *church order* (e.g. Peter Ackroyd on church discipline and Wallace Benn on episcopacy). The authors are eminently qualified to write on these subjects as preachers and pastors in the Puritan tradition themselves, and often as recognised scholars of the period. It is a joy that after a decade of circulating in booklet form these lucid and challenging lectures can now be brought together in one place and, we pray, continue to edify and inspire today's church with the wisdom of our forebears.

I would like to express immense gratitude to my scholar-pastor friends Adam Richardson, Marty Cowan, and Andrew Atherstone for graciously commenting on drafts of the introduction, saving it from various infelicities and helping to add colour and clarity that would otherwise be lacking. I am also very grateful to Margaret Hobbs, Janet Burrowes, Alison Brewis and their predecessors at the Latimer Trust who have made huge contributions to this project with the laborious and meticulous work of design, typesetting, and project management.

On behalf of the present Trustees of the St. Antholin's Lectureship Charity Trust (myself, Revd. Dr. Mark E. Burkill, and the Revd. William T. Taylor) it is my happy duty, then, to acknowledge and thank the preachers, pastors, and ambassadors who spent time and energy researching and crafting these lectures, and all those who have helped to bring them into this convenient and useful form.

Soli deo gloria!

Lee Gatiss
Cambridge

Foreword

St. Antholin's Lectureship Charity Lectures

In or about 1560 the parish of St. Antholin, now absorbed into what is the parish of St Mary-le-Bow in Cheapside and St Mary Alderbury, within the Cordwainer's Ward in the City of London, came into the possession of certain estates known as the "Lecturer's Estates." These were, it is believed, purchased with funds collected at or shortly after the date of the Reformation for the endowment of lectures of the Puritanical School of Divinity.

The first mention of the charity was an indenture, dated 24 June 1616, made between Richard Vane of the first part, the churchwardens of the parish of St. Antholin of the second part, and certain parishioners of the said parish of the third part.

Over the centuries the funds were not always used for the stated purpose, and in the first part of the nineteenth century a scheme was drawn up which revivified the lectureship, which was to consist of forty lectures to be given three times a year on the Puritan School of Divinity, the lecturer to receive one guinea per lecture. A further onerous requirement was that the lecturer had to be a beneficed Anglican, living within one mile of the Mansion House in the City of London.

Under such conditions the lectureship fell into disuse a long time ago, and it was not until 1987 that moves were put in hand with the Charity Commissioners to update the scheme. The first lecture under the new scheme was given in 1991.

Trustees: The Reverend W.T. Taylor
The Reverend Dr. M.E. Burkill
The Reverend L. Gatiss

The Grand Nursery of Puritanism: St. Antholin's as a Strategic Centre for Gospel Ministry

Lee Gatiss

Introduction 5
1. The Evil of "Impropriations" 5
2. The Collectors of St. Antholin's 13
3. The Fall of the Feoffees 26
4. Patronage, Stipends, and the Later History of St. Antholin's 39

LEE GATISS read Modern History at New College, Oxford before training for Anglican ministry at Oak Hill Theological College in London. He served a curacy in Northamptonshire before becoming Associate Minister of St. Helen's, Bishopsgate in the City of London in 2004. He holds a ThM in Historical and Systematic Theology from Westminster Theological Seminary in Philadelphia (USA) and his PhD at Cambridge University is on seventeenth century biblical interpretation. He is the Editor of *Theologian* (www.theologian.org.uk), Review Editor of *Churchman*, and Series Editor of the *Reformed Evangelical Anglican Library* as well as author of *The True Profession of the Gospel*.

Introduction

In my introduction to *Pilgrims, Warriors, and Servants*, the compilation of St. Antholin's Lectures for 1991-2000, I outlined something of the history of Puritan lectureships and that of St. Antholin's Church in London specifically.[1] They were established, we saw, to satisfy people's hunger for the word of God. St. Antholin's itself played an early and central role in the growth of preaching lectureships in the sixteenth century and the spread of Puritan theology. Yet during the next century, St. Antholin's also became a strategic centre for gospel ministry in England more generally, and indeed may well stake a claim to the title "the grand nursery of Puritanism."

In this introduction to the St. Antholin's Lectures for 2001-2010, therefore, we will look at the role St. Antholin's played in one particularly important episode in seventeenth century church history, when through bold initiative the Puritans tried to solve a universally recognised but seemingly intractable problem in church politics. We will see how this City church brought together its legal, financial, and ministerial connections as they sought to expand the reach of the gospel in their day. We will examine what they did when the Church of England was under financial pressure and many in the establishment were at the same time trying to force Puritanism out altogether, enforcing on it theologically dubious, avant-garde ideas of conformity. We will finish with a brief glace at the later history of that now demolished church and those famous preachers, shepherds, and ambassadors for Christ who were associated with it.

1. The Evil of "Impropriations"

Robert Crowley (d. 1588) was one of the earliest lecturers at St. Antholin's. He was known for combining a clear Protestant faith with compassion for the poor. In 1550 he published a set of epigrams and poems

---

[1] L. Gatiss, 'To Satisfy the People's Hunger for the Word: St. Antholin's as the Prototype Puritan Lectureship', in L. Gatiss (ed.), *Pilgrims, Warriors, and Servants: Puritan Wisdom for Today's Church*, St Antholin Lectures (1991-2000) (London: Latimer Trust, 2010), pp 3-22.

concerning abuses of various kinds, one of which lamented the misuse of the resources freed by Henry VIII's dissolution of the monasteries.

> As I walked alone
> And mused on thynges,
> That have in my time
> Bene done by great kings,
>
> I bethought me of Abbayes
> that sometyme I sawe,
> which are nowe suppressed
> all by a lawe,
>
> O Lorde (thought I then)
> What occasion was here,
> To provide for learninge
> And make povertye chere?
>
> The landes and the Jewels
> That hereby were hadde,
> Would have found godly prechers
> Which might well have ladde:
>
> The people aright
> That now go astraye,
> And have fedde the poor
> That famishe everye daye.[2]

Sir Francis Bigod (1507-1537), "a lover of evangelical truth,"[3] had argued similarly in 1535 that the tithes from monasteries should be used to provide adequate salaries to preachers.[4] They had been alienated from

---

[2] "Of Abbayes" is the first epigram of thirty-three (sic) in R. Crowley, *One and Thyrtye Epigrammes wherein are bryefly touched so many abuses, that maye and ought to be put away* (London, 1550).

[3] J. Bale, *Index Britanniae Scriptorum*, ed. R. L. Poole and M. Bateson (London: D.S. Brewer, 1902), p 72.

[4] F. Bigod, *A Treatise Concernynge Impropriations of Benefices* (London, 1535). The Council of Constance (1414-1418) and the Council of Trent (1545-1563) both recommended some steps towards the reversal of impropriations, though they were never followed through in practice according to T. Ryves, *The Poore Vicars Plea: Declaring, That a Competencie of Meanes is Due to Them out of the Tithes of their Severall Parishes, Notwithstanding the Impropriations* (London, 1620), pp 3-4. See also W. Kennett, *The Case of Impropriations, and of the Augmentation of Vicarages and Other Insufficient Cures, Stated by History and Law... With an Appendix of Records and Memorials Relating to that Subject* (London, 1704), pp 91-94.

the parishes in order to pay monks to pray for their dead patrons, "to the starving of the peoples souls" and the impoverishment of local church ministry.[5] Henry VIII's wife Anne Boleyn, it will be recalled, had fallen out with his chief minister Thomas Cromwell over this same issue in 1536. She wished to use the money to further the cause of reform rather than simply fill the king's coffers, and to endow various charitable enterprises.[6] In the mind of Puritans like Crowley, it was an obvious solution to suppress the old abbeys and use the cash thus released to "make poverty cheer" and to train "godly preachers" who would lead the people away from the superstitious doctrines promoted by the medieval system the monasteries represented. The sad conclusion to Crowley's epigram, however, is that "the people wyll not see but delyte to be blynde," and therefore "they are not worthy good preachars to have." Such preachers would, therefore, continue to be in need of decent provision even as believers would continue to crave the true spiritual sustenance that only a godly and learned ministry could bring.

The rights and resources of the dissolved monasteries were instead bestowed on local landowners and lords in return for their loyalty to the Tudor regime. As well as vast amounts of property, these often included the advowson of a local church (the ancient right of patronage which enabled the holder to present their chosen candidate to the bishop for his blessing and installation as Rector of the parish) and the right to the tithes from a local area which were intended to pay the minister's stipend. These were "impropriated" by their new lay owners.[7] By means of "fee-farming," these patrons could reserve a certain portion of the income from a benefice for their own personal use, and thus

---

[5] See W. Prynne, *The Remainder, or Second Part of a Gospel Plea (Interwoven with a Rational and Legal) for the Lawfulness & Continuance of the Antient Setled Maintenance and Tithes of the Ministers of the Gospel* (London, 1659), p 74.

[6] This is how it had worked out in other countries where the Reformation had taken hold, according to J. Selden, *The Historie of Tithes that is, the Practice of Payment of them, the Positive Laws Made for them, the Opinions Touching the Right of them* (London, 1618), p 486.

[7] J. Pilkington, *Aggeus and Abdias Prophetes* (London, 1562), p 55 says the name impropriations comes from the fact that "improperly thei be taken away and properly belong to the parishes." Impropriation was indeed later contrasted with the proper "appropriation" of the advowson by ecclesiastical authorities. J. Rainolds, *A Sermon upon Part of the Prophesie of Obadiah Touching the Destruction, as of Idumaeans, so of Papists* (London?, 1584), p 27 implies that the legal term in his day was "appropriation" but they were "named commonly, impropriations."

these resources were alienated from ecclesiastical use or made to serve purely individual interests. The historian and legal scholar John Selden (1584–1654) claimed this system had existed in France for a long time but only began in England under Henry VIII.[8] Richard Hooker lamented the swarms of "conscienceless and wicked Patrons" in the Church of England and estimated that their impropriations robbed the church of income totalling around £126,000 every year (a colossal sum). Yet although this was "extream sacrilegious injustice," he said, "we rest contentedly, and quietly without it, till it shall please God to touch the hearts of men, of their own voluntary accord to restore it to Him again."[9]

Needless to say, this was often the cause of great controversy, and clearly it was not just Puritans like Robert Crowley who lamented such a situation. The Reformer Hugh Latimer complained to King Edward VI that the devil had for seven hundred years conspired against preaching of the word of God, with "unpreaching prelates," with persecution, and "with impropriations," by means of which "he hath turned preaching into private masses."[10] In another sermon he also mentions a "great market-town" which raised tithes of fifty pounds per year, and yet the vicar was given only a small portion of this so that, "he is not able to buy him books, nor give his neighbour drink; all the great gain goeth another way."[11] Archbishop of York, Edwin Sandys (1519-1588) also complained during Elizabeth I's reign that, "Rome hath robbed Christ of his honour; and, by impropriations, given his

---

[8] J. Selden, *Table-Talk, being Discourses of John Seldon, Esq or His Sense of Various Matters of Weight and High Consequence, Relating Especially to Religion and State*, 2nd edn. (London, 1696), p 171.

[9] R. Hooker, *The Works of Mr. Richard Hooker... in Eight Books of Ecclesiastical Polity* (London, 1666), p 439, 445 near the end of Book VII section xxiv.

[10] G. E. Corrie (ed.), *Sermons by Hugh Latimer: Volume 1* (Cambridge: Cambridge University Press, 1844), pp. 202-203. The reference to seven hundred years is perhaps explained by the fact that it was Pope Adrian I (700-795) who first granted impropriations to the monasteries, according to T. Becon, *The Reliques of Rome: Contayning All Such Matters of Religion, as Have in Times Past Bene Brought into the Church by the Pope and his Adherentes* (London, 1563), Fol. 42-43 who claims this Pope, "moste unjustly and tyrantlike toke away [tenths and fruits] from the true owners, and gave them to the Cloysterers" whereas previously such resources would be given directly by the people to "their owne pastors and preachers." This medieval development is dated a little later by G. Carleton, *Tithes Examined and Proved to bee Due to the Clergie by a Divine Right* (London, 1606), pp 33-35.

[11] Corrie (ed.), *Sermons by Hugh Latimer: Volume 1*, pp 101-102.

patrimony to idle fat monks to feed upon. We have restored Christ to his honour and dignity: but we still hold from him his lands and living... Shall idle service be preferred to the true service of God? Shall false prophets be better regarded and rewarded than true preachers?" If this continued, he said, then the land was justly condemned for loving darkness when light had come into the world. "The gospel hath evil luck," he added, "it is never preached, but the patrimony thereof is pinched."[12] This was not an easy thing to preach either; Roman Catholic Queen Mary had promised to restore all the crown's tithes and impropriations, to augment small livings,[13] and better support the clergy but the Elizabethan government had immediately reversed this and taken back the income for the impoverished crown in 1559.[14]

Despite the widespread acknowledgement that this situation was lamentable, nothing was done by successive governments to put it straight. Some suggested radical reform – that bishops, deans, and chapters of Cathedrals should be abolished and the money used to finance a preaching ministry, schools, and poor relief. These proposals from the first *Admonition to Parliament* of 1572, however, did not attract serious support until the Long Parliament in the 1640s.[15] During a debate in the House of Lords in November 1601, Sir George Moore made it clear that "many Souls do not only languish but perish everlastingly for want of Spiritual Food," while Dr. James claimed the reason for this was that "in *England* there are above eight thousand eight hundred and odd Parish Churches, six hundred of which do but

---

[12] J. Ayre (ed.), *The Sermons of Edwin Sandys, Archbishop of York* (Cambridge: Cambridge University Press, 1841), p 45.

[13] Kennett, *Case of Impropriations*, pp 139-152.

[14] C. Hill, *Economic Problems of the Church: From Archbishop Whitgift to The Long Parliament* (Oxford: Clarendon Press, 1963), p. 245. Roman Catholic writers did not fail to make use of this fact; see P. Sarpi, *The Papacy of Paul the Fourth, or, The Restitution of Abby Lands and Impropriations an Indispensable Condition of Reconciliation to the Infallible See* (London, 1673), p 31. P. Heylyn, *Ecclesia Restaurata, or, The History of the Reformation of the Church of England* (London, 1660), p 54 says of Mary's promise, "This was well mov'd, and serv'd to entertain the time; but I find nothing in pursuance of it," i.e. it did not actually happen in practice. Cf. p 120.

[15] See J. Fielde, *An Admonition to the Parliament* (Hemel Hempstead?, 1572). Hill, *Economic Problems*, p 248.

afford competent living for a Minister."[16] The Millenary Petition of 1603 brought the problem to the attention of James I, and asked for the redirection of funds towards impoverished incumbents.[17] Francis Bacon wrote at this time that everyone saw the necessity for reform, but those who could change things were also those who benefited financially from the *status quo*, and so it was impossible.[18] It was, as they say, like asking turkeys to vote for Christmas.

In 1624 Henry Burton, Rector of St. Matthew's on Friday Street, a stone's throw away from St. Antholin's, complained that "by reason of the Impropriations, the Vicarages in many places, and in the properest Market townes, are so simple, that no man can live upon them, and therefore no man will take them."[19] Charles I was encouraged by Parliament at his accession a year later, "to enlarge the Word of God throughout all the parts of your Majesties Dominions, as being the most powerful means for planting of true Religion and rooting out of the contrary." In his reply, "he recommendeth to the House of Parliament, that care may be taken and provision made, That every Parish shall allow a competent maintenance for an able Minister; And that the Owners of Parsonages Impropriate would allow to the Vicars, Curates and Ministers in Villages and places belonging to their Parsonage, sufficient Stipend and Allowance for Preaching Ministers."[20] Yet although one or two proprietors voluntarily moved in this direction,[21] this was merely royal advice and nothing was accomplished immediately to put this vague recommendation on a more secure footing.

---

[16] S. D'Ewes, *The Journals of All the Parliaments During the Reign of Queen Elizabeth* (London, 1682), p 640.

[17] See T. Fuller, *The Church-History of Britain from the Birth of Jesus Christ until the year M.DC.XLVIII* (London, 1655), X.22.

[18] F. Bacon, *Certaine Considerations Touching the Better Pacification, and Edification of the Church of England* (London, 1604), F2-F3.

[19] H. Burton, *A Censure of Simonie* (London, 1624), p 101. J. Adamson, *The Noble Revolt: The Overthrow of Charles I* (London: Weidenfeld & Nicolson, 2007), pp 115, 117 comments on Burton that "His fate was emblematic of the fortunes of Calvinism in the English Church more generally post-1625... the sober, mainstream Calvinist under James, radicalized by his experience of the Church under Charles and Laud."

[20] See J. Rushworth, *Historical Collections of Private Passages of State* (London, 1659), i. 185-187 or (1680), i. 181-183.

[21] E. W. Kirby, 'The Lay Feoffees: A Study in Militant Puritanism', *The Journal of Modern History*, 14 (1942), pp 3-4.

Plans began to be made, however. Archbishop Richard Bancroft had had an audacious plan to reform the entire system and purchase impropriations but it died with him in 1610. There were Parliamentary bills in 1614 and 1621 which attempted reform but came to nothing. Later, William Laud wrote in his diary that "If I live to see the Repair of St Pauls near an End, I would move His Majesty for the like grant for the bringing in of Impropriations."[22] He intended to attack the problem by buying up impropriations (at the rate of "two a-year at least") for the Church, but only once his imposing and expensive cathedral project was complete. The money used for this, partly raised out of impropriations and ecclesiastical livings itself,[23] was ultimately wasted since St. Paul's was of course burned down a few years later during the Great Fire of London and had to be completely rebuilt. Even as Archbishop of Canterbury, however, Laud was unable to follow through on such a grand plan, although he did persuade King Charles I to give all the crown's impropriations in Ireland back to the Church there.[24] This may have been in response to "the poor vicar's plea,"[25] although William Prynne claimed that Laud, "did it onely to maintain the Pompe, Power, Pride, State of the Prelates and Clergy there; as he did in *England;* not to maintain, or set up godly Preaching Ministers, which he both here and there suppressed all he could."[26] In any case, the crown continued to

---

[22] J. Bliss & W. Scott (eds.), *The Works of the Most Reverend Father in God, William Laud, D.D. Sometime Lord Archbishop of Canterbury* (Oxford: John Henry Parker, 1847-1860), iii.255.

[23] See *A Commission from the Right Honourable the Lord High Chancellor, the Lord High Treasurer, the Lord Bishop of London, and the Dean of St. Pauls. To the Right Honorable the Lord Chief Justice of the Common Pleas, Mr. Justice Hyde, Mr. Attorney Generall and others. Concerning the Arrears of Impropriations, and other Ecclesiasticall Livings, &c. Granted by His Sacred Majesty to the said Lord High Chancellor, Lord High Treasurer, Lord Bishop of London, and Dean of St. Pauls. For and towards the Repair of the Cathedrall Church of St. Paul London* (London, 1662).

[24] Bliss & Scott (eds.), *Works*, iii.253. See H. R. Trevor-Roper, *Archbishop Laud: 1573-1645*, 2nd edn. (London: Macmillan, 1962), pp 109, 149-150 and P. Heylyn, *Cyprianus Anglicus, or, The History of the Life and Death of the Most Reverend and Renowned Prelate William, by Divine Providence Lord Archbishop of Canterbury* (London, 1668), p 269 for more on Laud's policy regarding ecclesiastical property.

[25] Ryves, *Poore Vicars Plea* was published in 1620 to persuade the crown of this very policy.

[26] W. Prynne, *Canterburies Doome, or, The First Part of a Compleat History of the Commitment, Charge, Tryall, Condemnation, Execution of William Laud, Late Archbishop of Canterbury* (London, 1646), p 535. Cf. p 386 where he claims the Irish re-appropriation was done "in an arbitrary, forcible and illegall way, to the undoing of many."

hold many benefices in England, as did other local magnates, while vast areas of the country were without what many would consider a clear and thorough biblical ministry.

Before we look at the Puritan solution to this problem, it is well worth putting it into perspective. There is a table of English and Welsh dioceses, showing the number of parishes and of impropriations in each, in the English edition of Bernhardus Varenius' and Nicolas Sanson's *Cosmography and Geography* (1682).[27] The numbers in this table correspond almost exactly with those scattered in the earlier works of Peter Heylyn, Ηρωολογια *Anglorum* (1641) and *Cyprianus Anglicus* (1668).[28] From here we discover that there were 9283 parishes in 27 dioceses.[29] Out of these, a massive 41% (3845) were impropriate, their tithes going somewhere other than the local ministry. Sir William Sanderson has almost the same numbers, but adds the important qualifier that the 3845 parishes were "either appropriated to the Clergy, or impropriated (as Lay-fines) to private persons."[30] It is difficult to know what proportion were appropriated by bishops and cathedral clergy to augment their incomes on the one hand and how many were in the hands of laymen, but John Selden appears to think the largest part, over a third of all parishes, were technically lay impropriations.[31] Others estimate that the percentage of advowsons (the specific right of

---

[27] B. Varenius & N. Sanson, *Cosmography and Geography... Illustrated with Maps* (London, 1682), p 119.

[28] See P. Heylyn, Ηρωολογια *Anglorum. Or, an Help to English History* (London, 1641), which purports to be by Robert Hall, which is one of Heylyn's pseudonyms, and Heylyn, *Cyprianus Anglicus*. Sanson and Heylyn disagree about the exact number of parishes in Salisbury, though they agree that 109 were impropriated.

[29] J. Speed, *The Theatre of the Empire of Great Britaine Presenting an Exact Geography of the Kingdomes of England, Scotland, Ireland, and the Iles Adioyning* (London, 1612), p 6 claims 9285 parishes (one extra in Carlisle).

[30] W. Sanderson, *A Compleat History of the Life and Raigne of King Charles from his Cradle to his Grave* (London, 1658), p 153. He thinks there are 9284 parishes, rather than 9283 and is followed very closely by the industrious imposter and antiquary T. Frankland, *The Annals of King James and King Charles the First* (London, 1681), p 387. The same figures appear in J. Godolphin, *Repertorium Canonicum, or, An Abridgment of the Ecclesiastical Laws of this Realm* (London, 1678), p 36 contrasting those "appropriated" to bishops, cathedral clergy, and colleges with those "impropriated" to the laity, but without putting numbers to either.

[31] Selden, *Historie of Tithes*, p 487. That is, over a third had been grabbed by "Antichrist of Rome" before the Reformation, and were now in "temporall mens hands."

presentation) in lay control was around 60-70% across the country as a whole.[32]

Durham had the highest proportion of impropriations (64%), with York (58%) and Llandaff (57%) close behind. His numbers were rounded, but Daniel Featley was surely correct when he complained in 1644 that, "Of the 9000 livings with cure in this Kingdom, there are above 4000 so castrated by sacrilegious appropriations, that in very many places in this Kingdom, that which remaineth for the incumbent is no way sufficient to support him and his family; either then his means must be pieced out with another living, or he perish for want of corporall, and his parishioners for want of spirituall food."[33]

2. The Collectors of St. Antholin's

Around this time, a group of Puritans, based in London at St. Antholin's Church, decided to begin this great work of re-appropriation themselves. The mis-direction of church funds away from local church ministry was to them a scandal. They had no problem with lay patronage and ownership of tithes, as such, but were concerned about putting them to a good and proper use, "for the meynteynance of preachers."[34] Their aim was to provide solid Puritan preaching in some of the darkest corners of the land, using whatever resources they could get their hands on, impropriated or otherwise. Bernard Gilpin, the so-called Apostle of the North, had complained in 1552 that "a thousand pulpits in England are covered with dust. Some have not had four sermons these fifteen or sixteen years."[35] Still, a century later, Roger Williams, the founder of Providence (Rhode Island), said that there were not just unbelieving 'Indians' in America but, "We have Indians at

---

[32] B. Donagan, 'The Clerical Patronage of Robert Rich, Second Earl of Warwick, 1619-1642', *Proceedings of the American Philosophical Society*, 120 (1976), pp 390-391.

[33] D. Featley, *Sacra Nemesis, the Levites Scourge* (Oxford, 1644), p 63. This testifies to the fact that the issue of pluralities (holding more than one benefice) was intimately connected to that of impropriations and lack of preaching. Today that is also true, in that ministers with a handful (or more) of financially barely-viable parishes are often unable to exercise a solid preaching ministry, and can become little more than mass priests haring around from one village to the next.

[34] I. M. Calder, *Activities of the Puritan Faction of the Church of England, 1625-33* (London: S.P.C.K. for the Church Historical Society, 1957), pp 73-74, 128.

[35] W. Gilpin, *The Life of Bernard Gilpin*, 2nd edn. (London, 1753), p 279.

home, Indians in Cornewall, Indians in Wales, Indians in Ireland... who can deny but that the body of this and of all other Protestant Nations (as well as Popish) are unconverted?"[36] This was an unacceptable situation for the Puritans, and one they sought vigorously to address. St. Antholin's would play a central part in one of their most audacious attempts to do so.

If we pause for a moment here, however, 'missionaries' is not perhaps the first word which comes to mind when one thinks of the Puritans. Keen disciples, passionate pastors, devotional writers, powerful preachers, precise theologians - yes. Radical revolutionaries and reformers even. But not missionaries. A recent *Companion to Puritanism* which features twenty in-depth studies by a stellar cast of the great and the good in Puritan studies today, on a whole host of subjects related to Puritanism, has no chapter on their missionary endeavours nor even an index entry for 'evangelism.'[37] Yet as far as the Puritans themselves were concerned, all their efforts in theology, in ministry, and even in politics were focused on bringing glory to God through the salvation of sinners, their biblical edification, and their establishment in the fellowship of the church until the Lord's return. In that sense, then, even if they did not use the words 'mission' or 'evangelism' as we would perhaps today, the Puritan story is the story of a persistent, determined, and spiritually-minded attempt to reach the lost for Christ.[38]

One author claims that "missionary enterprise [was] almost entirely absent," and "there was little or no missionary concern" amongst the seventeenth century Puritans. For such, apparently, the Christian world had to await "the triumph of Arminianism" and the

---

[36] R. Williams, *The Hirelings Ministry None of Christs, or, A Discourse Touching the Propagating the Gospel of Christ Jesus* (London, 1652), p 13.

[37] J. Coffey & P. C.-H. Lim (eds.), *The Cambridge Companion to Puritanism* (Cambridge: Cambridge University Press, 2008). The 1650 Act for the Better Propagation and Preaching of the Gospel in Wales does get a mention on p 168 and Baxter's evangelistic booklet *A Call to the Unconverted* is referenced on e.g. p 309. See also the brief section on pp 228-232 on Puritan tactics for bringing tepid baptised Christians to the boil.

[38] See further L. Gatiss, 'The Puritans as Missionaries', *Modern Reformation*, 20.2 (March/April 2011), pp 7-9.

enterprising Wesleys![39] Despite seeming polemically powerful, this is an entirely mythical reconstruction of history. The Puritans, and especially the Calvinists amongst them, saw the challenge of reaching the unevangelised edges of the archipelago and took it on with relish. The Geneva Bible, published in England just after the St. Antholin's Lectures began again following the Marian persecution, and beloved of the Puritans, claimed that "All townes and countries whence Gods worde, and good living is banished, are the throne of Satan, and also those places where the word is not preached syncerly, nor maners a right reformed."[40] Some outreach to areas outside of London happened almost naturally as Puritan merchants traded with other parts of the country, taking the gospel along with their wares.[41] Mission to areas outside the immediate gravitational pull of the capital was much slower. Preachers were sometimes sent by the Government to border counties as tools of military or economic policy, to remind the populace of their spiritual duties of loyalty to the crown and diligent labour. But this did not necessarily entail a call to fruitful obedience to the higher power of the messiah who died for sinners, and to de-throne Satan.

Later, evangelism abroad among Native Americans was supported by high profile Puritans such as John Owen, William Bridge, Thomas Goodwin, and Philip Nye.[42] Richard Baxter spoke movingly of his prayers for those in other countries without Christ.[43] One of the St.

---

[39] See G. F. Nuttall, 'The Influence of Arminianism in England', in G. O. McCulloh (ed.), *Man's Faith and Freedom: The Theological Influence of Jacobus Arminius* (Nashville: Abingdon, 1962), p 60.

[40] Geneva Bible note on Revelation 2:13.

[41] See J. E. C. Hill, 'Puritans and 'the Dark Corners of the Land'', *Transactions of the Royal Historical Society*, 13 (1963), p 78.

[42] See e.g. H. Whitfield, *Strength out of Weaknesse; or A Glorious Manifestation of the Further Progresse of the Gospel among the Indians in New-England. Held Forth in Sundry Letters from Divers Ministers and Others to the Corporation Established by Parliament for Promoting the Gospel among the Heathen in New-England* (London, 1652).

[43] In R. Baxter, *Reliquiae Baxterianae, or, Mr. Richard Baxters Narrative of the Most Memorable Passages of his Life and Times* (London, 1696), i.131 he says, "there is nothing in the World that lyeth so heavy upon my heart, as the thought of the miserable Nations of the Earth... No part of my Prayers are so deeply serious, as that for the Conversion of the Infidel and Ungodly World... There being no Employment in the World so desirable in my Eyes, as to labour for the winning of such miserable Souls: which maketh me greatly honour Mr. *John Eliot*, the Apostle of the Indians in *New-England*, and whoever else have laboured in such work."

Antholin's lecturers, Zachary Cawdrey (1618–1684), claimed that "Pious Persons have oft lamented" that the gospel had not followed English trade *abroad* as much as it ought to have done in "those vast Heathenish Inlands" of Africa and America. "Have we made so much as one solemn mission of pious and learned men (set apart for the work, with publick Fasting and Prayer) to preach the glad Tidings of Salvation in Jesus Christ... to those poor ignorant Heathen and Idolaters... or to the poor Negroes, which are detained in cruel slavery in our own plantations? I need not say what success we might expect upon the sending forth of such Evangelists fitted for the work... to be sure thereby the sincere Truth of the Gospel (cleared from the superstitions wherewith the Roman Missionaries beclog it) would be spread amongst those who yet sit in darkness and in the shadow of death." The sort of large scale project he envisaged was, however, "a project above my stock of braines to manage," he confessed. Yet he mentioned and commended it to his pious readers because it had "some affinity" to the subject of the book he had written. That book was called *A Discourse of Patronage*, and concerned the otherwise rather dry subject of impropriations, lay patronage, and the maintenance of evangelical ministry.[44]

In the mind of this St. Antholin's lecturer, then, impropriations and mission were most certainly related.[45] Impropriation of parish resources to monasteries in the first place had been a way of keeping the people in the ignorance and superstition of medieval Catholicism; John Rainolds (1549-1607) wrote of "*Impropriations* the first begotten childe of the *Pope* and *Sathan*."[46] Cawdrey, however, thought it was a

---

[44] Z. Cawdrey, *A Discourse of Patronage, being a modest enquiry into the original of it, and a further prosecution of the history of it* (London, 1675), pp 44-45.

[45] I am assuming that this Zachary Cawdrey is the Anglican who according to P. S. Seaver, *The Puritan Lectureships: The Politics of Religious Dissent, 1560-1662* (Stanford: Stanford University Press, 1970), p 280 was appointed a St. Antholin's Lecturer in December 1657. He held at the time the strongly parliamentarian parish of Woodford in Essex, whereas his father, also called Zachary Cawdrey (1577/8–1659), was Vicar of Melton Mowbray in Leicestershire. Interestingly, his grandfather Robert Cawdrey was behind the first monolingual English dictionary ever published (1604) while his uncle, the Petrean Daniel Cawdrey had backed William Castle's proposal to the Long Parliament for a missionary expedition to convert Native Americans as part of a godly foreign policy. See the entries in *Oxford Dictionary of National Biography* (hereafter *ODNB*) (Oxford: Oxford University Press, 2004) on each.

[46] J. Rainolds, *The Prophecie of Obadiah Opened and Applyed in Sundry Learned and Gracious Sermons* (Oxford, 1613), p 29.

redeemable institution. Godly, generous patrons, he said, were "under the Kings most sacred Majesty... to be nursing Fathers to Gods church and to deliver the poor starved, neglected souls of thousands."[47] He was not alone in making these connections. On the domestic front, Richard Sibbes, one of the greatest leaders of the Reformed Puritans in the seventeenth century, preached that,

> "If it were possible, it were to be wished that there were set up some lights in all the dark corners of this Kingdome, that might shine to those people that sit in darknesse, and in the shadow of death. One way is, To have a competent maintenance: to devise it for the poore Ministery; that they might live by the Gospell, that preach the Gospell: so by this meanes there might be a Church world without end."[48]

Sibbes himself therefore became one the leading lights in a group known as the Feoffees for the Purchase of Impropriations. The Rector of St. Antholin's, Charles Offspring, was also one of these Feoffees or trustees, along with prominent citizens in the City who supported the church, and so the Feoffees were also known (somewhat more memorably) as The Collectors of St. Antholin's.[49] They were a group of four lawyers, four businessmen, and four clergy who gathered together to plan the purchase of impropriations and the subsequent use of those resources for gospel ministry throughout the country. In a word, their strategy was to collect money to purchase the right to particular pulpits - both the right to choose the minister, and the right to collect the tithes from the parish and dispense them to him, or otherwise as they saw fit. They included John

---

[47] Cawdrey, *Discourse of Patronage*, p 38 alluding to Isaiah 49:23. Calvin had used this image to describe the duty of kings in the dedication, to the young King Edward VI, of his commentary on Isaiah (1550) and it was enthusiastically embraced by successive British monarchs.

[48] R. Sibbes, *The Saints Cordials: As they were Delivered in Sundry Sermons upon Speciall Occasions* (London, 1629), p 83. The motto on the title page of this sermon is "Uprightness hath boldness."

[49] See Rushworth, *Historical Collections*, ii.150 for this name given to the group during the legal proceedings against them. The word "feoffee" is from an early Middle English and Anglo-Norman word referring to the person to whom a fief or fee (the feoffment) is feoffed by a feoffor. In other words, a feoffee is a trustee, to whom a freehold of land is entrusted (or enfeoffed!). Sadly, the word seems to fade from common use by the end of the nineteenth century.

White, the great grandfather of John and Charles Wesley,[50] and William Gouge, a well-known London preacher and author of a vast commentary on Hebrews. Calvinists all, they saw St. Antholin's and the Feoffees' plan as part of the "fight to preserve the Calvinist basis of the Church of England."[51] Indeed, they were concerned about the threat which anti-Reformed theology posed to both Church and State; one of the chief lay Feoffees was Christopher Sherland of Gray's Inn, who according to Kirby "distinguished himself in the house of commons in the 1620's by his relentless warfare against Arminianism and popery."[52]

Other prominent Puritans were drawn in such as Thomas Taylor, John Davenport, and Thomas Gataker, who were also involved in international projects such as collections for the Protestants in the Palatinate and the organisation of support for Protestant ecumenist John Durie (1596-1680). Those involved also had links to the Massachusetts Bay Company, the Providence Island Company, and the Dorchester and New England Companies, while "interlocking matrimonial alliances" seem to have bound them closely together.[53] They were joined by serious men such as Sir Heneage Finch,[54] the Sheriff of London, and the Lord Mayor,[55] and according to Gouge's son, "they met very frequently, and spent much time in consultation about that businesse."[56] The Collectors of St. Antholin's made, according to Christopher Hill, "the greatest single attempt to put into practice the

---

[50] John Wesley's grandfather, Samuel Annesley, was married to John White's daughter Mary. See Newton E. Key, 'Annesley, Samuel (*bap.* 1620, *d.* 1696)', in *ODNB*. White was a "long-term critic of Arminianism" according to Jacqueline Eales, 'White, John (1590–1645)', in *ODNB*. Certainly his *The First Century of Scandalous, Malignant Priests* (London, 1643) was written against the "destructive Errours of Popery and Arminianisme" and took various Arminian ministers to task for their views (as well as behaviour).

[51] F. J. Bremer, *Congregational Communion: Clerical Friendship in the Anglo-American Puritan Community, 1610-1692* (Boston: Northeastern University Press, 1994), p 75.

[52] Kirby, 'The Lay Feoffees', p 6. Kirby is another historian who sees the Feoffees' project as a deliberately and self-consciously *Calvinist* endeavour.

[53] A. Milton, *Catholic and Reformed: Roman and Protestant Churches in English Protestant Thought, 1600-40* (Cambridge: Cambridge University Press, 1995), p 398. Hill, *Economic Problems*, p 255.

[54] Kirby, 'The Lay Feoffees', p 7. Finch was a strongly anti-Arminian lawyer.

[55] Hill, *Economic Problems*, p 255.

[56] See his narrative of his father's life in W. Gouge, *A Learned and Very Useful Commentary on the Whole Epistle to the Hebrewes* (London, 1655), c. This commentary is the fruit of thirty years of Wednesday lectures on Hebrews.

Puritan alternative solution for the economic problems of the church and the provision of a well-paid preaching clergy."[57] Or as one of their contemporaries put it, the Collectors' work "was a most charitable, and usefull & hopefull busines, and likely to have brought more advantage to the Ministery of England, then any one thing of that nature, which hath beene undertaken in any mans memory."[58]

This project seems to have its origins in the second decade of the seventeenth century,[59] but the Feoffees started to meet in earnest from 1625. In the eight years of their activity nearly £6400 was contributed to their fund and they spent over £8000, covering much of the deficit out of their own pockets.[60] A large proportion of the money came from individual donations. In 1627, 198 men and women subscribed over £1554 and asked the Feoffees to undertake the management of the St. Antholin's Lectures. To help endow the lectures, the trustees bought the impropriation of St. Andrew in Presteigne (then the county town of Radnorshire), 23 miles North-West of Hereford. This was just one of the 166 parishes in Hereford diocese (out of 313) which were at that time impropriated. This £1400 investment paid off, and the Feoffees were able not only to repair the chancel of the church itself,[61] and provide for ministry there, but also to subsidise the Lecturers and the Rector of St. Antholin's out of the profits from this parish. They increased the number of Lecturers to six and augmented their stipends to a more reasonable £30, so that an expository lecture could be delivered every weekday morning. The number of lecturers remained at six for the next two hundred years.[62]

A few miles to the North of Presteigne, another Feoffee, Rowland Heylyn, had already bought the impropriation of St. Alkmund in Shrewsbury in 1613.[63] The Feoffees were not focused solely on this

---

[57] Hill, *Economic Problems*, p 252.
[58] Anon, *Certaine Arguments and Motives of Speciall Moment... To Abolish that Unhappy and Unhallowed Government of our Church by Bishops* (London?, 1634), p 12.
[59] Rushworth, *Historical Collections*, ii.150.
[60] I. M. Calder, 'A Seventeenth Century Attempt to Purify the Anglican Church', *The American Historical Review*, 53 (1948), p 763.
[61] As they point out in their legal defence in Calder, *Activities of the Puritan Faction*, p 13.
[62] I. M. Calder, 'The St Antholin Lectures', *Church Quarterly Review*, 160 (1959), p 53.
[63] This was purchased from the crown, a point to remember as the story progresses. Calder, 'A Seventeenth Century Attempt to Purify the Anglican Church', p 769. Rowland Heylyn, who was born in Shrewsbury and whose father was of Welsh ancestry, was an ironmonger in the City.

part of the country but, writes Christopher Hill, "Nevertheless, it is significant that of the thirty-odd ministers whom they appointed or to whom they gave augmentations, nearly half were in Wales or on its borders. (Six or seven in Shropshire, three in Staffordshire, one each in Pembrokeshire, Radnorshire, Worcestershire and Gloucestershire.)"[64] In 1630, Rowland Heylyn and another London merchant also paid for a handy sized edition of the whole Bible in Welsh as well as a great deal of devotional and instructional literature in the Welsh language.[65] Parliament would later pass an Act which sought to use impropriations to provide for a better maintained preaching ministry in Wales,[66] but Heylyn and the Collectors of St. Antholin's began this work unofficially and on a smaller scale themselves. In many Welsh parishes tithes were worth £100 but the minister was paid a pittance, and this was true in other spiritually barren corners of the land such as the North East of England as well.[67] By augmenting the pay of the faithful men they planted in these pulpits (as lecturers or incumbents) to reasonable levels, the Trustees hoped to raise the standard of preaching in an area generally and attract more educated and diligent workers to these harvest fields. By funding lecturers in market towns where there was little or no preaching they also hoped to reach other business people with the gospel in the places that were central for them socially and economically.

Puritan private enterprise attempted to apply business nous to the spiritual issue of nationwide evangelism. The Feoffees were just one particularly well organised attempt to do this; London merchants with roots in Lancashire had previously tried to support half a dozen preachers there too, and there were sporadic instances of such

---

[64] Hill, 'Dark Corners', p 93.
[65] Ibid., p 91. This included a book called *The Practice of Piety* (in Welsh) and a Welsh dictionary.
[66] *An Act for the Better Propagation and Preaching of the Gospel in Wales* (London, 1650). See also A. Griffith, *A True and Perfect Relation of the Whole Transactions Concerning the Petition of the Six Counties of South-Wales, and the County of Monmouth for a Supply of Godly Ministers* (London, 1654) and A. Griffith, *Mercurius Cambro-Britannicus. Or, News from Wales, Touching the Glorious and Miraculous Propagation of the Gospel in those Parts* (London, 1652).
[67] See W. Vaughan, *The Spirit of Detraction, Conjured and Convicted in Seven Circles* (London, 1611), pp 93-94 who says the least of the 112 parishes in his vicinity (Carmarthenshire?) was worth £100 but paid only £5, "a beggarly annuity... Neyther will any Scholer of worth accept of such a meane rate." Cf. Hill, 'Dark Corners', pp 88-89.

patronage elsewhere.[68] One particularly impressive example was the merchant Richard Fishbourne (d. 1625) who was "puritan in some respects yet a faithful member of the Church of England."[69] He gave an enormous amount of money to endow lectureships and preaching generally, to augment ministerial stipends, and help the poor. According to his funeral sermon, however, his biggest bequest was that, "Hee hath given two thousand eight hundred pounds, to buy in certaine Impropriations, in some Northerne Counties, where there is least preaching."[70] This gift was even celebrated in a poem by William Strode:

> Now Henryes sacrilege is found to bee
> The ground that sets off Fishborne's charity,
> Who, from lay owners rescueing church lands,
> Buys out the injury of wrongful hands.[71]

Feoffee Richard Sibbes was in full sympathy with such charitable merchants like Fishbourne. "It is a world of hurt that comes to the Church by impropriations," he preached, "especially in the North parts."[72] It is no surprise then that gradually, the St. Antholin's Collectors' holdings came to extend as far north as Stafford and as far west as Haverfordwest, Pembrokeshire. The cost of buying up impropriations and advowsons (the specific right of a patron to present their candidate as minister) ranged from about £100 to over £2800, so they were by no means cheap or easy to obtain. Yet with the rents, glebe land, and tithes which came with such purchases, Ethyn Kirby was right to say that this was in some sense "a money-making scheme, although for pious purposes."[73] Given modern preoccupations with gender and common assumptions about the role of women in the seventeenth century and Puritanism particularly, it is worthwhile noting that this was not a male-only venture. As Kirby points out, in the accounts for the Collectors of St. Antholin's,

---

[68] See Hill, *Economic Problems*, pp 267-271.
[69] Margaret Forey, 'Fishborne, Richard (1562?–1625)', in *ODNB*.
[70] N. Shute, *Corona Charitatis, The Crowne of Charitie: A Sermon Preacht... at the Solemne Funerals of... the Mirroir of Charitie, Mr. Richard Fishburne* (London, 1626), p 34. See also G. S., *Anglorum Speculum, or The Worthies of England, in Church and State* (London, 1684), p 392.
[71] W. Strode, *The Poetical Works of William Strode (1600-1645)* (London, 1907), p 84.
[72] R. Sibbes, *Evangelicall Sacrifices in XIX. Sermons: The Third Tome* (London, 1640), p 81.
[73] Kirby, 'The Lay Feoffees', pp 11-12.

> "During the years 1626-32 nineteen contributions from women are listed, while fifty-six came from men. Many women, however, gave generously: Katherine Manning and Mrs. Burnell, both of St. Antholin's parish, gave £320 and £190, respectively; while a Mrs. Katherine Flood appears on the list with a contribution of £190. The largest amount given by one person was from Lady Wooley, who gave the feoffees in yearly payments the sum of £300 for increasing the vicar's stipend in Womersh, Surrey, and also £407 for buying land to found a lecture there."[74]

St. Antholin's itself was a key part of the Feoffees plans. They did not simply aim to buy pulpits, but to fill them with good preachers.[75] To that end, the central London Church became what contemporaries called "a practical seminary." One seventeenth century source (most likely the poet Samuel Butler) refers to the Puritan strongholds in certain Oxford and Cambridge colleges as "initiatory seminaries," and goes on to speak of the next plank of their strategy being to set up, "a *Practique Seminary,* and that was at St. *Antholines* here in *London*." This, he claimed, was like a spiritual Officer Training Corps, "being a place to traine up their young *Emissaries,* where they might take an Essay of their affections and abilities, and by the bewitchments of *gaine* and *popular applause* deeply ingage them in their Faction." St. Antholin's was important for the Feoffees for Impropriations because, says Butler, "from this *Seminary* were most of their new bought Impropriations fill'd... [they] had power to transplant their most hopeful Imps either into their purchased Impropriations, or else into a Lecture in some of the most populous places of the Kingdom, maintained by a borrowed

---

[74] Ibid., p 9. There were also donations from Susan Lancashire, Thomasine Owfield, Mrs. Gastrell, Mrs. Dobson, Mrs. Newporte, and Mrs. Stone according to the lists in Calder, *Activities of the Puritan Faction*, pp 29-34. There was significant *aristocratic* female patronage of Puritanism; as well as Lady Wooley we should also mention Jane, Lady Bacon who was patron to the prominent Puritan ministers Jeremiah Burroughes and William Greenhill (see their entries in the *ODNB*).

[75] A list of what they actually acquired can be found in Calder, 'A Seventeenth Century Attempt to Purify the Anglican Church', pp 764, 766 n16 and Calder, *Activities of the Puritan Faction,* p xv-xviii. They also considered or attempted to buy other places as platforms for Puritan ministry; they offered the Earl of Bedford £1000 for the advowson of St. Paul's, Covent Garden, for example, according to William Noy in ibid., pp 79-80.

portion from an Impropriation elswhere."[76] Archbishop Laud once referred to Emmanuel and Sidney Sussex colleges in Cambridge as 'the Nurseries of Puritanisme,"[77] but antiquary William Dugdale spoke of St. Antholin's as "the grand Nursery":

> And for an essay of those whom under colour of Preaching the Gospel, in sundry parts of the Realm, they determin'd to make instrumental for carrying on the work, they set up a Morning-Lecture at St. Antholines-Church in London; where (as Probationers for that purpose) they first made tryal of their abilities; which place was the grand Nursery, whence most of the Seditious Preachers were after sent abroad throughout all England, to poyson the People.[78]

Dugdale had his own agenda, of course, and pictures the Puritans here primarily as political troublemakers rather than religious missionaries. His book is "a highly partisan chronicle of events which has never found much recognition among historians, although it is useful for its copiousness and the precision of its dates." What's more, he made his own name compiling a three volume history of the monasteries in Latin which, when it first appeared, "evoked protests that it was a covert plea for the revival of Catholicism, and also that it might provide a basis for the recovery of former church lands that had been sold into private hands at the Reformation."[79] However, he was not alone in that generation in giving St. Antholin's pride of place in the Puritan

---

[76] S. Butler, *A Letter from Mercurius Civicus to Mercurius Rusticus, or, Londons Confession but not Repentance Shewing that the Beginning and the Obstinate Pursuance of this Accursed Horrid Rebellion is Principally to be Ascribed to that Rebellious City* (Oxford, 1643), p 6. He didn't use the actual phrase "Officer Training Corps" of course, but compared St. Antholin's to a spiritual "Artillery Garden," by which presumably he meant the Society of the Artillery Garden, a voluntary association of citizens who were trained in Dutch military practice and expected to provide a pool from which officers could be drawn for the trained bands.

[77] Prynne, *Canterburies Doome*, p 369.

[78] W. Dugdale, *A Short View of the Late Troubles in England Briefly Setting Forth, their Rise, Growth, and Tragical Conclusion, as also, Some Parallel Thereof with the Barons-Wars in the Time of King Henry III* (Oxford, 1681), p 37.

[79] Graham Parry, 'Dugdale, Sir William (1605–1686)' in *ODNB*. His *Monasticon Anglicanum* (3 vols., 1655, 1661, 1673) was published in English translation as *Monasticon Anglicanum, or, The History of the Ancient Abbies, and Other Monasteries, Hospitals, Cathedral and Collegiate Churches, in England and Wales* (London, 1693).

"conspiracy." Sir Roger L'Estrange, also no fan of the Puritans, repeated and heightened the accusations of Samuel Butler and wrote of "a kind of a *Practical Seminary* at St. *Antholines* in *London;* where their Disciples were in a manner, upon a Probation, for Abilities, and Affections."[80]

The plan seems to have been this: the Collectors of St. Antholin's aimed to train up a regiment of Puritan preachers by having them lecture weekly, that is, give an hour long expository sermon on a text of scripture at the early morning meetings at St. Antholin's. After a university education and up to six years of such intense training (during which time they would also have trained younger lecturers in these arts) they would leave to pastor a church themselves.[81] Several St. Antholin's Lecturers moved to places where the Feoffees had purchased the advowson.[82] In this way, St. Antholin's "the nursery of radical nonconformity in Elizabethan London,"[83] became the grand nursery of seventeenth century Puritanism.

John Morgan, in his survey of Puritan attitudes to education helpfully highlights one other aspect of the Collectors' work. They were, he says, "well aware of the contribution schooling could make to godly reform." Schooling, that is, of young children not just university educated ordinands, was also part of the godly agenda for bringing the gospel to the people of England. "It should be remembered," therefore, writes Morgan, "that the feoffees for impropriation, in addition to the church livings they gathered, also came to control the nomination of schoolmasters in several locations."[84] For example, they paid for a

---

[80] R. L'Estrange, *A Seasonable Memorial in Some Historical Notes upon the Liberties of the Presse and Pulpit* (London, 1680), p 2.

[81] Calder, *Activities of the Puritan Faction*, pp 79, 115.

[82] Seaver, *The Puritan Lectureships*, pp 234-235, 251 mentions one Zachary Symmes, a St. Antholin's Lecturer who moved to Dunstable in 1625 where the Feoffees had acquired the impropriation for St. Peter's, Dunstable, as well as John Archer who moved from St. Antholin's to Huntingdon. See also Calder, 'A Seventeenth Century Attempt to Purify the Anglican Church', p 767. Calder, 'The St Antholin Lectures', p 53.

[83] H. G. Owen, 'The London Parish Clergy in the Reign of Elizabeth I'. Unpublished PhD thesis, University of London (1957), p 325.

[84] J. P. Morgan, *Godly Learning: Puritan Attitudes Towards Reason, Learning, and Education, 1560-1640* (Cambridge: Cambridge University Press, 1986), p 174. Calder, 'A Seventeenth Century Attempt to Purify the Anglican Church', mentions several schools and there are other examples in J. T. Cliffe, *The Puritan Gentry: The Great Puritan Families of Early Stuart England* (London: Routledge, 1984), p 80.

schoolmaster and his house at Aylesbury "to teach freelie the Children of the poorer sort."[85] As Peter Adam pointed out in his exposé of Puritan tactics in the previous compilation of St. Antholin's Lectures, "Many preachers recognized their responsibility to train up the next generation. At Reading for example, Thomas Taylor maintained 'a little nursery of young Preachers, who under his faithful Ministry flourished in knowledge and piety.' Richard Greenham did the same at Dry Drayton, as did Richard Rogers at Wethersfield."[86] Producing the next generation of preachers was always felt to be important. Yet the Puritan project also aimed to reach the next generation at the earliest formative stages of their religious and social development, to inspire children with Puritan ideals of diligence, naturally, but also to inspire them with the grandeur of the gospel, its glory, and its urgency.

Hugh Peters (1598-1660) from Fowey in Cornwall is perhaps best known to posterity as an early American colonist and enthusiastic supporter of the regicide of Charles I. He later paid for his support of that infamous act with his own life after the Restoration of Charles II. Before that fateful deed, however, Peters himself mentioned in a sermon to Parliament another famous work he had been involved with, in an administrative capacity. "It was once my lot to be a Member of that famous, ancient, glorious work of buying in Impropriations," he preached, "by which work 40 or 50 preachers were maintained in the dark parts of this Kingdom. Divers Knights and Gentlemen in the Country contributed to this work," he said and then, urging the Lords and Commons to do even greater things in their day, he added, "and I hope they have not lost that spirit."[87]

That spirit did not confine itself to London alone, though there were strong concentrations of it at St. Antholin's and elsewhere. It was deliberately and studiously diffused throughout the country, strengthened by the zeal of the capital and emboldened, but not limited in its ambitions to that metropolis alone. The enterprising,

---

[85] Calder, *Activities of the Puritan Faction*, p 13.
[86] See P. Adam, 'A Church 'Halfly Reformed': The Puritan Dilemma', in L. Gatiss (ed.), *Pilgrims, Warriors, and Servants*, pp 205-206.
[87] H. Peters, *Gods Doings, and Mans Duty Opened in a Sermon Preached before Both Houses of Parliament, the Lord Major and Aldermen of the City of London, and the Assembly of Divines*, 2nd edn. (London, 1646), p 39. See his letter about the trustees in Calder, *Activities of the Puritan Faction*, pp 145-148.

entrepreneurial energy of the City saw in the legal peculiarity of impropriations an opportunity for expansion into the unreached corners of the country and the borderlands of unbelief. The generosity and gifts of hundreds of ordinary Puritan believers enabled them to put well-trained preachers into some populous but almost pagan areas of the country, in an attempt to reach the parts that others could not or would not evangelise. It was a bold initiative, but one that in the short term was destined to fail.

3.   The Fall of the Feoffees

The work of the Collectors of St. Antholin's ultimately foundered because it attracted the opposition of the most powerful churchman of the day: William Laud. Patrick Collinson calls Laud, "the greatest calamity ever visited upon the Church of England"[88] and it is not hard to see why from a Puritan perspective. His agenda for the church was somewhat different to theirs. This is exemplified perhaps by the way he related word and sacrament. For him, the eucharist, celebrated at an "altar," was much more important than the preaching of the word. For Laud, the altar was "the greatest place of God's residence upon earth. I say the greatest, yea, greater than the pulpit; for there 'tis *Hoc est corpus meum*, 'This is My body;' but in the pulpit 'tis at most but *Hoc est verbum meum*, 'This is My word'. And a greater reverence, no doubt, is due to the body than to the word of our Lord. And so, in relation, answerably to the throne where His body is usually present, than to the seat whence His word useth to be proclaimed."[89] At Oxford, Thomas Barlow (a future bishop of Lincoln and tutor to, amongst others, John Owen) wrote that in the late 1620s, "Arminianisme came into favour and soe in fashion... communion-table became a dull word (though in the text) and sacrifice and altar, and bowinge to it (though noe law of

---

[88] P. Collinson, *The Religion of Protestants: The Church in English Society 1559-1625* (Oxford: Clarendon Press, 1982), p 90.

[89] Bliss & Scott (eds.), *Works*, vi.57. For a similar evaluation and a sideswipe at modern Puritans who allegedly overvalue preaching and turn their churches into "mosques" focusing on the pulpit rather than on bread and wine, see N. T. Wright's provocative words in J. I. Packer & N. T. Wright, *Anglican Evangelical Identity: Yesterday and Today* (London: Latimer Trust, 2008), p 19.

God or man for it) were untimely urged."[90]

Laud aimed to build up the power, wealth, prestige, and dignity of the Church of England with various building projects. Yet, says Anthony Milton, "puritan nonconformists were Laud's chief target, and ceremonial conformity was the essence of his ecclesiastical policy... his determination to close off every remaining loophole and escape route meant that ceremonial conformity was imposed more systematically than ever before."[91] In 1632, as bishop of London, he tried to impose conformity on a parish next door to St. Antholin's, the Puritan stronghold of St. Mary, Aldermanbury. He ordered the Communion table to be railed off (and possibly moved altar-wise to the East End of the building), insisting that the Supper must not be taken "irreverently", that is, not sitting in the pews, but kneeling at the altar.[92]

Laud also interrogated and legally "silenced" various Puritan lecturers for their nonconformity. There was no spectacular purge, but he certainly created an "uncongenial atmosphere" for them,[93] and things were arguably more difficult for the Puritans under other Laudians such as Matthew Wren in Ely. Amongst those lecturers hauled in as part of Laud's shake-up in London were George Walker from St. Helen's, Bishopsgate,[94] Elias Crabtree of St. Peter's, Cornhill, and John Archer of St. Antholin's, who preached that it was not necessary to literally bow ceremonially at the mention of the name of Jesus, as Laud and others insisted.[95] Although Archer was suspended, the Collectors of St.

---

[90] Annotation by Barlow in his copy of Peter Heylyn's *Cyprianus*, a book about Laud (Bodl. Shelfmark NN Th 118), p 126. See K. Fincham & N. Tyacke, *Altars Restored: The Changing Face of English Religious Worship, 1547-c.1700* (Oxford: Oxford University Press, 2007), p 184.

[91] Anthony Milton, 'Laud, William (1573–1645)', in *ODNB*.

[92] Fincham & Tyacke, *Altars Restored*, p 188.

[93] Seaver, *The Puritan Lectureships*, pp 254-255.

[94] Ibid., p 261 says Walker was imprisoned for preaching that it was "sin to obey the greatest monarchs in things which are against the command of God."

[95] Ibid., pp 172, 227-228. On Crabtree, see P. Lake, *The Boxmaker's Revenge: 'Orthodoxy', 'Heterodoxy', and the Politics of the Parish in Early Stuart London* (Manchester: Manchester University Press, 2001), pp 59, 277-278 and 'The Will of John Juxon, Senior', *Camden Fifth Series*, 13 (1999), pp 171-86 (Juxon had donated £20 to the Feoffees in 1625 according to Calder, *Activities of the Puritan Faction*, p 29). He also appears in A. G. Matthews, *Calamy Revised: Being a Revision of Edmund Calamy's Account of the Ministers and Others Ejected and Silenced 1660-2* (Oxford: Clarendon, 1934), p 14.

Antholin's obtained for him the vicarage of All Saints, Huntingdon, "with the ready consent of the townspeople."[96] No wonder that around this time when Laud drew up his "to do list," item number three was "to overthrow the feoffment, dangerous both to Church and State, going under the specious pretence of buying in impropriations."[97] He considered them "the maine instruments for the Puritan faction, to undoe the Church."[98]

The Laudian attack on the Feoffees began on 11th July 1630 with a sermon at Oxford by one of Laud's henchmen, Peter Heylyn. In a "scathing denunciation," Heylyn accused the Feoffees directly of being the "Chief Patrons of Faction" who promoted dangerous innovations.[99] They were part of a nationwide conspiracy, he said. "And will they not in time have more preferments to bestow," he darkly insinuated, "and therefore more dependencies than all the Prelates in the Kingdom? Yet all this while we sleep and slumber, and fold our hands in sloth, and see perhaps, but dare not note it."[100] William Prynne claimed that Laud "suborned his flattering creatures to declaime against those Feoffees and their design in the Pulpit both at Court and elsewhere." Among them, he claims, was "his great Minion Peter Heylin [who]... discharged his venome against *Lecturers*, and those Feoffees in these bitter Invectives."[101] Heylyn may or may not have been put up to this assault on the Feoffees by Laud himself,[102] but they were certainly on the same page when it came to seeing their activities as a threat. Heylyn's sermon

---

[96] Seaver, *The Puritan Lectureships*, pp 251-252 which mentions how Thomas Foxley and William Martyn, two other St. Antholin's Lecturers, were also questioned and pursued by Laud.

[97] Bliss & Scott (eds.), *Works*, iii.253. Milton, 'Laud, William (1573–1645)' dates this list of "Things which I have projected to do if God bless me in them" to around 1630.

[98] W. Prynne, *A Breviate of the life of William Laud, Arch-bishop of Canterbury Extracted (for the most part) Verbatim, out of his owne Diary, and Other Writings, under his owne Hand* (London, 1644), p 17.

[99] See G. E. Gorman, 'A Laudian Attempt to Tune the Pulpit: Peter Heylyn and His Sermon Against the Feoffees for the Purchase of Impropriations', *Journal of Religious History*, 8 (1975), p 333.

[100] See Heylyn, *Cyprianus Anglicus*, pp 209-212. There is a similar account in J. Barnard, *Theologo-Historicus, or, The True Life of the Most Reverend Divine, and Excellent Historian, Peter Heylyn* (London, 1683), pp 146-149.

[101] Prynne, *Canterburies Doome*, p 386.

[102] Kennett, *Case of Impropriations*, p 200 thinks it probable. A. Milton, *Laudian and Royalist Polemic in Seventeenth-Century England: The Career and Writings of Peter Heylyn* (Manchester: Manchester University Press, 2007), pp 26-27 assesses the arguments.

was printed and he had a presentation copy bound in vellum sent to Laud, which certainly suggests some collaboration, premeditated or hoped for.[103] It was a significant opening act, and for Peter Heylyn himself it was personal, "a burning of his boats with prosperous branches of his own family" and with his past.[104] He was the great nephew of Rowland Heylyn, the Puritan former Sheriff of London and President of the Feoffees.[105]

With the younger Heylyn's assiduous assistance, Laud eventually succeeded in having a case against the Feoffees brought to the Court of Exchequer in 1633.[106] Thomas Foxley, one of the St. Antholin's Lecturers, although not a Feoffee was also named a defendant because of his work with the trustees. They were prosecuted by "the greatest and most famous Lawyer of that age",[107] William Noy (1577-1634) who had also made his mark as an MP for various Cornish constituencies including Fowey and St. Ives. As Attorney General he directed much of his prosecutorial zeal towards the Puritans and helped to create Charles I's so called "fiscal-feudalism" especially by certifying the legality of the notorious Ship Money.[108] Thomas

---

[103] Laud's copy is preserved as Magdalen College Archives MS 312. See also Trevor-Roper, *Archbishop Laud*, pp 108-109 who indicates that Laud encouraged Heylyn's further investigations.

[104] Milton, *Laudian and Royalist Polemic*, p 28. On Peter's early Puritan associations and connections, see Anthony Milton, 'Heylyn, Peter (1599–1662)', in *ODNB*.

[105] Ibid., p 27 says Rowland was Peter's "father's friend and kinsman." Hill, *Economic Problems*, p. 255 calls him Peter's uncle. An article on the family in *The Gentleman's Magazine: Volume 74, Part 2* (1804), p 723 says Rowland was the uncle of Henry Heylyn, Peter's father, which makes Rowland Henry's great uncle. Marc L. Schwarz, 'Heylyn, Rowland (1562–1632)', in *ODNB* says Rowland Heylyn "can be considered as one of the two most important lay members [of the Feoffees], served as treasurer and then in 1629 as president; in 1628 the feoffees met at his house." Heylyn, *Cyprianus Anglicus*, p 210 calls him Treasurer and the "casting Voice amongst them."

[106] The extent records of the lawsuit are reproduced in Calder, *Activities of the Puritan Faction*. The information, answers, and judgment in abbreviated form can be found in Rushworth, *Historical Collections*, ii.150-152. British Museum, Harleian MS. 832, eighty folios written on both sides, is apparently an eighteenth century copy of a contemporary account of the trial of the Feoffees and records proceedings on January 31st, February 7th, and February 11th 1633.

[107] Rushworth, *Historical Collections*, ii.213.

[108] See James S. Hart Jr, 'Noy, William (1577-1634)', in *ODNB*. H. Burton, *A Divine Tragedie Lately Acted, or A Collection of Sundry Memorable Examples of Gods Judgements upon Sabbath-breakers, and Other like Libertines* (Amsterdam, 1636), pp 43-46 uses Noy's early death in his morality tale as an example of God's judgment on those who persecute godly preachers.

Carlyle described Noy as a "morose, amorphous, cynical Law Pedant, an invincible living heap of learned rubbish."[109] The Feoffees were defended by William Lenthall, later to be the Speaker of the Long Parliament.[110] Puritans, Parliament, and City were growing closer together. Indeed, by their actions in regard to impropriations (both in England and in Scotland), the Laudian clergy, says Christopher Hill, "went out of their way to drive the men of property and the Puritans into one another's arms."[111]

Various charges were laid against the Feoffees by their opponents. They could be quite forceful in the ways they encouraged the existing incumbents of parishes they purchased the rights for (if they were not Puritans) to move on, for example.[112] Peter Heylyn somewhat bitterly (and conspiratorially) accused them of setting up lecturers "in all or most Market-Towns, where the People had commonly less to do, and consequently were more apt to Faction and Innovation than in other places; and of all Market-Towns, to chuse such as were Priviledged for sending Burgesses to the High Court of Parliament: Which that it might be done with the less charge to the People, who commonly love that Religion best which comes cheapest to them, it was agreed to raise a common Stock amongst them, for buying in such Impropriations."[113]

---

[109] T. Carlyle, *Oliver Cromwell's Letters and Speeches*, 2 vols. (London: Chapman and Hall, 1845), i.74-75.

[110] Hill, *Economic Problems*, p 263.

[111] C. Hill, *The Century of Revolution, 1603-1714* (London: Routledge Classics, 2002), pp 89-90. Though see also R. Brenner, *Merchants and Revolution: Commercial Change, Political Conflict, and London's Overseas Traders, 1550-1653* (London: Verso, 2003), pp 293, 381 n146 who notes that some previously supportive City merchants became less comfortable with Puritanism after the advent of Laud and that some merchants backed the Feoffees but sided against Parliament in the coming wars.

[112] See Calder, 'A Seventeenth Century Attempt to Purify the Anglican Church', pp 765-766 on the pay-off deal at St. John Baptist, Cirencester, where the existing incumbent had to be given large amounts of money before he would agree to move on in favour of the Feoffees' candidate. It was held against them at their trial that "they set themselues to remooue the Incumbent if he please them not." See Calder, *Activities of the Puritan Faction*, p 111. See also the "wearying of the incumbent" tactic used at Hertford and Dunwich, in Kirby, 'The Lay Feoffees', p 15.

[113] Heylyn, *Cyprianus Anglicus*, pp 109-110. See the same accusation regarding Parliamentary representation, at the hearing of 11th February 1633 in Calder, *Activities of the Puritan Faction*, p 100.

That Puritans targeted populous towns was an old accusation.[114] Defending the Feoffees and others who had done such things, one anonymous writer in 1634 said that they set up lectures in market towns and "other places of greatest resort," because that was where "they supposed they might do most good, and where there was greatest want of preaching."[115] The possible (but unquantified) effect on the return of MPs "was certainly a curious coincidence" says Christopher Hill,[116] though it is not quite clear, of course, that simply having a Puritan preacher in one of a town's parishes would by any means secure a Puritan population or a Puritan MP! Vague allusions to hidden, nefarious motives are always best when trying to create the impression of conspiracy.

Heylyn also insinuated that the Puritans' plan was "to have ready Sticklers in every place for the advancement of some dangerous and deep design."[117] As the Attorney General put it, "This is a growing Evill, A thing of dangeros Consequence."[118] This would have appealed to what Anthony Milton calls "Laud's constant paranoia."[119] Indeed, he did later confess that "I was... clearly of Opinion, that this was a cunning way, under a Glorious pretence, to overthrow the Church-Government, by getting into their power more dependency of the Clergy, than *the King*, and all *the Peers*, and all *the Bishops* in all the Kingdom had. And I did conceive the Plot the more dangerous for the fairness of the pretence; and that to the State, as well as the Church."[120] It is interesting to note who Laud thought ministers *should* be dependent on, i.e. bishops and the aristocracy.[121] There were some notable instances of aristocratic patronage of Puritan ministers, especially in Essex, which

---

[114] Hill, *Economic Problems*, p 261 traces it back to at least 1585 in some tracts attributed to Richard Bancroft.
[115] Anon, *Certaine Arguments*, p 13.
[116] Hill, *Economic Problems*, p 261.
[117] Barnard, *Theologo-Historicus*, p 147.
[118] Calder, *Activities of the Puritan Faction*, p 51. He later compared the Feoffees to the Jesuits, pp 61, 101.
[119] Anthony Milton, 'Laud, William (1573–1645)'.
[120] H. Wharton (ed.), *The History of the Troubles and Tryal of the Most Reverend Father in God and Blessed Martyr, William Laud* (London, 1695), p 372.
[121] Hill, *Economic Problems*, p 262 n2.

were hugely important to the spread and survival of the cause.[122] The Feoffees, however, while certainly in touch with the leading Puritan nobles,[123] represented the growing power, influence, and philanthropy of the middle classes.[124] Indeed, "merchants and tradesmen" account for around 72% of all charitable giving between 1601-1660 (with the nobility at only 2.5-5%).[125] They were the great benefactors and givers, so why should the Peers and Bishops have all the power over appointments?

Noy claimed that the Feoffees had a "vast appetite to get many Churches and to obtain supreme Patronage... aspiring to Regality," warning ominously that they "may get almost halfe the Churches in England."[126] He imagined they were after all 3000 impropriations in the country (underestimating the number of impropriations) at two or three per year. In Baron Trevor's opinion, "if they might bee permitted to go on, in two or .3. ages they might haue gotten most of the Churches in England."[127] These are strangely extravagant claims to make, when at this rate it would take over 640 years just to buy half the 3845 impropriated churches, which would then still be only 20% of the 9283

---

[122] See, for example, Donagan, 'Clerical Patronage of Robert Rich'. Donagan (p 390) comments, however, that the Earl's "Twenty-two livings were paltry compared with the one hundred and fifty at the disposal of the bishop of Lincoln or even the sixty in the gift of the bishop of Durham."
[123] Brenner, *Merchants and Revolution*, p 263. Brenner also mentions (p 405) Hugh Peter, who was a personal link between the Feoffees and the Earl of Warwick, thus bringing noble and middle class patrons of Puritanism together.
[124] There is an interesting illustration of these connections in the play by J. Mayne, *The Citye Match: A Comoedye. Presented to the King and Queene at White-hall. Acted since at Black-friers by His Maiesties Servants* (Oxford, 1639). The main protagonists, various members of the Seathrift family, are merchants, the father often going to the New World for trade. The daughter, known as "a rank Puritan" not only attends St. Antholin's every day but her schoolmistress is married to the Tuesday lecturer and her servant can "out pray a lecturer at Antlins." See e.g. pp 9, 36, 43. Members of the church are also depicted in another play by T. Randolph, *Poems with The Muses Looking-Glasse: and Amyntas* (Oxford, 1638). See *The Muses Looking-Glasse* p 38 for reference to "our Saint *Antlings.*"
[125] See the fascinating diagrams in Hill, *Century of Revolution*, p 322.
[126] Calder, *Activities of the Puritan Faction*, pp 100, 53.
[127] See "Opinions of the Barons" in ibid., p 112.

churches in England.[128] Yet this almost hysterical assessment in court of their potential has been repeated several times since. It is somewhat overblown to imagine that they would "in process of time… become the *prime Patrones*, for *number* and *greatness* of benefices,"[129] and that they "might have [redeemed all impropriate parishes] in fifty years, by the large summs soon advanced,"[130] or as the court put it "that they intended to the drawing to themselves in time the principal Dependency of the whole Clergie."[131] The numbers were simply too large for that,[132] although it might be fair to say this tended to make "a Church in a Church."[133] More realistically, providing for around 18 preachers in 11 counties between 1626 and 1633,[134] the Feoffees were aiming simply to secure an enclave, an expandable network of safe havens for Puritan preachers, within the wider church.

There is some truth in Laud's paranoid dislike of the Feoffees, of course, but in many ways it was a self-fulfilling prophecy. Some of these Puritans were not great supporters of episcopacy, including

---

[128] In terms of advowsons (rather than just impropriated tithes), K. W. Shipps, 'Lay Patronage of East Anglian Puritan Clerics in Pre-Revolutionary England'. PhD thesis, Yale (1971), pp 142-143 estimates that even in Essex, where Puritanism was very strong, Puritans (quite broadly defined) occupied only 40% of all *lay held* livings in 1630. In the unlikely event that this exceptional showing could, with a gigantic coordinated effort, be replicated across the country, it would still only come to about a quarter of the total number of parishes. In any case, it should also be remembered that the right conveyed by an advowson could only be exercised once the existing incumbent of the parish died or moved on, so it could take a long time to bring influence to bear in this way.

[129] Fuller, *Church-History*, p 143.

[130] Sanderson, *Compleat History of King Charles*, p 153.

[131] Rushworth, *Historical Collections*, ii.152. Calder, *Activities of the Puritan Faction*, p 139.

[132] Calder, 'A Seventeenth Century Attempt to Purify the Anglican Church', pp 760, 766 says of this "clever plan for the infiltration of the church" that "through clergymen selected by the feoffees and dependent upon them, the church established by Henry VIII was to be remodeled and purified." This again is somewhat overstated as an assessment of the likely impact of the Feoffees' plan, and seems to swallow the Laudian polemic against them too easily.

[133] Calder, *Activities of the Puritan Faction*, p. 113 (Baron Trevor) rather than p 103, "a new Religion" (William Noy). Baron Denman, p. 116, says "We knowe the begining, but the end what it may be, if they should goe on we doe not knowe It may be transcendent."

[134] T. Webster, *Godly Clergy in Early Stuart England: The Caroline Puritan Movement c.1620-1643* (Cambridge: Cambridge University Press, 1997), p 82. Though see Peters, *Gods Doings and Mans Duty*, p 39 who claims 40-50 preachers were put in place.

Feoffee John White whose book exposing "scandalous, malignant priests" was intended to reveal the inevitable corruption that resulted from that system.[135] This was written in 1643, however, and we should beware of thinking that they were all as convinced of the case against episcopacy before this and willing to push it. Indeed, Laud's suppression of the Feoffees was one of the key things which persuaded those who were otherwise more than willing to work within the established order that more radical reform was inevitable.[136] However, all the lecturers and ministers appointed by the Feoffees had been licensed by their bishops,[137] (this was one of the Feoffees' rules in fact),[138] and they taught the people "to bee *obedient to God,* and *loyall to their Soveraigne.*"[139] There was as yet no real "Conspiracy against the Lawe of the Kingdome, Against the Regall power, and against the Ecclesiasticall state" as Lord Chief Baron Davenport alleged.[140] However, "the truth is," said one anonymous commentator in 1634, "they feared, but without cause, that this [buying in impropriations] would in time have clipped their wings, & have abridged their authority, whereof they are much more jelous then of Gods glory; and that caused them to set the matter so much to hart."[141] As William Prynne commented,

> "That it would introduce a Ministry independent on the Bishops, is a false surmise, since none were recommended to officiate or preach at any of the purchased impropriations, but by speciall license of the Bishops in whose [diocese] they were, and none were presented to them but conformable men, free

---

[135] White, *First Century,* A2 says the intention of the book was "To open thine eyes and clearly convince and satisfie thee that the Parliament had good, and very great cause ... to declare and resolve, that the present Church Government by Arch-bishops, Bishops, their Chancellours, Commissaries, Deanes, Arch-deacons, and other Ecclesiasticall Officers, depending upon the Hierarchie, is evill and justly Offensive and burdensome to the Kingdome, a great Impediment to the Reformation and growth of Religion, and very prejudiciall to the State and Government of this Kingdome, and therefore to be taken away."
[136] See Seaver, *The Puritan Lectureships,* pp 259, 266, who says "the attempt to suppress the preachers had succeeded only in heightening their militancy to the point where some were prepared to preach revolution."
[137] Fuller, *Church-History,* p 143.
[138] See Calder, *Activities of the Puritan Faction,* pp xiii, 16, 17, 48, 74, 85, 97, 107, 109, 111, 135.
[139] Anon, *Certaine Arguments,* p 12.
[140] Calder, *Activities of the Puritan Faction,* p 117.
[141] Anon, *Certaine Arguments,* p 13.

from all just exceptions, & if he could justly except against ought in their proceedings, Master White deposeth, he offered that he himselfe should rectifie it, so as the work might proceed"[142]

Yet over time the enmity of the establishment, which refused to allow them a space within which to grow and flourish, eventually pushed the Puritans to oppose both bishops and monarchy much more forcefully. Both Laud and Charles I would lose their heads as a result.

The Feoffees were convicted on two technicalities. First, they had become what Noy termed an "Apocrypha Incorporation."[143] That is, they had formed themselves into the kind of self-perpetuating corporation which properly required either Parliamentary or Royal approval. They had considered applying for incorporation by Act of Parliament in 1628 but the idea had not been followed up, and was perhaps considered unnecessary or bureaucratically burdensome.[144] It is this which accounts for their lack of an official legal name and office. As Noy said, "They will not stand to any name, They will not be called by any Comon name, neither feoffees nor Collectors of St Antholins nor the Nationall Vestry."[145] Secondly, however, they were charged with breach of trust, partly for buying advowsons and funding schools rather than just buying impropriations, and partly for having subsidised the St. Antholin's lectures.[146] As Fuller recounts it, "they diverted the charity, wherewith they were intrusted, to other uses, when erecting a Lecture every morning at St. *Antholines* in *London*. What was this but *lighting candles to the Sun, London* being already the *Land of Goshen,* and none of those *dark* and far *distant corners,* where *Soules* were ready to *famish* for lack of the *food* of the *word?* What was this but a bold *breach* of their *trust...?*"[147]

---

[142] Prynne, *Canterburies Doome*, pp 538-539. Cf. p 387. See also the defence case in Rushworth, *Historical Collections,* ii.151.

[143] Fuller, *Church-History,* p 143.

[144] Calder, 'A Seventeenth Century Attempt to Purify the Anglican Church', p 762.

[145] Calder, *Activities of the Puritan Faction,* p 50 in the hearing of 31st January 1633 and the defence on p 92 on 11th February 1633. The endorsement on Hugh Peter's letter of 1627 in ibid., p 148 does refer to "the feofment of S. Anthins" and a letter from Lady Wolley on the next page is similarly endorsed with the phrase "feoffees of St Antlins."

[146] Noy asserted that their trust did not allow them to meddle in buying and maintaining schools (ibid., p 79). The Barons agreed that they had "misimployed" funds "not according to their trust," and such was the decree against them (ibid., pp 106, 113, 120, 140).

[147] Fuller, *Church-History,* p 143.

It is true of course that there was more preaching in London than anywhere else in the country. One man, it is reported, was able to hear nineteen sermons in just one week in the capital![148] Richard Sibbes, one of the clerical Feoffees, even said once that, "I think there is no place in the world where there is so much preaching."[149] Yet the Feoffees replied that they had not been specifically confined by their feoffment to buy impropriations (the right to the tithes) and not also advowsons (the right of presenting the minister), and that many of the contributors did in fact live in London and so were entitled to benefit. In fact, as Kirby points out, "The largest gifts came from St. Antholin's parishioners."[150] Presteigne had been bought deliberately to fund the Lectures at St. Antholin's, with money given for that specific purpose.[151] In any case, as we saw above, funding lectures in London was not an accident or an indulgence, but a crucial part of the strategy, since St. Antholin's was being used as a seminary to provide men for the Puritan parishes in the provinces. Prynne summed up the legal response to this charge by saying, "That some of the revenues of purchased Impropriations were contributed towards the maintainance of Saint *Antholins* Lecturers, is true; but that it was a mis-imploying by them contrary to trust, or that any unworthy or unconformable Ministers were put into them, is a grosse falshood, disproved by Master *White* upon Oath: However, had it been true, he [Laud] should then have reformed the abuse, not utterly destroyed the good work, so much conducing to Gods glory, and the peoples edification."[152]

There were also complaints that the money from the purchased impropriations did not return directly to the parishes but was

---

[148] J. Spurr, *English Puritanism 1603-1689* (Basingstoke: Macmillan, 1998), p 38. See also Hill, 'Dark Corners', p 78 on the word being "plentifully preached" in London.

[149] M. Dever, *Richard Sibbes: Puritanism and Calvinism in Late Elizabethan and Early Stuart England* (Macon, Ga.: Mercer University Press, 2000), p 80 citing the sermon called *Lydia's Conversion* in Sibbes' *Works*, 6:527.

[150] Kirby, 'The Lay Feoffees', p 9.

[151] See their defence in Calder, *Activities of the Puritan Faction*, pp 11, 14, 66, 131 and the accounts on p 34. Noy seems to concede this point on p 52 but the Chancellor of the Exchequer, Lord Cottington, objected to funds from one parish being used to pay a Lecturer in another, p 122.

[152] Prynne, *Canterburies Doome*, p 539.

redistributed by the Feoffees, who retained control over it.[153] This is not quite true, as some of the money collected in the localities where the Feoffees operated did not pass through their hands but went straight to the curate or incumbent, as at Hertford, Haverfordwest, Kinver, and Dunwich.[154] Yet even when all the impropriations had been confiscated as a result of the trial, and control of them transferred to the king and to Laud, "The tithes were still not restored to the parish from which they originated" though this is what the Exchequer had decreed.[155] Neither did they answer the setting up of this supposedly illegal corporation by establishing a legal one, despite agreeing in principle with the idea of buying in impropriations. "Alas!" says White Kennett, "we know nothing of any Steps of Redress that were taken in this matter; and we never heard of any Legal Corporation establish'd, in lieu of that voluntary Society, which was thus dissolv'd."[156] Instead, we read in Prynne's account that,

> "Mr William Kendall, Mr Iohn Lane, and Mr Tempest Miller, severally deposed at the Lords Bar, that the Archbishop [Laud] in the presence of them and divers others, speaking of the Feoffees of Impropriations, said; that they were the bane of the Church; and then uttered these words in a vaunting manner, I was the man that did set my self against them and (then clapping his hand upon his brest, said) I thank God I have destroyed this work."

Prynne comments on these reports that Laud "did not only subvert this pious project to propagate the preaching of the Gospell, but boasted of it, and had so much shamelesse Impiety, as to thanke God himselfe for effecting it."[157] Ultimately it seems, however, that "Laud was more successful at frustrating others than at carrying out his own plans."[158]

---

[153] Heylyn, *Cyprianus Anglicus*, pp 210-212. Kennett, *Case of Impropriations*, p 195. This was a technical point against the Feoffees in the hearing against them on 31st January 1633, where Noy attempted to prove that their trust was to maintain "perpetuall Vicars" rather than "datiue and remooveable men," that is, stipendary lecturers; see Calder, *Activities of the Puritan Faction*, pp 51, 81.
[154] Calder, *Activities of the Puritan Faction*, pp 21, 132-133.
[155] Hill, *Economic Problems*, pp 264-265 n6; Calder, *Activities of the Puritan Faction*, p 141.
[156] Kennett, *Case of Impropriations*, p 204.
[157] Prynne, *Canterburies Doome*, p 388.
[158] Hill, *Century of Revolution*, p 87. Cf. the same conclusion in Hill, *Economic Problems*, p 264 on the regime as a whole.

The Collectors of St. Antholin's were suppressed. They were personally refunded about £1000 which the accounts showed they had donated from their own pockets, but the right of presentation and patronage in each of the schools and parishes they had invested in, including Presteigne, was forfeited to the king. Criminal proceedings and severe punishment were threatened but the king wisely held back from allowing this.[159] The management of the St. Antholin's Lectures returned to the churchwardens of St. Antholin's itself.[160] The publicity aroused by the court case, however, gave prominence to the Feoffees' project and provoked further pledges of generosity. One lady sent a promise of £1000 to them just a week before they were wound up.[161]

One large bequest made in 1631 did not quite pass through all the administrative hurdles in time to actually make it into the Feoffees accounts before they were disbanded. Sadly, the money did not eventually go to St. Antholin's either (I speak as a Trustee of the St. Antholin's Lectureship Charity)! John Marshall, a baker, left a significant sum to the Collectors of St. Antholin's to build a church in Southwark, pay for a lecture in Stamford, Lincolnshire, and a scholarship for a Southwark man to train at Oxford or Cambridge. The rest was to buy up impropriations.[162] Through a somewhat convoluted history, the trustees who ended up with Marshall's inheritance after the Restoration did eventually pay for Christ Church, Southwark in 1670 (and indeed again after the building sank into the Lambeth Marsh, and then yet again in 1959 after the second building was bombed in 1941). That church's website says that today, "The Trustees generously support the maintenance of the building and the cost of some of the ministry based here."[163]

However, John Marshall's money (originally donated to the Feoffees for "the Mayntenance and Continuance of the sincere preaching of God's most holie Word in this Land for ever") went even further than this. In 2010, according to *its* website, the charity set up by Marshall's will (and funded solely from his endowment) gave some £660,000 to various projects, benefiting 30 churches and 190

---

[159] Calder, *Activities of the Puritan Faction*, p 123.
[160] Calder, 'The St Antholin Lectures', p 55.
[161] Hill, *Economic Problems*, p 261.
[162] See Calder, *Activities of the Puritan Faction*, p xiv n1.
[163] http://www.christchurchsouthwark.org.uk/history.html (accessed 25th August 2011).

parsonages.[164] It pays for clergy house repairs, burglar alarms, and such things, rather than University scholarships, preaching lectures, and gospel ministry directly – the physical rather than the spiritual fabric of the church. As the current Trustees said in a recent Annual Report, "It is certainly impressive that John Marshall's Will should have created grants worth some £60 million at current prices."[165] In 2010, the accounts showed the charity had total funds of around £16 million. It is a worthy and impressive reminder of a Puritan project from the 1620s, though without the theological edge which made the Feoffees Marshall originally donated so controversial.

4. Patronage, Stipends, and the Later History of St. Antholin's

The failure of the Feoffees' project was another factor which encouraged Puritan migration to New England.[166] At least one St. Antholin's Lecturer went there, and a lecturer from Shrewsbury (Rowland Heylyn's home town) emigrated to Amsterdam. Zachary Symmes, at St. Antholin's in the 1620s became the incumbent of a Feoffee church in Dunstable but after the dissolution of the Feoffees he packed up and moved to Charlestown in 1634.[167] Perhaps the Feoffees had foreseen their own demise, or at least planned for it as a possibility, which is why they were also so involved in the Dorchester Company, the New England Company, and the Massachusetts Bay Company. "One of the objects of all three trading companies," remarks Isabel Calder, "was the founding of a refuge for Puritans across the Atlantic."[168] They had seemingly failed to carve out a refuge for themselves in England and Wales, but perhaps they might find more opportunities for gospel

---

[164] His will, the 1855 Marshall's Charity Act, and recent financial information can all be read on the website: http://www.marshalls.org.uk/about.html.
[165] p 5 of the 2010 Annual Trustees' Report for Marshall's Charity.
[166] Calder, 'A Seventeenth Century Attempt to Purify the Anglican Church', p 761.
[167] Calder, 'The St Antholin Lectures', p 54. Hill, *Economic Problems*, p 260.
[168] Calder, *Activities of the Puritan Faction*, pp xxiv and 29 where we learn that John White of Dorchester, an influential Patriarch amongst the Puritans and instrumental in setting up the Dorchester Company, was one of the early donors to the feoffees. See also D. Underdown, *Fire from Heaven: Life in an English Town in the Seventeenth Century* (London: HarperCollins, 1992), pp 108-109 on White's collections for the clergy of Dorchester.

growth in the colonies? In any case, they were probably not surprised by the setback of 1633. As Seaver astutely points out, "Puritans thrived on failure. They advertised their defeats and issued dire warnings of the imminent demise of godly England, if not the end of the world... they learned to live with failure. But this is not to say that they adopted a spirit of accepting passivity."[169]

Laudian policy, says Patrick Collinson, was "as much responsible as any puritan excess for destroying the comprehensiveness of the Church of England and its fully national character."[170] The revolution, however, was just around the corner. In 1640, the Commons Committee for Preaching Ministers under the chairmanship of John White, a former Feoffee, was instructed to reverse the decree against the Collectors of St. Antholin's.[171] The Lectures continued to be well endowed, but the Feoffees' confiscated funds were eventually diverted to army pay.[172] In 1645, Archbishop Laud was executed; another former Feoffee, Samuel Browne, had been a prominent member of the committee which drew up the articles for his impeachment,[173] and indeed, one of the articles against him was that he campaigned against the Feoffees.[174] With the Puritans now in the driving seat, the State itself took on the task which the Collectors of St. Antholin's had begun two decades earlier.[175] Parliamentary Commissioners sitting at Goldsmith's Hall in London under the Chairmanship of Sir Anthony Irby MP began to address the issue of paying preachers. They were able to purchase or leverage a good number of impropriations from "delinquents", that is Royalist supporters upon whom fines had been levied. In part payment

---

[169] Seaver, *The Puritan Lectureships*, p 290.
[170] P. Collinson, *The Elizabethan Puritan Movement* (Oxford: Clarendon Press, 1990), p 247. Cf. Seaver, *The Puritan Lectureships*, p 262 on how Laud and his colleagues "contributed in large measure to the creation of a revolutionary situation."
[171] The copy in the Public Record Office was "criss-crossed with ink lines" in March 1647. Calder, *Activities of the Puritan Faction*, p 125.
[172] Hill, *Economic Problems*, p 267.
[173] Ibid., p 267.
[174] Prynne, *Canterburies Doome*, p 39.
[175] Hill, *Century of Revolution*, p 162.

of these fines, they handed over large amounts of income (totalling around £9000 per annum) to augment the income of preachers.[176]

As part of his programme for the reform of the entire English legal system after the execution of Charles I, the attorney and pamphleteer, William Leach (d. 1655) proclaimed "the funeral of simony, impropriations, and tithes."[177] Oliver Cromwell's Law reformer, William Sheppard, said "I wish [tithes] were taken away... but I suppose this will ask time."[178] Cromwell was wary of abolishing tithes and concerned that "lay impropriators should be compensated," possibly because much of his own income in Huntingdon and Ely had come from administering tithes,[179] but also because he was aware of the complexity of this issue and the strength of feeling aroused by it. Some Oxford and Cambridge colleges had, for example, exchanged lands and revenues with Henry VIII in return for monastic impropriations, which resources, if the latter were to be confiscated, should properly be returned to them.[180] Many different ideas were discussed in those heady days for the better maintenance of preachers but, as with ecclesiastical and indeed constitutional reform today, it seems many could agree on

---

[176] See *Impropriations Purchased by the Commissioners Sitting at Goldsmiths-Hall, For Compositions with Delinquents... For Augmentation of the Maintenance of Preaching Ministers in Severall Parishes within this Kingdome* (London, 1648). See also *An Answer to the Severall Petitions of Late Exhibited to the High Court of Parliament and to His Excellency the Lord General Cromwell by the Poor Husband-men, Farmers and Tenants in Severall Counties of England for the Taking Away of Tithes Paid to Priests and Impropriators* (London, 1652), pp 3-4. J. Ley, *Exceptions Many and Just Against Two Injurious Petitions Exhibited to the Parliament... Not Only Against Tithes, but against All Forced or Constrained Maintenance of Ministers* (Oxford, 1653), p 5.

[177] W. Leach, *The Funerall of Symonie, Impropriations, and Tithes... Published by many welwillers to Christianity and learning (and competent maintenance for the true labourers therein) and just right and equitie* (London, 1653).

[178] See W. Sheppard, *The Parsons Guide: or The Law of Tithes* (London, 1654). N. L. Matthews, *William Sheppard, Cromwell's Law Reformer* (Cambridge: Cambridge University Press, 2004), p 107.

[179] J. S. Morrill, 'The Making of Oliver Cromwell', in J. S. Morrill (ed.), *Oliver Cromwell and the English Revolution* (London: Longman, 1990), p 23.

[180] The errata and addenda of H. S. Spelman, *The Larger Treatise Concerning Tithes Long Since Written and Promised by Sir Hen. Spelman, Knight; Together with Some Other Tracts* (London, 1647), lists Christ Church, New College, Magdalen, and Queen's in Oxford, as examples. See also *An Answer to the Severall Petitions... for the Taking Away of Tithes Paid to Priests and Impropriators*, pp 5-6 which mentions that many of those loyal to Parliament during the civil wars owned impropriations.

the need for change but there was no consensus on what it should look like in detail.

Moving now to the perspective of our own day[181], it is interesting that in 1653 Samuel Clarke spoke of "The mischiefs which would ensue if tithes were brought into a common treasury, and ministers reduced to stipends."[182] The tithe system formally ended quite some time ago, of course, but it is only comparatively recently that historic glebe lands were taken away from local churches by the central administration in return for a promise that ministry there would continue to be funded.[183] Now, the freehold rights of Rectors are also being removed, and we have yet to see what mischief (or good) this may cause in the long term. Equalisation of stipends may generally have been a good thing in that it has removed an economic disincentive for clergy to work in certain poorer areas (and the unhelpful temptation to seek better endowed livings). However, the relatively recent innovation of the "parish share" or "quota" system, very much a centralising solution, does indeed appear to have caused various problems for the Church of England. It has been keenly opposed by many descendents of the Puritans who baulk at the idea of financially supporting a system which seems to like their money but not the gospel which inspires their generosity.

Today's Puritans have sometimes taken radical action on this front to resist centralisation and the alienation of a church's money from the ministry of the parish, much as their forefathers might have done. Many have even set up trusts (feoffments!) to which

---

[181] Bridging the gap to our own day with regards to church property and finance, tithes, stipends, and such things is best done by consulting G.F.A. Best, *Temporal Pillars: Queen Anne's Bounty, The Ecclesiastical Commissioners, and the Church of England* (Cambridge: Cambridge University Press, 1964) which covers the period from the late seventeenth century until 1948, and Andrew Chandler, *The Church of England in the Twentieth Century: The Church Commissioners and the Politics of Reform 1948-1998* (Woodbridge, Suffolk: Boydell Press, 2009).

[182] S. Clarke, *An Item against Sacriledge: or, Sundry Queries Concerning Tithes* (London, 1653).

[183] By virtue of The Endowments and Glebe Measure 1976, glebe (the area of land in a parish used to support the clergyman) ceased to belong to the incumbent of the benefice as of 1st April 1978. Such property now belongs to the various Diocesan Boards of Finance. The Church Commissioners were charged by the Measure with replacing a benefice's endowment income with a guaranteed annuity towards the minister's stipend (with similar provisions for Archdeacons, Curates, and some Lay Assistants).

congregations may give, separate from the parish's accounts, to pay for additional teaching ministry (unordained preachers, youth workers etc) which can then no longer be controlled by the denominational bureaucracy. As Spurr comments regarding Puritan lecturers, however, they may on the one hand have been "less vulnerable to pressure from their bishop, but on the other they were open to pressure from their lay paymasters."[184] The advantage of episcopacy over congregationalism is that there is supposed to be someone for curates, lecturers, associate ministers, and vicars to appeal to for help if things go wrong at parish level; one possible danger of a lack of extra-congregational oversight (or of ordinations by far distant bishops) is that some ministers may be at the mercy of difficult local relationships, with no hope of redress or impartial intervention. Glee at circumventing diocesan demands for cash needs, of course, to be tempered with care for the human resources thereby released.

Quotas placed on how many stipendiary curates a diocese is allowed also mean that some parishes, which can afford to pay for their preachers, have been asked to go without such ministry for a "fallow year" or more. Such a system, supposedly designed to achieve a "fair" distribution of clergy amongst the dioceses, would seem in many instances to put a cap on growth and be a tactic employed merely to manage decline.[185] It seems insufficiently flexible to meet the challenges of church growth and in particular the needs of new and sometimes unconventional congregations (or so-called "Fresh Expressions"). Certainly it can store up resentment and tension in the long term or add to pre-existing friction, as can the fact that parish share paid into diocesan coffers can often be set well above the actual costs of providing

---

[184] Spurr, *English Puritanism 1603-1689*, p 71.
[185] The "Sheffield formula" (so-called because it was designed by a former Bishop of Sheffield) intended to "Enable the Church, over a period of years, to use the manpower that was available in the most effective way possible, and in a manner which would ensure fairer shares between dioceses than the existing distribution, based on historical patterns rather than present needs" according to *Church Statistics: Some Facts and Figures about the Church of England* (London: The Central Board of Finance of the Church of England, 1991), p 16. Since 1975 this has been the major instrument used by the Church of England to effect changes in rural/urban clergy deployment. Quotas are decided by the House of Bishops based on a number of factors such as diocesan populations and areas, numbers on electoral rolls, number of churches, and (since 1988) average Sunday attendances.

stipendiary ministry in a church, and is used to pay for ministry elsewhere.

Evangelical protestations about such financial matters have not always gone down well with other churches, as they did not during the Puritan era. We can be perceived to be rich, smug, and detached and need to work hard to counter that impression. More local approaches to conscientious giving beyond the parish, to support good ministry elsewhere, have gained supporters, however, particularly as the liberal agenda has been more forcefully pushed at various levels in the national Church. Like those who gave to support the Collectors of St. Antholin's, we like to know our money will be well-used and not squandered on those who will not feed people's souls with the saving word of God.

Evangelicals have, in the past, also taken an active interest in the issue of church patronage. Perhaps the most significant name in this respect is Charles Simeon (1759–1836) who greatly strengthened the position of evangelicalism in the Church of England through the purchase of advowsons. Once Simeon got a taste of what could be done in this regard there was no stopping him, and he was able to purchase advowsons in many places, including fashionable watering-places such as Cheltenham, Bath, and Bridlington, and industrial centres such as Northampton, Birmingham, and Bradford. The Municipal Corporations Act of 1835 compelled the corporations to dispose of livings in their gift, and this enabled Simeon and his trust to increase their holdings. Leonard Cowie says that "By the time of his death the trust possessed twenty-one livings, a number which increased to 150 during the next century."[186]

Other bodies such as CPAS and the Church Society also possess patronage rights in a number of churches across the country, and although (since 1924) these cannot be bought or sold, and patrons' rights have been somewhat watered-down in recent years, this allows such evangelical bodies a significant degree of influence over clergy appointments if they choose to make use of it.[187] As Simeon said to the Bishop of Salisbury in 1835, concerning the appointment of the right

---

[186] Leonard W. Cowie, 'Simeon, Charles (1759–1836)', in *ODNB*. See the classic study of W. D. Balda, 'Spheres of Influence: Simeon's Trust and its Implications for Evangelical Patronage.' PhD thesis, University of Cambridge (1981).

[187] A useful, popular level survey of patronage legislation since the eighteenth century can be found in B. Palmer, *Serving Two Masters: Parish Patronage in the Church of England since 1714* (Lewes: Book Guild, 2003).

people to parishes, "*This* is the great reform wanted in our Church; and if generally carried into effect by all who have patronage in the Church, it would supersede all occasion for any further reform. If it did not stop the mouths of Dissenters, it would diminish their numbers, and effectually prevent their increase."[188]

Anglican Evangelicals sometimes appear keener these days to plant new churches entirely outside "the system." This weakens their impact within the Church of England and puts their reforming agenda there somewhat at odds with their plans for growth. It might be better to consider integrating these two things where that is possible, though there is an understandable reluctance on the part of many to invest too much in a Church of England which seems to them hell-bent on making life as uncomfortable as possible for those of classic Reformed Anglican convictions. Perhaps, like the Collectors of St. Antholin's, we need a two-track approach, and to pursue growth within the system as vigorously as possible while also considering what might happen if we are pushed out. This may be costly, as it was for the Feoffees. Any trusts used to fund and coordinate such work should, if we are to learn any lessons from the suppression of the Feoffees, have their purposes very carefully and properly defined. The legal opinion of a good property lawyer could be invaluable; and we need always to recall that financial investments made for the sake of growth can go up as well as down – we cannot trust a fragile economic system to help us anymore than the Feoffees could trust William Laud!

In any event, passivity is not an option. While opportunities remain for gospel ministry and influence within the established church they should be enthusiastically grasped and energetically developed. As with the Feoffees' use of surplus resources from Presteigne and other parishes to subsidise ministry elsewhere, churches with the ability to financially help others in need of clear gospel ministry should actively seek out opportunities to do so. Similarly, the Feoffees' strategic use of St. Antholin's as base for training ministers who were then deployed in the darker corners of the land should remind bigger churches everywhere (not just the capital) that they have a responsibility not to hoard their human resources but put them to use in evangelising the

---

[188] W. Carus & C. P. McIlvaine (eds.), *Memoirs of the Life of the Rev. Charles Simeon: with a Selection from his Writings and Correspondence* (Pittsburgh, 1847), p 752.

nation as a whole. There are huge numbers of un-evangelised people in the capital, of course, but they are usually much closer to a gospel-preaching church (and therefore within the sound of the gospel) than millions of unreached, spiritually-famished people outside the urbanised South-East of England. How can we, like our seventeenth century forebears, strategise for their salvation, and the strengthening of churches North of the Watford Gap?

The history of St. Antholin's and those who ministered there should encourage us along these paths. On another occasion, we might consider some of the other great names associated with this now demolished church on Budge Row, Watling Street. We might narrate how William Kiffin (1616-1701), a founding father of the particular Baptists, was converted to Puritan theology after hearing a lecture at St. Antholin's one morning. We may hear how John Wesley preached at St. Antholin's on May 25th 1738, the very morning after his heart was "strangely warmed," but also how, very soon afterwards, Richard Venn (1691-1739), Rector of St. Antholin's in the early eighteenth century forbade any further Methodists from preaching there. His son, the more famous Henry Venn, was a St. Antholin's Lecturer, and Wesley was there again several times before his death as, it seems on occasion, was William Wilberforce.[189] The great evangelist George Whitefield preached on justification by faith alone at St. Antholin's in 1738.[190]

We could also recall how Richard Johnson (1755-1827) was colonial chaplain to New South Wales, arriving with the first fleet to celebrate the very first Anglican church service there under "a great tree" at Sydney Cove on February 3rd 1788. After his Australian mission, he returned to England in 1800 and eventually became Rector of St. Antholin's.[191] He was followed sometime later by William Goode, who was Rector of the church 1835-1849. In his day, Goode was "widely acknowledged as the most able and learned champion of the evangelical party within the Church of England... For almost forty years he took a prominent part in nearly every major controversy in the Church of England. His writings reveal a formidable polemicist with a deep

---

[189] See Calder, 'The St Antholin Lectures', pp 60-61.
[190] See L. Gatiss (ed.), *The Sermons of George Whitefield: Part 2*, The Reformed Evangelical Anglican Library Volume 1.2 (Watford: Church Society, 2010), pp 238-249 (Sermon 46 on 1 Corinthians 6:11).
[191] See John N. Molony, 'Johnson, Richard (*bap.* 1755, *d.* 1827)', in *ODNB*.

knowledge of patristic, medieval, and Reformation literature, and a firm grasp of the intricacies of both historical theology and ecclesiastical law."[192] Puritan Reformed theology seems never to have departed from St. Antholin's, despite many setbacks, and neither was it ever bereft of that bold ingenuity and outward-looking, entrepreneurial spirit which brought it to prominence in the sixteenth and seventeenth centuries.

The story of the decline, demolition, and eventual rebirth of St. Antholin's is, however, a story for another day.

---

[192] See Stephen Gregory, 'Goode, William (1801–1868)', in *ODNB*.

Word and Spirit: The Puritan-Quaker Debate

Peter Adam

1. Setting the scene: Puritan England in the 1650s 51
2. The Fundamental Issue: Word and Spirit 55
3. Consequences and Clarifications 60
4. Historical Reflections 84
   - 4.1. *Word and Spirit in the Reformers* 84
   - 4.2. *Enlightenment heat and Quaker light* 86
   - 4.3. *Puritans and Quakers: friends or foes?* 86
   - 4.4. *What Puritans believed about the Bible* 87
   - 4.5. *Quakers, Puritans, and Gospel truth* 87
5. Contemporary Reflections 88
   - 5.1. *Quaker patterns of using the Bible* 88
   - 5.2. *Modern Spirit-Word dichotomy* 89
   - 5.3. *Contemporary Evangelical confusion* 90
   - 5.4. *Christ and the Bible* 93

PETER J. H. ADAM served several curacies in Melbourne, Australia and studied in England at both London and Durham Universities, gaining a PhD from the latter on the practice of the imitation of Christ with special reference to the theology of Dietrich Bonhoeffer in 1981. After several years as a tutor at St. John's College, Durham he returned to Australia and was minister of St. Jude's, Carlton for 20 years and Anglican Chaplain to Melbourne University. He became Principal of Ridley Mission and Ministry College, Melbourne in 2002 and has published several books on biblical spirituality and exposition including *Hearing God's Words* and *Written for Us*.

This lecture is dedicated to the ministers and people of St. Antholin's Budge Row, London, who preached the Gospel, taught the Holy Scriptures, defended the faith, and worked for the spread of the Gospel and the conversion of their nation.

I am grateful for help from Ian Breward, Keith Condie, and Rhys Bezzant, and from the Library staff of the State Library of Victoria, and Monash University.

In quotations from 17th Century documents I have used the original spelling.

1. Setting the scene: Puritan England in the 1650s

Richard Baxter, in memorable words, complained of the 'giddy and turbulent sectaries' who disturbed the life and ministry of the church in his days.

In the St. Antholin's Lecture for 1998, "The Church 'Halfly Reformed,'" I addressed the difficulties the Puritans had in continuing to reform the national church. Here I turn to their difficulties with the Quakers, prominent among the 'giddy and turbulent sectaries.' 'Giddy' because they seemed erratic in ideas and practice; 'turbulent' because they caused turmoil within the Puritan movement and nation; and 'sectaries' because they were separatists, that is, they formed their own churches.

This lecture does not represent original historical research, but an attempt to provide an 'Anatomy' of the important theological issue that divided Puritans from Quakers in the 1650s, that of Word and Spirit.

By Puritan I mean those who were the leading edge of the move to convert sinners, reform the church, and change the nation. Puritans were 'the hotter sort of Protestants.' Their aim was to achieve, in Patrick Collinson's words,

> [T]he bright Elizabethan vision of a godly commonwealth, instructed in one doctrine from the pulpit of every parish church, and corrected by one uniform and wholesome discipline.[1]

When the Puritan movement began within the Church of England, the parish of St. Antholin's Budge Row in London quickly became a powerhouse of Reformed and biblical teaching, of expository preaching, of evangelistic strategy, and of Puritan hopes.

There were different brands of Puritans within the Church of England in the 1650s. They included convinced Anglicans committed to the further reformation of the Church of England along the lines of

---

[1] Patrick Collinson, *Puritanism and the English Church* (London: Jonathan Cape, 1967), p 465.

Archbishop Ussher's 'Reduced [i.e. Synodical] Episcopacy'; those committed to the Presbyterian restructuring of that Church; and various kinds of Independents and Baptists. There was some continuity between more radical Puritans and the Quakers, as we shall see.

Within the Puritan movement there was a strong contrast between conservative Puritans who worked for the reform of the National Church, who were hierarchical in thought, and who were reluctant to leave its ministry; and the radical Puritans who were egalitarian, and who tended to form new ecclesial bodies. There was a range of attitude to preaching and teaching in the church, from the conservative view that only properly ordained men could preach, through the view that any gifted person could preach even if they were untrained 'tub-preachers,' to the idea that all men and women should speak for God.

Quakers, like Baptists, objected to church buildings which they called 'steeple-houses.' Quakers followed the ideas of some Independents in denying the sacraments. Some Independents allowed women ministers, as some Baptists allowed women prophets like Anna Trapnel. For conservative Puritans, preaching was the exposition of the Bible. For Independents and Baptists, 'prophecy' meant exhortation based as much on personal testimony as on the Bible. For Quakers, women as well as men could prophesy, but from their hearts, not from the Bible.

Conservative Puritans approved of the compulsory tithe system, because it paid the stipends of the ministers. Radical Puritans and Quakers were generally opposed to these tithes. Quakers, like radical Puritans, were against 'tyrannicall Kings and bloody Bishops,' against magistracy and ministry that opposed them.

It was painful for conservative Puritans to be accused of compromise by the radical Puritans and the Quakers, to be out-flanked by them in the matter of reformation. Conservative Puritans wanted to distance themselves from their more radical friends, lest their own moves for further reform be compromised. There can be few more painful debates than between fellow-reformers who disagree about the method, shape, and speed of reform.

So from one perspective the Quakers were Radical Puritans, and this is a helpful insight, as Geoffrey Nuttall has shown in *The Holy Spirit in Puritan Faith and Experience*.[2]

The complementary truth, the perspective of this Lecture, is that the Puritans, conservative or radical, followed a different faith to the Quakers, and this difference resulted from opposing views on Word and Spirit. We cannot be accused of importing an alien distinction into the debate, because both Puritans and Quakers were strongly aware of the differences between them, and regarded their battle as of fundamental and critical significance. Their sociological similarities should not blind us to their deep theological differences. The titles of their tracts indicate the strength of their controversy: *The Boasting Baptist Dismounted and the Beast Disarmed, The Quaker Quashed and his Quarrel Quelled, George Fox Digg'd out of his Burrow.*

Puritan was the name of a family grouping, out of which grew the Quaker movement. The conflict between Puritans and Quakers was especially painful because the Puritans were enjoying political influence in the 1650s, and also because it was a time of last-days intensity.

Most Protestants believed at this time that the 1000-year reign of Christ had continued till 1100; then the Papacy or Antichrist had become powerful; then the Reformation marked the beginning of the end. They were witnessing the Fall of Antichrist, the conversion of the Jews, the rule of the saints, and the second Coming of Christ. The political edge to this was the expectation of the Fifth Monarchy [following the four- Assyria, Persia, Greece, and Rome], which would be the rule of Christ and his saints on earth.

The Quaker fight against the Puritans was part of 'The Lamb's War,' as they termed it. Both sides felt a last-days intensity about their conflict. As Archbishop Ussher complained, 'nothing is so familiar nowadays ... as to father upon Antichrist whatsoever in church matters we do not find to sort with our own humours.'[3]

It is also significant that many early Quakers began their life within Puritanism, often as the children of Puritan parents. They often

---

[2] Geoffrey Nuttall, *The Holy Spirit in Puritan Faith and Experience*, with an introduction by Peter Lake (Oxford: Basil Blackwell, 1992).
[3] Christopher Hill, *The English Bible and the Seventeenth Century Revolution* (London: Penguin Books, 1993), p 317.

began with a deep conviction of sin, but found no gospel relief within Puritan faith. Quakers felt frustrated with Puritans, and Puritans felt betrayed by Quakers. Richard Baxter describes those moving on from Puritanism in these words: 'I had far rather that men continued Separatists and Anabaptists than turned Quaker or plain apostates.'[4]

The success of the Quaker movement over ten years was astonishing. In the ten years from 1652 it grew from a few people to 40,000, if not 60,000. By 1662 there were as many Quakers as Catholics in England.[5]

The Quaker Stephen Crisp describes his life in his allegory *A Short History of a Long Travel from Babylon to Bethel*,[6] similar to John Bunyan's *Pilgrim's Progress*. Crisp was dissatisfied with Puritan preachers, and discovered them to be blind guides, physicians of no value, and hireling shepherds because they were paid by compulsory tithes. They were people of a book, the Bible, and so demonstrated that they themselves did not know the way of truth. Crisp then tried the Independents, then the Anabaptists, before hearing the Quaker message. Then 'the new man was made, and so peace came to be made, and so it pleased the Father to reveal his Son in me.'

Some Quakers began in meetings of Seekers, people on the edge of Puritan churches who were as yet unsatisfied, convinced that the church and ministry they knew was deficient, and searching for a deeper knowledge of God. They met to read the Scriptures, and then wait for a further direct revelation of God in silence.[7]

The Quakers we are studying are those of the 1650s. Quaker ideas since that date have varied greatly, and modern Quakers would not all identify with their 17th Century antecedents.

---

[4] Richard Baxter, *The Quakers Catechism* (1655), A4.
[5] B. Reay, 'Quakerism and Society', in McGregor, J. F., and Reay, B. [eds.], *Radical Religion in the English Revolution* (Oxford: Oxford University Press, 1984), p 141.
[6] Owen C. Watkins, *The Puritan Experience* (London: Routledge & Kegan Paul, 1972), pp 160-164.
[7] Hugh Barbour, *The Quakers in Puritan England* (New Haven and London: Yale University Press, 1964), pp 31, 32.

2. The Fundamental Issue: Word and Spirit

As we have seen, there were very close connections between the Puritans and the Quakers, and many Quakers came from a Puritan background. What was their fundamental disagreement? It was about the crucial issue of the way in which God speaks to his people. The Puritans believed that God spoke through the Bible, and the Quakers believed that God spoke immediately, and not through the Bible. Both agreed that believing and obeying God's words was crucial: they disagreed about the way in which God communicated his words to his people.

The Puritans believed that the Spirit's words were the Bible. William Bridge wrote that 'the written word of God is our appointed Food, our daily Food.'[8] They regarded the Scripture as inspired by the Holy Spirit, and self-authenticating. In the words of John Arrowsmith, 'Holy men of God ... spake as they were moved by the Holy Ghost. They wrote accordingly.'[9]

According to John Ball, the Bible was inspired in both matter and form: 'to be immediately inspired is to be, as it were, breathed, and to come from the Father, by the Holy Ghost, without all means.'[10] So to wait on God's words in the Bible and through the preacher is a sign of humility before God. Jeremiah Burroughs reminded his congregation 'you come to tender up your homage to God, to sit at God's feet and there to profess your submission to him.'[11]

However in Margaret Fell's account of her conversion to Quaker experience, we find the Quaker distinction between what God has said through Christ and the Apostles, and what God is now saying to the child of Light inwardly:

> And then he [George Fox] went on, and opened the Scriptures, and said The Scriptures were the prophets' words, and Christ's, and the apostles' words, and what as they spoke they enjoyed and possessed and had it from the Lord. And said, 'Then what

---

[8] H. D. McDonald, *Ideas of Revelation, An Historical Study 1700 to 1860* (London: Macmillan & Co., 1959), p 203.
[9] McDonald, *Ideas of Revelation*, p 202.
[10] McDonald, *Ideas of Revelation*, pp 202,203.
[11] Jeremiah Burroughs, *Gospel Worship* (Ligonier: Sole Deo Gloria Publications, 1990), p 197.

had any to do with the scriptures but as they came to the Spirit that gave them forth? You will say, Christ saith this, and the apostles say this, but what canst thou say? Are thou a Child of Light, and hast thou walked in the Light, and what thou speakest is it inwardly from God?' I cried in my spirit to the Lord, 'We are all thieves, we are all thieves, we have taken the scriptures in words, and know nothing of them in ourselves.'[12]

George Fox, in his anti-Puritan tract *The Great Mistery Of The Great Whore Unfolded, and Antichrist's Kingdom Revealed unto Destruction* claimed that having the Scriptures was no use without the Spirit:

> And who have the Spirit of God, have that which is infallible ... Now many may have the scriptures, and if they have not the Spirit that gave them forth, they do not worship God in the Spirit.[13]

The Quakers also called the indwelling Spirit the Light of Christ. The Quakers believed that God gave the Light of Christ to everyone, and identified that Light with salvation in Christ. The Puritans believed that it was important to distinguish between the light of general revelation that God gave to all, and the saving light of Christ found in the gospel. So Baxter wrote about this inner Light:

> [Do] you mean it is sufficient to leave men without excuse [that we maintain as well as you], or is every man's light sufficient to his salvation? Or is it now sufficient to all who have never heard the gospel? If so, is not the gospel a vain a needless thing? If the world has sufficient light, what need they your teaching, of discourse, or conviction? If all have sufficient light within them, what need they any converting grace?[14]

The Quakers however meant that the saving Light of Christ came to everyone directly from God, and was not limited to those who had heard the Gospel of Christ by hearing or reading the Bible.

The debate also turned on whether Puritans believed in personal and immediate revelations. So Baxter claimed:

---

[12] William C. Braithwaite, *The Beginnings of Quakerism* (London: Macmillan and Co., 1912), p 101.
[13] George Fox, *The Great Mistery of the Great Whore Unfolded* (1659), p 28.
[14] Baxter, *The Quakers Catechism*, p 8.

> I own all divine revelations, and disown all diabolical ones, so far as I know them. I own all those blessed revelations contained in the holy Scriptures, for they were infallibly sealed by multitudes of uncontrolled miracles and a spirit of holiness. I believe that the scriptures or laws of Christ being finished and sealed [1 Tim. 6: 13, 14], and that these are able to make men wise to salvation without any more additions, and therefore no more is to be expected. But yet I believe:
>
> 1. That God has not tied himself from revealing particular matters in subserviency to scripture extraordinarily, as divers murders have been revealed, and the like matters of fact.
>
> 2. And I believe that all true Christians have the illuminating, sanctifying spirit of Christ to help them to know all the meaning of scripture which is of flat necessity to salvation.[15]

The Quakers did not make use of what the Spirit had said to others in times past in the Bible, and would only use what God was saying to them in the present age. They objected to believers saying David's Psalms, because these were the Spirit's words to David, not to people today. Baxter replied:

> If all scripture is written for our use and learning, why may we not speak to God in the words of David's psalms as well as any other scripture?[16]

Of course both believed in the work of the Spirit within. In the words of the Puritan Richard Sibbes, 'The Spirit of God must work in us spiritual sense, sight and taste, that we may see, discern, and relish heavenly things.'[17] Puritans as well as Quakers expected spiritual life and vitality in their ministry. As Baxter wrote, there is nothing more indecent 'than to be a dead preacher speaking to a dead people the living truth of the living God.'

The distinction between them was in their use of the Bible. John Knott, in *The Sword of the Spirit*, describes the Digger Winstanley's use of Scripture in words that also describe that of the Quakers.

---

[15] Baxter, *The Quakers Catechism*, pp 12, 13.
[16] Ibid., p 13.
[17] John R. Knott Jr., *The Sword of the Spirit: Puritan Responses to the Bible* (Chicago and London: University of Chicago Press, 1980), p 48.

- Where the orthodox Puritan divine, instructed by Perkins, painstakingly collected parallel texts and tested his interpretations by the analogy of faith, Winstanley followed his intuitions of the Spirit in rendering what he saw as the truth behind the letter, not so much expounding scripture as re-creating it by fashioning his own highly individual version of the Fall and redemption of Man.

- Winstanley approached the Bible as a poet might, alive to the power of images and the symbolic force of names ...

- Winstanley could let his imagination range freely over Scripture because the words of the text had no fixed meaning for him.[18]

In fact the words and messages that the Quakers received and passed on to others were frequently in words that originated in the Scriptures. They had learned enough from the Scriptures to know that, in the words of Barbour; 'the Bible was the Spirit's characteristic vocabulary.'[19] Over 70% of their writings used biblical language.[20] Their Puritan background meant that in many cases the Bible formed an unconscious safeguard on their understanding of what God was saying to them. Quaker leaders were so immersed in the Scriptures as a result of their Puritan upbringing that the manifestation of the Spirit to which they bore witness was tested by the written Word in ways of which they were not conscious.[21]

However the use of biblical words and phrases was also deceptive, in that it concealed the wide gap between Puritan faith and Quaker experience. For the use of biblical phrases does not ensure that the Bible's message is being communicated. Indeed, the use of biblical phrases may have obscured the fact that the Quaker message was a radical departure from Puritan faith. For the Quakers' use of the Bible was of course selective. They sensed vitality in those passages that corresponded to their own vivid experience and felt coldness when Puritans expounded them.[22]

The 20th Century Quaker Harold Loukes makes a very revealing

---

[18] Knott, *The Sword of the Spirit*, pp 96, 97.
[19] Barbour, *The Quakers in Puritan England*, p 121.
[20] Ibid., p 157.
[21] McDonald, *Ideas of Revelation*, p 178.
[22] Knott, *The Sword of the Spirit*, p 157.

point when he writes that:

> Quaker propaganda was full of Biblical quotation, but not by way of appeal to authority so much as a persuasive device. Those who listened took the Bible as authority. Friends [i.e. Quakers] appealed to it to destroy its authority.[23]

The Puritan objections to Quaker claims were not only about their view of revelation, but also about the consequences of this error in the remainder of their beliefs. Richard Baxter claimed that the Quakers and the Papists had at heart the same theological system, because both replaced the authority of the Scripture by a human authority. He claimed that the Papists had infiltrated and seduced the Quakers, and that Quakers were conscious or unconscious agents of Papistry.

> If you ask me how I know it is Papists who thus seduce them, I can answer: 1. Because they do the Papists work, and maintain their cause ... [T]he disgracing and secret undermining [of] the sufficiency of the scripture, the decrying of the ministry, the unchurching of our churches, the slighting of justification by imputed righteousness ... the crying up the light within us, and the sufficiency of common revelation, the setting up the strength of man's free will, the asserting the necessity of a judge of controversy above scripture [which they are content should be the spirit of revelation awhile, till they can boldlier exchange that for the Pope] ... the doctrine of perfection without sin in this life. All this the Papists have taught the Quakers.[24]

Whether or not there was in fact some connection between the Roman Catholic Church and any Quakers, Baxter is making a theological point about the similarities of belief in these two systems.

The Puritan objections to the Quaker view were matched by Luther and Calvin's objections to the prophets of their times. So Luther said of the Zwickau prophets, that he would not believe them 'though they had swallowed the Holy Ghost, feathers and all' or 'even if it snow miracles everyday.'

The Quakers did not expect that the Spirit would contradict his past revelations in the Bible, but denied that the Spirit spoke through the Bible

---

[23] Harold Loukes, *The Quaker Contribution* (London: S. C. M., 1965), p 28.
[24] Baxter, *The Quakers Catechism*, C3.

today. Ironically, though they would assert that God spoke to all, they would not accept the Puritan witness that God spoke to them through the Bible.

3. Consequences and Clarifications

If Revelation is immediate, as the Quakers claimed, then we should note the following consequences and clarifications.

3.1 Revelation is immediate, so the Bible is obsolete

The Puritan Francis Higginson wrote *The Irreligion Of The Northern Quakers* in 1653. The Quaker movement grew initially in the north of England, and attracted many from Puritan congregations.

Higginson attacked the attitude to Scripture that resulted from the Quaker conviction that revelation is immediate:

> 1. They hold that the holy scripture, the writings of the prophets, evangelists, and apostles, are not the word of God, and that there is no written word of God; but they say, using a foolish distinction of their own coining, that they are a declaration of the word only in those that have the faith.

> 2. They hold that their own speakings are a declaration of the word [Christ] in them, thereby making them, though they be for the most part full of impiety and nonsense, to be of equal authority with the holy scriptures.

Higginson also noted Quaker opposition to exegetical preaching and teaching of the Scriptures, and their attack on this style of Puritan ministry:

> 3. They hold that no exposition ought to be given of the holy scripture, and that all such exposition of scripture is an adding to it, and that God will add to such a one all the plagues written in that book. Opening, and applying the scripture, is one thing they mainly declaim against, wherever they come.

> 4. They teach poor people that whosoever takes a text of scripture and makes a sermon of it or from it is a conjurer, and

that his preaching is conjuration.[25]

When Higginson mentions conjuration, he is replying to the language Quakers used to attack exegetical preaching, for example George Fox's words in *Saul's Errand to Damascus* of 1653:

> All that study to raise a living thing out of a dead, to raise the spirit out of the letter, are conjurers, and draw points and reasons, and so speak a divination out of their own brain. They are conjurers and diviners, and their teaching is from conjuration, which is not spoken from the mouth of the Lord, and the Lord is against all such, and who are of God are against all such.[26]

Fox is claiming that the Scripture is dead, and that it represents the letter rather than the spirit. He describes exegesis of the Scripture as conjuring and divination, so clearly forbidden in the Old Testament.

William Dell makes the point even clearer, 'the believer is now the only book in which God writes his new testament.' As Barbara Siddall said of the Bible, 'not the Word of God but onely a dead letter.'[27]

The Quakers regarded the Bible as valid for its time, as the record of how God spoke to the people who wrote it. However it was now obsolete, and a distraction from hearing God's words at the present time, as George Fox wrote.

> The Spirit that gave forth the Scriptures teaches us how to pray, sing, fast, give thanks, to praise and worship, and how to honour and glorify God. And so the Spirit of Truth, which gave forth the Scriptures is our director, guide, leader and comforter.[28]

For Fox, the Spirit was sufficient revelation.

> And we found this light to be a sufficient teacher to lead us to Christ ... and in all things we found the light which we were inlightened withal ... to be alone and onelie sufficient to bring to

---

[25] Francis Higginson, *A Brief Relation of the Irreligion of the Northern Quakers* (1653), p 4.
[26] George? Fox and James Nayler, *Saul's Errand to Damascus* (1653), p 7.
[27] Reay, 'Quakerism and Society', p 146.
[28] Jonathan Fryer (ed.), *George Fox and the Children of Light* [Journal and Epistles of George Fox] (London: Kyle Cathie, 1991), p 225.

life and eternal salvation.[29]

The Puritans recognised the danger of this attitude to Scripture. It was, in the words of Thomas Shepherd:

> the precipice of all delusion [to] forsake the scriptures and wait for a spirit to suggest immediately God's inmost thought toward me.[30]

Yet the idea that God could speak outside Scripture was also found within those who would be regarded as Puritans. So Oliver Cromwell claimed that: 'As well without the Written Word as with it God doth speak to the hearts and consciences of men.'[31] John Goodwin went even further when he wrote that:

> reformation according to the word of God must give way to the wind to blow where it listeth and give liberty to the spirit of God to do with his own what he pleaseth.[32]

H. D. McDonald, in his historical study *Ideas of Revelation*, points out that there is a similarity between the view that certain knowledge derives from human reason, and the view that certain knowledge comes from immediate revelation.[33] Both look for certainty within the individual, either within reason or within feeling.

The orthodox response to both attitudes has been to assert the authority and effectiveness of the more objective revelation in Scripture. This was certainly the response of the Puritans.

So John Owen asserted the inspiration of Scripture as he described the human authors of Scripture: 'They invented not the words themselves, suited to the things they had learnt, but only expressed the words they received.' Owen claimed that the work of the Spirit is found in the Scriptures: '[The Spirit never] speaks to us of the Word, but by the Word'

Here the point is present efficacy of the Bible, the way in which the Spirit speaks today. The Quakers did not deny that the Bible was

---

[29] Fox, *The Great Mistery of the Great Whore Unfolded*, To the Reader.
[30] Spurr, *English Puritanism 1603-1689* (Basingstoke and London: Macmillan Press, 1998), p 7.
[31] Geoffrey F. Nuttall, *The Puritan Spirit: Essays and Addresses* (London: Epworth Press, 1967), p 175.
[32] Spurr, *English Puritanism*, p 111.
[33] McDonald, *Ideas of Revelation*, chs 2-4.

written by inspiration of the Spirit. They claimed that the same Spirit indwelt every believer, and that to use the Bible was to use non-immediate and therefore obsolete revelation.

John Owen's reply was based on the idea that the Bible is self-authenticating as effective present revelation, that God gives the testimony of the Spirit to render effective the revelation, and that this is 'the public testimony of the Holy Ghost, by and in the Word, and its own divine light, efficacy and power.'[34]

Other Puritans rejected the Quaker claims of immediate revelation as 'Jack-in-the-Lantern,' 'Will-o' the wisp.' George Fox claimed that through his teaching:

> the Lord's power was over all and people were turned to God by his spirit, with which they came to know Christ, and God, and the Scriptures.[35]

Of course he meant they had gained a Quaker perspective, with its distinctive attitude to the Bible. His own perception that Christ enlightens everyone was not gained from the Scriptures [what he calls 'the letter'], but by direct and immediate inspiration.

> These things I did not see by the help of man, nor by the letter, though they are written in the letter, but I saw them in the light of the Lord Jesus Christ, and by his immediate Spirit and power, as did the holy men of God, by whom the Holy Scriptures were written.[36]

The Quakers believed that the Scripture was inspired but is now obsolete, and that only present and immediate revelation is valid, while the Puritans believed that the inspired Scripture remains the effective word of God. The Quakers believed in the sufficiency of the Light within, while the Puritans believed in the sufficiency of the Scriptures.

3.2 Revelation is immediate, so salvation history occurs now

Another consequence of immediate revelation is that as the present

---

[34] McDonald, *Ideas of Revelation*, pp 197-199.
[35] George Fox, *The Journal of George Fox*, (ed. John L. Nickalls; London: Religious Society of Friends, 1975), p 124.
[36] Nuttall, *The Holy Spirit in Puritan Faith and Experience*, p 52.

replaces the past in verbal revelation, it does also in salvation history. God's works as well as God's words become contemporary.

It is this present aspect of saving history which lay behind the often inflated language used of the early Quaker leaders, Fox and Nayler.

Here are some examples of the language used to address George Fox:

> • let not that beastly power which keeps us in bondage seperate thy bodyly prsence from us, who reigns as king above it & would reioyce to see thy kingly power here triumph over it

> • Grant that I may live with thee for ever & be cload with thy righteousnesse

> • he is a blessings to ye nations and ye Joy off his people ye second appearance of him whoe Is blessed for ever.[37]

> • Deare Geoff who art the father of the faithfull ... I know thee whome thou art, who was ded and is alive & for ever lives.[38]

In 1656 James Nayler rode into Bristol welcomed by his followers with shouts of "Hosanna to the Son of David". These actions of the Quakers were inspired by the Scriptures, but meant that the focus of attention was on the progress of God's kingdom through them now, rather than through salvation history recorded in the Scriptures. The immediacy of verbal revelation was matched by the immediacy of salvation history.

Geoffrey Nuttall wrote that Fox:

> so 'telescopes' the divine processes of creation and redemption as inevitably to reduce the significance of the coming of Christ and His Holy Spirit in history.[39]

In the words of the 20th Century Quaker H. G. Wood, there are three defects within Quakerism from its beginning. These are 'the tendency to distrust the intellect, to suspect the outward, and to neglect the historical.'[40] He also comments that William Penn's writings lacked 'an

---

[37] Nuttall, *The Holy Spirit in Puritan Faith and Experience*, pp 181, 182.
[38] Watkins, *The Puritan Experience*, p 147.
[39] Nuttall, *The Holy Spirit in Puritan Faith and Experience*, p 159.
[40] R. Newton Flew, *The Idea Of Perfection in Christian Theology* (New York: Humanities Press, 1968), p 290.

adequate conception of the history of salvation.'[41]

If the past had been caught up into the present, so too the future has also been made present in the Quaker experience. So Watkins comments that the Quaker is already in the Celestial City, so the battle is external not internal.[42] The future is experienced completely now within the immediacy of divine revelation, so the only remaining battle is in the world, and not within the believer.

John Owen noted the vital connection between the historical revelation in Christ and the Holy Scriptures in his reply to the Quakers. He pointed out that Christ and Scripture have the same formal content, that is, the saving will of God.[43] Christ sends the Spirit, so the message of the Spirit will be that of Christ. As Christ is sufficient for salvation, so the Scriptures are sufficient for knowledge of salvation. As God's saving work in Christ is found in history, so God's revelation of the meaning of that work is also found in that same history.

3.3 Revelation is immediate, so Christ's saving work is internal, not historical

It was not just that the Quakers' focus on God's immediate saving work resulted in a lack of regard for the saving work of Christ on the cross. They believed that the Puritan emphasis on the atoning work of Christ on the cross was an evasion of personal responsibility, a way of excusing sin, and an avoidance of costly moral perfection. So the Quakers saw the great Puritan doctrines of imputed righteousness and substitutionary atonement as an evasion of the agony of facing personal sin, repenting of it, and becoming perfect.[44]

So although the Puritans had a reputation for demanding great moral change in believers, from the perspective of the Quakers their trust in the atoning work of Christ on the cross meant in practice that they accepted continued sinning too easily. Their message could be

---

[41] Nuttall, *The Holy Spirit in Puritan Faith and Experience*, p 159.
[42] Watkins, *The Puritan Experience*, p 205.
[43] Carl R. Trueman, *The Claims of Truth: John Owen's Trinitarian Theology* (Carlisle: Paternoster Press, 1998), pp 70-75.
[44] Barbour, *The Quakers in Puritan England*, p 106.

ridiculed as 'Christ died outside the gates of Jerusalem, and then all is well.'[45]

So in *Saul's Errand*, a Quaker tract of 1653, the answer to the question 'Whether a believer be justified by Christ's righteousness imputed, yea, or no?' is that: '"He that believeth is born of God"; and he that is born of God, is justified by Christ alone without imputation.'[46]

And in Edward Burrough's *Declaration to All the World of our Faith* there is no mention of the atoning work of Christ, even though he asserts that 'salvation, justification and sanctification are only in [Christ].'[47]

In his *The Idea of Perfection in Christian Theology*, Newton Flew comments:

> Fox knows, like his later followers, that the Cross is no 'dead fact, stranded on the shore of the oblivious years,' but an inward living experience in the heart of the believer, refashioning his life into perfect love.[48]

For the Puritan, the Cross derives its internal power to transform from its external reality in the history of salvation. However it is also true that Fox did later assert his belief in the historic saving work of Christ.

> Christ gave himself, his body for the life of the world: he was the offering for the sins of the whole world, and paid the debt, and made satisfaction.[49]

In general Fox and his associates were more radical in their assessment of the atoning death of Christ in the 1650s. They reverted to more orthodox views by the 1670s, as is demonstrated in Robert Barclay's Catechism and Confession of Faith of 1673.[50]

Moderate Quakers asserted both the historic work of Christ and the importance of his immediate work in the believer. Radical Quakers placed so much emphasis on Christ's immediate work that they denied

---

[45] Watkins, *The Puritan Experience*, p 162.
[46] Fox and Nayler, *Saul's Errand to Damascus*, p 12.
[47] Barbour and Roberts, *Early Quaker Writings*, p 299.
[48] Flew, *The Idea Of Perfection in Christian Theology*, p 291.
[49] Fox, *The Great Mistery of the Great Whore Unfolded*, Response to Jeremy Ives.
[50] Hugh Barbour and Arthur O. Roberts [eds.], *Early Quaker Writings 1650-1700* (Grand Rapids: Eerdmans, 1973), pp 314-349.

his historic and external work on the cross.

The Quakers believed that the coming of the Light to the believer resulted in such a radical transformation that perfection was attained. The Puritans believed that though forgiveness was found in the atoning death of Christ, complete moral transformation would only occur at the return of Christ. For the Quaker, all was in the present: for the Puritan, faith in Christ involved trusting in his saving death and resurrection in the past, and waiting for his return in the future, for the personal, corporate, and creational transformation that he will bring at that time. Barbour comments on the Quakers:

> The effect was to make the actual historical events of Jesus' life mainly an example, at times only a symbol or type, of the recurring events on every Christian's pilgrimage.[51]

3.4 Revelation is immediate, so the Golden Age is now

The Quaker experience was so vivid and powerful for those involved that they assumed that they were living in a Golden Age. This view is characteristic of those living in a time of revival of religion.

There were three possible interpretations of the significance of a Golden Age. It could be: i. 'the last days,' interpreted as a time of great revival, ii. a return of the primitive age of the founding of Christianity; or iii. the third age, the age of the Spirit.

i. The Puritan Richard Sibbes spoke of these 'latter times' in which there was:

> a reformation of religion, after our recovery out of popery ... a second spring of the gospel [through] the revelation of Christ by the Spirit, which hath the Spirit accompanying it.[52]

Arthur Dent in 1603 thought that his was the last age, that of the war between the armies of Christ and the Antichrist.[53] In the words of John Milton:

> God is decreeing to begin some new and great period in His

---

[51] Barbour, *The Quakers in Puritan England*, p 146.
[52] Nuttall, *The Holy Spirit in Puritan Faith and Experience*, p 104.
[53] Christopher Hill, *A Turbulent, Seditious and Factious People: John Bunyan and his Church* (Oxford: Oxford University Press, 1988), p 94.

> Church, even to the reforming of the Reformation itself: what does He then but reveal Himself to His Servants, and as His manner is, first to His Englishmen [sic!].[54]

Iain Murray has described the Puritan hope of the last days in terms of evangelism and revival, including the conversion of the Jews.[55] This expectation also lay behind the Quaker movement, which claimed to represent a worldwide revival of true Christianity in the last days.

ii. Franklin Littell writes of that Primitivism which was a feature of the Anabaptists, part of the radical reformation movement in Europe.[56] The restoration of the primitive age is an important clue to Quaker faith. Dismissing traditions is understandable when the first fine careless rapture is being recovered. The title of William Penn's book *Primitive Christianity Revived* captures this Quaker hope.

The call for further reform in the church could be an expression of the Quaker desire to go beyond the Scriptures. It could also be a recognition that the principle of *semper reformanda* meant that the achievements of the 16th Century Reformers should not preclude further reformation.

If there was a revival of the first days, could it be that revelations should continue? Puritans believed that extraordinary revelations that happened in the days of the Apostles should not be expected today. They believed that God's saving works, words, and signs were all tied to salvation history. Quakers asserted that God's saving work was immediate and in the present, and that signs should accompany this revelation.

iii. William Erbury wrote of his Quaker age in terms of the third age, that of the Spirit.

> God under the Law and to the Fathers before, was known, as the Father. In the Gospel, God was known, as the Son; of the knowledge of the Son was peculiar to the Gospel-dispensation. The third will be pure Spirit, when nothing but Spirit and power

---

[54] Nuttall, *The Holy Spirit in Puritan Faith and Experience*, p 121.
[55] Iain H. Murray, *The Puritan Hope: Revival and the Interpretation of Prophecy* (Edinburgh: The Banner of Truth Trust, 1971).
[56] Franklin H. Littell, *The Origins Of Sectarian Protestantism* (New York: The Macmillan Company, 1964), ch 2.

> shall appear, when God shall be all in all ... the presence of the Lord, and his power, was more spiritual, in inward and eternal things; ... Therefore the third dispensation ... will be more spirituall yet.[57]

Of course the idea of the third age of the Spirit was immensely attractive to the Quakers, because it enabled them to dismiss obsolete features of the first two ages, and to help to shape the new age in which they lived. It necessarily meant that they devalued the Puritans and others who went before them. No wonder Richard Baxter complained in *The Quakers Catechism*:

> And yet more unmatchable pride and impious infidelity is it, to damn all the church and people of God for this 1600 years at least ... who can believe that Christ hath no church until now, and that all the ministers of the gospel for 1600 years were the ministers of the Devil?[58]

3.5 Revelation is immediate, so God is unity not Trinity

Why did the Quakers tend towards Unitarianism? The reasons included the following:

i. The loss of historical revelation and the Bible meant that they did not pay close attention to the shape of the biblical revelation, and to the clues within it that the revelation of God's unity is only part of the story,

ii. Their suspicion of clerical education meant that they were less likely to learn from the lessons of theology and church history.

iii. Their concentration on the present human person as the focus of immediate Divine revelation meant that they limited themselves to the economic revelation, to God as experienced, and this resulted in an undifferentiated perception of God.

There were two immediate causes of their unconscious Unitarianism, two fatal identifications. In Nuttall's words 'they identified the Logos or eternal Christ with the Spirit'; and they identified

---

[57] Nuttall, *The Holy Spirit in Puritan Faith and Experience*, p 106.
[58] Baxter, *The Quakers Catechism*, C1.

the Logos or Spirit in Christ with the Spirit within them.[59]

Thus they failed to distinguish between the presence of God in Christ and in themselves.

One sign of this failure was the assumption of personal infallibility and perfection for all those indwelt by the Logos, the Light, Christ, the Spirit. Another sign was the acceptance of Messianic language and divine descriptions by Quaker leaders. One Quaker addressed Margaret Fell in these words:

> O thou daughter of God ... thou art comely in thy beauty ... clothed with the sun and moon under thy feet ... thou art in thy life and glory to be above all things desired after.[60]

Hugh Barbour comments that Fox merged Christ and the Spirit, and asserted that Christ was not distinct from the Father.[61] For many, there was no distinction between the members of the Trinity. 'God and the Spirit hath no Person, nor cannot be truly distinguished into Persons.'[62] The Digger Winstanley claimed that Father, Son, and Spirit are 'three names given to one spirit.'[63]

For the Puritans, the Quaker views both diminished the unique incarnation of the Son of God, and also elevated every believer into a Christ figure. Richard Baxter claimed that 'The very person of Jesus Christ [some Quakers] blaspheme, and speak allegorically and equivocally when they mention his name and nature.[64]

No wonder John Owen wrote that one only needed to 'Convince any of them of the Doctrine of the Trinity, and all the rest of their Imaginations vanish into Smoak.'[65]

3.6 Revelation is immediate, and this revelation is universal

The Quakers had an extraordinarily vivid sense of a missionary call to the whole world. By 1660 Quakers had visited:

---

[59] Nuttall, *The Holy Spirit in Puritan Faith and Experience*, p 175.
[60] Ibid., p 183.
[61] Barbour, *The Quakers in Puritan England*, p 145.
[62] Ibid., p 145.
[63] Knott, *The Sword of the Spirit*, p 92.
[64] Richard Baxter, *One Sheet against the Quakers*, (1657), p 3.
[65] Nuttall, *The Holy Spirit in Puritan Faith and Experience*, p 162.

> Germany, America, and many other islands and places, as Florence, Mantua, Palatine, Tuscany, Italy, Rome, Turkey, Jerusalem, France, Geneva, Norway, Barbadoes, Bermuda, Antigua, Jamaica, Surinam, Newfoundland.[66]

Their defining ideas included belief that Christ had enlightened everyone in the world, and the loss of the particularity of salvation history meant that everyone in the world had equal access to God in the Light within.

So Fox's letter to Quakers in captivity included these instructions:

> get the Turks and Moors Language, that you might be the more inabled to direct them to the Grace and Spirit of God in them, which they have from God, in their hearts.[67]

Fox firmly believed in 'that of God in every man,' and so the task of the Quaker missionary was to alert people to the God within, to encourage them to respond to this God, and to learn from their witness of their internal revelation. John Woolman, Quaker missionary to the American Indians, wrote of his purpose in these words:

> That I might know and understand their life, and the Spirit they live in, if happily I might receive some instruction from them, or they be in any degree helped forward by my following the Leadings of Truth among them.[68]

This universal vision was fundamental to Quakers. William Penn wrote of Fox's vision on Pendle Hill in 1652:

> He had a vision of the great work of God upon the earth, and of the way that he was to go forth in public ministry, to begin it. He saw people thick as motes in the sun, that should be brought home to the Lord, that there might be but one shepherd and one sheepfold in all the earth.[69]

The usual Puritan response to the notion of 'that of God in everyman' was to understand this to be the light of nature, the general revelation of

---

[66] Ibid., pp 160, 161.
[67] Ibid., p 160.
[68] Loukes, *The Quaker Contribution*, p 122.
[69] Fox, *The Journal of George Fox*, p xl.

God, or the conscience. They claimed that this was not saving knowledge of God, and they assumed that the Quakers were entirely too optimistic about the possibilities of people responding to this dim revelation. In this they missed the point of the Quaker claim, which was that this was universal, supernatural, and saving revelation, given directly and immediately to all people by God.

The Quakers effectively equated God's general and special revelation: the Puritans retained that useful distinction. Richard Baxter commented:

> All that come into the world of nature, he enlighteneth with the light of Nature ...; And all that come into the world of grace he enlighteneth with the light of supernatural revelation.[70]

For Quakers there was no such distinction, because God's saving revelation was immediate to every person in the world. However although they believed that God's revelation was universal, they would not accept the Puritan witness that God spoke to them through the Bible.

3.7 *Revelation is immediate, so the believer is indwelt by the Holy Spirit and therefore infallible*

The Quaker democratisation of Christianity removed any distinction in roles between the human authors of Scripture and any believer. Both had the same infallible Spirit and immediate revelation. Indeed for the Quaker, it was a sin to follow what the Spirit had said to a Bible writer: the Quaker call was to follow the Spirit within.

Geoffrey Nuttall writes that one of the main issues of dispute between Puritans and Quakers was 'whether or no the presence of the Holy Spirit involved intellectual infallibility and moral perfectibility.'[71] The vital question was where the infallible Spirit was to be found: in the Bible, or in the child of Light? So in The Quakers Catechism of 1655, Richard Baxter wrote:

> Your twelfth query is whether we have the same infallible spirit as the holy men of God had, who spoke forth the scriptures.
>
> Answer: But we hear the croakings of your Papist guides in that

---

[70] Baxter, *The Quakers Catechism*, p 7.
[71] Nuttall, *The Holy Spirit in Puritan Faith and Experience*, p 155.

word 'infallible'; that's the pillar of their kingdom, and the master-point of their new religion, that their church is infallible. But I will answer you and your master together in a word.

1. The prophets and apostles had infallible inspirations of new matters of divine verity, not before revealed, because they were to be God's penmen and messengers of such new revelations; I have none such that I know of.

2. The Prophets and apostles were guided infallibly in the manner as well as the matter, so that every word that they wrote to the churches was infallibly true. I have no such infallibility, nor your grandfather the Pope neither.[72]

In his *An Answer To A Book Called The Quakers' Catechism*, James Nayler replied:

> Thou says the Prophets and Apostles were guided infallibly in the manner and matter, so that what they writ to the Church was true; but thou hast no such infallibility. I say, if thou had such a Spirit, your pulpits would have more truth, and thy book not so full of lies as it is ... for the Spirit of God is but one, and who hath it hath an infallible guide in matter and manner, if he keep to it ... so far as any are led by the Spirit, it guides into all truth if it be not erred from.[73]

The Quaker apologist Samuel Fisher claimed to possess infallible guidance, and sinlessness: Richard Baxter's reply was that 'I am one that is sick and have need of the Physician'.

The Quaker complaint against the Puritans was that they preached a 'miserable salvation' in that 'all of them cried out "No Freedom from Sin on this side of the Grave."'[74]

Both Quaker and Puritan believed that people needed divine healing. The Quaker believed that this was fully achieved when a person received the fullness of the Light, and the Puritan believed that while they were justified by faith and reconciled to God, full transformation of believers would happen at the return of Christ.

---

[72] Baxter, *The Quakers Catechism*, pp 9, 10.
[73] James Nayler, *An Answer to a Book called the Quakers Catechism* (1655), p 22.
[74] Watkins, *The Puritan Experience*, p 166.

3.8 Revelation is immediate, and only those who have responded to this immediate revelation are in Christ's church

It is important to recognise that the Quakers were not offering a complementary form of revelation to the Bible, but a replacement. They focussed more on the process of revelation (its immediacy) than the content. For them the immediacy of the revelation was a non-negotiable fundamental. This meant that only those who responded to this internal mode of revelation belonged to Christ. Not only were they the only ones who belonged to Christ, but their task was to wage war on those who claimed any other process and source of revelation, such as the Puritans. The Quakers' battle was the Lamb's War. In Fox's words:

> And thus we became followers of the Lamb whithersoever he goes, and he hath called us to make War in righteousness for his names sake against Hell and death ... against the Beast and the False Prophet ... we war in truth, and just judgement ... with the sword that goes out of the mouth ... and shalt slay the wicked.[75]

The Quaker claim was an exclusive claim to be Christ's people. Richard Baxter recognised the significance of this claim, and refuted it by claiming to belong to the church of Christ, the Catholic church.

> [We are] Sincere Catholic Christians, saved from Infidelity and Impiety: Having one God, one Mediator between God and man, one Holy Spirit: being a member of that one Catholic Church, which is not confined to the sect of the Papists, or the sect of the Anabaptists, or any sect, but containeth all the true Christians in the world, though some parts of it be Reformed and pure, and others more deformed and corrupt; having one Catholic rule, the Word of God; and one Catholic love to all Christians in the world.[76]

He also points to the Christological significance of their claim:

> They renounce the Church that we are of: and that is the only

---

[75] Fox, *The Great Mistery of the Great Whore Unfolded,* To the Reader.
[76] Richard Baxter, *One Sheet for the Ministry, Against the Malignants Of All Sorts* (1657), pp 1, 2.

> Church on earth, containing all true believers in Christ.
>
> And if Christ had not a Catholick Church before then, and ever since his Ascension, he ceased to be Christ in Office, the Head and Saviour of the Church: For no Church, no Saviour; no Body, no Head; no School, no Teacher; no Kingdom, no King; No Wife, no Husband.[77]

He rightly recognises that the claim to be the new and true people of Christ is actually a claim to have found a new Christ. A 'new Catholic Church' means a 'new Christ.'

He also claims the connection between the Christ of the historical revelation and the work of the Spirit, the Christological content of the Spirit's work:

> The Spirit is not given now to make us a new Religion, or new Gospel (Galatians 1:8, 9) but to cause us to believe and receive the old one.[78]

So the Quaker claim to be the only people of God fighting the Lamb's War not only unchurched all others who claim to be believers, but also changed their understanding of Christ and the work of the Spirit.

3.9 Revelation is immediate, so structures and 'means' are a hindrance

Francis Higginson described Quaker meetings in these words:

> They have no singing of psalms, hymns, or spiritual songs – that is an abomination. No reading or exposition of holy scripture, that is also an abhorrency. No teaching or preaching – that is in their opinion the only thing that is needless. No administration of sacraments – with them there is no talk of carnal things ... Sometimes after they are congregated, there is [altum silentium] not whisper among them for an hour or two together. This time they are waiting which one of them the Spirit shall come down upon in inspirations and give utterance to.[79]

---

[77] Ibid., p 2.
[78] Richard Baxter, *One Sheet Against the Quakers* (1657a), p 3.
[79] Higginson, *A Brief Relation of the Irreligion of the Northern Quakers*, p 11.

The immediacy of revelation meant that God would not use past words, such as the Bible, and would not use what Puritans called 'means' such as the sacraments. In both private and corporate spirituality, the believer must wait in silence for the immediate revelation of God within.

This was in contrast with the Puritans, who greatly valued God-given 'means.'

In his biography of the Puritan pastor Richard Greenham, John Primus points out the importance of the Bible to Greenham as 'the Librarie of the holy ghost.' When quoting Scripture Greenham's usual introduction is 'the holy Ghost here telleth us ....' The Holy Spirit was the author of Scripture, but also works within us so that we not only hear 'the letter,' but also 'the Spirit'

Greenham also developed a strong doctrine of 'means,' which sprang naturally from his observation that God normally works through creaturely agency. For Greenham the 'means' include the Word, prayer, sacraments, discipline, affliction, and the Sabbath. If God uses 'means,' then we should use what God has provided. We break the first commandment by 'a negligent and carelesse use of the meanes to serve God in his providence.' He confesses to God, 'I have not loved the meanes as I should doe.' He usually refers to 'means' as 'means to faith,' or 'means to godliness'.

He contrasts his own view of God using 'means' with the views of the Papists on the one hand, and the sect the Family of Love on the other.

> Seeing the Lord hath joyned together the meanes of godlines and godlines itselfe, let us not separate them, either with the superstitious Papists, resting on the worke wrought ... neither with frantike heretikes despise the meanes, as though without them we could live in obedience to God, or in love to our brethren.

The 'frantike heretiks,' the Family of Love, despised the 'means': so later did the Quakers.

Of all the 'means,' the Bible and its preaching is the chief. So preaching is the 'most principall and proper meanes to beget Faith in us.' Hence the Puritan critique of ministers who would not preach: 'dumb dogges that cannot barke,' in William Perkins' phrase. If the Bible is a 'means,' so then is the preacher:

> where a faithfull Minister is that doth sincerely and purely preach the word, it is all one as if the Lord himselfe dwelt personally among us.

Finally the Sabbath was a 'means' given by God on which there was special time to receive all the other 'means.' In his *Treatise of the Sabbath*, Greenham explained that the Sabbath was 'the school day, the faire day, the market day, the feeding day of the soule.'[80] The Sabbath was the day to hear the Bible read and preached, to pray, to meditate on the work of God in one's life, to receive the sacrament, and to give to those in need. Greenham shows us that use of God-given 'means' was crucial to Christianity.

Jane Turner gave an account of her journeys in faith, as she moved from formalism and what she called 'Legal Righteousness' as a Presbyterian, to free grace as a Baptist. She then experimented with Quaker views, but moved back from them, despite their 'Angel-like appearance,' partly because they did not recognise that God used 'means.' She knew that 'ordinarily [God] works by means, and leaves no ground in Scripture to expect him out of means.'[81] In McDonald's words:

> The Puritans did not regard the Bible as a mere record of revelation. It is itself the revelation of God in which and through which God comes savingly to the soul.[82]

No wonder then that the Puritans were so scandalised that the Quakers despised the 'means,' especially the Bible. As we have seen, the Quakers regarded the Bible as valid for the people whose experience was recorded in it, but as a distraction for the believer today. They dismissed it with the language of letter and spirit: 'The Letter kills ... but the Spirit only gives Life.'[83]

They not only dismissed the Bible, but also the ministers who taught from it, as we have seen. Because the teaching of the Bible was not the task of the minister, and because they distrusted the use of reason and education, they therefore criticised the training that

---

[80] John H. Primus, *Richard Greenham: the Portrait of an Elizabethan Pastor* (Macon, Georgia: Mercer University Press, 1998), pp 86, 87, 127, 129, 131, 137, 150.
[81] Watkins, *The Puritan Experience*, pp 48, 88ff, 90.
[82] McDonald, *Ideas of Revelation*, p 202.
[83] Barbour, *The Quakers in Puritan England*, p 159.

ministers received, which was one of the glories of the Puritan movement.

However while the Quakers warned against Puritan and other ministers, they were of course receptive to the ministry of words of other Quakers. This ministry of words was not a ministry of teaching or preaching the Bible, but that of another Quaker speaking what God had immediately and directly put in their heart to say. In Fox's words:

> And whereas some have objected, that, although Christ did speak both to his disciples and to the Jews in the days of his flesh, yet since his resurrection and ascension he doth not speak now; the answer is, that as God did then speak by his Son in the days of his flesh, so the Son, Christ Jesus, doth now speak by his Spirit ... They who neglect or refuse to hear the voice of Christ, now speaking from heaven in this his gospel day, harden their hearts.[84]

For the Quaker, all the Lord's people were prophets, so believers would receive God's immediate words directly and through others, and would speak God's immediate words to others.

3.10 *Revelation is immediate, and this revelation is received in the emotions*

One of the crucial questions about immediate revelation is 'By what aspect or part of the human person is it received?' Possible answers include the conscience, the intellect or reason, the emotions, or the will. The answer to the question has great significance for the attitudes adopted by those who are expecting the revelation.

If revelation is mediated to and through the intellect or reason, then the attitude adopted by the believer will be one of intellectual inquiry and alertness. There may also be the use of debate and argument as part of the process of revelation.

If revelation is mediated through the emotions, then aids to emotional receptivity will be used, and emotional intensity will signify significant revelation.

---

[84] Fox, *The Journal of George Fox*, p 666.

If revelation is primarily to the conscience, then a sense of guilt will be the infallible sign of the presence of revelation, and moral transformation the sign of its long term effects.

According to John Spurr, 'Puritanism combines the rapture of being saved, with the rationality of a complex account of why God saves some.' He comments further that 'the combination of reason and feeling was inherently unstable.'[85]

It may have been unstable, but it was a more positive way than limiting immediate revelation to the emotions. Puritans valued mind, emotions, and conscience as parts of the human person addressed by God. According to the Puritan Richard Greenham:

> the seat of faith is not in the brain, but in the heart, and the head is not the place to keep the promises of God, but the heart is the chest to lay them up in.[86]

Robert Blair wrote against merely 'notional' knowledge in favour of 'spiritual' knowledge:

> A Great deal of this brain frothy foamy knowledge cometh to little ... This true and spiritual knowledge is affectionate and practical; as it floweth from the Spirit of Grace, so it carries with it a stream and current of holy affections, and stirreth up to endeavours and earnestness in holy practice.[87]

Richard Sibbes spoke of the 'sweet motions' of the Spirit, but also made the point that the Holy Spirit works on the reason as well as the will. 'For though God work upon the will, it is with enlightenment of the understanding at the same time.'[88] We find the same ideas in Richard Baxter:

> The Spirit of God supposeth nature, and worketh on man as man; by exciting your own understanding and will to do their parts.

And again:

> The Spirit worketh not on the will but by the reason: he moveth not a man as a beast or stone, to do a thing he knoweth not why,

---

[85] Spurr, *English Puritanism*, p 6.
[86] Ibid., p 6.
[87] Watkins, *The Puritan Experience*, pp 97, 98.
[88] Knott, *The Sword of the Spirit*, p 54.

but by illumination giveth him the soundest reason for the doing of it.

And so Baxter allows for the use of hearing and studying the scriptures, using both the 'means' of the Bible, and also the use of the mind and understanding:

> The Holy Spirit assisteth us in our hearing, reading, and studying the Scriptures, that we may come, by diligence, to the true understanding of it; but doth not give us that understandings, without hearing, reading, or study.

What is received by faith will then be known in experience:

> The way to have the firmest belief of the Christian faith, is to draw near and taste, and try it, and lay bare the heart to receive the impression of it, and then, by the sense of its admirable effects, we shall know that which bare speculation could not discover. Though there must be a belief on other grounds first, so much as to let in the word unto the soul, and cause us to submit our hearts to its operation, yet it is this experience that must strengthen and confirm it.[89]

No wonder that Baxter's *The Saints' Everlasting Rest*, in which he encouraged the contemplation of heaven, includes a long explanation of the trustworthiness of Scripture, the true basis of the hope of eternal life.

> The Quakers rejected both the Scriptures as the source of the knowledge of God, and also the use of human reason in any form, because they knew that revelation was mediated through the emotions, and not through the rational mind. In George Fox's words:

> we met together often and waited upon the Lord in pure silence ... hearkened to the voice of the Lord, and felt his word in our hearts.[90]

So James Nayler condemned the Puritan ministers who had spent:

> so many Years at Oxford and Cambridge ... to know what unlearned men, Fishermen, Ploughmen and Herdsmen did mean when they spoke forth the Scriptures.[91]

---

[89] Nuttall, *The Holy Spirit in Puritan Faith and Experience*, pp 169, 170, 47.
[90] Fox, *The Great Mistery of the Great Whore Unfolded*, To the Reader.
[91] Barbour, *The Quakers in Puritan England*, p 157.

William Bayly claimed that 'It was the Serpent who led my mind out wholly to delight in the Art of Arithmetick, and the study and practise of navigation.'[92] Even the learning of Hebrew, Latin and Greek was suspect, because as George Fox wrote, 'The tongues of Hebrew, Greek & Latin, were set up over Christ by Pilate who crucified him.'[93]

The Quaker experience was of the immediate power of God, and a person open to this power was described as 'tender.' So George Fox claimed:

> But both priests and people were astonished at the wonderlul power that broke forth; and several of the priests were made tender, and some did confess to the power of the Lord.

Fox also wrote, as we have seen, that he knew the truth 'in the light of the Lord Jesus Christ, and by his immediate Spirit and power.' And his task was:

> to turn people to that inward light, spirit, and grace, by which all might know their salvation and their way to God; even that divine Spirit which would guide them into all truth.[94]

William Dewsbury wrote that his knowledge of God came by 'the inspiration of the Spirit of Jesus Christ.'[95]

Whereas the Puritans believed that the Word of God that was Scripture addressed the whole person, including mind, emotions, and will, the Quakers believed that the immediate revelation of God was received through the emotions, and that reason and learning were enemies of that revelation. It was not the case that Puritans were rationalists and Quakers emotionalists. The difference was that the Puritans included reason, and the Quakers excluded it.

3.11 *Revelation is immediate on the emotions, and physical signs mark its presence*

The presence of revelation was evident because the power of God within the human person produced 'quakings,' as well as other physical signs of the internal reality.

---

[92] Watkins, *The Puritan Experience*, p 230.
[93] Fox, *The Great Mistery of the Great Whore Unfolded,* Reply to Francis Higginson.
[94] Fox, *The Journal of George Fox*, pp 42, 34, 35.
[95] Nuttall, *The Holy Spirit in Puritan Faith and Experience*, p 53.

The Puritan Francis Higginson described these physical signs in these words:

> Now for their quakings, one of the most immediate, notable fruits and accidents of their speakings. Though their speakings be a very chaos of words and errors, yet very often while they are speaking, so strange is the effect of them in their unblest followers, that many of them, sometimes men, but more frequently women and children, fall into quaking fits.
>
> The manner of which is this: those in their assemblies who are taken with these fits fall suddenly down, as it were with a swoon, as thought they had been surprised with an epilepsy or apoplexy, and lie grovelling on the earth, and struggling as it were for life, and sometimes more quietly as though they were departing. While the agony of the fit is upon them their lips quiver, their flesh and joints tremble, their bellies swell as though blown up with wind, they foam at the mouth, and sometimes purge, as though they had taken physic. In this fit they continue sometimes an hour or two, sometimes longer, before they come to themselves again, and when it leaves them they roar out horribly with a voice greater than that of a man – the noise, those say who have heard it, is a very horrible fearful noise, and greater sometimes than any bull can make.
>
> The speaker, when any of them falls in this fit, will say to the rest, 'Let them alone, trouble them not, the Spirit is now struggling with the flesh, if the Spirit overcomes they will quickly come out of it again, though it is sorrow now, it will be joy in the morning' ... These quakings they maintain and in their books and papers call them the marvelous works of the Lord.[96]

The Quaker Robert Barclay described the same signs with more sympathy:

> there will be such a painfull travel found in the soul, that it will even work upon the outward man, so that ... the body will be greatly shaken, and many groans, sighs and tears ... Sometimes the Power of God will break forth into a whole meeting ... and

---

[96] Higginson, *A Brief Relation of the Irreligion of the Northern Quakers*, pp 15, 16.

thereby trembling will be upon most ... which as the power of truth prevailes, will from pangs and groans end with the sweet sound of thanksgiving and praise.[97]

John Gilpin in his tract *The Quakers Shaken* describes being thrown from his chair during a Quaker meeting, lying on the ground all night, unable to resist the power of God that acted upon him. He later returned to the Bible and Presbyterianism.[98]

We should not imagine that these physical signs were the only evidence of the presence of Christ and the Spirit in a person. Moral change was also a necessary sign of true spiritual experience for the Quakers.[99]

However quaking was taken to be a certain sign of the presence of the Light of Christ, an external and physical sign of the internal and invisible Christ.

The Puritans on the other hand did not look for physical signs: their tests were inward conviction and assurance, and gradual moral transformation. So Richard Baxter was suspicious of physical quaking as a definitive sign of the presence of God. In his Quakers Catechism he wrote:

> Your twenty-third query is whether do you own trembling and quaking which the scripture witnesseth? Answer: I own the fear of the Lord, which is the beginning of wisdom ... but I think that the great quaking that was in the army of the Philistines was no virtue or blessing to them, nor any sign of God among them [1 Samuel 14: 15].[100]

So we can see that the Quaker view of revelation was that of immediate and direct revelation to the human person; that it was therefore in the present and not in the past; that it was within the person, and not by external means except by another Quaker; that it was received through the emotions, and not through reason or rational thought; and that the evidence of its presence was the physical sign of quaking.

On the other hand the Puritan view was that revelation of Jesus Christ was given through salvation history culminating in the coming of Christ, that it was mediated through the Spirit-given Scriptures, and

---

[97] Barbour, *The Quakers in Puritan England*, p 36.
[98] Ibid., p 118.
[99] Ibid., p 119.
[100] Baxter, *The Quakers Catechism*, pp 23, 24.

received by faith by the human person, in mind, emotions, understanding, and will.

From the perspective of sociology, Radical Puritans and Quakers looked much the same, like radical reformers. However from the perspective of theology, they were different breeds, and the gulf between them arose from their different views of how revelation is mediated to humanity. The main protagonists, Puritans and Quakers, were vividly aware of this theological gulf between them, and regarded it as of critical and fundamental importance.

4. Historical Reflections

4.1. *Word and Spirit in the Reformers*

The different attitudes of Puritans and Quakers to Spirit and Word may have their roots in an earlier difference between the Reformers about the nature of the Bible. In Luther's opinion, there was a great gulf between his view of the Bible, and that of Zwingli. Luther held that the Bible was the means God used to communicate his truth, whereas Zwingli held that the Bible was a sign of the truth that God communicated by the Spirit. Luther summarised his own view in these words:

> The Word ... is the power of God, which makes all who believe on it blessed ... God works through His Word, which is like a vehicle or a tool whereby we learn to know Him in our heart.

He described Zwingli and his followers' view as:

> They separate the man who preaches and teaches the Word from God who makes it effectual ... and they mean that the Holy Spirit is given and works without the Word, which is, as it were, an external symbol, sign and mark, and meets the Spirit who is already and always waiting in the heart ... The External Word is ... a picture, which enlightens, witnesses and interprets ... They reject the oral Word and the power and efficacy of the Sacraments entirely.[101]

Zwingli distinguished between *Verbum Dei externum* and *Verbum Dei*

---

[101] T. H. L. Parker, *The Oracles of God: An Introduction to the Preaching of John Calvin* (London and Redhill: Lutterworth Press, 1947), pp 47, 46.

internum. The external Word of God is that which is read and preached, and is a sign and witness, which prompts us to attend to the internal Word, and helps us understand it. In Zwingli's words 'What is heard is not that Word by which we believe.' G. W. Bromiley says of Zwingli's views:

> It is in the heart of the believer or unbeliever that it is decided whether at this or that point ... the letter of Scripture is also the living Word of God, the sign is conjoined with the thing signified.[102]

Here the hearing of the Bible read and preached is not an actual 'means,' but an accompanying instruction. This separation between external Word and internal Spirit makes it easier to break the connection between the two. McDonald notes that the separation between the Word and the Bible in which the Bible contains the Word is found in the Puritan John Goodwin, but that this was an eccentric view among Puritans.[103]

Zwingli wants to refute an *ex opere operato* view of preaching, but in doing so runs the danger of failing to recognise that the Bible is God's words 'intrinsically as well as instrumentally,' in the useful phrase of J. I. Packer.

Calvin asserts both the efficacy of the external Spirit-inspired Word and the necessity for the internal work and testimony of the Spirit. In this he honours the 'means' which God uses, Bible and preacher, as well as pointing to our own powerlessness and our dependence on God's work in our hearts, minds, and lives.[104]

Too close an identification of Spirit and Word falls down when we reflect that the Spirit indwells believers even when they are not thinking the words of Scripture. Too radical a separation between Spirit and Word diminishes two of the 'means' that God has provided and chosen to use, Bible and Bible-teacher.

---

[102] G. W. Bromiley (ed.), *Zwingli and Bullinger*, [vol. XXIV of The Library of Christian Classics] (London: SCM Press, 1953), p 36.
[103] McDonald, *Ideas of Revelation*, pp 199-206.
[104] John Calvin, *Institutes of the Christian Religion*, (ed. John T. McNeill; trans. Ford Lewis Battles; 2 vols; Library of Christian Classics 20-21; Philadelphia: The Westminster Press, 1960), IV.xiv, viii, and I.vii, i.

4.2. Enlightenment heat and Quaker light

William Temple once wrote that the most significant moment in Western Society was when René Descartes went into his stove, to emerge with the basis for all knowledge in the statement, 'I think, therefore I am.' We could assert that the first Quaker who said, 'I feel, therefore I know' was equally significant.

The decision to replace the external authority of Bible or Church by an internal authority was of great importance, whether the internal authority was that of reason or emotion.

We can see Puritanism degenerate in both these ways in the 17th Century. Cambridge Platonists were former Puritans who believed in the supremacy of reason, 'the candle of the Lord'; and Quakers were former Puritans who believed in emotion, 'the Light of Christ.' Both departed from the authority of the Bible. Both replaced that authority with an internal authority. Reason and emotion are perhaps closer than we might expect.[105] Later Deists and Enthusiasts both followed the revelation within.

4.3. Puritans and Quakers: friends or foes?

It is possible to see the Quakers as yet one more example of radical and sectarian Puritans in an age in which many radicals flourished. This is the perspective of Geoffrey Nuttall in his analysis of Puritan faith and experience.[106] It is also the perspective of those who make a sociological analysis, such as R. J. Acheson.[107] However the complementary truth is the viewpoint of this Lecture. There was a radical difference between Puritans and Quakers over the focus of revelation, the external Bible or the immediate light of Christ. But this difference resulted in radically diverse forms of religion, not least in their views of Christ and the Spirit, as well as salvation history and eschatological existence. The proponents themselves were aware of the radical opposition between them. They regarded each other as foes, not friends. Sociologically they were close: theologically they were very different.

---

[105] McDonald, *Ideas of Revelation*, pp 32-34, 68.
[106] Nuttall, *The Holy Spirit in Puritan Faith and Experience*.
[107] R. J. Acheson, *Radical Puritans in England 1550-1660* (London and New York: Longman, 1990).

4.4. What Puritans believed about the Bible

The great danger of writing about the Puritans if you are sympathetic to them is that of creating them in your own image. However I wish to summarise the Puritan view of Scripture, which they held to despite the attacks of the Quakers. They believed that the Bible was:

- authoritative and powerful; an effective 'means' used by God; the present and contemporary words of God; God's words 'intrinsically as well as instrumentally'
- the way in which God addresses every aspect of us; will, reason, emotions, and character
- to be understood in terms of God's gradual revelation of Christ; to be read in its original historical context; self-interpreting
- originally inspired in words as well as content, as well as Spirit-empowered in the present
- infallible in its teaching; sufficient and complete
- God's word through his Spirit about his work through his Son; God's Spirit-words about his Son-work.

4.5. Quakers, Puritans, and Gospel truth

The Quaker theological approach, dependent as it was on personal perceptions of immediate revelation, was essentially fluid, and resulted in a wide range of theological positions. George Fox was more radical in the 1650s, but by the end of his life had adopted more traditional theology, with greater emphasis on the Bible.[108]

The Quaker movement has had two broad streams. One is 'liberal,' the result of depending on internal perceptions of revelation in the world of Western rationalism. In the long term, listening as an emotional experience cannot be sustained, and is transformed to a more rational intuition that reflects the worldview of the age.

The other stream is more conservative and evangelical, more

---

[108] Barbour and Roberts, *Early Quaker Writings*, pp 43, 44.

dependent on the Bible. There was a revival of evangelical Quakerism in England in the 19th Century led by J. J. Gurney, and represented in the United States of America by the Evangelical Friends Alliance.[109]

However if the Quakers had difficulty in maintaining Gospel truth, so did the Puritans, many of whose descendants soon became Socinians and Unitarians.

Semper reformanda, continued reformation by the Bible, is the only remedy against theological decline.

5. Contemporary Reflections

We conclude this 'conversation with the past' with four contemporary reflections.

5.1. *Quaker patterns of using the Bible*

We now find the following patterns across many Christian traditions.

5.1.1. *The Bible as example of process.*

We should notice that for Quakers the Bible was an example of the process of immediate revelation. The believer today should follow their example and find out what God is now saying. There is a parallel to the modern belief that the Bible writers give us an example of theological reflection, and that we should follow their example by doing our own theological invention and reflection.

5.1.2. *The Bible and internal spirituality.*

The idea that the Bible history of salvation provides models for us to follow in our own internal spiritual journey was common to Philo and the Quakers, and is common today. The result is a preoccupation with the internal, and neglect of historical revelation.

---

[109] Ibid., pp 43-46.

5.1.3. *The effect of the dismissal of the Bible.*

While the early Quakers retained many biblical ideas because of their Puritan upbringing, the next generation moved well away from biblical faith. This move was obscured by their continued use of biblical language. People need great discernment to recognise that the use of biblical phrases does not necessarily indicate the presence of biblical faith.

5.1.4. *The poetic use of the Bible.*

Using Bible images as the raw material from which we create our own version of Christianity, is as popular now as it was in the days of the Quakers, and is now defended by modern theories about the meaning of texts. However neither Quakers nor modern theorists appreciate their own texts being treated in this same way!

5.1.5. *The third age of the Spirit.*

The Quaker confusion about salvation history had bad effects on them, but one of the most unfortunate aspects of it was the notion that they lived in the third age, the age of the Spirit, which replaced both the age of the Father [the Old Testament], and the age of the Son [New Testament]. The idea of this third age was articulated by Joachim of Fiore, and was influential from 1000 AD. Of course it meant that both the Old and New Testament were now obsolete, and that Jesus was no longer trusted as the focus of God's activity.

5.2. *Modern Spirit-Word dichotomy*

In his book *Ideas of Revelation* H. D. McDonald shows the different ways in which the Spirit-Word debate has surfaced since the 17th Century. One interesting example is what we might call a midway position between Puritans and Quakers, in which revelation is discerned within the Bible, but not identified with it. For example he shows how S. T. Coleridge in the 19th Century dismissed the idea of biblical infallibility, but claimed that:

> the words of the Bible find me in the greater depths of my being; and that whatever finds me brings with it such an irresistible evidence of its aving proceeded from the Holy Spirit.

McDonald adds:

> There is no human soul, Coleridge teaches, unilluminated by the light of God. For the Christian when this light is turned on to the Scriptures, certain passages become radiative: and what becomes so illuminative becomes authenticated for us.[110]

We can also see the similarity between these views and those of Barth and Brunner. McDonald writes that Brunner insists on the complete separation of Christ as the Word of God from the Bible as human testimony or 'witness' to that revelation. He adds that the Bible points to divine revelation, and can 'bear' it in part.[111] We determine in what texts this revelation occurs, and no doubt assess this as much by emotion as reason.

Though this theology may look as if it respects the revelatory significance of the Bible, it is a matter of subjective feeling or opinion whether or not any part of the Bible is functioning as revelation. The illumination and discernment of the believer have replaced the inspiration and authority of the Bible.

On the other hand it is inadequate to respond to these ideas with an assertion of the original inspiration of the Bible without also asserting that the Bible is also, in Kevin Vanhoozer's words, God's contemporary speech-act.[112] The historic words of God are also his powerful and effective words to us today.

5.3. *Contemporary Evangelical confusion*

5.3.1. *Bible words no guarantee.*

It is still possible to be bewitched by the sound of biblical words and phrases, and believe that Bible words mean Bible truth. On the contrary, Bible words can be used to convey ideas that are very far from the Bible.

---

[110] McDonald, *Ideas of Revelation*, pp 173, 174.
[111] Ibid., p 191.
[112] Kevin Vanhoozer, 'God's Mighty Speech-Acts: The Doctrine of Scripture Today', in Philip E. Satterthwaite and David. F. Field (eds.), *A Pathway into the Holy Scriptures* (Grand Rapids: Eerdmans, 1994), pp 143-181.

5.3.2. Evangelical in name and Quaker in practice.

True Evangelicals not only believe the Bible, but also use it in every part of their ministry, and expect that God will use it in their ministry. The popularity of Quaker writers like Richard Foster and M. Scott Peck indicates that in practice Evangelicals may still trust the feeling of the Spirit within more than the Spirit's words in Scripture. The key question as we have seen, is whether or not the Bible is used as the central and sufficient 'means' provided by God, or whether reason, research, personal testimony, emotions, or feelings replace it.

5.3.3. Reaction inadequate.

To react against Quaker ideas by asserting mere intellectual orthodoxy is inadequate. It is one the tragedies of Protestantism that it is so often governed by reaction against error than by a sincere desire to live out biblical faith and practice.

It is not enough to respond to emotionalism by resorting to intellectualism. Reacting against error will always lead to another error. Biblical faith is at once more demanding and more satisfying than any merely human stance.

5.3.4. Last days theological confusion no surprise.

We should not be alarmed by the presence of 'giddy turbulent sectaries' in our own day. We live in a gullible age, in which the novel, the contemporary and the immediate predominate. There is little sympathy for careful biblical and theological reflection, and it is easier to start something new than to reform what is old. This should not surprise us: the Bible warns us that the last days will be characterised by doctrinal and moral confusion, by misplaced enthusiasms. Our task is to believe and preserve biblical faith, preach it, and live it, to the glory of God our Saviour.

5.3.5. Theology necessary?

There was a profound theological disagreement between Puritans and Quakers. Ignoring theology does not work, and those who do so will be all the more effectively hindered by their unconscious theological system.

The Quakers came to grief because they would not recognise the need for intellectual clarity, the good use of reason, and the benefit of informed theological thinking. The Reformers and the Puritans were strengthened because they intentionally engaged with what Alister McGrath calls 'The Great Tradition' of orthodox biblical faith.[113]

Historic Credal Christianity [Baxter's 'Catholic Faith'] is a needed remedy against confusion. This does not mean that the Bible is insufficient. It does mean that the Bible is best understood from within the long-term history of the people of God.

5.3.6. God's presence and physical signs.

The Quaker belief that God was most surely present when we feel that he is present is common today. The idea that God's presence is always accompanied by intense emotional awareness or by physical signs such as quaking or falling down is now popular in and beyond the charismatic movement.

We would do well to heed the warning of Jonathan Edwards, that 'Great effects on the body certainly are no sure evidences that affections are spiritual.'[114]

5.3.7. Golden silence?

Of course there is good reason to create times of silence to meditate on God in our noisy and word-filled world, in our over stimulated environment. They are good reasons to stop and engage in a 'royal waste of time,' meditating on the goodness, grace, and love of God.

But waiting in silence can have another more sinister connotation, that of the Quaker belief that God's words in Scripture, valid for their day, are now obsolete or insufficient. This silence is not golden but leaden, unresponsive to God, and open to deception.

---

[113] Alister E. McGrath, 'Engaging the Great Tradition', in John G. Stackhouse Jnr. (ed.) *Evangelical Futures* (Grand Rapids: Baker, Leicester: IVP, Vancouver: Regent College Publishing, 2000), pp 139-158.
[114] Jonathan Edwards, *The Religious Affections* (Edinburgh: Banner of Truth, 1986), p 59.

5.4. Christ and the Bible

I have argued that the difference between the Puritans and Quakers on the method that God uses to bring revelation to us was of fundamental importance, because the issue of the means of revelation influences all other doctrines. It leads to radically different understanding of the place where the Spirit reveals Christ, and so to radically different understanding of Christ and his work.

If the historical revelation of Christ is lost because the historical revelation of that work through Christ's Spirit in Scripture is lost, then all is lost. Without the Bible the remembered Christ becomes the imagined Christ.

We must receive God's Spirit-words about his Son-work. The Bible comprises God's words through his Spirit about his work through his Son.

Bibliography

Primary Sources
From EEB 1641-1700, University Microfilm, Ann Arbour, Michigan.
Baxter, Richard [1655], *The Quakers Catechism.*
Baxter, Richard, [1657a], *One Sheet against the Quakers.*
Baxter, Richard [1657b], *One Sheet for the Ministry, Against the Malignants Of All Sorts.*
Fox, George? and Nayler, James [1653], *Saul's Errand to Damascus.*
Fox, George [1659], *The Great Mistery of the Great Whore Unfolded.*
Higginson, Francis [1653], *A Brief Relation of the Irreligion of the Northern Quakers.*
Nayler, James [1655], *An Answer to a Book called the Quakers Catechism.*

Modern editions.
Baxter, Richard [1974], *The Autobiography of Richard Baxter* [Reliquiae Baxterianae], ed. N. H. Keeble, London: J. M. Dent.
Baxter, Richard [1981], *The Practical Works of Richard Baxter*, [reprint of the 1863 edition, Blackie and Sons], Grand Rapids, Michigan: Baker Book House.
Burroughs, Jeremiah [1990], *Gospel Worship*, Ligonier: Soli Deo Gloria Publications.
Calvin, John [1960], *Institutes of the Christian Religion*, ed. John T. McNeill. Translated by Ford Lewis Battles. 2 vols. Library of Christian Classics 20-21. Philadelphia: The Westminster Press.
Edwards, Jonathan [1986], *The Religious Affections*, Edinburgh: The Banner of Truth Trust.
Fox, George [1975], *The Journal of George Fox*, ed. John L. Nickalls. London: Religious Society of Friends.
Fryer, Jonathan (ed.) [1991], *George Fox and the Children of Light* [Journal and Epistles of George Fox], London: Kyle Cathie.

Goodwin, Thomas [1979], *The Work of the Holy Ghost in Our Salvation*, Edinburgh: The Banner of Truth.

Woolman, John [no date], *The Journal with other Writings of John Woolman*, Everyman Edition, London: J. M. Dent.

Secondary Sources

Acheson, R. J. [1990], *Radical Puritans in England 1550-1660*, London and New York: Longman.

Adam, Peter [1998], *The Church 'Halfly Reformed': The Puritan Dilemma*, London: The St. Antholin's Lectureship.

Anderson, Marvin W. [1987], *Evangelical Foundations, Religion in England 1378-1683*, New York: Peter Lang.

Barbour, Hugh [1964], *The Quakers in Puritan England*, New Haven and London: Yale University Press.

Barbour, Hugh, and Roberts, Arthur O. [eds.] [1973], *Early Quaker Writings 1650-1700*, Grand Rapids, Michigan: William B. Eerdmans.

Bohn, Ralph P. [1955], *The Controversy between Puritans and Quakers to 1660*, University of Edinburgh, Ph.D.

Braithwaite, William C., [1912], *The Beginnings of Quakerism*, London: Macmillan and Co.

Bromiley, G. W. (ed.) [1953], *Zwingli and Bullinger*, [vol. XXIV of The Library of Christian Classics], London: SCM Press.

Collinson, Patrick [1967], *Puritanism and the English Church*, London: Jonathan Cape.

Durston, Christopher and Eales, Jacqueline (eds.) [1996], *The Culture of English Puritanism 1560-1700*, Basingstoke and London: Macmillan Press.

Flew, R. Newton. [1968], *The Idea Of Perfection in Christian Theology*, New York: Humanities Press.

Hill, Christopher [1988], *A Turbulent, Seditious and Factious People: John Bunyan and his Church*, Oxford: Oxford University Press.

Hill, Christopher [1993], *The English Bible and the Seventeenth Century Revolution*, London: Penguin Books.

Knott, John R. Jr. [1980], *The Sword of the Spirit: Puritan Responses to the Bible*, Chicago and London: University of Chicago Press.

Knox, R. A. [1950], *Enthusiasm: A Chapter in the History of Religion*, Oxford: Clarendon Press.

Littell, Franklin H. [1964], *The Origins Of Sectarian Protestantism*, New York: The Macmillan Company

Loukes, Harold [1965], *The Quaker Contribution*, London: S. C. M.

McDonald, H. D. [1959], *Ideas of Revelation, An Historical Study 1700 to 1860*, London: Macmillan & Co.

McGrath, Alister E. [2000], 'Engaging the Great Tradition,' in John G. Stackhouse Jnr. (ed.) *Evangelical Futures*, Grand Rapids: Baker, Leicester: Inter-Varsity Press, Vancouver: Regent College Publishing, pp. 139-158.

Murray, Iain H. [1971], *The Puritan Hope: Revival and the Interpretation of Prophecy*, Edinburgh: The Banner of Truth Trust.

Nuttall, Geoffrey F. [1967], *The Puritan Spirit: Essays and Addresses*, London: Epworth Press.

Nuttall, Geoffrey [1992], *The Holy Spirit in Puritan Faith and Experience*, with an

introduction by Peter Lake, Oxford: Basil Blackwell.
Packer, J. I. [1990], *A Quest for Godliness: The Puritan Vision of the Christian Life*, Wheaton, Illinois: Crossway Books.
Parker, T. H. L. [1947], *The Oracles of God: An Introduction to the Preaching of John Calvin*, London and Redhill: Lutterworth Press.
Powicke, Frederick J. [1924], *A Life of the Reverend Richard Baxter 1615-1691*, London: Jonathan Cape.
Primus, John H. [1998], *Richard Greenham: the Portrait of an Elizabethan Pastor*, Macon, Georgia: Mercer University Press.
Reay, B. [1984], 'Quakerism and Society,' in McGregor, J. F., and Reay, B. [eds.], *Radical Religion in the English Revolution*, Oxford: Oxford University Press, pp. 141-164.
Samuel, D. N. (ed.) [1979], *The Evangelical Succession*, Cambridge: James Clarke.
Spurr, John [1998], *English Puritanism 1603-1689*, Basingstoke and London: Macmillan Press.
Trueman, Carl R. [1998], *The Claims of Truth: John Owen's Trinitarian Theology*, Carlisle: Paternoster Press.
Vanhoozer, Kevin [1994], 'God's Mighty Speech-Acts: The Doctrine of Scripture Today,' in Satterthwaite, Philip E. and Field, David. F. (eds.), *A Pathway into the Holy Scriptures*, Grand Rapids, Michigan: Eerdmans, pp. 143-181.
Wakefield, Gordon S. [1957], *Puritan Devotion*, London: Epworth Press.
Wallace, Dewey D. Jr. [1987], *The Spirituality of the Later English Puritans*. Macon, Georgia: Mercer University Press.
Watkins, Owen C. [1972], *The Puritan Experience*, London: Routledge & Kegan Paul.

Ussher on Bishops: A Reforming Ecclesiology

Wallace Benn

James Ussher Biography 99
Introduction... 102
1. A Study of the Original Documents 103
2. Reduced Episcopacy...111
      2.1 Propositions for godly rule in the church 112
3. Conclusion: An Evaluation of Ussher's Views on Episcopacy and Church Government............................. 113

Appendix: Episcopal and Presbyterial Government Conjoined..116

WALLACE P BENN is the Anglican Bishop of Lewes in the Diocese of Chichester. He was educated at St. Andrew's College and University College, Dublin and then trained for ordination at Trinity College, Bristol. After curacies on the Wirral and in Cheadle, he was Vicar of St. James the Great, Audley in Staffordshire and then of St. Peter's, Harold Wood in Essex. He was consecrated in 1997, and in 2002 (the year of this lecture) he also made a famous appearance in the popular BBC television motoring series *Top Gear*, coming third in the "Fastest Faith" driving competition.

The short biography of James Ussher, Archbishop of Armagh, is taken from *Puritan Profiles* by William Barker (Professor of Church History at Westminster Theological Seminary, Philadelphia), published by Mentor, an imprint of Christian Focus Publications 1996, and used by kind permission.

The collected works of Ussher are to be found in *The Whole Works of the Most Rev. James Ussher* edited by C. R. Elrington and J. H. Dodd (Dublin: Hodges, Smith 1847-64) in 17 volumes. An accessible paper on Ussher and the Irish Articles is to be found in *The Evangelical Roots of the Church of Ireland: James Ussher and the Irish Articles* by E. Culbertson (Church of Ireland Evangelical Fellowship No. 14 1999). There is an Usher bibliography to be found at: http://www.ucc.ie/acad/classics/CNLS/bibliography /ussherbibl.html

Wallace Benn, St. Patrick's Day, 2002

James Ussher (January 4, 1581 – March 21, 1656)

Early in 1647 the House of Commons resolved, 'That Dr. James Ussher shall have leave to preach at Lincoln's Inn, according to the desire of his petition,' and also, 'That Dr. James Ussher shall have leave to go to sit with the Assembly of Divines as one of the said Assembly.' This was a remarkable action since Ussher, Archbishop of Armagh and Primate of the Anglican Church of Ireland, had not only declined his original appointment to the Assembly in June of 1643, but he had boldly preached against the legality of the Assembly because it lacked the King's approval. There is no indication that Ussher ever attended the Assembly, but the fact that such favour could be granted to a committed royalist shows the respect in which he was held by Puritans.

The reasons were at least threefold: his Calvinistic theology, his godliness and his pre-eminent scholarship. He had for a long time associated with a network of Puritan clergymen, and his defence of the Anglican Church against the historical claims of the Church of Rome were greatly appreciated. His Irish Articles, adopted by the first convocation of the Irish Protestant clergy in 1615, served as a model for much of the Westminster Confession of Faith, not only in their anti-Roman Catholic sentiment (denouncing the Pope as 'the man of sinne' and rejecting 'the sacrifice of the Masse' as 'most ungodly'), but also in their inculcating of the Puritan view of the Sabbath and in their teaching of absolute predestination and perseverance. At the same time they make no mention of three orders in the ministry or of the necessity of episcopal ordination. Alexander F. Mitchell comments:

> In these Articles ... we have the main source of [the Westminster Confession] and almost its exact prototype in its statement of all the more important and essential doctrines of Christianity. In the order and titles of many of its chapters, as well as in the language of whole sections or subdivisions of chapters, and in many single and *voces signatae*, occurring throughout their Confession, the Westminster divines appear to me to have followed very closely in the footsteps of Ussher and his Irish

brethren.[1]

Mitchell also claims an influence of Archbishop Ussher's theology on the Westminster Catechisms. Even though not present at the Assembly, clearly Ussher was an influence upon it.

Ussher was born in Dublin on January 4, 1581. A precocious scholar he was among the first students to enter the new Trinity College, Dublin in 1594. Before receiving his B.A. in 1597, he had begun to draw up a biblical chronology, in Latin, through the Hebrew monarchy, which would become the basis of his famous chronology included in many later editions of the English Bible. In April 1599, when he was still only eighteen years old, he effectively engaged in a disputation at Trinity College with Henry Fitzsimon, a Roman Catholic prisoner in Dublin Castle. This led to a systematic reading of the church fathers which took eighteen years to accomplish.

Ussher was made a fellow in 1599, received his M.A. on February 24, 1601, and was assigned to give the catechetical lecture on the Romish Controversy on Sunday afternoons at Christ Church, Dublin. He was ordained deacon and priest on December 20, 1601. In 1602 and again in 1606, and thereafter every three years – staying one month each in Oxford, Cambridge and London, he went to England to purchase books for the Trinity College library. He received the B.D. in 1607 and was appointed the first professor of divinity at Trinity College. In 1609 he made the acquaintance of the scholar and later Parliamentary member of the Westminster Assembly, John Selden.

His first publication was *De ... Ecclesiarum ... Successione (The Succession and Standing of the Christian Churches in the West)*, published in 1613, in which he sought to carry on the argument of John Jewel's *Apology for the Church of England* by showing the continuity of doctrine in England over against Roman deviations down to 1270. In 1613 Ussher married Phoebe Challoner and on March 2, 1615 he was chosen Vice-Chancellor of Trinity College.

It was at this time, when he was thirty-four, that Ussher was assigned the task of drafting the Irish Articles for the Anglican Church in Ireland. Having served at the rectories of Fingles, Assey, and Trim,

---

[1] A.F. Mitchell & J. Struthers, *Minutes of the Sessions of the Westminster Assembly of Divines* (London: William Blackwood and Sons, 1874), p xlvii.

he was consecrated Bishop of Meath and Clonmacnoise in June of 1621. Granted leave by James I to pursue his studies of British ecclesiastical antiquities, Ussher stayed in England for more than two years, from December 1623 until early 1626. During this time he was appointed Archbishop of Armagh on March 22, 1625.

Between 1628 and 1640 he engaged in correspondence with William Laud, with whom he had cordial agreement in 'love of learning, in reverence for antiquity, and in opposition to Rome' even though he differed with his Arminian theology: 'and though Ussher had none of Laud's passion for uniformity, he fully recognised the duty of allegiance to constituted authority.' He later would attend Archbishop Laud before Laud's execution on January 10, 1645.

In March 1640 Ussher preached before the Irish Parliament and then left Ireland, as it turned out, for the last time. Staying first at Oxford, he was called to London to assist in the ecclesiastical settlement connected with the opening of the Long Parliament in November of 1640. He prepared a draft of a modified scheme of Episcopacy, which gained the favour of some moderate Puritans, eventually of Charles I, and then of Charles II. It was published in 1656, after Ussher's death, as *The Reduction of Episcopacie unto the Form of Synodical Government Received in the Ancient Church*. On December 22, 1641 he preached before the House of Lords. The rebellion in Ireland having destroyed his property there, except for his library, Ussher was given the Bishopric of Carlisle, the revenue from which he received until the autumn of 1643. He preached in London at St. Paul's, Covent Garden and then moved in 1642 to Oxford, where he preached frequently at St Aldate's or at All Saints' Church.

When his response to the summons to participate in the Westminster Assembly was to preach against its legality, the House of Commons confiscated his library, but Daniel Featley with John Selden's assistance rescued the books, though many papers and all his correspondence were lost. He left Oxford on March 5, 1645 and took refuge in Wales for a year before returning to London, where he was guest of Elizabeth Mordant, now Dowager Countess of Peterborough, whose husband, John Mordant, first Earl of Peterborough, he had won back from Roman Catholicism more than twenty years earlier.

As mentioned earlier, Parliament approved his appointment at the beginning of 1647 as preacher at Lincoln's Inn, 'one of the most lucrative preaching positions in London.' In November of 1648 he there denounced Parliament's treatment of the King. In January 1649, from Lady Peterborough's house in St. Martin's Lane, 'just over against Charing Cross,' he saw the beginnings of Charles's execution, but fainted when 'the villains in vizards began to put up his hair.'

Oliver Cromwell sought Ussher's advice in the 1650s. Ussher attended Selden's deathbed in November 1654. He gave up preaching after September 1655, due to failing sight and difficulty in speaking from loss of teeth. He died on March 21, 1656. Cromwell ordered a public funeral at Westminster Abbey, the Anglican service being used at the grave.

His several portraits show him in skull-cap and large ruff. 'He was of middle height, erect and well made, of fresh complexion, and wore moustache and short beard.' Gilbert Burnet said of him: 'No man had a better soul.' 'Love of the world seemed not ... in his nature.' 'He had a way of gaining people's hearts and of touching their consciences that look'd like somewhat of the apostolical age reviv'd.' He proved attractive to kings, Cromwell, and everyone in between. His biographer concludes: 'His Augustinian theology commended him to the puritans, his veneration for antiquity to the high churchmen; no royalist surpassed him in his deference to the divine right of kings. All parties had confidence in his character, and marvelled at his learning.'

Introduction

Anglican Evangelicals have in recent years neglected the doctrine of the church outside the local congregation. When recently trying to find some serious evangelical writing about bishops, I discovered that the last time, to my knowledge, something scholarly was in print was the Islington Conference Papers of 1966!

The result of this neglect is twofold. On the one hand, Evangelicals 'promoted' in the structures of the Church have no sufficient ecclesiology to help them and sometimes, to fill the vacuum, adopt a more 'Catholic' ecclesiology at this point, which they should know better than to do. On the other hand good faithful evangelical clergy are disenchanted not only by the difficulties they have with some bishops but feel sceptical of the historic ecclesiological position of the Anglican Church from the time of the Reformation. 'If we had a clean piece of paper we would do things differently', or, more extremely,

'What on earth is the point of bishops?' This is sometimes not only a disappointment with the way the office is practised in our day, which is a very legitimate concern, but a more fundamental scepticism of the whole ecclesiological framework of the Church. So some stay as Anglican because it is still 'the best boat to fish from' or because the alternatives are worse, rather than because of a basic conviction that our Reformers got things substantially right in the government of the Church. 'I'm fine in my Parish, but I don't know how to handle things outside it' said one incumbent to me.

When I discovered Ussher's works in the library of Lambeth Palace I was surprised and delighted. Here was an evangelical who had thought hard about church government scripturally, and in post-apostolic times, and had remained a convinced Anglican. He was the outstanding Reformed and Evangelical scholar of his day, who was also an eminent patristic scholar, and he lived at a time (post 1640) when there was a wide dispute amongst Evangelicals about how the government of the church should be run. Ussher 'almost persuaded' the other leaders at the Westminster Conference, Presbyterian & Independent, to follow his understanding. And his arguments, though not always unique to him, were found to be very attractive to the great Richard Baxter. Ussher typifies the ecclesiological position held by Anglican Puritans in his day and is their best spokesman.

So why had I never heard some of his reasoning before about bishops and church government? After investigation I concluded that we have forgotten our heritage and it is time that Ussher is allowed to speak again. He is an enormous help to us in forming a bigger evangelical ecclesiology in our day.

My desire is that Ussher should be allowed to speak for himself and though his arguments, especially from patristics, are dense and detailed, the cumulative effect is helpful and instructive. I personally find his biblical arguments for an episcopal form of government very convincing, and they are backed up by the practice of the early church in post-apostolic times.

1. A Study of the Original Documents

As I have already stated, my aim is to let James Ussher speak, and for his arguments to have a wider audience. In 1644 he wrote *The Original of Bishops and Metropolitans Briefly Laid Down* as part of a symposium entitled *Confessions and Proofs of Protestant Divines of Reformed Churches, that Episcopacy is in Respect of the Office according to the Word of God...*

Let me quote the first two paragraphs, which are crucial to his argument:

> The ground of episcopacy is derived partly from the pattern prescribed by God in the Old Testament: and partly from the imitation thereof brought in by the apostles and confirmed by Christ himself in the New. The government of the Church of the Old Testament was committed to the priests and Levites; unto whom the Ministers of the New do now succeed, in like sort as our Lord's-day hath done unto their Sabbath, that it might be fulfilled which was spoken by the Prophet, touching the vocation of the Gentiles 'I will take of them for priests, and for Levites, saith the Lord.'

> That the priests were superior to the Levites, no man doubteth: and that there was not a parity, either betwixt the priests or between the Levites themselves, is manifest by the word of God, wherein mention is made of the heads and rulers both of the one, and of the other. (1 Chronicles 24 v 6, 31 and Ezra 8 v 29).

Ussher goes on to remind us that the Levites were divided into 3 families – over each one a 'ruler' or 'leader' was appointed (Numbers 3: 24, 30, 35). The priests were also divided by David into 24 'courses,' and they likewise had their heads. In the New Testament these are described as the 'chief priests' (Matthew 2:4, 27:1), and are not to be confused with the High Priest who was a type of Jesus, that 'great high priest who has gone through the heavens, Jesus the Son of God' (Hebrews 4:14). The chief officer of the priests, and also the Levites is called 'bishop', interestingly, in the LXX of Nehemiah 11:14, 22. Further, of Levi it was said 'They shall teach Jacob your rules and Israel your law; they shall put incense before you and whole burnt offerings on your altar' (Deuteronomy 33: 10).

Though the latter part of the sentence is removed in the New Covenant, the former part of the sentence remains. Bishops and presbyters are to be 'able to teach' (1 Timothy 3:2). Also says Ussher, 'by just analogy inferred,' those who waited at the altar were partakers with the altar, so likewise the Lord had ordained that those who preached the gospel should live by the gospel (1 Corinthians 9:13, 14). The differences between the Old Covenant leaders and the New Covenant leaders should not blind us to some similarities in principle. Ussher asks, is there any good reason that 'what was instituted by God in the Law, for mere matter of government and preservation of good order (without all respect of type or ceremony) should now be rejected in the Gospel as a device of Antichrist?'

We need to consult with Christ and see what he says about things that don't suit us! Here is a key point in Ussher's argument. 'Stars' are mentioned in Revelation chapters 2 and 3, and these are explained as the 'angels' of the seven churches in Revelation 1:20, which Christ holds in his right hand (Revelation 2:1; 3:1). 'How great therefore is the dignity of true pastors, who are both stars, fixed in no other firmament than in the right hand of Christ, and (called) "angels."' Now according to Acts 20 there were many presbyters (v 17) made bishops or overseers by the Holy Spirit to feed the church of God (v 28). So Ussher reminds us that there were a number of elders/presbyters/overseers in the church in Ephesus and he acknowledges that 'bishop' was interchangeable with 'presbyter' in those days ('That name (i.e. bishop) being in those days common to all the presbyters'). But according to the Book of Revelation one of this number of presbyters/ bishops was given an eminency and called the 'angel' of the church, and 'that such a one was to be esteemed as a star fixed in no other firmament, than in the right hand of Christ.' Here Ussher criticised a certain Reformer, whom he respected, for saying the 'star' was not one but the whole college of presbyters. And he quotes Beza with approval who like Ussher felt this was a 'wresting of the plain words of our Saviour.' Beza said that the star/angel equalled the president over the rest of the pastors in Ephesus. 'To the angel, that is, to the president, as whom it behoveth specially to be admonished touching those matters; and by him both the rest of his colleagues, and the whole church likewise.' This president the church fathers afterwards called 'bishop.' Ignatius called this president 'bishop' no more than 12 years later, according to Ussher.

The Council of Chalcedon says that from Timothy there had been 27 bishops till then at Ephesus (the angel in Revelation 2 must be one of these!). Beza confessed that Timothy was president of the presbyters (i.e. bishop) in line with Eusebius and Polycrates. The latter was himself once bishop of Ephesus (some 36/37 years after John wrote Revelation, according to Ussher). Ignatius was bishop of Antioch at the same time John wrote Revelation. According to timing specified by Eusebius and Jerome, 12 years later than they say Revelation was written, Ignatius wrote a letter to Ephesus (on his journey to martyrdom in Rome) and made mention of the then bishop, Onesimus. He refers to the bishop, and to the presbytery as 'so conjoined with their bishop, as the strings are with a harp.' Ignatius in the same journey wrote to the Church at Smyrna and here again he greets the bishop and the presbyters (and he tells them that no one is to administer the sacraments or anything pertaining to the church, without the consent of the bishop).

Polycarp who was bishop of Smyrna later wrote to the Philippians. Irenaeus spoke of hearing Polycarp talk of his conversation with St. John. Irenaeus said that Polycarp conversed with those who had seen Christ, and was taught by the apostles, and made bishop of the Church in Smyrna, by the apostles (he lived long and was martyred), before John wrote Revelation. So who but Polycarp could be the angel of the church in Smyrna (he was martyred 74 years later)? Tertullian said that the heretics of the 2nd century are later than the bishops to whom the apostles committed the church (churches of Corinth, Athens, Jerusalem etc. had bishops appointed). In Jerusalem, according to Hegesippus, James was made bishop.

This Hegesippus, who wrote the most ancient history after Acts, said there was no heresy in the church of any substance till the death of Symeon who was martyred in the time of Emperor Trajan, and was bishop of the Church in Jerusalem after James. He says that the church was called a 'virgin' till then. Symeon, who was very old when he died, was probably born before Jesus! Heretics came into the church when the generation that had heard the Lord had died away. Episcopacy was, says Ussher, held in esteem in the early days.

Ussher was an expert in the early church Fathers and his point here is to show how soon after the end of the New Testament episcopacy was established (and maybe even before). Here Ussher returns to the heart of his argument:

> But to return unto the angels of the seven churches, mentioned in the Revelation of St. John: by what hath been said, it is apparent, that seven singular bishops, who were constant presidents over those churches, are pointed at under that name. For other sure they could not be, if all of them were cast into one mould, and were of the same quality with Polycarp, the then angel of the church in Smyrna: who without question was such, if any credit may be given herein unto those that saw him and

were acquainted with him.

> And as Tertullian in express terms affirmeth him to have been placed there by St. John himself ... so doth he elsewhere, from the order of the succeeding bishops, not obscurely intimate, that the rest of that number were to be referred unto the same descent. Also Tertullian says, 'We have the churches that were bred by John. For although Marcion do reject his Revelation; yet the order of the bishops reckoned up into their original, will stand for John to be their founder.'

It was believed that St. John went to Ephesus and there wrote his Gospel, after the Revelation, according to Irenaeus, and continued his work in Asia (with the help of the seven bishops) according to Eusebius. Clement of Alexandria says he ordained bishops over many churches – 'When St. John, Domitian the tyrant being dead, removed from the island of Patmos unto Ephesus, by the entreaty of some he went also unto the neighbouring nations; in some places constituting bishops, in others founding whole churches.'

Hierapolis was one of those neighbouring churches where Papias was bishop (he was a hearer of St. John and companion of Polycarp according to Irenaeus; and he also conversed with the disciples of the Apostles, and with those who had heard Christ).

Here then is Ussher's conclusion: 'Neither can any man be so simple as to imagine, that in the language of Clement of Alexandria the name of a bishop should import no more than a bare presbyter ...' And he quotes the emperor Hadrian writing about the state of things in Egypt, who makes distinct mention in his letter of the 'presbyters of the Christians,' and those 'who call themselves bishops of Christ.'

> And thus having deduced episcopacy from the apostolical times, and declared, that the angels of the seven churches were no other, but such as in the next age after the apostles were by the fathers termed bishops; we now further enquire, why these churches are confined unto the number of seven ...

These seven churches had some degree of eminency among the churches in Asia (and so all the rest of the churches are in some way understood under them or in relation to them). We cannot imagine that there was no more than seven churches after all the effort in Asia of Paul and others (Acts 19:10)!

> So that in all reason we are to suppose, that these seven churches, comprising all the rest of them, were not bare parochial ones, or so many particular congregations, but diocesan churches, as we use to call them, if not metropolitical rather. For that in Laodicea, Sardis, Smyrna, Ephesus and Pergamum, the Roman governors held their courts of justice, to which all cities and towns about had recourse for the ending of their suits, is noted by Pliny. And besides these, which were the greatest, Thyatira is also by Ptolemy expressly named a metropolis, as Philadelphia also is, in the Greek acts of the council of Constantinople ... Which giveth us good ground to conceive, that the seven cities, in which these seven churches had their seat, were all of them metropolitical, and so had relation unto the rest of the towns and cities of Asia, as unto daughters rising under them.

These seven churches were diocesan or metropolitan churches. There were other churches with bishops in the Asian province at the time Ignatius wrote his epistles. It seems that Ignatius who calls himself the bishop of Syria, as well as of Antioch, had a wider responsibility, and that he wrote to the bishop of Rome, who had at that time a presidency over the churches that were in the Roman province (and the other bishops there). So it was that metropolitan responsibility developed later on – the great Council of Nicea confirmed the primacy of the bishops of Alexandria, Rome, and Antioch, (Cyprian was called Archbishop of a Province by Tertullian). Eusebius had the superintendency of the churches in Crete, which derived, he said, from the time of Titus. Ussher quotes Paul writing to Titus, whom he believed to be a bishop figure: 'This is why I left you in Crete so that you might put what remained into order, and appoint elders in every town as I directed you' (Titus 1:5). Ussher reminds us that Calvin says on this verse: 'We learn out of this place, that there was not then such an equality betwixt the ministers of the church, but that there was some one who was president over the rest, both in authority and in counsel.' Furthermore Bishop Jewel says on Titus 'Having the government of many bishops, what may we call him but an Archbishop?'

Ussher interestingly quotes the Synod of Nicea at this point – 'that no bishop should intrude himself into any other province, which had not formerly and from the beginning been under him or his predecessors.' Going back to Numbers he reminds us that Moses 'having set apart the three families of the Levites for his own service, and constituted a chief, as we have heard, over every of them: he placed immediately over them all, *not* Aaron the High Priest, but Eleazar his son.' – 'Eleazar the son of Aaron the priest was to be chief over the chiefs of the Levites, and to have oversight of those who kept guard over the sanctuary' (Numbers 3;32). So he is a 'president of the presidents'! So Ussher says that one can argue for an archbishop's role, as being in tune with 'that reverend opinion of the primitive bishops of the Christian Church,' and expressive of the patriarchal government of the church in Scripture. This he says has not got apostolic commendation but is a legitimate way to run the growing associations of the church and he points out that Bucer said it was legitimate and Calvin himself was not really against it either.

At the end of his article Ussher reminds his readers of the testimony of Ignatius who wrote to the church in Philadelphia no later than twelve years after St. John wrote to the same church (Revelation 3:7). Ignatius wrote of 'one bishop, with the presbytery and the deacons' and that he delivered this, as the voice of God – 'Take heed unto your bishop, and to the presbytery and the deacons.'

There is a following short article added to Ussher's by one named simply 'WC.,' and called *The Apostolic Institution of Episcopacy; Deducted out of the Premises*. At the time of writing, I have not discovered who this person is but his summary of the arguments is helpful and in what he writes he clearly has the approval of Ussher himself.[2]

The essentials of episcopal government are this – 'An appointment of one man of eminent sanctity and sufficiency to have the care of all the churches within a certain precinct or diocese; and furnishing him with authority, not absolute or arbitrary, but regulated and bounded by laws, and moderated by joining to him a convenient number of assistants. To the intent that all the churches under him may be provided of good and able pastors.' But he says that he is not so enamoured by this form of government that if it was contrary to Apostolic teaching or the doctrine of Christ, or unhelpful in the reformation of men's lives, that he would hold out for it! 'For obedience

---

[2] [Editor's Note] This was written in 1641 and published in 1644 by William Chillingworth (1602-1644), author of *The Religion of Protestants: A Safe Way to Salvation* (Oxford, 1638)

to our Saviour is the end for which church government is appointed.' But if it may be demonstrated, or at the least that it is probable that the following are true then it should be welcomed and defended.

> 1. That it is not repugnant to the government settled in and for the church by the Apostles.
>
> 2. That it is compliable with the reformation of any evil in church or state.
>
> 3. That there is no record of our Saviour against it.

He then addresses further the first point and comes to a key conclusion:

> That this government was received universally in the Church, either in the apostles' time, or presently after, is so evident and unquestionable, that the most learned adversaries of this government do themselves confess it.

This government also helps 'to avoid the confusion which often times ariseth out of equality.' Furthermore:

> That seeing Episcopal government is confessedly so ancient and so catholic, it cannot with reason be denied to be Apostolic.
>
> For so great a change, as between presbyterial government and Episcopal, could not possibly have prevailed all the world over, in a little time. Had Episcopal government been an aberration from, or a corruption of the government left in the churches by the Apostles, it had been very strange, that it should have been received in any one church so suddenly, or that it should have prevailed in all for many ages after ... Had the churches erred they would have varied. What therefore is one and the same amongst all, came not sure by error, but tradition.

This is a fundamental deduction with which Ussher would have been in complete agreement.

I think that this is a very powerful argument in its place. Far more likely, this government was received, he argues, because it shows no observable alteration. Furthermore he argues forcibly – 'and besides that the contagion of this ambition should spread itself and prevail without stop or control, nay, without any noise or notice taken of it, through all the churches in the world; all the watchmen in the meantime being so fast asleep, and all the dogs so dumb, that not so much as one should open his mouth against it?' He concludes:

Episcopal government is acknowledged to have been universally received in the church, presently after the Apostles' times. Between the Apostles' times and this presently after, there was not time enough for, nor possibility of so great an alteration. And therefore there was no such alteration as is pretended. And therefore episcopacy, being confessed to be so ancient and Catholic, must be granted also to be Apostolic. *Quod erat demonstrandum!*

2. Reduced Episcopacy

In his tract *The Reduction of the Episcopacy unto the Form of Synodical Government Received in the Ancient Church* (1656), Ussher is concerned to commend a form of government that is not repugnant to Holy Scripture and is in accord with the ancient practice of the church. As the subtitle of the tract states he wants to try and mend differences in the church between godly people and prevent divisions over the matter of church government. He appeals to all 'sober conscientious persons,' 'to all the Sons of Peace,' in order that the peace of the church might be recovered. He spoke against a background of sharp division over church government between Anglicans, Presbyterians, and Congregationalists (Independents).

He wants to understand episcopal government in a moderate Presbyterian way and return to the role of presbyters not only in preaching the word and dispensing the sacraments but also in matters of ruling and discipline. He wants episcopal and presbyteral government to be conjoined. He argues from his familiar line that in Acts 20 the elders are plural and shepherd (or rule) the flock. In Revelation the president of these elders is called the angel of the Church in Ephesus (Revelation 2:1). Ignatius, about 12 years later than when this was written, calls this 'angel' the bishop. All the Elders were involved in ruling and disciplining and they were involved in the common government of the church. The bishop was the chief president (whom Tertullian later called 'summus sacerdos'). He reminds readers that the Fourth Council of Carthage concluded 'that the Bishop might hear no man's cause without the presence of the clergy: and that otherwise the bishop's sentence should be void, unless it was confirmed by the presence of the clergy' (confirmed in our own land by canons of Egbert Archbishop of York in Saxon times).

It is true, he says, that in the English church this form of government has long been disused but he argues that it is still profitable. Every pastor has a right to rule the church, and in the first place the name 'rector' (ruler) was given for this reason. Synodical conventions of the pastors of every parish would easily relate well with the presidency of bishops of each diocese and province.

Ussher seems to be taking the biblical principal of plurality of eldership in the local church with the need for a presiding elder (a first amongst equals), which he sees as equally biblical, and applying it not just locally but at every level of church life (Deanery/Diocese/Province/Nation). He works from the local to the national and not the other way around. He also sees the need for discipline and good government in the church and understands that this will be commended to the church when it is not people acting in isolation but in collaboration with others at each level. This is no prelatical model – it is collaborative and co-operative. It is also connectional, seeing the church as more than the local congregation, for the need when serious issues face a local church of having agreement with as wide a group of responsible godly elders as possible. It has a firm place for episcopal leadership but prevents it being authoritarian and élitist. It sees a presbyteral college at work throughout the church which needs the chairmanship and authority of a bishop. Here is someone standing back from the controversies of his time and attempting to argue for a pattern of government that applies biblical principles and practice to the needs of the church of his day in a way that is in accord with ancient practice. He sees the best in each form of government but can see a happy synthesis really working, just as it did in the early church.

2.1. *Propositions for godly rule in the church*

1. In every parish the rector or incumbent pastor, churchwardens and sidesmen should note those who live 'scandalously' in the congregation. Then they should be given appropriate admonition and reproof: if this was not heeded, their case would be presented to the next monthly synod; in the meantime they would be debarred from access to the Lord's Table.

2. Suffragans had already been appointed – and one might be appointed to every deanery (into which each diocese is subdivided). This suffragan could meet every month with all the rectors and conclude all matters brought to them. To such a synod the rector and

churchwardens might present 'such impenitent persons.' If they remain 'contumacious and incorrigible,' then they might be excommunicated by the synod. Also, all things concerning the parish on doctrine and 'new opinions' might be dealt with here, with a right of appeal to the diocesan synod.

3. The diocesan synod would meet once or twice a year. All suffragans and rectors (or a certain select number) would meet with the bishop. Here matters of greater importance might be taken into consideration, and the orders of monthly synods revised. If any matter did not receive 'a full determination' it might be referred to the next provincial or national synod.

4. The provincial synod could consist of all the bishops and suffragans and 'such other clergy as should be elected out of every diocese within the province.' The Archbishop of either province could be moderator of this meeting (or one bishop appointed by him to take his place). All matters before this synod would be decided by common consent, and it would be held every 3 years. Also, he says, it would be possible to have a national synod whenever so desired.

Ussher is arguing (in a very modern fashion) for local deaneries to have power and responsibility, and he is arguing for synodical government in the church at every level which in a number of interesting ways is parallel to the development of synodical government in the church of our day. It is noteworthy however that his concern is for the discipline and ordering of the church in a godly and biblical way. His synods would have had teeth and a focused concern!

3. Conclusion: An Evaluation of Usher's Views on Episcopacy and Church Government

1. Ussher's biblical arguments are important and impressive. He is not afraid to learn from the pattern established by God in the ordering of the church in the Old Testament. He is very clear however about the pitfalls of this and is careful to explicitly avoid any identification with the High Priest other than Jesus himself.

2. His noting of the plurality of elders in the Ephesian church and the singular 'angel' in Revelation 2:1ff, and his explanation of this as a presidency amongst the presbyters, is compelling. It makes sense. Here

is an episcopal system that is not prelatical, but presbyterian and argued from the ground up, rather than in 'Catholic' ecclesiology, from the top down. He argues for a 'Reformed Catholicism' in church government as being in line with the practice of the early church. Furthermore his understanding of the Revelation Chapters 2 and 3 references to 'angel' as early episcopacy places warrant for this form of government (carefully understood) within the pages of the Bible itself. He sees it as deducible from the Old Testament principles of relationship and association (how the Old Testament church worked) and also evidently there in the practice recorded by John and by implication approved of by Christ in the Book of Revelation.

3. The further argument that any novelty in church government would have been queried or somehow resisted in the post-apostolic church is a very telling one.

4. In a world full of dissension about ecclesiology Ussher wants peace between godly, sober-minded people. He wants to include presbyterians and congregationalists and share their concern for church order and discipline (in doctrine he was a Calvinist and a Puritan). But he is not Anglican just because it is the best boat to fish in, nor does he see bishops as merely deacons, nor episcopacy as a necessary evil which given a clear piece of paper should be abandoned. Understood rightly, in a presbyterian sort of way, he believes that it is in accord with the teaching of the New Testament, and therefore legitimately and universally accepted in the post apostolic church. It is not just the best form of church government but the biblically and historically preferred option.

5. In his own day, his elastic-sided (ecclesiologically speaking) church gathered around a Reformed understanding of the faith, and episcopally led and governed, sought to persuade presbyterians and congregationalists by seeing (and indeed sharing) their fundamental concerns, without giving in to all their arguments. His synodical vision is only now being implemented in the church, but our outworking lacks his concern for godly discipline and gospel rule in our church.

6. He was called 'that miracle of learning' James Ussher. He was the outstanding scholar of his time. He was the probable author of the 104 Irish Articles (sadly neglected), which became, it is now recognised, the framework for the great Westminster Confession of Faith. His evangelical credentials are unassailable.

7.   He was esteemed by Cromwell (though he was a royalist), offered sanctuary by Cardinal Richelieu when pressed because of his political views, a friend of Archbishop Laud (though he disagreed with him), and extremely highly thought of by the Puritan pastors of his day with whom he shared his biblical Calvinism. He was a sharp debater and a profound scholar but was a gracious and cordial man to all his theological opponents. In this he is a grand and good example of 'grace and truth.'

In a day when our ecclesiology is often 'pragmatic' (outside our doctrine of the local congregation) he gives us a bigger vision of the local church (having a number of house churches and congregations) and gives us a biblical and historical reason not to be ashamed to believe in episcopal government, and to work for its reform along the lines he suggests. He would have been rightly horrified by the modern and novel suggestion that bishops are mere deacons, but he would perhaps have been even more horrified by the monarchical and authoritarian episcopal model which has been too often seen in the church. He would have encouraged respect for our system of government (not dismissiveness), have applauded many synodical developments, but have called us to a deeper concern for gospel truth, holiness and discipline in our church, which ought to be embracing of those who differ on secondary matters but sharp and clear about the fundamentals.

Appendix

The Reduction of Episcopacy unto the form of Synodical Government Received in the Ancient Church:

Proposed as an Expedient for the compromising of the now Differences, and the preventing of those Troubles that may arise about the matter of Church Government.

By J A Usher, *Armachanus*

And now published, seriously to be considered by all sober conscientious persons, and tendered to all the Sons of Peace and Truth in the three Nations, for recovering the Peace of the Church, and settling its proper Government.

Tolle jam nominis crimen et nihil restat nisi criminis nomen,
Tertullian, Apology.

Contra rationem nemo Sobrius; contra Scripturam nemo Christianus; contra Ecclesiam nemo pacificus Senseris, Augustine, On The Trinity.

1656

Episcopal and Presbyterial Government Conjoined.

By Order of the Church of England all Presbyters are charged[3] to minister the Doctrine and Sacraments, and the Discipline of Christ as the Lord has commanded, and as this Realm has received the same; and that they might the better understand what the Lord had commanded therein[4], the Exhortation of St. Paul to the Elders of the Church of Ephesus is appointed to be read unto them at the time of their Ordination; 'Take heed unto your selves, and to all the flock, among whom the Holy Ghost has made you overseers, to Rule[5] the Congregation of God, which he has purchased with his blood.'(Acts 20:28)

Of the many Elders, who in common thus ruled the Church of Ephesus, there was one President; Whom our Saviour in his Epistle to that Church in a peculiar manner styles the Angel of the Church of Ephesus;[6] and Ignatius, in another Epistle written about twelve years after unto the same Church, called the Bishop thereof, betwixt which Bishop and the Presbytery of that Church, what an harmonious consent there was in the ordering of the Church government, the same Ignatius does fully there declare, by the Presbytery with St. Paul[7] understanding the Company of the rest of the Presbyters or Elders, who then had a hand not only in the deliverance of the Doctrine and Sacraments, but also in the administration of the Discipline of Christ, for further proof whereof, we have that known testimony of Tertullian in his Apology for Christians.[8]

---

[3] The form of Ordaining of Ministers.
[4] Ibid. from Acts 20:17, 28.
[5] ποιμαίνειν [poimainein] – so taken in Matthew 2:6 and Revelation 12:5 & 19:15.
[6] Revelation 2:1.
[7] 1 Timothy 4:14.
[8] 'In the same place also exhortations are made, rebukes and sacred censures are administered. For with a great gravity is the work of judging carried on among us, as befits those who feel assured that they are in the sight of God; and you have the most notable example of judgment to come when any one has sinned so grievously as to require his severance from us in prayer, in the congregation and in all sacred intercourse. The tried men of our elders preside over us, obtaining that honour not by purchase, but by established character.' Tertullian, *Apology*, Chapter 39.

In the Church are used exhortations, chastisements and divine censure. For judgement is given with great advice as among those who are certain they are in the sight of God; and it is the chiefest foreshowing of the judgement which is to come, if any man have so offended that he be banished from the Communion of Prayer, and of the Assembly, and of all holy fellowship. The Presidents that bear rule therein are certain approved Elders, who have obtained this honour, not by reward, but by good report; who were no other (as he himself elsewhere intimates) but those from whose hands they used to receive the Sacrament of the Eucharist.[9] For with the Bishop who was the chief President (and therefore styled by the same Tertullian in another place *Summus Sacerdos* for distinction sake)[10] the rest of the Dispensers of the Word and Sacraments joined in the common government of the Church; and therefore, where in matters of Ecclesiastical judicature Cornelius Bishop of Rome used the received form of gathering together the Presbytery[11]; of what persons that did consist, Cyprian sufficiently declares, when he wishes him to read his letters[12] to the flourishing Clergy which there did preside or rule with him, the presence of the Clergy being thought to be so requisite in matters of Episcopal audience that in the fourth Council of Carthage, it was concluded, that the Bishop might hear no man's cause without the presence of his Clergy, and that otherwise the Bishop's sentence should be void, unless it were confirmed by the presence of the Clergy[13], which we find also to be inserted into the Canons of Egbert[14], who was Archbishop of York in the Saxon's times, and afterwards into the Body of the Canon Law itself.[15]

True it is, that in our Church this kind of Presbyterial

---

[9] 'We take also, in congregations before daybreak, and from the hand of none but the presidents, the sacrament of the Eucharist.' Tertullian, *The Chaplet or De Corona*, Chapter 3.

[10] 'Of giving baptism, the chief priest [*Summus Sacerdos*] (who is the bishop) has the right: in the next place, the presbyters and deacons.' Tertullian, *On Baptism*, Chapter 17

[11] 'The whole of this transaction therefore being brought before me, I decided that the presbytery should be brought together; (for there were present five bishops, who were also present today;) so that by well-grounded counsel it might be determined with the consent of all what ought to be observed in respect of their persons.' *The Epistles of Cyprian: Epistle 45* Cornelius to Cyprian.

[12] *The Epistles of Cyprian : Epistle 55* to Antonianus About Cornelius and Novatian.

[13] *Fourth Council of Carthage*, Canon 23 (Greek numbering).

[14] *Canons of Egbert*, Chapter 43.

[15] Gratian's *Decretals Causa* xv.Q7.

government has been long disused, yet seeing it still professes that every Pastor has a right to rule the Church (from when the name of Rector also was given at first unto him) and to administer the Discipline of Christ, as well as to dispense the Doctrine and Sacraments, and the restraint of the exercise of that right proceeds only from the custom now received in this Realm, no man can doubt but by another Law of the Land this Hindrance may be well removed: And how easily this ancient form of government by the united Suffrages of the Clergy might be revived again, and with what little show of alteration, the Synodical conventions of the Pastors of every Parish might be accorded with the presidency of the Bishops of each Diocese and Province; the indifferent Reader may quickly perceive by the perusal of the ensuing Propositions.

1. In every parish the Rector or Incumbent Pastor together with the Churchwardens and Sidesmen[16] may every week take notice of such as live scandalously in that Congregation, who are to receive such several admonitions and reproofs, as the quality of their offence shall deserve; and if by this means they cannot be reclaimed, they may be presented unto the next monthly Synod; and in the mean time debarred by the Pastor from access to the Lord's Table.

2. Whereas by a Statute in the 26th year of King Henry the eighth (revived in the first of Queen Elizabeth), Suffragans are appointed to be erected in twenty six places of this Kingdom, the number of them might very well be conformed unto the number of the several rural Deaneries into which every Diocese is subdivided; which being done, the Suffragan (supplying the place of those who in the ancient Church were called *Chorepiscopi*) might every month assemble a Synod of all the Rectors, or Incumbent Pastors within the Precinct, and according to the Major part of their voices conclude all matters that should be brought into debate before them.[17]

To this Synod the Rector and Churchwardens might present such impenitent persons, as by admonition and suspension from the Sacrament, would not be reformed; who if they should still remain contumacious and incorrigible, the sentence of Excommunication might be decreed against them by the Synod, and accordingly be

---

[16] The Parochial government answerable to the Church Session in Scotland.
[17] The Presbyterial monthly Synods, answer to the Scottish Presbyteries or Ecclesiastical meetings.

executed in the Parish where they lived.

Hitherto also all things that concerned the Parochial Ministers might be referred, whether they did touch their doctrine or their conversation; as also the censure of all new Opinions, Heresies, or Schisms, which did arise within that Circuit; with liberty of Appeal, if need so require, unto the Diocesan Synod.

3. The Diocesan Synod[18] might be held once or twice in the year, as it should be thought most convenient: Therein all the Suffragans and the rest of the Rectors or Incumbent Pastors (or a certain select number) of every Deanery within that Diocese might meet, with whose consent, or the Major part of them, all things might be concluded by the Bishop or Superintendent (call him whither you will) or in his absence by one of the Suffragans whom he shall depute in his stead to be Moderator of that Assembly.

Here all matters of greater moment might be taken into consideration, and the Orders of the Monthly Synods revised, and (if need be) reformed: And if here also any matters of difficultly could not receive a full determination; it might be referred to the next Provincial or National Synod.

4. The Provincial Synod might consist of all the Bishops and Suffragans, and such other of the Clergy as should be elected out of every Diocese within the Province; The Primate of either Province might be Moderator of this meeting (or in his room, some one of the Bishops appointed by him) and all matters be ordered therein by common consent as in the former Assembly.

This Synod might be held every third year, and if the Parliament do then sit (according to the Act for A Triennial Parliament) both the Primates and Provincial Synods of the Land might join together, and make us a National Counsel:[19] Wherein all appeals from inferior Synods might be received, all their Acts examined, and all Ecclesiastical constitutions which concern the state of the Church of the whole Nation established.

END

---

[18] Diocesan Synods answerable to the Provincial Synods in Scotland.
[19] The Provincial and National Synod answerable to the General Assembly in Scotland.

The Form of Government here proposed, is not in any point repugnant to Scripture; and that the Suffragans mentioned in the Second Proposition, may lawfully use the power both of jurisdiction and Ordination, according to the Word of God, and the Practice of the ancient Church.

Strangers to Correction: Christian Discipline and the English Reformation

Peter Ackroyd

1. Introduction 125
   - 1.1 *The search for the true church* *127*
2. Reformation Church Discipline 129
3. Martin Bucer (1491-1551) 130
4. Peter Martyr Vermigli (1499-1562) 133
   - 4.1 *Brotherly correction* *135*
   - 4.2 *Excommunication* *136*
   - 4.3 *Peter Martyr on discipline: summary* *138*
5. Church Discipline in the Edwardian Reformation .. 138
   - 5.1 *The Stranger churches* *139*
   - 5.2 *A Stranger's critique* *140*
   - 5.3 *The Reformatio Legum Ecclesiasticarum* *142*
6. Conclusion: Strangers to Correction 146

Abbreviations and references 147

PETER M ACKROYD has been Vicar of Wootton, near Bedford, since 2002. After an early career in international banking and private equity, he trained for Anglican Ministry at Wycliffe Hall in Oxford. He was curate of St. James, Denton Holme in Carlisle before serving as Ministry Secretary of the Proclamation Trust, based in London. His doctoral studies at New College, Edinburgh were in the doctrine of the church in the writing of Peter Martyr Vermigli, with particular reference to church discipline and the Edwardian Reformation. Peter and his wife JoJo have three children. He is a Trustee of the Latimer Trust.

1. Introduction

In October 1552, as the reign of Edward VI entered its last nine months, the chancellor of the University of Oxford, Richard Cox, penned a revealing letter. His correspondent was a longstanding friend, Henry Bullinger, the leader of Zurich's Reformation. His subject was the progress of the Reformation in England.

As Cox wrote, the prospects for reform in England seemed strong. The 1552 *Prayer Book,* embedding the gospel of justification by faith unambiguously in her religious life, was within weeks of its introduction. Cranmer's *Articles of Religion,* the forerunner of our *Thirty-Nine Articles,* were on the brink of adoption as the church's doctrinal yardstick. Though Cox knew that the task of winning English hearts and minds for evangelical religion had scarcely begun, he had reason to hope that, gradually but irreversibly, the gospel would be heard more often and more widely than ever before. The revolution was well under way.

Yet the optimism in his letter was guarded, and his caution takes us to our subject in this lecture. There was one area of reform where England was ominously dragging her feet:

> the severe institutions of Christian discipline we most utterly abominate. We would be sons, but we tremble at the rod. Do pray stir us up, and our nobility too, by the Spirit which is given to you, to a regard for discipline; without which, I grieve to say it, the kingdom will be taken away from us, and given to a nation bringing forth the fruit thereof.[1]

Cox's reference was to the obstacles facing a final official document which was being prepared to stand alongside the *Articles, Prayer Book,* and *Ordinal.* Alongside seven others, he was on the drafting committee preparing a new code of church law, to give the church the clear legal framework it had lacked ever since Henry VIII's declaration of its

---

[1] Cox to Bullinger, 5 Oct 1552, *Original Letters Relative to the English Reformation* (ed. H. Robinson; 2 vols; Cambridge: Parker Society, 1846-1847), I. 123; *Epistolae Tigurinae de Rebus Potissimum ad Ecclesiae Anglicanae Reformationem Pertinentibus Conscriptae* (Cambridge: Parker Society, 1848), p 80.

independence from Rome. Yet Cox's report reveals that opposition to this vital component of church renewal was strong. And it focused on the thorny question of Christian discipline: England's leadership seemed determined to remain 'strangers to correction.' There is a contemporary resonance to this apparently remote sixteenth century debate. It has been recently and publicly suggested that in the church 'we don't solve our deepest problems just by better discipline but by better discipleship.'[2] So put, who could disagree? For many, the mere mention of church discipline is sufficient to trigger alarm, either from legitimate apprehensions over the ecclesiastical abuse of power, or more commonly from a spirit of the age hostile to the suggestion that discipleship has moral boundaries which the church must delineate. Yet the antithesis is one which neither the Reformers, nor their Puritan successors whose divinity this lectureship perpetuates, would recognise. For them, a church which lacked a functioning system of discipline was incapable of fostering authentic discipleship. For the advocates of reform, it was not an optional extra.

My aim in this lecture is to set out the Reformers' vision of the discipline they regarded as vital to a church's health, and to compare their prescription with the intentions of the Edwardian Reformation. The discussion will focus on the contributions to the debate made by two significant reforming 'strangers' who played more than a walk-on role in England's reformation under Edward VI: a German-speaker from Alsace, Martin Bucer, and an Italian-speaker from Florence, Peter Martyr Vermigli. Both served the regime as theological consultants, as well as pioneering the teaching of evangelical biblical studies in Cambridge and Oxford respectively.

We will see through their eyes that the portrayal of ecclesiastical discipline as repressive and incompatible with the gospel was far from the Reformers' vision. As for Cox, discipline for them was Christian discipline, not church discipline. The distinction is significant. For the Reformers and their Puritan successors, discipline was no more than the necessary public, pastoral expression of the mutual responsibility which believers share to encourage and maintain lives shaped by the contours of the gospel.

---

[a] http://www.archbishopofcanterbury.org/sermons_speeches/030227.html (accessed 26/03/03).

1.1. The search for the true church

The church setting, however, was important. All the Reformers came to recognise that they were in new territory, seeking to restore the 'true church.' The institutional church had failed in its principal task, to proclaim the gospel of justification by faith, and Rome's rejection of this analysis therefore transformed a soteriological dispute into an ecclesiological crisis. The Reformers were driven to redefine the church Christologically, distinct from the historic institution. The church was the gathering of all believers in Christ. Its unity, catholicity, apostolicity and holiness inhered in its connection to Christ, not in the outward hierarchy.

This redefinition of the church in turn generated the idea of the marks. The church was the assembly of believers, but since faith is not visible, the church was to be discerned in the exercise of the ministry through which faith is born and nourished. Hence the definition of the church in the 1553 *Forty-Two Articles:*

> The visible church is a congregation of faithful men in which the pure Word of God is preached and the Sacraments be duly administered according to Christ's ordinance in all those things that of necessity are requisite to the same.[3]

The true church was now one in which the marks were exercised, a view which England derived from the continent: like several other provisions, this article can be traced to the 1530 *Augsburg Confession.*

Indeed, in Cranmer's restoration of the true church in England, links with the Continental Reformation were deliberately fostered. Bucer and Martyr were not the only foreign scholars to cross the Channel. Such 'strangers' reinforced the links between England's evangelicals and the continent, and provided added resource and impetus for the process of reform. Their teaching in the universities had a dramatic impact. Some were closely involved in the revision of the *Prayer Book.* And many of them added their voices to the calls for the reform of discipline.

In Martyr's case, his influence over the next generation of

---

[3] Article Twenty (which survived unchanged as Article XIX of the 1571 *Thirty-Nine Articles*).

England's evangelical leadership was perhaps even greater. It can be traced, for example, in the writings of John Jewel, Elizabethan bishop of Salisbury, and author of the *Apology of the Church of England*. He was also the author of the Homily for Whitsunday in the Elizabethan 1563 second book of homilies, which defines the church as follows:

> The true church is an universal congregation or fellowship of God's faithful and elect people, built upon the foundation of the apostles and prophets, Jesus Christ himself being the head corner-stone. And it hath always three notes or marks, whereby it is known: pure and sound doctrine, the sacraments administered according to Christ's holy institution, and the right use of ecclesiastical discipline. This description of the church is agreeable both to the scriptures of God, and also to the doctrine of the ancient fathers; so that none may justly find fault therewith.[4]

Jewel had been one of Peter Martyr's students in Oxford, and followed him to Strasbourg and then to Zurich during Mary's reign. His definition closely reflected Martyr's preference for a three-mark doctrine. Though the *Thirty-Nine Articles* of 1571 was to retain Cranmer's two-mark doctrine, England's Reformers, not least in the Puritan tradition, continued to see discipline as an indispensable component of healthy church life. The Puritan seventeenth century congregationalist John Robinson, for example, devoted a substantial part of his catechism to church discipline, which he observed: 'is to be used by every particular Church, according to the rules of Christ.'[5] Indeed, concern for the legitimate exercise of church discipline was a common feature of most shades of Puritan opinion in both the Elizabethan and Jacobean eras.[6]

---

[4] *Certain Sermons or Homilies Appointed to be Read in Churches* (Oxford: Clarendon, 1822), p 428.

[5] John Robinson, *A Briefe Catechisme concerning Church Government: An Appendix to Mr Perkins His Six Principles of Christian Religion* (London, 1642), A6v. Robinson quotes Martyr's commentary on the exercise of discipline in 1 Corinthians 5.4 in *A Just and Necessarie Apologie of Certain Christians no lesse contumeliously then commonly called Brownists or Barrowists* (Amsterdam, 1625), p 33.

[6] See, for example, Stephen Brachlow, *The Communion of Saints: Radical Puritan and Separatist Ecclesiology 1570-1628* (Oxford, 1988), for a survey of Puritan approaches to church government including the exercise of discipline.

What accounted for this preoccupation with an issue which to many modern eyes sounds arcane and repressive? The simple answer was that the Reformers found the exercise of discipline both commanded and exemplified in Scripture. Their aspiration to return the church to its apostolic foundation entailed fidelity to this ordinance. Before returning to the English situation, we will therefore briefly examine their approach.

2. Reformation Church Discipline

Obedience to the dominical commands of Matthew 18.15-17 was the starting point for the Reformers. Though this text had shaped the practice of public penance in the early church, by the medieval era moral conduct had come to be supervised mainly through the system of sacramental penance. Public discipline, culminating in excommunication, had become the province of the church courts, and had fallen into widespread disrepute by the early sixteenth century.

The Reformers, while repudiating sacramental penance, recognised that the Matthean text was binding, and were also strongly influenced by I Corinthians 5. Discipline was now seen as an aspect of pastoral care. Since (following Luther) the freedom of the Christian was to be exercised in service of others, this included the work of helping one another in obedience to Christ, and embraced correction alongside instruction and encouragement. This recovery of the restorative purpose of church discipline distinguished their approach from much traditional practice.

Attempts to realise the ideal spawned a plethora of approaches. In the writings of Martin Luther, and the churches which came to look to him and to Phillip Melanchthon as their primary interpreters of Scripture, there was a pronounced reluctance to revive a formal disciplinary structure. Luther's view of the church's task as being primarily educational was decisive here.

In southern Germany and Switzerland, however, a different approach emerged, represented by Bucer and Martyr among many others. Space precludes a detailed examination of the varied disciplinary practices of these churches. However, one development was particularly significant. The early Swiss Reformation, under the leadership of Zwingli and his successor Bullinger, saw ecclesiastical discipline as the responsibility of the civil community, which they were not ashamed to identify with the church of Matthew 18. However, in Basel and then in Strasbourg, an alternative approach developed, in which pastors lobbied for church control of moral discipline and involved lay elders in its exercise. It was this tradition which, largely through the ministry of John Calvin in Geneva, was ultimately to dominate the Reformed churches. In Edward VI's day, Geneva's hegemony lay in the future, but the springs from which Calvin's disciplinary reforms flowed were also those which fed England's Reformers.

3. Martin Bucer (1491-1551)

A Reformer of wide sympathies and prodigious energy, Martin Bucer, whose career was spent mainly as the leader of Strasbourg's church, was involved in schemes of church reform in Lutheran, proto-Reformed, and Catholic jurisdictions. Invited to England by Cranmer, his last major work *De Regno Christi,* was a prescription for the completion of the reform of England's church. He died in Cambridge in early 1551.

Bucer's distinctive understanding of discipleship was decisive for his interpretation of discipline. 'Living for others' characterises the Christian. Discipline is therefore primarily the exercise of mutual care, a means of Christian formation rather than a corrective instrument.[7]

Bucer's 1538 *Von der waren Seelsorge* heralded the maturity of his pastoral thought. Here, discipline and teaching together constitute the pastoral office. Formal discipline takes its place as part of a programme of pastoral care which embraced mandatory catechetical instruction, fraternal admonition, the use of public penitential discipline, and a form of non-sacramental confirmation. Discipline is therefore a broad category, understood to embrace admonition, penance and excommunication. Moreover, Bucer had accepted, under the influence of Basel, the notion that lay elders should share responsibility for discipline with the church's pastors. In one scheme, the exercise of pastoral care, including discipline, was in the hands of what amounted

---

[7] Gottfried Hammann, *Entre la Secte et la Cité: Le Projet de l'Eglise du Réformateur Martin Bucer* (Geneva: Labor et Fides, 1984), p 154.

to a presbyteral consistory.[8]

Bucer's commitment to fraternal admonition as the principal part of discipline was a constant. Indeed, it was more important to him to encourage fraternal correction, informal as well as ministerial, than to prescribe procedures for excommunication. He came to see formal discipline, including public penance and excommunication, as essential for the church, but looked to other instruments – catechising, confirmation, admonition – to accomplish the main goals of Christian discipline.

De Regno Christi summarises Bucer's conception of discipline. He describes it as the third function of the church, alongside teaching and the administration of the sacraments. It is also a broad category, embracing life and manners, penance, and 'sacred ceremonies.' The discipline of life and manners is a pastoral function, and requires that:

> not only the public ministers of the churches (though these principally) but even individual Christians should exercise a care for their neighbours. By the authority and magisterium of our Lord Jesus Christ, each person should strengthen and advance his neighbours wherever this is possible, and urge them to progress in the life of God, as his disciples, in his faith and knowledge. And if any fall into error of doctrine or some vice of life or manners, whoever can should with utmost zeal recall such persons from all false doctrine and depraved activity, both for the purity of Christian doctrine and the sedulous conformity of all life to the will of God.[9]

On the basis of Matthew 18, all Christians share responsibility for encouraging both right belief and godly conduct:

> For Christ, our master and governor, lives in each Christian. In each, therefore, and through the ministry of each, he seeks and saves the lost. On this account it is necessary that whoever are really of Christ should have a vigilant care for their brethren on his authority and power and eagerly exhort whomever they can

---

[8] Amy Nelson Burnett, *The Yoke of Christ: Martin Bucer and Christian Discipline* (Kirksville, MO: Sixteenth Century Journal Publishers, 1994), pp 185-91.

[9] *De Regno Christi*, ed. & tr. in *Melanchthon and Bucer*, ed. W. Pauck, *Library of Christian Classics* 19 (Philadelphia: Westminster, 1969), p 240.

to their duty, and keep all from sins according to their ability or rescue those who have fallen into them.[10]

The discipline exercised by pastors and elders is supplementary to this mutual ministry of fraternal correction and encouragement among believers. It remains a weighty responsibility:

> Those whom the Lord has put in charge of his sheep should therefore ponder seriously the fact that from their hands will be required whatever sheep perish by their negligence.[11]

Indeed, Bucer calls on the church's ministers to restore the public exercise of excommunication over serious public sin:

> the faithful ministers of Christ should not tolerate in the company of Christ, nor admit to the sacraments of Christ, those whom they cannot and should not acknowledge by their fruits, according to the precepts of the Lord, to be his true disciples and followers.[12]

The purpose of such ostracism is to induce genuine repentance. It is justified by Christ's command in Matthew 18.17, by Paul's instructions to Corinth, and by the need to preserve the church from sin's contagion. Ministers and elders, who are to act with the consent of the congregation, have authority both to exercise this sanction and to restore those who prove themselves genuinely penitent:

> It is within the office of rectors and elders in the churches to urge not only a true repentance of spirit concerning sins but also the doing of penance and the showing of its fruits, and to bind by the authority of Christ; and they are not to dissolve that bond until these persons have shown good faith to the Church concerning their true repentance and conversion to the obedience of Christ through those worthy fruits of repentance.[13]

> Let us also observe [...] that the Holy Spirit wished the whole Church to be gathered, in the spirit of Paul, for that man not only to be excommunicated by the common judgment of all, but also by the ministry of the same apostle 'to be handed over to

---

[10] Ibid., p 241.
[11] Ibid.
[12] Ibid., p 242.
[13] Ibid., p 244.

Satan.' [...] Saint Paul in the Spirit of God urged the Corinthians no less gravely to receive him into the the favour of the Lord and of the Church, once he had sufficiently demonstrated his repentance of spirit for his sin.[14]

The goal of restoration should govern the use of the sanction. In particular, while offenders are excluded from the sacraments and from normal social intercourse with fellow believers, they are encouraged to attend church services, so that through hearing the Word of God they would be moved to repentance and prayer.[15] Bucer concludes, summarising his view of evangelical excommunication from II Thessalonians 3:6, 11-15:

> From this text we realise how much authority has been given to us in order to apply to sinful brethren this remedy of salutary abstention and avoidance and how much the Lord wishes this very thing to work in healing the wounds of the brethren. For those who are not entirely hopeless it is an intolerable torment of mind to be excluded from the company of the brethren and of the whole church, and to be avoided by all, like men profane and alien to Christ our Lord. When such pressure is used, sinning brethren are moved to repentance and brought back to their duty much more effectively than by other punishments. [...] ... let us think over how much we harm both the sinning brethren and the entire church when we deprive those brethren who are involved in misdeeds of this medicine of holy severity.[16]

4. Peter Martyr Vermigli (1499-1562)

Though Bucer was the most distinguished foreign scholar to participate directly in England's Reformation, Peter Martyr (as he was normally known) was arguably more influential. Whereas Bucer had been in England for less than two years when he died in 1551, Martyr spent nearly six years as Cranmer's confidant. Moreover, many of the Marian exiles, several of whom ultimately became leaders in Elizabeth's church, continued to look to him for counsel.

---

[14] Ibid., p 246.
[15] Ibid., p 243.
[16] Ibid., p 247.

Among the most consistent advocates of a three-mark doctrine of the church, Martyr outlined his views on discipline extensively in his 1551 commentary on I Corinthians. Commenting on I Corinthians 1:2, he offers a characteristic definition of the church:

> And to define it, we say that it is a body of believers, and of the regenerate, whom God gathers together in Christ, through the word and Holy Spirit, and governs through ministers by purity of teaching, by the lawful use of the sacraments, and by discipline.[17]

While the church owes its origin to divine initiative, it owes its order and to the divine provision of ministry, through teaching (doctrina), sacraments, and discipline.

Martyr defines discipline itself as:

> nothing else but a power of the church, granted by God, by which the will and actions of believers are made conformable to the divine law, which is done by instruction, admonitions, correction, and finally by punishments, and also by excommunication if necessary.[18]

In Martyr's thought, unambiguously, the authority is given to the church, not the magistrate. Further, the instruments of discipline are several, and are closely related to the ministry of the word. Teaching, warnings, and correction have priority. Penalties and excommunication are held in reserve, and in any case securing willing adherence to biblical precept, rather than punishment of wrong, is the primary object.

It is naturally in his commentary on 1 Corinthians 5 that Martyr gives sustained attention to the question of discipline, notably in a lengthy an excursus, *Concerning Excommunication*.[19]

---

[17] Peter Martyr Vermigli, *In Selectissimam D. Pauli Priorem ad Corinthios Epistolam Commentarii* (3rd ed.; Zurich: C. Froschauer, 1572 [1st ed. 1551]), 5r; *The Common Places of the most famous and renowned Divine Doctor Peter Martyr, divided into foure principal parts* (trans. Anthonie Marten; London: H. Denham and H. Middleton, 1583), IV.1.1.

[18] Comments on 1 Corinthians 10:10, Vermigli, *Corinthios*, 132r; *Common Places* IV.5.1.

[19] *De Excommunicatione*, in Vermigli, *Corinthios*, 66r-69v. The locus is translated in *Common Places* IV.5.2-18.

4.1. Brotherly correction

Like Bucer, Martyr distinguishes the informal exercise of discipline – which he terms 'brotherly correction' – from the formal disciplinary process, involving the church's pastors and elders, which culminates in excommunication. Both form part of the church's disciplinary office. In his earliest printed work, he had taken Matthew 18.15-17 to refer primarily to brotherly correction, and though the Corinthians commentary devotes considerable attention to excommunication, Martyr continued to regard this as no more than the final step in the disciplinary process.[20]

Indeed, to proceed to excommunication without the use of private admonition is to deprive the sinner of the opportunity for repentance. Thus *correctio fraterna* is an opportunity repeatedly to impress on the sinner the gravity of his offence, the impending divine anger and punishment, and his scandalising of the church, in the hope of inducing repentance. This is more likely to be accomplished if rebuke is administered gently, patiently and out of loving concern. If repentance is forthcoming, no further action is required: the penitent is won back to Christ, and discipline has achieved its end.[21]

In his later commentary on Samuel Martyr maintained his position that the Matthean verses refer primarily to this universal responsibility: the ministerial exercise of discipline is always preceded by its informal exercise in the congregation. His definition of the function reflects this pastoral concern:

> Reproving is an action pertaining to discipline, whereby of charity we are earnest with them that are fallen as touching their sins, warning them to repent according to the manner and form set forth by Christ, to the intent that evil may be taken away

---

[20] Peter Martyr Vermigli, *Una Semplice Dichiartione Sopra Gli XII Articoli Della Fede Christiana* (Basel: Johan Hervagius, 1544), 154; *Early Writings: Creed, Scripture, Church* (ed. J. C. McLelland with a biographical introduction by P. M. J. McNair, 1994), p 71, Vol. 1 of J. P. Donnely, J. C. McLelland and F. A. James, *The Peter Martyr Library*, Sixteenth Century Essays and Studies (Kirksville, Mo.: Sixteenth Century Journal Publishers/Truman State University Press, 1994-).

[21] Vermigli, *Corinthios*, 66v; *Common Places* IV.5.4.

from among us.[22]

Thus Martyr consistently advocated a mutual discipline to be exercised informally throughout the church. If the teaching and administration of the sacraments are in the hands of duly chosen ministers, the third mark is for every believer to share in.

4.2. *Excommunication*

Commenting on I Corinthians 5:2, Martyr observes that it is not sufficient for the church merely to grieve over open, serious sin. It ought to resort to excommunication, since this power has been granted it by Christ. Indeed, churches which fail to exercise this discipline are themselves sinful, as are magistrates who hinder its use rather than encouraging it, since excommunication is the church's *supremus gladius*. Through it the church is able to go beyond lamenting sin, and remove it. Despite historical abuse, it was in origin a good instrument, instituted by Christ himself.[23]

It is defined at the beginning of the locus *Concerning Excommunication*:

> Excommunication is the casting out of an offender from the fellowship of believers, by the judgment of the leaders and with the whole church consenting, by the authority of Christ and the rule of holy Scripture, for the salvation of the one cast out, and of the people of God.[24]

Though Martyr insists that discipline is to be exercised over a wider range than merely public, serious offences, 'lighter sins' are excluded. On the other hand, sins that are originally private become a public concern when the sinner does not respond to warnings, and are therefore referred to the whole church. Moreover, excommunication is also to be used in cases of heresy, as Bucer had also argued.[25]

Turning to the effects of excommunication, Martyr's emphasis falls on the social ostracism excommunication entails. The sanction cuts

---

[22] Vermigli, *Common Places*, IV.5.1; *In Duos Libros Samuelis Prophetae* (Zurich: Froschauer, 1564), 17r.
[23] Vermigli, *Corinthios*, 62r.
[24] Vermigli, *Corinthios*, 66r-v; *Common Places*, IV.5.2.
[25] Vermigli, *Corinthios*, 66v-67r; *Common Places*, IV.5.5.

off the offender from the fellowship of believers. The nature of this ostracism is, however, governed by the restorative purpose of the sanction. Excommunication does not absolve believers from the obligation to treat an offender with charity and mercy, in regard to both his physical and spiritual needs. Indeed, the conduct of both church and individual is to be governed by the goal of restoration. The offender should continue to receive admonition, instruction and reproof. Social and sacramental ostracism is to be tempered by the requirement to keep the excommunicate within earshot both of preaching and of continual encouragement to repent.[26]

Theologically, excommunication recognises the separation which Martyr understands persistent sin to effect between an offender and God. He does not shrink from referring to this as a loss of communion with God. Excommunication follows and recognises the forfeiting of spiritual *communio.* Its effect is to remove the earthly fellowship of the church, making public the grievous sin that has already separated the sinner from God.[27] The church's judgment ratifies and declares this spiritual separation. However, it also provides the means by which repentance can be most effectively secured as God, through his church, seeks restoration.

Excommunication is therefore a hopeful sanction. Since in this world there is always hope for a sinner's salvation, there is every ground for optimism over its outcome. Exhortations, comfort, and prayer continue to be the charitable duties of the church towards him. The object of excommunication is to bring the offender to a genuine repentance which restores him not only to the fellowship of believers, but also to communion with God.[28]

In describing the process of excommunication. Martyr invokes a distinctive understanding to church government. The church's leaders are progressively more prominent in the disciplinary process, but the *plebs Christi* retains a decisive role. First, informal brotherly admonition culminates in warnings given in the presence of witnesses. If this fails, an offender is reported to the rulers *(praefecti, presbyteri)* of the church, for further warning. If he remains impenitent, the matter is

---

[26] Vermigli, *Corinthios,* 69r-v; *Common Places,* V.5.18.
[27] Vermigli, *Corinthios,* 67r; *Common Places,* IV.5.
[28] Vermigli, *Corinthios,* 67r.

then referred to the people. If still obdurate, he is excommunicated with the consent of the whole church.[29]

Excommunication for Martyr is one of the weighty matters of church government which require congregational agreement. The involvement of the people is not notional. Without such consent, it cannot be exercised.[30] However, while sentence is in the hands of the people, he is careful to point out that they are directed by the counsel of the teaching presbyters and their lay counterparts, since ultimate responsibility for the ministry of warning, correcting, and caring for Christ's flock is shared by this group.[31]

To summarise, excommunication is a pastoral function exercised by the church independently of the civil power. Its scope is all serious sin, including heretical belief. Its purpose is the church's purity and the salvation of the sinner, and its gravity requires the consent of the congregation both for its exercise, and for the restoration of the repentant.

4.3. Peter Martyr on discipline: summary

The breadth of Martyr's aspirations for discipline is striking to the modern reader. The church's third mark is assigned an ambitious role. Discipline is a divine command and also a power given to the church. It intends to achieve the ordering of the whole life of believer and church, so that both conform to orthodox doctrine. Through its administration by ministers and people in accordance with Scripture, God maintains the purity and health of the church, and enables the restoration of the fallen believer. To fail to exercise such a healthy, God-given instrument is to disobey God. A church without a functioning discipline is both defective and disobedient.

5. Church Discipline in the Edwardian Reformation

Cox's lament reflects the frustration of many evangelicals over England's reluctance to implement the sort of discipline advocated by

---

[29] Vermigli, *Corinthios*, 66v.
[30] Ibid., 68v.
[31] Ibid., 62v.

Bucer, Martyr, and many others. It was unquestionably a genuinely perplexing issue. On one hand, the 1552 *Prayer Book* suggests that Cranmer himself aspired to a restoration of the sort of public Lenten penance practised in the early church.[32] On another, as we shall see, the draft canon law code vacillated between Reformed and traditional approaches. Even if it had been enacted, it would scarcely have provided the English church with a functioning discipline along thoroughly Reformed lines. And yet in the heart of London there were already churches vigorously implementing evangelical discipline.

5.1. *The Stranger churches*

The most prominent London Stranger churches, with Dutch and French speaking congregations, were formally established in 1550 under the overall leadership of the Polish pastor Jan Laski.[33] Their composition and leadership meant that semi- autonomous Protestant communities were now tolerated in the heart of London, generously endowed by the government. Their royal charter established their freedom 'freely and quietly to practice, enjoy, use and exercise their own rites and ceremonies and their own peculiar ecclesiastical discipline, not withstanding that they do not conform with the rites and ceremonies used in our kingdom.'[34]

In accordance with this freedom, they lost little time in introducing church government on Reformed lines, under pastors and lay elders, including a formal system of consistorial discipline. 1552 saw the publication of a short set of liturgies for the French Stranger church, which included a rite for the public reconciliation of the penitent excommunicate. Indeed, the wide range of institutions and forms described in Laski's 1555 *Forma ac Ratio* mostly derive from London

---

[32] This aspiration survives in the opening paragraph of the *Commination, or Denouncing of God's Anger and Judgements Against Sinners* in the *Book of Common Prayer.*

[33] The first officially sanctioned Stranger church in London was established primarily for Italians, under the leadership of another emigré, Bernardino Ochino, in January 1548; Diarmaid MacCulloch, *Tudor Church Militant* (London: Allen Lane, 1999), pp 79-81; idem, 'Peter Martyr and Thomas Cranmer,' in *Peter Martyr Vermigli: Humanism, Republicanism, Reformation* (ed. Emidio Campi; Geneva: Droz, 2002), pp 181-182.

[34] Quoted in Andrew Pettegree, *Foreign Protestant Communities in Sixteenth-Century London* (Oxford: Clarendon, 1986), p 35.

Stranger church practice, and include similar disciplinary rites.³⁵ These prescribe a graduated system of brotherly correction before moral failure is brought before the ministers and elders. A sensitive and flexible, but also comprehensive instrument, this system established for the first time an ecclesiastical discipline on Reformed lines in England.

The ministers of the churches hoped that they would have a wider influence as a spur to further reform in England. In the event, Laski proved to be something of a gadfly for the evangelical establishment, and the autonomy of the Stranger churches was also a source of friction with London's church leadership, especially Bishop Nicholas Ridley. Laski remained influential, for example being made a member of the greater commission for canon law reform, though his conduct, and persistent tension with Ridley, did not always commend his counsel.

5.2. *A Stranger's critique*

In any event, the patterns of discipline very publicly advocated by the evangelical 'strangers' – England's foreign scholars and pastors – were not adopted with enthusiasm by the Edwardian regime. This is evident both from the growing and unconcealed alarm among many of the 'strangers' that England was dragging her disciplinary feet, and in the very cautious and, from an evangelical perspective, unsatisfactory disciplinary provisions of the draft code of ecclesiastical law.

A few illustrations from Peter Martyr's pen make the point. In summer 1549 he was commissioned by Cranmer to draft two sermons against the popular rebellions which had broken out, partly in response

---

[35] *La Forme des Prieres Ecclesisatiques and Doctrine de la Penitence Publique* (London, 1552), ESTC 16572.3, 16572.7. The latter includes *La Forme de la Penitence Publique*. Laski's 1555 *Forma ac Ratio Tota Ecclesiastici Ministerii, in Peregrinorum, Potissimum vero Germanorum Ecclesia*, in *Joannis à Lasco Opera tam Edita quam Inedita*, ed. A. Kuyper, (2 vols.; Amsterdam, 1886), II, p 1-283, includes both a *Ritus ac Forma Publicae Poenitentiae ante Excommunicationem*, p 184-194, and a *Ritus Recipiendi Rursus in Ecclesiam Excommunicatos post Data Manifesta Signa Verae Resipiscentiae*, p 208-222. Both of these rites derive from London Stranger Church practice.

to the new *Prayer Book*.³⁶ His analysis of the causes of the rebellion includes criticism of both church and state for tolerating sin and failing to live by the gospel which both officially professed. National repentance, on the part of both the nobility and their subjects was necessary. The means to this was not only vigorous preaching and instruction, especially of the young, but also the determined exercise of 'evangelical discipline.' Martyr commends both brotherly correction and excommunication as essential to the restoration and maintenance of peace and order, observing that, if this is to be implemented, pastors will need to be assisted by elders.³⁷

Martyr's recommendations fell on stony ground. Though Cranmer drew extensively on his analysis for a landmark sermon against the western rebels, he omitted his prescription for reform.³⁸ It is scarcely surprising, therefore, to find the Italian lamenting to Bucer some eighteen months later:

> But this is a matter of the deepest concern – that while they are occupied with those subjects of small importance, those things in the Church, which ought to be considered as the prow and the stern, remain neglected! For, as to establishing order in parishes, and [taking care] that doctrine and discipline may be ministered everywhere among the people – not a syllable! For my own part, I expect little fruit; because I cannot perceive, in any other way, among those who ought to govern the Church, any interchange of counsels or deliberations.³⁹

---

[36] Martyr's sermons are in manuscript in the Parker Library, Corpus Christi College, Cambridge, CCCC MS 340.73-95, *Hoc luctuoso tempore,* and CCCC MS 340.115-31, *Oratione perstrinximus.*

[37] CCCC MS 340.127-8.

[38] Cranmer's English redaction of Martyr's sermons, in a scribal hand with marginal notes by the archbishop, is also in the Parker Library: *A Sermon concerning the Time of Rebellion,* CCCC 102.409-82. An editorial comment states that it derives from Martyr's Latin drafts; ibid., 410. It is printed in Thomas Cranmer, *Works of Archbishop Cranmer* (ed. J. E. Cox; 2 vols.; Cambridge: Parker Society, 1846-1848), vol. 2, pp 190-202.

[39] Martyr to Bucer, early February 1551, *Gleanings of a Few Scattered Ears, during the Period of the Reformation in England* (ed. G. C. Gorham; London: Bell & Daldy, 1857), p 232. Bucer himself, writing to Hooper in November 1550, had similarly bewailed the silence on ecclesiastical discipline: *Gleanings of a Few Scattered Ears,* p 202. Other foreign scholars active in pressing this issue included Pierre Alexandre, whose 1553 *Tractatus Perutilis et Necessarius de Vera Ecclesia Disciplina et Excommunicatione,* is among the Yelverton manuscripts in the British Museum, BL Add MS 48040, fols 213r-248v.

After his return to the continent, Martyr appears to have ascribed the failure of England's Reformation to this reluctance to embrace discipline:

> Very many churches could serve you as examples of how we labour in vain without that discipline; they did not want to shoulder this so salutary yoke during the foundation stage of their reformation; later they could never be brought in line by any just rule touching their morals and life. [...] It is then a serious disaster and certain destruction for the churches if the sinews of discipline are missing from them.[40]

5.3. *The Reformatio Legum Ecclesiasticarum*

England's Reformation was certainly not without a disciplinary framework. Retention of the traditional, episcopal government of the church entailed the retention of its elaborate system of church courts. The reform of canon law – given the title *Reformatio Legum Ecclesiasticarum* by John Foxe on its attempted revival in 1571 – was a comprehensive attempt to clarify the law which governed the church and which its courts would enforce. Although torpedoed by political circumstance in the closing months of Edward VI's reign, the draft code survives, in both manuscript and published form.[41]

Its disciplinary provisions are intriguing. They reveal not so much agreement on the nature of England's church discipline, as division and indecision. Space precludes a detailed description, but a few salient features illustrate the point.

First, though excommunication itself is freshly defined along broadly evangelical lines, its retention for a wide range of offences, procedural as well as moral, reveals an inherent institutional conservatism. On the one hand, the moral offences against which it may

---

[40] Martyr to the Polish Lords Professing the Gospel and to the Ministers of their Churches, 14 Feb 1556, Peter Martyr Vermigli, *Loci Communes D Petri Martyris Vermilli* ... (4th ed.; London: Thomas Vautrollerius, 1583) p 1111-1112; Peter Martyr Vermigli, *Life, Letters and Sermons* (ed. J. P. Donnely), p 147, Vol. 5 of Donnely, McLelland, and James, *Peter Martyr Library*.

[41] Text and English translation in Gerald Bray ed., *Tudor Church Reform: The Henrician Canons of 1535 and the Reformatio Legum Ecclesiasticarum* Church of England Record Society 8 (Woodbridge: Boydell, 2000).

legitimately be employed are prescribed by the Pauline 'vice lists,' in line with Reformed practice. On the other hand, excommunication is also retained, throughout the code, as a procedural sanction. Such provisions mean the disciplinary tenor of the whole document is more medieval and punitive than evangelical: for example, excommunication is to be exercised against those who assault clergy, church wardens who neglect their duty, and those who refuse to take an oath in a church court.[42]

This impression is reinforced by the language used. While its restorative intent is acknowledged, the emphasis falls more heavily on its punitive aspect:

> by reading the sentence of excommunication [the minister] shall inform the people that the person so restricted ought to be thrown out of the church as if he were a corpse, and not partake of the Lord's supper, or attend the divine services, or associate with Christians, but should be thrown out of the bosom of the church, the common mother of Christians, and amputated from the body of Christ and shunned by heaven and earth alike, bound over to the devil and his equally wicked servants, and consigned to the eternal tortures of the flames unless he effects his salvation from the bonds of Satan.[43]

Excommunication in the *Reformatio* is accordingly more a 'vibrating thunderbolt' than an instrument of evangelical persuasion, and altogether lacks the Reformers' emphasis on the need to labour for the salvation of the offender.[44] Further, little more than lip-service is paid to the notion that the exercise of such discipline requires congregational consent: excommunication is a judicial sanction, exercised by the bishop or his surrogates.[45]

However, while most of the disciplinary titles display few signs of evangelical influence, some sections reveal reforming priorities. In one, the *Reformatio* prescribes a pattern of services to be used weekly in

---

[42] Definition at Bray, *Tudor Church Reform*, pp 462-463. For examples of the code's attention to the judicial processes of excommunication, see Bray, *Tudor Church Reform*, pp 552-553, 640-641, 676-677, 726-727, 730-731.
[43] Ibid., pp 468-469.
[44] Ibid., pp 468-469, 476-491.
[45] Ibid., pp 462-467.

every parish, and embedded within this is provision for a parochial discipline on Reformed lines. As well as advocating public penance for open sin, the title institutes a weekly consultation on how those 'accused of depraved morals and whose evil life has been noted, may first of all be challenged in the gospel by sober and virtuous *men,* acting in brotherly love according to the commandment of Christ.' Such discussion and discipline is to be carried out by the minister and elders *(seniores)* in each parish. If their warnings are heeded, no further action is required. Persistence in sin, on the other hand, is expected to lead to more severe treatment, which 'we see has been designed by the gospel [ie, Matthew 18.17] for their contumacy.'[46]

The mention of regular public penance echoes Bucer's blueprint, while the inclusion of the detailed procedure for parochial discipline also suggests Martyr's hand. In any case, the mention of elders, without parallel elsewhere in the code, shows that a plural oversight of parochial discipline along Reformed lines was contemplated. However, this is otherwise absent from the *Reformatio.* Indeed, the provision for such presbyteral discipline is in contrast with the more traditional provisions of the title on church wardens. Here, wardens as episcopal officers are instructed to report notorious sinners directly to the bishop.[47]

Finally, the most surprising element in the entire code is its inclusion of a liturgy, or *Formula,* for the reconciliation of excommunicates.[48] This provides a rite for the restoration of the penitent offender to the fellowship of the local congregation. It bears no trace of the judicial phraseology of the rest of the code. With scarcely any reference to the penal character which excommunication bears elsewhere in the *Reformatio,* its tenor is one of pastoral care for, and solidarity with, the sinner and a yearning for his reconciliation to the church. He is addressed repeatedly as 'dearest brother.' Indeed, the liturgy is a confession of mutual slavery to sin, vulnerability to temptation, and dependence on divine mercy. It urges each believer to pray for preservation from temptation, and reminds them of the need to offer and seek forgiveness. The excommunicate's humility and confession are to call forth a corresponding attitude on the part of the

---

[46] Ibid., pp 340-343.
[47] Ibid., pp 370-371.
[48] *Formula reconciliationis excommunicatorum,* Bray, *Tudor Church Reform,* pp 477-491.

listening congregation. Significantly, its focus is on securing congregational consent. Though the bishop's assent to absolution is mentioned, without the willing consent of the congregation the offender cannot be restored.[49]

This unusual section displays most clearly the efforts of the 'strangers' to introduce evangelical disciplinary practice to England's church. Its theology and pastoral tone correspond to Martyr's own emphases, while its opening homily bears a close resemblance to a sermon in the French Stranger church 1552 liturgies. Whereas in the rest of the code the sanction is a judicial process under the control of the courts, this liturgy envisages a pastoral, parochial, and evangelical approach to restoration from excommunication. However, like the provisions for parochial discipline, it appears anomalous by comparison with the rest of the code. It is probably best understood as a relic of an early stage of the drafting process, a moment when England's evangelical leadership openly contemplated adopting a discipline on Reformed foundations: most of the formal disciplinary titles were added towards the end of the drafting process, and revert to a more traditional approach.

This brief survey suggests that the *Reformatio* displays the interplay of conservatism and change in the English Reformation. It was to be a powerful statement of England's emerging ecclesiological identity, the production of a regime confident of its control of the process of reform and determined to complete it. Yet it displays both an unexpected ambivalence to the direction which reform was taking across the Channel, and the persistence of a distinctively legal approach to church government, epitomised in its attitude to discipline. Of course, city-state models of reform in any case were of limited use in a realm as large as England, as *De Regno Christi* implicitly acknowledged. Yet this consideration alone is inadequate to account for the conservative approach of most of the code's disciplinary provisions. The predominant approach is judicial and penal, rather than congregational, presbyteral, and reformative. Ecclesiastical discipline in the *Reformatio* is a judicial process, administering a graded series of penalties, rather than an essentially pastoral function.

If, as the inclusion of the *Formula* suggests, the code's drafters

---

[49] Bray, *Tudor Church Reform*, pp 476-483.

were sympathetic to a continental solution when they began their work, in its final form the *Reformatio* suggests that they drew back from this course. Discipline was far from ignored. However, the ecclesiastical discipline which was to be integral to England's church order would be very different from the Christian institution which Martyr and his peers held was crucial to the health of the true church.

6. Conclusion: Strangers to Correction

By continental standards, England's Reformation began late. At the moment when its political momentum was at its height, its leaders were able to draw on the expertise and support of a wide range of continental sympathisers and supporters. Through Cranmer's advocacy and the generosity of the Edwardian regime, it was even able to import high-level theological brain-power – England's Protestant 'strangers' – to add experienced pastoral and intellectual impetus to the pace of change. As has recently been recognised, a great deal was achieved, the spiritual identity of the nation was decisively altered, and the foundations laid for England to become a thoroughly Protestant nation within fifty years.[50]

However, despite this revolution, I have argued the English church remained 'strangers to correction,' despite its advocacy by Bucer, Martyr, Laski and their friends. Through a combination of political inertia, deliberate isolation and, it seems from the comments of contemporaries, plain reluctance to submit to the words of Scripture, England drew back from adopting a reformed church polity. Their grand vision of a Christian discipline pleasing to the Lord of the church, and obedient to his command, in which every member of the church shares responsibility for the health of the whole body, arguably awaits fulfilment yet.

---

[50] MacCulloch, *Tudor Church Militant*, pp 11-14, 157-167, 185-222.

Abbreviations and references

Works of Peter Martyr Vermigli

Cor In Selectissimam D. Pauli Priorem ad Corinthios Epistolam Commentarii, 3rd edn. (Zurich: C. Froschauer, 1572 [1st edn. 1551]).

CP The Common Places of the Most Famous and Renowned Divine Doctor Peter Martyr, Divided into Foure Principalle Parts, tr. Anthonie Marten (London: H. Denham and H. Middleton, 1583).

LC Loci Communes D Petri Martyris Vermilii ... 4th edn. (London: Thomas Vautrollerius, 1583 [1st edn. 1576])

Sam In duos Libros Samuelis Prophetae ... (Zurich: Froschauer, 1564)

USD Una Semplice Dichiaratione Sopra Gli XII Articoli Della Fede Christiana (Basel: Johan Hervagius, 1544)

PML The Peter Martyr Library, ed. Donnelly, J.R, McLelland, J.C. and James, F.A., Sixteenth Century Essays and Studies (Kirksville, MO: Sixteenth Century Journal Publishers/Truman State University Press, 1994-)

PML 1 Early Writings: Creed, Scripture, Church, ed. McLelland, J.C. with a biographical introduction by McNair, P.M.J. (1994)

PML 5 Life, Letters and Sermons, ed. Donnelly, J.P. (1999)

Other works

ET Epistolae Tigurinae de Rebus Potissimum ad Ecclesiae Anglicanae Reformationem Pertinentibus Conscriptae (Cambridge: Parker Society, 1848)

Cox Cranmer, Thomas, Works of Archbishop Cranmer, ed. Cox, J.E., 2 vols (Cambridge: Parker Society, 1846-48)

Gorham Gleanings of a Few Scattered Ears, during the Period of the Reformation in England ..., ed. Gorham, G.C. (London: Bell & Daldy, 1857) OL Original Letters relative to the English Reformation, ed. Robinson, H., 2 vols (Cambridge: Parker Society, 1846-7)

TCR Tudor Church Reform: The Henrician Canons of 1535 and the Reformatio Legum Ecclesiasticarum ed. Bray, G., Church of England Record Society 8 (Woodbridge: Boydell, 2000)

"Decalogue" Dod and his Seventeenth Century Bestseller

David Field

1. "Decalogue" Dod 151
   - 1.1 The first thirty years *151*
   - 1.2 Ministry at Hanwell and beyond 152
   - 1.3 Preaching 153
   - 1.4 Physician of souls and godly guide 155
   - 1.5 Nonconformist but no separatist 156
   - 1.6 After Hanwell 157
   - 1.7 Dod's Stature 159
2. ... and his seventeenth century bestseller 159
3. Dod's *Decalogue* as an example of Puritan practical divinity 163
   - 3.1 Human life, as well as Christian theology, is the 'art of living to God' 163
   - 3.2 The gravity of spiritual matters requires that we be in earnest about them 165
   - 3.3 The presentation of Christian truth must be Scripture-saturated 168
   - 3.4 True religion begins in the heart 169
   - 3.5 ... yet, as preached and as lived, the Christian life is immensely action-oriented 169
   - 3.6 ... and realistic and thoughtful in regard to human affliction 175
   - 3.7 These things will only be understood and lived if taught plainly and directly 176

4.	Dod's treatment of particular commandments	179
5.	Dod's views on law and obedience	185
6.	A handful of other gems from Dod's *Decalogue*	194

Conclusion... 200

Appendix: Doctrines dispersed in this book gathered together. 201

Further Reading 204

DAVID P FIELD read theology at Oxford and began ministry in Felixstowe, Ipswich, and as a lecturer at a theological college in Nigeria. After completing a PhD in English Puritanism at Cambridge he was Pastor of Horsley Evangelical Church in Surrey (1991-1996). Following several years as a head hunter he was a lecturer at Oak Hill Theological College in London (2000-2009) before returning to Executive Search with Perrett Laver. David is married to Sue, has three daughters, and is the author of *Rigide Calvinisme in a Softer Dresse: The Moderate Presbyterianism of John Howe, 1630-1705* (Rutherford House, 2004) as well as various theological articles.

1. "Decalogue" Dod ...

1.1. The first thirty years

John Dod was born in around 1549 near Malpas in Cheshire, the youngest of seventeen children.[1] In the mid-1560s he went up to Jesus College, Cambridge where he was elected a scholar and, some years later, a fellow. He was known as a learned man, witty and cheerful, and an accomplished Hebraist. His performance at one public disputation prompted a number of visiting Oxford scholars to invite him to become a member of their university. He declined the invitation.

We know little of Dod's early spiritual life, but at some point while a fellow at Jesus, a false accusation was brought against him of having defrauded the college of a sum of money due from one of his pupils. Dod fell into a severe fever and while ill 'his sins came upon him like armed men and the tide of his thoughts was turned.'[2] Dod was cleared of the charge and he thereafter began to preach at a weekly lecture set up by the godly of Ely.

It was around this time that the incident of the Sermon on Malt occurred. As recounted by the *Dictionary of National Biography*, Dod 'had preached strongly at Cambridge against the drinking indulged in by the students and had greatly angered them. One day some of them met "Father Dod" as he was called, passing through a wood, seized him, and set him in a hollow tree, declaring that he should not be released until he had preached a sermon on a text of their choosing. They gave him the word "malt" for a text and on this he preached, beginning, "Beloved, I am a little man, come at a short warning to deliver a brief discourse, upon a small subject, to a thin congregation and from an unworthy pulpit," and taking each letter as a division of his sermon.'

Whilst at Cambridge, Dod became a part of Laurence

---

[1] The main seventeenth century source for Dod's life is Samuel Clarke's account in his *Lives of Sundry Modern Divines* appended to *A General Martyrologie* (1677). The outline given here follows that given in DNB with additional details from Brook, Haller, Webster, and Collinson (see Further Reading).

[2] Samuel Clarke, *Lives*, pp 168-9, cited by William Haller, *The Rise of Puritanism* (New York: Columbia University Press, 1938) p 56.

Chaderton's group[3] and thus acquainted with and a friend of such key figures in the Elizabethan Puritan movement as Thomas Cartwright, Arthur Hildersham, Richard Greenham, and William Whitaker. He was given the responsibility, along with Hildersham, of taking care of Cartwright's papers after his death and, indeed, preached Cartwright's funeral sermon. Cartwright himself had referred to Dod as 'the fittest man in the land for the pastoral function, able to speak to any man's capacity and never out of the pulpit.'[4]

1.2. Ministry at Hanwell and beyond

In 1585, perhaps upon Dod's marriage to his first wife, Anne, stepdaughter of Richard Greenham and sister of the later renowned sabbatarian Nicholas Bownde,[5] Chaderton recommended Dod to Sir Anthony Cope, patron of St Peter's, Hanwell in Oxfordshire. Cope was, in Knappen's words, 'collecting a fine assortment of Puritan ministers'[6] and in addition to bringing Dod to Hanwell, he secured, at around the same time, the appointment of Robert Cleaver as minister of nearby Drayton.[7] Here Dod was to serve for almost twenty years and the shape and character of his ministry at Hanwell and, in subsequent pastorates led Haller to make the remarkable claim that 'no one probably did more than he to fix by personal influence and example the way of life and style of preaching followed for generations by the rank and file of the Puritan ministry.'[8]

Certainly his ministry made a great impact upon many people and in many ways. At his funeral sermon it was said that he gave himself at Hanwell to 'much fasting and prayer and as his seed-time was painful, so his harvest was gainful, hundreds of souls being converted to his ministry.'[9] A number of local ministers, resenting the

---

[3] Tom Webster, *Godly Clergy in Early Stuart England* (Cambridge: Cambridge University Press, 1997), p 20.
[4] Cited by Haller, *The Rise of Puritanism*, p 58.
[5] Anne was to bear Dod twelve children. After her death he married for a second time.
[6] M. M. Knappen, *Tudor Puritanism* (Chicago: University of Chicago Press, 1939, 1966), p 292.
[7] http://hanwellvillage.com/church_history.htm accessed 27th July 2011
[8] Haller, *The Rise of Puritanism*, p 58.
[9] Jacqueline Eales, "A Road to Revolution: The Continuity of Puritanism, 1559-1642" in Christopher Durston and Jacqueline Eales, *The Culture of English Puritanism 1560-1700* (London: Macmillan, 1996), p 195.

popularity of Dod's preaching, forbade their parishioners to go to hear him. Instead, perhaps, they went to the weekly lecture at Banbury (a town which, according to Collinson, was fast-becoming a 'by-word for puritanism') where Dod was one of four lecturers.[10] Others included Robert Cleaver and, later, Robert Harris and Henry Scudder. Dod was influential in knitting together a community of clergy in the area and himself took tutees at his own household seminary.[11]

1.3. Preaching

Dod's preaching was all that the puritans looked for. It was godly, learned, plain, pithy, affectionate, and practical. His method was typical and formative of Puritan preaching:

> John Dod would stand up to preach with nothing more in his hand than 'the Analisis of his Text, the proofs of Scripture for the Doctrines, with the Reasons and Uses.' His manner was to begin by 'opening a verse or two, or more at a time, first clearing the drift and connection, then giving the sense and interpretation briefly, but very plainly, not leaving the text until he had made it plain to the meanest capacity.' Next he cleared and exemplified the doctrines by reference to scripture itself, the preacher, 'opening his proofs, not multiplying particulars for oppressing memory, not dwelling so long as to make all truth run though a few texts.' Finally he spoke 'most largely and very home in application, mightily convincing and diving into men's hearts and consciences, leaving them little or nothing to object against it.'[12]

His main themes were so clear that he became known as 'Faith and Repentance' Dod. His directness was such that on one occasion 'a person being enraged at his close and awakening doctrine, picked a quarrel with him, smote him in the face and dashed out two of his teeth.' At this, 'this meek and lowly servant of Christ, without taking the least offence, spit out the teeth and blood into his hand, and said, 'See here, you have knocked out two of my teeth without any just provocation; but on condition I might do your *soul* good, I would give

---

[10] Patrick Collinson, *Godly People* (London: The Hambledon Press, 1983), p 484.
[11] The words are from Webster, *Godly Clergy*, p 28.
[12] Haller, *The Rise of Puritanism*, pp 134-135.

you leave to dash out all the rest.'[13] And his insight into souls was so searching that 'some said he must have had spies and informers at work for him.' His reply, we are told was 'that the Word of God was searching, and that if he was shut up in a dark Vault, where none could come at him, yet allow him but a Bible and a candle, and he should preach as he did.'[14]

Others were less appreciative and yet, again, his response tells us much about the man, his priorities, and his character:

> When someone complained at the length of his sermons, his rejoinder was that if 'Gentlemen will follow hounds from seven in the morning till four or five in the afternoon, because they love the cry of dogs, we should be content though the Minister stood above his hour.' And he added, 'methinks it is much better to hear a Minister preach than a kennel of hounds to bark.'[15]

His preaching was not, however, his whole ministry. After sermon any who wished to could go back to his house to eat and to rehearse and further apply the sermon. Dod loved to be with people and he loved to talk. He became known for his pithy sayings and later in the seventeenth century broadsides of 'Dod's Droppings' were widely sold, providing biblical counsel, almanac style, for generations to come.

Dod was also ready at all times to meet with needy souls. Haller, following Clarke, describes his practice:

> His habit was to use the church edifice itself for his pastoral study. There, perplexed souls would find him and if he thought them bashful, he would meet them and say, 'Would you speak with me?' And when he found them unable to state their question, he would help them out with it, taking care to find the sore: but would answer and deal so compassionately and tenderly, as not to discourage the poorest soul from coming again.[16]

---

[13] Benjamin Brook, *The Lives of the Puritans* (3 vols.; London: James Black, 1813), vol III, p 6.
[14] Haller, *The Rise of Puritanism*, p 132, following Clarke, *Lives*.
[15] Ibid., p 60.
[16] Ibid., p 58.

1.4. Physician of souls and godly guide

Indeed, over the years at Hanwell and afterwards, Dod 'built up a national reputation as a godly guide.'[17] On several occasions he helped dying believers to assurance. After early failures in which Dod declared that 'the Devill's rhetoricke taught her against herself,' Dod and Thomas Hooker between them even brought the famously melancholic Joan Drake of Esher out of her spiritual distress before her death in 1625, something which John Preston, James Ussher, Richard Sibbes, and Ezekiel Culverwell had all attempted without success.[18]

Dod became a good friend of John Preston, and it was after Dod persuaded him that 'English *preaching* was like to work more and win more souls to God' that Preston declined to become the Lady Margaret Divinity Professor at Cambridge.[19] Later, in July 1628 and knowing that he had little time left to live, Preston asked to be taken to Fawsley in order to receive dying comfort from Dod. A few days later Dod preached Preston's funeral sermon.[20]

His counsel was sought by several puritans, as they tried to make up their minds in the 1630s whether or not to leave the country for New England. In 1633 he dissuaded George Hughes and John Ball from doing so. John Cotton and Thomas Hooker, on the other hand received a different reply. Dod explained that he believed it was legitimate to leave although as an elderly man he did not intend to do so himself: 'When Peter was young he might gird himself and go whither he would; but when he was old and unfit for travel, then indeed God called him rather than to suffer himself to be girt of others, and lead along to prison and death.' Cotton expressed concern for the congregations of those pastors who left and Dod at once replied, 'that the removing of a minister was like the draining of a fish pond: the good fish will follow the water, but eels, and other baggage fish, will stick in the mud.'[21]

---

[17] Eales, 'A Road to Revolution', p 193.
[18] Webster, *Godly Clergy*, p 50. Hooker gained not only spiritual insight but also a wife from the case: he met, fell in love with, and subsequently married Mrs Drake's woman-in-waiting, Susannah Garbrand.
[19] Haller, *The Rise of Puritanism*, p 73.
[20] Paul Seaver, *The Puritan Lectureships* (Stanford: Stanford University Press, 1970), p 265; Webster, *Godly Clergy*, pp 13, 42.
[21] Webster, *Godly Clergy*, pp 277-278; see also p 169.

1.5. *Nonconformist but no separatist*

Collinson describes Dod as a 'nonconformist within the Church of England' and in this sense he is the typical early English puritan.

> When Simeon Ashe and John Wall wrote a commendatory epistle for one of [Samuel] Clarke's earliest ventures, in December 1649, they expressed interest in the further publication of the 'characters' of such as Preston, Sibbes, Dod, and Hildersham who all their lives had 'kept a due distance from Brownistical separatism and were zealously affected towards the *Presbyterial* Government of the Church.'[22]

His zeal for presbyterial government is unsurprising given his membership of Chaderton's group and his closeness to Cartwright back in the 1570s. Another indication of his nonconformity was his setting up of three benches at St Peter's, Hanwell for the reception of the elements of the Lord's Supper (this so that the elements would not be received kneeling).[23] Three times he was suspended from the ministry and on numerous other occasions he was cited. In 1616 he approved of Henry Jacob gathering a covenanting church in Southwark.[24]

> Moreover, Webster tells us:
>
> There is a small hint of the practice of particular church discipline in the refusal of John Dod to read out in church the sentence of the ecclesiastical court on a fornicator of his flock because the young man had already taken penance before his fellow parishioners before he had been examined by the archdeacon in 1633.[25]

And yet, for all this, Dod was no separatist. Spurr refers to a communication of 1637 in which:

> A group of thirteen English nonconformist clergy, headed by the aged Dod and Cleaver, wrote to the New England clergy

---

[22] Collinson, *Godly People*, p 516. Clarke's *Lives of Sundry Eminent Persons* appended to his General Martyrologie would, of course, provide exactly the account which Ashe and Wail sought.
[23] http://hanwellvillage.com/church_history.htm accessed 27th July 2011.
[24] Webster, *Godly Clergy*, p 295.
[25] Ibid., p 234.

reminding them that when they had all lived in the same kingdom, they had jointly 'maintained the purity of worship against corruptions, both on the right hand and on the left.' But now they had heard that their brethren in New England taught that set prayers were unlawful, and the godly should not 'join in prayer' or 'receive the sacraments' where such a 'stinted liturgy is used.' Did not this lend support to their opponents' charges that 'nonconformists in practice are separatists in heart?'[26]

Dod would have none of it. Nonconformist in practice he certainly was and he suffered for it. Separatist in heart he emphatically was not, looking as he did for reform of the national church according to the Word of God.

1.6. *After Hanwell*

In January 1604, Dod, along with another thirty or so Puritan ministers held private meetings alongside the Hampton Court Conference. The outcome of the Conference itself was a great disappointment to the Puritan party and over the next few years around three hundred ministers lost their livings. That Dod and Cleaver feared exactly this is clear from the Epistle Dedicatory of *A Plaine and Familiar Exposition of the Tenne Commandements*, dated September 1604. They give three reasons for dedicating the work to their patron, Sir Anthony Cope, and all three reasons have some foreboding about them:

> First, to testifie our unfained thankfulnesse for all the singular favours, which we have received at your hands, for the space of these twentie yeares. Wherein you have always shewed yourselfe as willing to ayde and defend us in our just cause, as you were carefull to make choice of us, at our first entrance into our places.
>
> Secondly, because we know not how soone we shall finish the dayes of our Ministerie, we thought it our dutie to give some taste, and to leave some testimony thereof unto the world, to witnesse your godly desire to discharge the trust committed unto you, and our faithfull endevours to performe the dutie belonging unto us.

---

[26] John Spurr, *English Puritanism, 1603-90* (Basingstoke: Macmillan, 1998), p 93.

> Lastly, for that having formerly heard whatsoever is here set downe in writing, and also having throughly knowne the manner of our doctrine and conversations, you are best able even of your owne knowledge, to make our defence to any that shall unjustly except against us.

Their anxieties were justified. Shortly afterwards, Dod was suspended from his living by Bishop Bridges of Oxford. For some while he remained in the area, supporting his successor, Robert Harris, later Master of Trinity, Oxford, and member of the Westminster Assembly, and also preparing works on the Proverbs for publication. The first of these was issued in 1606 and Dod states simply, 'we are now more willing to make some work for the press because we have no employment in the pulpit.'[27]

Taking into account what has already been said about Dod's preaching ministry and his counsel to many seeking godly guidance, the story of the next forty years is quickly told. He held positions in Fenny Compton in Warwickshire and then in Canons Ashby in Northamptonshire between 1607 and 1611, being 'silenced' by Archbishop Abbot in 1611. Little is known of the next twelve years of his life beyond the publication of a series of books on the Proverbs with Cleaver.

In 1624, however, he was settled as Rector of Fawsley in Northamptonshire under the protection of Sir Richard Knightley, the Puritan squire of Fawsley Hall. His preaching and lecturing, his cure of souls, his encouragement of godly learned ministers and his writing continued over the next twenty years. At over ninety years old he wrote to Lady Mary Vere and offered if he 'might any way be helpful to your Ladyship to resolve you of any doubts or questions in your heart, I should be glad ere my departure, now at hand, to do you any service this way.'[28]

In August 1645, at around 95 years of age, he died.

---

[27] Dod and Cleaver, *A Plaine and Familiar Exposition of the Ninth and Tenth Chapters of the Proverbs of Salomon* (London, 1606), Epistle Dedicatorie.
[28] Eales, "A Road to Revolution," p 194.

1.7. Dod's Stature

Little man though he was, Dod was a giant. Collinson, possibly the foremost living scholar of Elizabethan Puritanism calls him, simply, 'the great John Dod.'[29] Numerous writers refer to him as a 'puritan patriarch.' By personal contact and involvement he was at the heart of English Puritanism from the 1570s right through until the 1630s. Thomas Cartwright, Arthur Hildersham, Richard Greenham, Laurence Chaderton, William Gouge, Ezekiel Culverwell, William Perkins, John Preston, Richard Sibbes, John Cotton, Thomas Hooker: the list of those who honoured him as personal friend and leader of the movement itself reads like a roll-call of Puritan greats. Archbishop Ussher declared, 'Whatever some affirm of Mr Dod's strictness, and scrupling some ceremonies, I desire that when I die my soul may rest with his.'[30] Further, by personal example and influence he advanced the cause of a learned and godly ministry and of biblically mature personal religion as few others have done in the history of this nation. And in his best-selling book, Dod's *Decalogue*, he provides us with classic puritan practical divinity, the pure embodiment of the genre, and a powerful example of what is great about English Puritanism. It is to that book that we now turn.

2. ... and his seventeenth century bestseller

A *Plaine and Familiar Exposition of the Tenne Commandements* by John Dod and Robert Cleaver was first published in 1604 and became a publishing phenomenon of the seventeenth century. In the Epistle Dedicatory to their patron, Sir Anthony Cope, the authors explain the circumstances which occasioned the book's publication. In 1603, some enthusiastic hearers of Dod's and Cleaver's sermons on the commandments had 'published their notes (as themselves could gather them in the time of the Sermon) without our knowledge or consent, and many faults were escaped in writing and printing which by due care and foresight might have been prevented: therefore both for our clearing, and the better satisfying of the Christian Reader, we were compelled to

---

[29] Patrick Collinson, *The Elizabethan Puritan Movement* (London: Jonathan Cape, 1967), p 456.
[30] Brook, *Lives of the Puritans*, vol III, p 5.

review and refine the whole Treatise. Wherein we have jointly laboured as near as we could to set down every thing, without addition or detraction, as it was first delivered in the public Ministry.'[31]

The book proved to be immensely popular, running to nineteen editions over the next thirty years and, according to Collinson, making Dod and Cleaver 'the most successful co-authors of the century.'[32] Other than the Bible and the Psalm-book, it was the most commonly-owned book in early Plymouth Colony,[33] and in his well-known description of 'the poorest or smallest library that is tolerable,' Richard Baxter places 'Mr Dod. on the Commandments' in his list of must-have 'affectionate practical English writers.'[34]

One of the earliest published commendations of the work combines quaintness with accuracy. William Gamage, a Welsh gentleman vicar-poet wrote two 'centuries' of epigrams in 1613. One of them was for a friend who had lent him 'Dod and Cleaver on the Decalogue' and ran as follows:

> Dod with his Cleaver cleaves the stonie rocke
> Of our hard harts through their laborious paine:
> And plaines the way most plaine for Christ his flock,
> That leads o're hils to the celestiall plaine.
> These paire of friends with thankes I send againe,
> Though two in Name, in Nature yet not twaine.[35]

The contents of the book are easily described. After the Epistle Dedicatory and 'A Friendly Counsel to the Christian Reader' in verse, the body of the work consists of eleven sections, namely, one section on the prefatory words of Exodus 20:1-2 and then one section on each of the commandments. These sections are on average thirty pages long

---

[31] Dod and Cleaver, *Exposition*, p A2. All footnotes that follow with nothing other than a page number refer to the *Exposition*. Spelling has been modernized and some small editorial changes made for the sake of clarity.

[32] Collinson, *Godly People*, p 496.

[33] http://www.mayflowerhistory.com/History/religion.php accessed 27th July 2011.

[34] Richard Baxter, *A Christian Directory in Practical Works*, vol.1 (Morgan, Pa.: Soli Deo Gloria, 2000), p 732.

[35] William Gamage, *Linsi-Woolsie or Two Centuries of Epigrammes*, (Oxford: Joseph Barnes, 1613), Second Century, Epigram 12, "To his lo: friend Mr. M. Hop: for the loane of Dod, and Cleaver on the Decalogue." This material is to be found at http://www.philological.bham.ac.uk/gamage/text2.html accessed 27th July 2011.

with the longest being the sixty-four page treatment of the fifth commandment and the shortest the nine-page treatment of the tenth commandment. The main body of the work is followed by a thirteen-page catechism borrowed from another author and giving such readers as are 'wearied with the larger Discourse upon the Commandments a compendious abridgement of all the substantial points of Religion.'[36] The book closes with a versified meditation on God's name from Exodus 34, a table of 'Doctrines dispersed in this Book gathered together'[37] and finally an index, 'A Table of the principal things contained in this Exposition.'

As to the genre of the book, it is that most characteristic of Puritan published works, the printed sermon series, and is therefore shaped by the distinctively Puritan method of sermon structuring. The Puritan sermon had three parts: exegetical, doctrinal, and applicatory. In the first, relatively brief, exegetical part, the setting, the words and the divisions of the text would be explained. Next would follow 'doctrine' and 'use,' sometimes just one doctrine followed by between two and five uses, and at other times a whole series of doctrines, each applied with a number of uses. The doctrinal part would be built around and upon a didactic proposition either stated in or deduced from the text and this would then be explained, confirmed, and illustrated with reasons given and objections dealt with. The uses would bring the doctrine to bear upon the lives of the hearers. Common types of use were for trial ('where do I stand in relation to this teaching, this promise, threat, encouragement or warning?'), for reproof ('if this is true then the following beliefs and behaviours are shown to be wrong'), for consolation ('if this is true then the following people should feel encouraged'), and for consideration ('if this is true then think, think, think about what follows from it').

Various influences shaped this Puritan method of preaching: the prophesyings of the 1570s; the spiritual brotherhood of the Cambridge circle: Chaderton, Cartwright, Hildersham, Dering, Greenham, Perkins, Ames, and scores and scores of Puritan ministers up and down the country who had learned pastoral ministry from these giants; the published distillation of method by Perkins and Ames

---

[36] Epistle Dedicatorie, p A3.
[37] See Appendix.

(influenced by Ramus); the ease with which the method could be understood and practised; and its success in enabling hearers truly to hear the Word of God, to remember what they had learned, to think doctrinally, to see the demand of Scripture upon the details of their belief conduct and experience and to reason with themselves and with others in accordance with Reformed divinity. And all these influences made the Puritan way of handling and communicating the truth of Scripture the method for the moment, a moment, indeed, which lasted a century and more. Dod's *Decalogue* reflects just this method.

Ames speaks for all Puritans in his assertion that 'the chief scope of the sermon is the edification of the hearers.'[38] Theological innovation, unreachable exegetical certitude, man-pleasing rhetorical impressiveness were all set aside for the sake of plain declaration and powerful application of the Word. Ames again,

> They faile therefore who stick to a naked finding out and explication of the truth ... neglecting use and practice, in which Religion, and so blessedness, doth consist, [they] doe little or nothing edifie the conscience.[39]

There is little question but that Ames would have been well-pleased with Dod's *Decalogue*. It was not original and nor was it theologically distinctive but it was an early example of its type, an example which was followed many times over in the decades ahead. It did not break new ground theologically or exegetically but neither did it stick at the level of an expository lecture. It was intended by its authors to change lives by the plain statement and direct application of the truth and, in God's hands, it achieved this to a remarkable extent and degree in the decades after it was published.

It is astonishing, then, given the very great influence of this book in the seventeenth century, that it has not been reprinted since. In introducing it, therefore, I wish much more to provide a taste than an analysis. (Analysis can follow if a way can be found of getting Dod's *Decalogue* reprinted.) I will do this in four ways and, as much as possible, in Dod's own words. Over the next pages, then, we will firstly, explore Dod's *Decalogue* as a splendid example of Puritan practical divinity; secondly, comment briefly upon Dod's treatment of particular

---

[38] William Ames, *Marrow of Sacred Divinity* (1641), p 157.
[39] Ibid., p 157.

commandments; thirdly, consider the challenge to us of Dod's views about law and obedience to law as categories of Christian thinking and living; and fourthly, enjoy a sampling of gems from Dod's *Decalogue* leaving us, hopefully, with an appetite for more.

3. Dod's *Decalogue* as an example of Puritan practical divinity

This great work exemplifies what is best about Puritan practical divinity in a hundred ways. Here are just seven.

3.1. *Human life, as well as Christian theology, is the 'art of living to God'*[40]

The Puritan vision of Christian discipleship was, quite simply, God-centred. A life of communion with God and service to him is a life of utmost blessedness and yet the focus of attention must be God himself rather than the blessedness. Our confidence comes from him, from his greatness and perfection:

> This must teach us earnestly to seek his love and favour, which if we have, nothing can hurt us: For in him we live, move, and have our being. Having his love, we have all power, wisdom, and counsel on our side. If he be perfect in himself, and all creatures have what ever they have, from him, what need we fear (he being with us) what all the creatures can do against us? Seeing that all their power is derived from him, and used at his direction.[41]

This sense of the greatness and the reality of God brings boldness:

> We may learn not to be afraid or ashamed to stand for [the commandments], as also to practise them in our lives, though the atheists and profane sinners of the world mock and scoff at us never so much for the same. For what need we be ashamed to maintain those words which God himself was not ashamed in

---
[40] The phrase, of course, is William Ames': *Marrow*, pp 1-3.
[41] Dod, *A Plaine and Familiar Exposition of the Tenne Commandments*, p 13.

his own person to speak?[42]

> This serves therefore exceedingly to condemn their dastardliness, that are afraid to keep the Sabbath, or to do any other religious duty, because they should be counted and called Puritans. But is it not better that men should hate us without cause than that God should have a quarrel against us upon a just cause? Is it not much better that they should scoff at us for good, than that God should plague us for evil?[43]

And confidence:

> Nothing has any power to do a man any good but God.[44]

Furthermore, the whole of life is to be lived in the knowledge that God not only sees all that we do but also that he is dealing with us in all things. In avoiding rash anger, for example, the Christian must:

> labour to get wisdom always and in every thing to behold God's providence, to see his hand ruling every thing and to persuade ourselves that all things come to pass according to his purpose and direction and then we shall not so soon fret against men though it be unjust with men, yet it is just with God and though we have not deserved it at their hand and so they wrong us, yet we have deserved that at God's hands and much more too: he does us no wrong at all though he appoints such evil instruments to afflict us.[45]

One of the key lessons of God's unchangeableness is that the record of God's dealings with people in the pages of Scripture can be directly applied to our own lives.[46] God afflicts and prospers, blesses and curses, delays and delivers now as he did in Scripture times. This is not naïve; if anything, and so soon in the early modern period, Dod has moved through suspicion to the second naivete. He knows that God is exalted and majestic but this grounds rather than undermines a confidence that he is intimately involved with human beings in the details of their lives. He knows that reading providence is no easy task,

---

[42] Ibid., p 7.
[43] Ibid., p 7.
[44] Ibid., p 272.
[45] Ibid., p 235.
[46] Ibid., p 14.

that the righteous are afflicted for a variety of reasons and that the human heart is deceitful beyond knowledge but this leads him to humility in interpreting how God deals with men and women rather than to abandoning the belief that he does so.

Thus, life with our eyes towards God is life as life should be.

3.2. *The gravity of spiritual matters requires that we be in earnest about them*

The matters of eternity weigh more heavily than the transient. Only a fool would prefer stubble to gold or value a dumb beast more highly than a human soul. How, for example, should one decide where to live?

> This also serves much for the reproof of them that only look to their bodies and present estate, without any regard to their souls: and therefore whithersoever their commodities lead them there they plant themselves. Be the towns or families never so superstitious, that is not respected, so that gain and honour may arise to them from thence, there they will dwell, and there they will match their children.[47]

And we therefore argue from the greater to the lesser to comfort ourselves in temporal affliction:

> Has he removed the tyranny of sin, which would have damned our souls and cannot he give us refreshing from the misery of our bodies? If God deliver from sin, death and hell, never faint, as though he could not, or would not rid us from outward afflictions. If he have overcome the greater, the lesser shall not withstand him. If God grant us freedom from those things that are simply evil (as sin is) and the cause of all ills then it is easier to succour us against those which are medicines against evil and are often turned into blessings.[48]

Self-examination

If the teachings of Scripture are true then one cannot be too serious about spiritual realities. It is vital that individuals know where they

---

[47] Ibid., p 20.
[48] Ibid., p 22.

stand spiritually and self-examination is a key means to this which Puritan preachers constantly urged upon their hearers. For example, Dod tells us that since obedience is rendered by those who know God to be their God, this raises the question as to how a person is to know whether or not he or she is the Lord's. To find out, self-examination is necessary in order to seek certain marks. Dod lists several:

> So that, if God the Father has regenerated us, and Christ has killed our sins; and the holy Ghost has made us ashamed of them, to confess them, likewise if it work in us love, and patience, and moderation of our affections, and make us able to pray to God, then God is our God, and this will make us obey: but if this be shaken, all is shaken: for this is the foundation of all obedience.[49]

And in describing them more fully it becomes clear that attention must be given to spiritual experience as well as to outward conduct:

> Also God the Son, Christ Jesus, where he comes, he kills sin, he abates our lust and worldliness, and works a fresh spring of grace and holiness: but if we feel no work of death in us to mortify our sin, then how can we know that he died for us?[50]

Particular circumstances, too, will prompt self-examination. For example:

> When we see that God does not bless us according to his promises made to those that keep his commandments, then we must examine our selves diligently concerning our obedience to this his law, whether we live not in some sin, or whether some old sin lie not in us, which has never been repented of Wherefore, when he strikes us, we must begin to examine our obedience.[51]

Universal Obedience

Spiritual seriousness shows itself not only in self-examination but in endeavours after universal obedience. After all, if the Ten

---

[49] Ibid., p 18.
[50] Ibid., p 17.
[51] Ibid., p 11.

Commandments are the demands of God, obedience must be universal:

> Whence it is to be learned, that whosoever will have any true comfort by his obedience to God's law, must not content himself to look to one, or two: but must make conscience, and have a care to keep them all and every one.[52]

Partial obedience is insincere because in reality it is serving self rather than recognising the loving authority of God. And partial obedience is also unstable:

> And this was Herod's case, he did many things according to John's preaching, and did hear him gladly, and for some other commandments was reasonably willing to be ruled: but for the seventh he must needs have a dispensation; and he kept this resolution that let all the preachers in the world say what they could, he would not be brought to leave his incest, nor to part with his brother's wife. Therefore we see how soon he fell to break, first the third commandment, in swearing sinfully to that light and wanton woman, to give her whatsoever she should ask, and then also he grew to persecute John and cut off his head: so, taking liberty to himself to break the seventh commandment, he cast off all care and regard of the rest.[53]

A further aspect of this universal obedience and earnestness about spiritual realities is, of course, the famed Puritan concern for detail, the response to the charge that Puritans were 'precisians' being, simply, 'I serve a precise God.' Dod expresses this concern too. On the tenth commandment:

> The least motion after the least thing of our neighbour's is sin there is nothing so small but it is something though the matter be small wherein one offends, yet it is not a small matter to offend God.[54]

And he proves that 'the first motion and inclination of the heart to any sin is a sin' because:

> These lusts break God's commandments, and are against the

---

[52] Ibid., p 9.
[53] Ibid., p 9.
[54] Ibid., p 337.

law of charity, and come from an evil cause, and bring with them such evil effects, therefore the least evil imagination arising in the heart, without any agreement of the mind to put it into practice, is sin, and deserves the curse of God.[55]

3.3. The presentation of Christian truth must be Scripture-saturated

This may be briefly stated. The whole of Dod's *Decalogue* demonstrates the Puritan conviction not only that Scripture is the best interpreter of Scripture but also that the preaching of one Scripture is an occasion for instruction in other Scriptures besides. To give illustrations of various human traits and behaviours from Scripture stories will thus simultaneously strengthen doctrinal grasp and increase the Bible knowledge of the hearer. Within the first few pages of the book Dod is using as illustrations, Eglon listening to Ehud, David listening to Abigail, and Balak listening to Balaam; Jacob examining himself; Esther and the Jews being delivered on the day of their greatest threat; Herod obeying many commands but not all and thus falling into judgment; David, Zechariah, and Elizabeth yielding true though not perfect obedience; and Lot being vexed in Sodom.

And this cross-referencing is for interpretation as well as for illustration: Dod is unafraid, for example, to use the Old Testament case law in expounding the Ten Commandments, whether with regard to the due penalty for adultery, the twenty per cent to be added to what was stolen when making voluntary restitution, or the application of kidnapping laws to the treatment of servants.

Dod is at home everywhere else in Scripture too. Passages from the Old Testament prophets are frequently used and the book of Proverbs is a particularly favourite source of illustration and example: it is unsurprising that Dod's next published work was an exposition of some chapters of Proverbs itself. To listen to his preaching was a workshop for the Bible student as well as a workout for the Christian disciple.

---

[55] Ibid., p 330f.

3.4. True religion begins in the heart

One of recurring themes of the whole work is that true obedience is spiritual and inward and must both proceed from a renewed heart and affect a person's inner thoughts and affections and motivations as well as his outward conduct.

> Therefore all the obedience performed to God, must proceed from within, and come from the heart, else it shall be no whit acceptable to him. That which grows without, if it come not from the root of sincerity within, shall afford no comfort to our souls in the time of trial. But if we will have our outward obedience to bring forth any fruit to our own souls, or glory to God, we must look that it have its beginning from an upright, sound, and faithful heart.[56]

There is real insight into the mixed motives which characterise the sinner. On anger:

> We must never be moved without a just cause and we [must] proportion our anger to the sin committed against God and not to the injury done to us, for that proceeds from pride and is no better than revenge.[57]

None are exempt. On the false gods of preachers:

> For a man may preach and exhort others to the love of God and yet if he do this for vain-glory and not for God's glory, to get promotion to himself and not salvation to God's people, he at that very time sets up an idol in his heart.[58]

And it is because of this that the 'how to' sections of the work often begin with the exhortation to appeal to God for his purifying work upon the heart.

3.5. ... yet, as preached and as lived, the Christian life is immensely action-oriented

Faith is a busy, active, productive grace:

---

[56] Ibid., p 8.
[57] Ibid., p 234.
[58] Ibid., p 29.

> But men will say they have faith, and believe in God: which if they had, it would bring forth obedience and have works. For how can they choose but obey God, if they hold this sure, that God loves and regards them, and will give them reward for every good thing that they do? And this every one must perform, that will say, God is my God.[59]

True repentance will bear fruit:

> We cannot be assured of pardon for that which is past nor perseverance in a better course, unless there be true repentance. And true repentance never goes before but willingness to make restitution follows presently after.[60]

There is, therefore, a resolve to clear any and all obstacles put in the way of obedience. They may be obstacles of understanding (why does God punish the children for the sin of the fathers?)[61] or of nervousness, such as the fear that Sabbath-keeping may cost us too much:

> Better it were that we should hazard some part of our outward estate than the wrath of God to fall upon us. 'But when our corn or hay lies in hazard like to be spoiled by ill weather, what will you have us do then?' Trust in God's providence, who as he has commanded you to rest, so he will see that you shall be no loser by your resting faithful obedience was never any man's hindrance, but negligence and infidelity brings all their misery.[62]

Or, indeed, it may be the obstacle of plausible-sounding excuses for sin. With regard to taking something very small from another's goods:

> Yet men have excuses for this their stealing. As first, 'it is a small thing, you should not make so much ado about so little a matter.' Is it a small thing? Then, the more wretched and abject sinner you, that will corrupt yourself for so small a thing.
>
> 'Oh, but he can spare it well enough.' God has absolutely forbidden to take any man's goods without any such exception as this, 'unless he can spare it.'

---

[59] Ibid., p 18.
[60] Ibid., p 299.
[61] Ibid., p 76.
[62] Ibid., p 143.

> 'It will do him no harm.' This is not the question whether it will hurt him or not: it offends God, he has forbidden it and therefore if you do it you sin against God and hurt your own soul.
>
> 'It will do me good.' That is not true, it will hinder you rather and bring a further curse on you than before.[63]

In addition to removing excuses and doubts, Dod energetically provides encouragements and motivations. The God who gave the command will also give the power to obey:

> Also this serves for the singular comfort of all God's children that since all these be God's commandments, even all as well as any one, therefore they shall have power to obey them all, as well as one. For that God that has enabled us to keep some, can as well strengthen us to keep all the rest: because that power which we have to obey one, is not from our selves, but from the work of God in us. And indeed God does not give us these laws, that we should imagine that we can obey them of our selves, but that (seeing our own wants) we should go to him for help.[64]

And if any fear that there are some sins which they simply will not be able to defeat, some duties which are beyond them, Dod will strengthen their hands:

> So that no man ought to discourage himself in respect of the corruption and frailty that cleaves most fast to him. But oh, will some say, for other things I have some hope that I shall overcome them: but I shall never get the better of this or that sin while I live. Well then, other sins you hope you can overcome: but whither have you power – to subdue them by any virtue of your own, or from the working of God's Spirit in you? If you say, from your self, then you speak ignorantly and foolishly: for flesh cannot kill any sin, this must be the work only of God: but if you say that Christ Jesus did give help to you against them, why should you doubt of victory against this? He that gave you ability to over-rule your flesh in some things, cannot he give the like in all? Yea, this very mercy, that he has

---

[63] All four of these quotations are from Ibid., p 286f.
[64] Ibid., p 11.

given you a disposition and power to obey him in one commandment is a sure testimony to you that he will do the like in the rest: so that by humble, faithful and fervent prayer, you crave this grace at his hands. This therefore which he says, 'God spoke all these words,' is a marvellous encouragement to the saints that therefore seeing their wants in any duty they may go to God and say, 'Lord, you are the author of all these commandments alike and the keeping of them all pertains to me as well as to any other: you know, O Lord, that there is no power in me to obey the least of them; therefore I come now for help and grace from you to make me obedient to all as well as you have to some.' So we shall obtain grace to keep every one as well as any one.[65]

Warnings may be given:

This is also for the terror of the wicked. Is God Jehovah, constant and unchangeable? Then look what plagues proud persons have had heretofore, the same they shall have now, unless they repent and get pardon in Christ.[66]

Basic Bible truths will be rehearsed:

The want of this persuasion, that God looks always fully upon us, is the cause why men have so many covetous, so many crafty and cruel thoughts and such impure cogitations. Yea, many are not afraid nor ashamed to think and say that, 'Thought is free.' But they shall find that though it be free from men, it is not free from God.[67]

And the unexpressed objections or beliefs hindering obedience will be brought to the surface and exposed:

Consider the deceitfulness of our own hearts. One thinks now that if he had a fairer house he should be more at quiet but may not this be a false persuasion? May not God cross him with sickness and diseases, with shame and disgrace, with troubles and horror of conscience? And then the walls will not comfort him, the roof and covering will not bring him any peace. It is

---

[65] Ibid., p 12.
[66] Ibid., p 15.
[67] Ibid., p 30.

> not the dwelling that will bring quietness, nor the change of the house that can settle the heart: unless we change our covetousness and wickedness for contentedness and goodness, we shall have great grief and vexation in great and fair houses and in the midst of our abundance. But if our heart be good and reformed, we shall live quietly and die blessedly in whatsoever house or place we live and die.[68]

This was not called *practical* divinity for nothing. In his *Exposition of the Ten Commandments* Dod deals with an astonishing array of specific life situations in which biblical wisdom is needed. He gives warnings against standing surety unwisely; he comments on enclosure, the use of lots and the timely payment of wages; he insists that husbands should never criticise their wives in front of others; he explains why sodomy and oppression of the poor are alike; he shows that bad ministers are soul-murderers; and he describes the characteristics of rash and sinful anger.

Three further examples may be of interest. What are the marks of the godly application of corporal punishment?

> First, let it be seasonable and done in time for indeed a small twig and a few blows when he is a child and not hardened in sin will do more good than many rods and abundance of stripes afterwards. Secondly, it must be done in great compassion and mercy not in bitterness, to ease oneself with the pain of the child, for that is rage and cruelty. Thirdly, it must be done with prayer, that God would give them wise hearts to give due and seasonable correction and their children also soft hearts to receive it humbly and meekly and to their profit.[69]

What must a person say who has stolen but no longer has the means of making restitution?

> Yet I resolve with myself and make a covenant with mine own conscience, that if ever I have it, I will pay him and if I had it now, I would defer no longer, he should have it now. In the meantime I will not cease to supply that by my prayers which by reason of poverty is wanting in my payment; that my humble

---

[68] Ibid., p 333.
[69] Ibid., p 179f.

> suit to God for him may as much profit him as my sin against God and against him has damaged him.[70]

Who is to be given what when you draw up your will?

> Let this be the first and main rule: that those children be best respected which are best, and those have most goods given them that have most grace in their hearts.[71]

No unreal heavenly-mindedness here. Common sense and down-to-earth realism shine out on every page. How are we and how are we not to judge others:

> But yet this must be known by the way, that though love will not allow suspicion yet it does not thrust out discretion. It judges not rashly but it judges justly. It is not so sharp-sighted as to see a mote where none is, nor so purblind but it can discern a beam where it is.[72]

And even in matters of what today we might call 'spirituality,' Dod knows how sinners work. He describes how Popery proceeds in trying to win adherents to its false worship:

> For as an adulterer will first strive to draw the wife's mind from her husband by accusing his government and dealings as hard and unjust, and afterwards endeavour to entice her to his lure, so it is with these spiritual adulterers. First, they will do what they can to bring us to dislike God's service and his ministers and ministries (as indeed our love to Christ and his Word and ministers is not so hot, for the most part, but that a few clamorous and false accusations will quickly cool it). And then, having withdrawn us from the true worship of God, we are easily caught and persuaded to anything. So that no opinion can be so fantastical and heretical but if the author of it can bring us out of our liking with God's service and his ministers we shall be ready enough to embrace and follow it.[73]

---

[70] Ibid., p 300.
[71] Ibid., p 185.
[72] Ibid., p 304.
[73] Ibid., p 59.

3.6. ... *and realistic and thoughtful in regard to human affliction*

Christian preaching and living must be active and confident, it is true, and yet this does not mean that they are to be activist or triumphalist. Few groups in the history of the church so far have wrestled as deeply, experientially, and systematically with questions of suffering and affliction as the Puritans. Compassion, realism and confidence in God mark their treatment of the subject. Dod, again, is typical. Having just described how God blesses obedience, he goes on:

> Oh, but this makes me doubt whether I am God's child or not, because I have such long and fiery troubles: if God loved me would he afflict me thus? But outward ease is no sure sign of God's favour, else none should have been so much in God's favour as the Sodomites, Canaanites and such like: for they had all the ease, wealth, and outward prosperity of the world. But let us keep God's favour, let us fear him and pray to him and then our long and strong crosses shall bring long and strong comforts.[74]

And since afflictions *will* come then it is Christian wisdom to prepare for them:

> Let us learn hence to prepare for crosses, since God's children may be sore afflicted: else little do we know how they will sting us when they come. It is our best course therefore to get wisdom while the price is in our hands, to labour to get patience and to acquaint ourselves with God, that we may seek him and wait for deliverance at his hands. For that makes crosses tedious and grievous, when they hit us on the bare: whereas if we had patience to bear them and wisdom to make a good use of them, and faith to empty our hearts by prayer, they would be easy. Nothing makes afflictions so burdensome as when they meet with an heart in which remains some sin unrepented or some passion not subdued.[75]

And on the same theme:

---

[74] Ibid., p 22.
[75] Ibid., p 23.

Prepare therefore for crosses and we shall be able to bear them. But if we go on in a fool's paradise and think indeed this world is a vale of tears to others but to me it shall be a place of pleasure: they must have trouble but I must have ease: then, when, instead of joy, we find grief that we look not for, and we dream of credit but there comes nothing but contempt; we imagine that God should lift us up higher and higher and he casts us down lower and lower; this casts us into such desperate passions, that we are neither fit to serve God nor man.[76]

3.7. *These things will only be understood and lived if taught plainly and directly*

In some ways this is a further element of the action-orientation discussed above: the demand that preachers be 'plain.' When matters of life and death and more were at stake then clarity and directness were demanded. Never minding the sneers of the elegant rhetoricians, the Puritan minister (who was, recall, generally well-acquainted with the original languages and university-educated) was determined that the word of God should be heard by all.

And the godly hearer, marked by the dual conviction that preaching was the release of the Word and that the Word was really that of God, should not be stumbled by the ordinariness of the messenger:

> We shall in truth show ourselves to believe, that God is the Author of these words, if we can be content to endure that these precepts should be pressed and urged upon us, though by one that is our inferior, and baser in outward respect then ourselves. So then, will we show that we do in truth believe that these be the words of God? Then must we, when any man shall press any of these laws upon us, straightways yield and stoop to them, and then in deed we confess that God spoke all these words. But if we begin to shift and cloak and colour, and distinguish, then we declare evidently, that our heart is not persuaded that God is the author of them.[77]

---

[76] Ibid., p 23.
[77] Ibid., p 5f.

3.7.1. *Directness*

A large part of Puritan plainness was directness. Hearers were spiritually sleepy and needed waking up. Dod could hardly be more direct.

On avoiding evil company:

> Ministers and other faithful professors will not willingly come into ill company and among ill persons and hear ill words because they know the curse of God be on those that do so and fear their own weakness and frailty.[78]

On the use of images as 'laymen's books':

> But what be the lessons they teach? Even lies. And what get the scholars of these teachers? Even the curse of God.[79]

On theft by stealth:

> So many things as a man gets by stealth from his neighbour, so many curses he gets to his soul.[80]

On rationalization:

> Where lust has dominion, it whets the wit to speak for it, and the devil helps: but if God's Spirit come once, it drives men to a plain confession, and casts down Satan's strongest holds and then lust rules the wit no more.[81]

On whom you serve:

> For he that does God's work, he worships God and he that does the Devil's work, he worships the Devil.[82]

3.7.2. *Illustrations*

When it comes to what we might call illustration, Dod's way is again both plain and direct. When he wishes for examples and stories, he finds them in Scripture and thereby deepens his hearers' knowledge of

---

[78] Ibid., p 60.
[79] Ibid., p 61.
[80] Ibid., p 286.
[81] Ibid., p 18.
[82] Ibid., p 68.

the Word. When he needs analogies they come not from literature but from everyday life.

On radical dependence upon God as a motive for obedience:

> We see, among men if there be one whose estate depends wholly upon his landlord's courtesy, that may put him out and beggar him when he please, how careful is he to please him and have his favour lest (through his displeasure) he should be turned out of all? So it is with all the men on earth: they be all God's tenants and that at will: no man holds anything by lease for an hour: our breath is not our own but his. It is at his appointment what shall become of our souls and bodies whether they shall be saved or damned. And he is such a God, whose anger is an eternal anger, and his wrath an eternal wrath, and his plagues everlasting plagues: therefore how careful and diligent should we be to please him? And then we show ourselves to believe his eternal and unchangeable truth, power, justice, goodness and mercy when it is our greatest care to seek his favour and always to endeavour to do the things that are pleasing in his sight.[83]

From the second commandment on the evil of inventing our own ways of worshipping God:

> He is a good servant that does his master's will, not his own.[84]

From the eighth commandment on hiding the possessions of others:

> A man were as good put a coal of fire into the thatch of his house or in the barn as bring any stolen goods among his goods.[85]

Here, then, we have a presentation of practical Christianity which is theocentric, deeply serious about spiritual realities, and Scripture-saturated. It begins with the depths of a person's heart and extends to action and change in every area of life. It is careful and compassionate in the face of suffering and presented with clarity and energy. These are, in fact, the characteristics of true religion as understood by the Puritans.

---

[83] Ibid., p 13.
[84] Ibid., p 70.
[85] Ibid., p 286.

Dod's *Decalogue*, that is to say, is a perfect example of Puritan practical divinity.

4. Dod's treatment of particular commandments

In his comments on Exodus 20.1-2, Dod gives some 'Rules for the better understanding of the whole Law'[86] telling us that the law is spiritual and makes demands upon the inner person; that it is perfect and requires comprehensive obedience; that 'whatsoever the law commands, it forbids the contrary'; that 'many more evils are forbidden and many more good things are commanded in every commandment than in words is expressed' and that 'where the law commands or forbids anything, it commands and forbids all means and occasions leading thereto.'[87] In the body of the work he applies these principles thoroughly, yielding a directory for the conduct of the Christian in every area of life.

4.1.1. *The First Commandment*

Dod's treatment of the first commandment is foundational in content and the most sermonic in style. As he does with all the others he treats the requirements of first commandment as both negative and positive. Negatively:

> To have none other gods is, not to have anything whereon we set our delight or which we esteem more than God.[88]

Positively:

> We are commanded four special things: to know God, to love him, to fear him, to trust in him. If we have these things in our hearts, then God bears the sway there and is the chief commander of our souls and bodies.[89]

---

[86] Ibid., p 24f.
[87] Forty years later the Westminster Divines would gives a very similar list of 'rules for the right understanding of the ten commandments' in Q.99 of the *Larger Catechism*.
[88] Dod, *Exposition*, p 26.
[89] Ibid., p. 30f.

4.1.2. *The Second Commandment*

Unsurprisingly, Dod's emphasis in his exposition of the second commandment is anti-Roman. He states a form of the regulative principle of worship and spends much time arguing against the use of images, the Mass, the sign of the cross, prayers to and for the dead, swearing by the Mass, instituting holy days while neglecting the Sabbath, and in any other way showing 'fond love' or making oneself wiser than God.

A brief discussion of less ordinary means of worship, namely, fasting, vows, and the use of lots leads to a general exhortation to spiritual worship and, in dealing with the phrase, 'that love him and keep his commandments,' an important discussion of the possibility of true, though not perfect obedience.

4.1.3. *The Fourth Commandment*

The brother-in-law of the great sabbatarian, Nicholas Bownde, does not disappoint. He gives more space to the treatment of the fourth commandment than to any other, bar the fifth, and deals with numerous objections to Christian sabbatarianism including the claims that the change of day, or Christ's attitude to the sabbath, or Colossians 2.16, or the ceremonial dimension of the Sabbath somehow show that the fourth commandment was dispensed with in a way that the other nine were not.

4.1.4. *The Fifth Commandment*

Dod bases a discussion of a whole range of social relationships upon the fifth commandment and is typical of Reformed commentators in so doing. He writes of the relative duties of parents and children, masters and servants, husbands and wives, ministers and their congregations, magistrates and their people.

4.1.5. *The Sixth Commandment*

An outline of the teachings of the sixth commandment is typical of Dod's treatment of others. He divides the requirements of the commandment into things prohibited and things required. The chapter is structured as follows:[90]

1. Things prohibited
   a) omission of good
      i. to body
         - the omission of works of mercy
         - failure of charity
         - failure to pay wages
         - sodomy and lack of charity are alike
      ii. to soul
         - bad ministers are guilty of soul murder
         - fathers must not omit good to the souls of those in their household
         - and masters must seek the spiritual welfare of their servants
   b) practice of evil
      i. Inward
      a) rash anger
         - what it is: anger which hinders the doing of good to another or which is conceived without sufficient cause or exceeds in the time or in the measure;[91]
         - how to keep from rash anger
         1. Meditate upon our own sin and vileness: 'None are more eager and passionate against the slips of others than those that are most slack and negligent to examine their own great sins.'[92]
         2. 'Labour to get wisdom always and in every thing to behold God's providence, to see his hand ruling every thing and to persuade ourselves that all things come to pass according to his purpose and direction.'[93]
         3. 'Avoid the occasions that will provoke us to it.'
         4. 'Mark and observe those that be stirred up with passionate anger, beholding their countenance, how unseemly and disfigured it is, how rude their actions, how absurd their words, how base and contemptible all

---

[90] Ibid., pp 231-256.
[91] Ibid., p 234.
[92] These six points are to be found on Ibid., p 235f.
[93] See above, 1.a) for the full paragraph

their behaviour is. And the sight of this in another will be some means to loathe it in himself.'

5. 'Consider what testimony the word of God gives of this hastiness and of forward and unquiet persons: ... so much fury, so much folly; the more chafing, the less wisdom.'

6. 'Weigh the punishment which it deserves and draws upon us.'

b) envy
- definition of envy: 'bitter affection against the prosperity and the pre eminence of another.'[94]
- examples of envy: Cain, Joseph's brothers;
- causes of envy: 'The causes are pride, and abundance of self-love, but exceeding want of true love. For love envies not but self-love and pride would have all themselves and think that they are wronged if another have anything more than they.'[95]
- the remedy against envy: 'The way to keep out this monster is to get store of charity into our hearts for then we are armed and fenced against repining at another's good. When shall you have a loving mother grudge at her child's beauty, goods, good name or such like? When will she think her child does too well and be sorry because he is in so good an estate? Surely never. And why? Because she loves it. And this is a buckler against all envy.'[96]

ii. Outward
a) gesture
b) word
c) deed
    i. to strike to hurt without death
        - the wickedness of revenge with regard to the attacked, the attacker and God
    ii. actual murder

---

[94] Ibid., p 236.
[95] Ibid., p 237.
[96] Ibid., p 238.

- secret murder
- all murder
- self-murder, proceeding from pride, unbelief and cruelty

2. Things required
    a) Inward
        i) meekness
        - the parts of meekness
            a) forgiveness
            b) construing the best
            c) being peaceable
        ii. compassion and pity
        - the example of Jesus and Paul
        - compassion to soul and compassion to body
    b) Outward
        i. amiable behaviour – modesty and love
        ii. defend the oppressed and succour those that suffer wrong
            - various failures of this and the excuses given
        iii. show mercy to the needy
            - store up treasure in heaven to have a merciful and generous heart here
            - rules for works of mercy
                a) just
                b) cheerful
                c) to the household of faith
3. Things to avoid which lead to a breach of the sixth commandment
    a) pride
    b) covetousness
    c) riotousness and drunkenness

On eleven occasions in the book, Dod provides his own diagrammed outline, usually representing only one half of his treatment of the commandment in question. Three examples will give a taste:

4.1.6. *The Seventh Commandment*

Things forbidden in the commandment are:
1. Inward – all unchaste lusts
2. Outward [taking a fourfold division from Galatians 5:19 in the Geneva Bible]
    a) adultery

b) fornication
    i. unnatural
      A. with others [sodomy and bestiality]
      B. with oneself
    ii. natural – in marriage
      A. entering unlawfully [marrying another of a contrary religion; within the degrees of consanguinity; without consent of parents]
      B. using
        1. out of time
        2. immoderately
  c) uncleanness
  d) wantonness
    i. things pertaining to the body
      A. apparel
      B. food
      C. sleep etc.
    ii. body itself in
      A. parts
        1. hand
        2. eye
        3. foot etc.
      B. whole – as in dancing immodestly

4.1.7. *The Eighth Commandment*

Things forbidden are either
  1. Inward – as the desire of the heart
  2. Outward
    a) public
      i. Church
      ii. Commonwealth
    b) private
      i. ill-using of a man's own goods
        A. wastefulness
          1. excess in anything
          2. idleness
          3. suretyship
        B. niggardliness
      ii. unjust pursuit of other men's goods by
        A. some show or colour of law

1. crafty bargaining
   2. usury
  B. some means without colour as
   1. by force
   2. thieving

4.1.8. *The Ninth Commandment*

The things commanded are either
  1. Inward, contrary to suspicion: a charitable opinion and our neighbour which must be showed by
     a) taking doubtful things in the best part
     b) defending his name if we hear him slandered
     c) being grieved when we hear true report of his ill deed
  2. Outward
     a) general, to speak the truth from one's heart and that,
        i. with a good affection
        ii. to a good end
     b) special, touching
        i. others – to speak of
           A. faults before their face
           B. virtue behind their back
        ii. ourselves – to speak sparingly either of our
           A. faults or
           B. good deeds

5. Dod's views on law and obedience

John Dod, in respect of the use of Old Testament law, was a mainstream Puritan and typically Reformed.[97] He believed that the law had a threefold use: to restrain the evil-doer, to drive the sinner to Christ, and to instruct the righteous in ways pleasing to God. He believed that law was an inescapable concept in a universe with a God who was neither

---

[97] John Calvin, *Institutes*, II.vii; Francis Turretin, *Institutes*, Eleventh Topic; Westminster Confession, Chapter XIX; Heidelberg Catechism, Questions 92-115; William Perkins, *The Whole Treatise of the Cases of Conscience* (1606); Edward Elton, *An Exposition of the Ten Commandments* (1623); William Ames, *Marrow of Sacred Divinity* (1641); Anthony Burgess, *Vindiciae Legis* (1646); Thomas Shepard, *Theses Sabbaticae* (1649); James Durham, *The Law Unsealed* (1676).

morally indifferent nor silent. God has standards and reveals those standards and those revealed standards represent authoritative moral demands upon his creatures. He further believed that the Ten Commandments represented a distinct and special summary of God's universal moral law which in addition to being written by the finger of God on stone was also stamped upon the conscience of all humankind. These commandments were specially given to Israel not to show that they were not binding upon all humankind but rather to show that they could only be kept by a redeemed people.

No human being, the Lord Jesus Christ excepted, has ever kept these Ten Commandments, the summary of which is the twofold love command, and thus all men and women deserve the curses announced by the law. The Lord Jesus Christ came not to set aside the moral law but rather to keep it, confirm it, expound it, and intensify it and to bear the punishment due to the elect for their transgression of it. And more, he came to enable his redeemed people to keep it themselves and thus enjoy the blessings of obedience. The law, after all, was not a malicious imposition of a spiteful tyrant but the loving, righteous, wise instruction of a Fatherly God who loves to bless. Obedience to it by the pardoned and renewed people of God represents the path to true human maturity and to the flourishing not only of individuals but of societies. Those individuals and societies that live by the law of God will enjoy the blessings of God and those that do not will suffer the curse of God.

Many times in his life Jesus, who declared that Scripture cannot be broken and who lived by every word that came from the mouth of God, sang, 'Oh, how I love your law! It is my meditation all the day' and 'I open my mouth and pant, because I long for your commandments' and 'Seven times a day I praise you for your righteous rules.' Far from setting aside the law, Jesus by his Spirit causes the law, which his servant Paul calls holy, righteous, good, and spiritual and says he delights in his inner man, to be written upon the hearts of his people. He gives them the new hearts which are essential to a life of loving God which is, of course, a life of obeying his not-burdensome commands. He also gives them all manner of encouragements and motivations to obey, knowing that obedience is a blessing and a delight to the renewed people of God. Those with new hearts will seek to please God with their every thought, word, and deed and will pursue universal obedience in the fear and love of God.

The Ten Commandments are expounded in the case law which

helps us to understand specific applications. They are spiritual and require heart obedience. They bring positive and negative requirements, touch the inner life and the outer life, direct the individual by himself and in all his roles, responsibilities and relationships. Even now no believer perfectly obeys the requirements of the law – far from it – and yet true and sincere obedience is possible and God is – and does not merely pretend to be – truly pleased with it, rewarding it with all manner of blessings in this life and the next. Such is his providence, however, that the righteous continue to suffer much affliction which, it should be understood, God allows and uses for their real good; and also that the curse which rests upon the unrighteous is rarely manifest in its full force this side of judgment.

This is the Reformed synthesis and Dod's *Decalogue* is fully in tune with it. He pays almost no attention to what some would see as 'negative' statements about the law on the simple grounds that the law is negative only when misunderstood and misused by sinners. Rightly understood and rightly used by the right people it is nothing but a good gift of a loving God whose will for the faithful, who delight in and constantly meditate upon the law, is prosperity, life, maturity, and true humanness; in a word, blessing.

After this synopsis, let us hear these things in Dod's own words.

The very first sentence of the book, referring to Exodus 20:1-2 makes plain Dod's basic position:

> These words contain a preparation to stir us up with all care and conscience to keep the law of God.[98]

We are to 'keep the law of God,' we are to do so 'with all care and conscience' and we need to be 'stirred up' to do so.

The law in question is expressed in the Ten Commandments which 'must be exceedingly reverenced because God's own voice did speak them' and because 'God himself wrote them with his own finger.'[99] There is no expression of God's perfect standards for humankind quite like the Ten Commandments. In them there is a

> wonderful and perfect holiness [which] shows who is the maker

---

[98] Dod, *Exposition*, p 1.
[99] Ibid., p 3.

of them, because there is no good duty, which God bound Adam to perform, but is comprehended and commanded in one of these: and there is no sin that we are bound to abstain from and eschew, which is not forbidden in some of these ten words. It was above the wit of men or angels to contain in so few words, the whole perfection of our duty to God and man.[100]

Indeed:

> this law is so absolute, and sets out so full and complete a righteousness, that if one could fulfil them all, he should be fully acceptable to God, and need not flee to Christ to be his Redeemer.[101]

The Ten Commandments summarize the moral law and thus they:

> are written and engraven in every man's conscience for, God has not left himself without witness: but in every man's bosom, and everyone's nature, has planted so much of his law, as will serve to leave them without excuse. Who can raze these laws out of their own consciences, though they do what they can, and strive never to much to extinguish this natural light?[102]

Since this is a summary of the moral law, rather like the twofold love command, then Dod will go so far as to claim that:

> all the punishments that are at any time inflicted upon the world, have come from the disobedience against this law; and all the mercies and benefits which men enjoy, proceed from the obedience yielded to it. For when God sets down his curses and blessings, do they not run thus? If you observe and keep these Commandments, then you shall be blessed in soul, and body, in children, in cattle, in field, and in all things you put your hand to. Contrariwise, if you will not obey but neglect them, then you shall be cursed in all things.[103]

And Christ did not come to set these laws aside, neither in their substance nor in their (positive and negative) sanctions, but rather:

---

[100] Ibid., p 3.
[101] Ibid., p 3.
[102] Ibid., p 4.
[103] Ibid., p 4f.

> Christ himself came into the world to keep these laws. For they require a perfect and absolute obedience, as they are perfect; which seeing no man could do, therefore Christ took our flesh upon him to fulfil them; that as Adam by his disobedience had cast us out of Paradise, so he by his obedience, might bring us into heaven: and he came not only to perform them himself fully, but also to make his saints able to obey them, though not in perfection, and without any defect, (for that only he himself could do) yet in truth and sincerity for that he requires of all his members.[104]

The law is spiritual and has intensive reach: 'It reaches therefore to the inward parts of every man and lies close upon his conscience.'[105]

> It is all from God and therefore requires universal obedience:

> Though one be no thief, nor adulterer, yet if he be a Sabbath breaker, he breaks the whole law. For if one ask him why do you not commit adultery? and he say, 'because God commands that I should not'; then he would keep the Sabbath also, for they be both alike in the commandments of God: but if it be not because God commands, then he does not obey the law, but serve himself. Therefore he that makes no conscience of all God's laws has no soundness and fidelity in him, because he does not remember that God spoke all these words.[106]

> And therefore he has no sound heart that allows himself in the breach of any one, and addicts not himself to keep them all.[107]

Though binding upon all, it is only the redeemed who are able to keep the law truly (and even they, not perfectly) and they also have the strongest incentives for doing so – incentives of redeemed status, covenant relationship with God, and assurance of his goodness towards them:

> Almighty indeed I am, infinite, eternal and perfect, yet so as that I abase myself to take care for you, to have a loving heart towards you, and to be your father and to make you my child, to

---

[104] Ibid., p 5.
[105] Ibid., p 8.
[106] Ibid., p 10.
[107] Ibid., p 11.

be your husband also and to make you my spouse; one that have promised to give you all good things and to remove all ill things from you: this is to be your God. If God had set down only his infinite majesty and greatness and his glorious incommunicable name, that would have feared us and made us flee from him: but now he encourages us by this, that he is our God and gives us these commandments for our own benefit and because he loves us, to submit ourselves to him and with all willingness to serve him.[108]

The commandments are given for our good:

> [He] gives us these commandments for our own benefit and because he loves us, to submit ourselves to him and with all willingness to serve him.[109]

And there are, as mentioned above, some important 'rules for the better understanding of the whole law,'[110] namely:

> The first is, that the law is spiritual, reaching to the soul and all the powers thereof. For it charges the understanding to know the will of God: it charges the memory to retain and the will to choose the better and leave the worse. It charges the affection to love the things to be loved and to hate the things to be hated.

> Secondly, the law is perfect and requires full obedience of the whole man, not only commanding the soul but the whole soul, not only to know, retain, will and follow good, but also to do the same perfectly. So in condemning evil, it condemns all evil and in commanding good, it commands all good in the fullest measure and longest continuance.

> Thirdly, whatsoever the law commands, it forbids the contrary. As where all the false means of God's worship are forbidden, all the true means are commanded. And where the sanctification of God's name is required, there all abuse of his holy name is condemned. And the law that forbids murder and cruelty does as strongly command compassion and mercy: and so all the rest.

---

[108] Ibid., p 16.
[109] Ibid., p 16.
[110] Ibid., p 24f.

> Fourthly, many more evils are forbidden and many more good things are commanded in every commandment than in words is expressed: as under idolatry is contained all means of false worship: by killing all hindering of life and all unmercifulness.
>
> Fifthly, where the law commands or forbids anything, it commands and forbids all means and occasions leading thereto: as in the second commandment we are forbidden to be present in body at idolatrous service or to reserve any special monument of idolatry or to be companions with idolaters. And on the contrary we are here required to use good books written according to God's word and to be companions of the true worshippers of God which be special means of keeping this commandment.

Although it is true that these laws were given to Israel on their deliverance from Egypt, the greater deliverance which the new Israel enjoys makes them all the more compelling:

> For that is more excellent than the deliverance out of bondage, by how much the state of unregeneration is more grievous than their corporal thraldom. In that, men tyrannized over them; in this, the devil, sin and death. There, the body only was tormented; here the soul deadly wounded. There was some intermission; this is perpetual, day and night. There death made an end of this misery; here it begins it. That was felt, and therefore they were willing to be relieved; this spiritual servitude is not perceived and therefore they will neither seek help nor receive it when it is offered.[111]

And Christians understand the Ten Commandments better than old Israel because 'Christ [is] the Law-Maker and therefore also the best expounder of it.'[112]

For any foolish enough to think that redemption can be found in the law, there are only two possibilities, which quickly resolve to one: render perfect, total, constant, flawless obedience to each and every law of God in its comprehensive requirement or fall under the curse. When thinking of those redeemed by Christ, however, we may speak in

---

[111] Ibid., p 26.
[112] Ibid., p 257.

another way. Dod calls it 'a sincere (but not perfect) obedience.'[113] The issue for the believer is no longer one of perfect obedience or death. Rather it may be one of sincere and true obedience which enjoys the blessing. Dod brings Scripture examples to bear:

> Why then should not every Christian hope to be able to yield obedience to God, in whatsoever God commands him? As God witnesses of David that he was a man after his own heart in all things, save in the matter of Uriah: for there he sinned presumptuously, his heart was upright in all things else. And likewise as it is spoken of Zachariah and Elizabeth that they were perfect and unblameable in all things: not that they were quit from all infirmities (or had not their faults as well as other saints) but they were upright and sincere, their heart was true with God and so God can and will give grace unto all his, to obey every one of his commandments with a true and upright obedience.[114]

Dod anticipates the obvious objection:

> Some will object that if the love of God consist in the keeping of his commandments then it should seem that none love him because in many things we offend all. But for resolving of this know that there is a great difference between these two, to keep God's commandments and to fulfil his commandments. For keeping denotes a truth, fulfilling a perfection. Perfection, Christ only had; but truth, every Christian must have. This true keeping must be known by these notes. First, we must aim at all, there must be a full purpose and true desire to keep [each] one. Secondly, this obedience must be done willingly, with a free and cheerful heart. Thirdly, the end of our actions must be good, to show our loyalty to God, to approve our hearts to him in obedience to his commandments and not for any other end or intent of our own.[115]

The obedience of Christians is never perfect but this does not mean that it is not real, nor that God is not truly pleased with it:

---

[113] Ibid., p 29.
[114] Ibid., p 12.
[115] Ibid., p 83.

> He requires not of his children that they should perfectly fulfill his law, for that Jesus Christ has done for them already, but that they should constantly and faithfully endeavour to know and keep it according to that measure of grace and strength which God has given them. If we will stand to be justified by our own righteousness then we must either have perfection or confusion. But if we trust to Christ, then we are under grace and there is mercy in Christ, rewarding all our good, pitying and passing by all our infirmities.[116]

And the announced sanctions still apply:

> For in the Law, God threatens that if we be disobedient to him and his commandments, we shall be cursed in soul, body, wife, children, and all that we put our hand to. But, on the other side, if we be upright and with a perfect heart set ourselves to follow God's commandments, then we shall be blessed in soul, body, wife, children and all that belongs to us, so that the blessing of God shall meet us at every turn.[117]

The closing paragraph of the book sums up much what we have just studied:

> And so much for the exposition of the law which must serve to this end, that seeing our own unrighteousness and insufficiency, we should be humbled in our souls before the judgment seat of the Almighty, and then to fly to Christ to be our righteousness and sufficiency. And finally, to make this the rule of our life and a lantern to our feet, that though we cannot attain to the perfection which the law requires, yet we may have that uprightness which God accepts in Jesus Christ. For if we have respect to all the Commandments, and labour faithfully to keep them (though we cannot perfectly fulfill them) then shall we constantly enjoy all those blessings and graces which God has promised to his righteous servants, all the days of our life: and when we have finished this short and troublesome pilgrimage, we shall for ever inherit that glorious kingdom which our Lord Jesus Christ has purchased for us with his most precious blood. Unto whom, with the Father and the Holy

---

[116] Ibid., p 85f.
[117] Ibid., p 81.

Ghost, three persons, and one only wise, holy, and eternal God, be ascribed all power, praise and glory for evermore. Amen.[118]

6. A handful of other gems from Dod's *Decalogue*

That the Puritans ever came to be widely portrayed as sour, holier-than-thou, repressive, world-denying, spiritually proud, pleasure-haters who could never say anything briefly runs so far counter to the truth of the matter that only the father of lies could have generated and nurtured such hostile prejudice. Lovers of biblical Christianity, who are necessarily lovers of much that the Puritans stood and lived for, must fight battles for words and perceptions as well as for hearts and lives. Happily, Dod's *Decalogue* provides us with some powerful weaponry with which to attack anti-Puritan prejudice.[119]

Humility and judgmentalism

Dod's Puritanism has no place for Pharisaical judgmentalism:

> None are more suspicious of other men's truth and fidelity than they who have been the greatest deceivers and defrauders of others.[120]

> When one never examines his own life then he is most ready to pry into another man's conscience and he that (for the most part) spares himself will lay the heaviest load upon another.[121]

> James 3:17 – He shows the cause why the best men never forward to judge nor hasty to pass sentence upon other men even because they, having good hearts and desiring to be as good as they seem to be, have so much to do in fighting and striving with their own corruptions as that they have no leisure to examine other men's dealings which belong not to them, but

---

[118] Ibid., p 338.
[119] Leland Ryken, *Worldly Saints* (Grand Rapids: Zondervan, 1986), does a fine job of refuting some of the most common errors about the character of Puritanism.
[120] Dod, *Exposition*, p 303.
[121] Ibid., p 303.

would rather reform the things which be amiss in themselves.[122]

The godly are not only slow to judge, but also deeply consciousness of sin:

> [We have] continual humiliation for that our nature and the whole frame of our soul is such as no minute (almost) goes over our head but some evil and vain motion or other goes through our heart and springs our of the sink and puddle of our flesh.[123]

Enjoying the good gifts of creation

Puritan Dod celebrates the good gifts of creation.

Husbands and wives:

> The first duty of the husband is to dwell with his wife: that, since there is a near and dear society between them, and of all others the nearest (for so she is to him as the Church is to Christ, flesh of his flesh and bone of his bone) therefore he must be willing constantly and kindly to converse with her, to walk with her, talk with her and let her have all comfortable familiarity with him: that she may see he delights in her company and may well know that of all others she is his most loved and welcome companion ... This reproves those foolish men (indeed not worthy to carry the name of husbands) that can take more delight in any vain, riotous and unthrifty company and take more pleasure in any lewd exercises than in the society of the loving and kind wife; that are never so merry as when the wife is absent and never dumpish and churlish but with her. Such also as dwell with hawks and hounds and drunkards and gamesters not with their wives: these shall carry the brand and name of fools.[124]

On the eighth commandment:

> They be thieves that will not thankfully use his benefits, but defraud and starve themselves.[125]

> Proverbs 21.20: [the wise man] has joy and comfort and a

---

[122] Ibid., p 303.
[123] Ibid., p 331.
[124] Ibid., p 204f.
[125] Ibid., p 281.

> blessing in the use of them and he has not for necessity only but also for delight for refreshing and recreation.[126]
>
> It is our duty to take part of those things that God has given us and with a thankful and cheerful heart to enjoy his kindness.[127]
>
> It is a most miserable and base thing for one to restrain himself of his lawful liberty in meat, drink, apparel and honest recreation.[128]

And of those who are too busy working or saving to enjoy good things:

> This men commonly call good husbandry and thrift for a man to wear out and waste himself with immoderate travail and to pinch and starve his household by miserable sparing; but it is plain theft in the sight of God for one to spend himself and pull a want upon himself when he may live in plenty. God's marks be found upon him for a wicked man and a cursed sinner when he has much but can use nothing ... miserable bondslaves to lucre and covetousness.[129]

Real obedience flows from assurance and is a matter of delight

Neither the alleged anxiety nor sourness of Puritans find a place with Dod.

> The doctrine hence gathered is that if ever we will obey God in soundness then we must know him to be our God, to have a tender care over us, to love us and that we shall speed best when we yield most obedience to him.[130]
>
> Therefore if ever we would yield any cheerful obedience to God, let us labour to feel the truth of that which God speaks, that he is our God, our Saviour, and has done, and always will do more for us, then any other can, and therefore we will obey him above all.[131]

---

[126] Ibid., p 294.
[127] Ibid., p 295.
[128] Ibid., p 279.
[129] Ibid., p 281.
[130] Ibid., p 16.
[131] Ibid., p 17.

On assurance and obedience:

> [Papists make] this a certain point of their religion, that no man stands certain of salvation: and by this means they hinder men from cheerful obedience, and cut off all sound thankfulness.[132]

> It is a most tedious thing to a Christian heart to obey the Devil's commandments but most joyous to follow God's to pray, to hear the Word, to read, confer, or do works of mercy and the rest of that kind, it is even a recreation and delightful exercise for him.[133]

On sabbath-keeping and recreation:

> Is it not a recreation for a Christian to hear the voice of Christ.[134]

The shortest way to defeat sin is to embrace righteousness

Joyless repression is no spiritual weapon for Dod. Rather the expulsion of sin is achieved by the glad embrace of what is good for us.

Idolatry:

> We must labour to get the true and sound knowledge out of his word and a fervent love of him: for till then a man is in danger to fall to idolatry then we are safe from idols when we have gotten a fervent love of Christ.[135]

Covetousness:

> Let us learn to set our minds on work always with some good meditation and holy desires and thoughts if we do not by grace direct our heart towards God and man, corruption will draw it to all disorder and confusion. Therefore it is that many are so troubled with ill motions and continual boiling of ill thoughts because the heart is not busied and taken up with some good thing.[136]

---

[132] Ibid., p 19.
[133] Ibid., p 84.
[134] Ibid., p 136.
[135] Ibid., p 69.
[136] Ibid., p 332.

Lust:

> If married persons give fervent and pure love one to the other, this will keep them safe. For it is not the having of a wife but the loving of her that makes a man live chastely. Pure love is a gift of God and a spark that comes from heaven and has this virtue to make a man live chastely.[137]

> To delight then and rejoice in the pure Word of God and to embrace it in one's heart, this will so satisfy the mind and content the soul with sweet comfort and delight ... for no man can live without his delight.[138]

Social justice

Whilst affirming God's hierarchical ordering of human society, the Puritans were no mere social traditionalists.

On the equality of servants and masters:

> Both were made in the womb, both had one nature, one Creator and Redeemer. In all the former respects there is no difference of bond or free but there is an equality between the servant and master. The servant, if he be elect and holy has as much right in the blood of Christ and shall have as good part on the glory of Christ in heaven as the master.[139]

On coercive redistribution as theft:

> Ill kings would take away the people's vineyards and fields and olives to bestow them on their servants and on whom it pleased them. This is not mercy, nor to be accounted liberality, neither does it deserve any better name than theft.[140]

On the justice of enjoying earnings:

> Let the calling be good and the means good and then a man may with a good conscience take the blessing and fruits thereof.[141]

---

[137] Ibid., p 263.
[138] Ibid., p 263.
[139] Ibid., p 335.
[140] Ibid., p 253.
[141] Ibid., p 298.

On right regard for servants:

> The most contemptible servant in the world is of more worth, by nature, than the most excellent brute beast.[142]

And, briefly ...

And finally, Dod, like many another of the great Puritan communicators, knew how to be pithy and brief.

On transgressions of the first commandment:

> That is every man's God that every man's heart is most set upon.[143]

> And self as our chief idol: So that every carnal man sets up himself he does nothing but seek and serve himself and therefore is his own idol, and another god to himself.[144]

On the need for inward religion:

> If we say and swear and protest never so much that we love and fear him, if this be not in our soul, it is not before his face.[145]

Nothing is worse than sin:

> One had better therefore die the death than use any bodily gesture of reverence to an idol.[146]

On parents and children:

> The best way for any man to do good to his children is to be godly himself.[147]

> It is better to be the child of a godly than a wealthy parent.[148]

> Every man is a bishop in his own house.[149]

---

[142] Ibid., p 336.
[143] Ibid., p 26.
[144] Ibid., p 28.
[145] Ibid., p 29.
[146] Ibid., p 68.
[147] Ibid., p 81.
[148] Ibid., p 82.
[149] Ibid., p 233.

Idleness as theft:

> An idle man is a thief to himself: he does that to himself that if another should do it all men would take heed of him for a notorious stealer.[150]

How covetousness gets a grip:

> The ground of covetousness is this that men have a false and foolish imagination that wealth will bring some happiness and if they have a great store of riches then they should be in good safety.[151]

Wantonness of the eye:

> Reading loving books of dalliance and filthiness.., is a kind of contemplative fornication.[152]

Greater and lesser enemies:

> So that if Christ have washed us from our sins, the worst and sorest enemy (for all the world cannot wash away one sin) then never fear these less matters.[153]

The hatred of God:

> False love is true hatred: and in that they do those things which God hates and forbids, whatever their pretence is, they are haters of God. Sinful fond affection is hatred.[154]

On possessions:

> The want of them shall not hurt us, if God be with us; for we live by his blessing.[155]

Conclusion

It is no surprise that people travelled for miles to hear this man preach. The

---

[150] Ibid., p 277.
[151] Ibid., p 271.
[152] Ibid., p 268.
[153] Ibid., p 22.
[154] Ibid., p 79.
[155] Ibid., p 29.

clarity and order, the depth and reach, the urgency and considered-ness, the seriousness and joy of his presentation of life with and for God are compelling.

And it is no surprise that Dod's Decalogue became a seventeenth century bestseller. It was quintessential Puritan practical divinity from a master of the art of living to God and teaching others to do the same. John Dod had a profound knowledge, both of the Word of God and of the heart of the sinner, and was resolved that the one should so impact the other that all of human life should come to be lived under and, according to the holy, righteous, and good laws of God by men and women who had been pardoned and renewed by his grace in Christ and through the Spirit. Dod's work was both formative and typical of the Puritan approach to the Christian life as well as massively popular in his own day. It provides a fine example and sets a humbling standard for those called to be physicians of the soul by being teachers of the word. And it lays out, for all those who are privileged to read it, a vision of the all-encompassing renewal of the human individual and human society which God brings about in his redeeming and restoring work through his authoritative and life-giving Word.

Appendix: Doctrines dispersed in this book gathered together

Doctrines out of the Preface

1. God is, after a peculiar manner, the author of the Ten Commandments.
2. Obedience to all and every one of God's commandments, and not to some, brings sound comfort.
3. If ever we will obey God in soundness, then we must know him to be our God.
4. It is a mercy of God to be saved from dwelling in idolatrous places.
5. God will deliver his children from all miseries.

Doctrines out of the first commandment

1. The more goodness God exercises towards us, the more nearly we should cleave to him.
2. Nothing should withdraw us, or anything in us, from God.

3. We must not only carry ourselves well before men, but our hearts also must be upright in God's sight.
4. Every man is enjoined to know God revealed in the word, both in essence, persons, properties, and actions: and according to this knowledge, to compose all his actions.

Doctrines out of the second commandment

1. Man's nature is prone to idolatry and superstition.
2. He that would avoid idolatry, must avoid idols.
3. God's services may not be communicated to any other.
4. Idolatry is offensive to God, and dangerous to men.
5. We must stand for God's pure worship against all idolatry and superstition.
6. Ungodly parents are the greatest enemies children have.
7. All false love is hatred.
8. He that will do good to children must be godly himself.
9. They only be lovers of God, that be doers of his will.

Doctrines out of the third commandment

1. Great care is to be had of us, that the holy Name of the Lord be not dishonoured.
2. Right swearing, an holy service of God.
3. He that takes the name of God in vain, and repents not for it, draws down God's judgements upon himself.

Doctrines out of the fourth commandment

1. That the Sabbath day is moral and perpetual.
2. He that will conscionably keep the Sabbath when it comes, must prepare to be ready for it.
3. The Sabbath must be employed in holy exercises.
4. That all the Commandments are just and equal.

5. Man may not take that to his use which God has set apart for himself.
6. No worldly business great or small must be done upon the Sabbath, all earthly cares, questions and works must be cut off.
7. That it belongs to all Governors, to see that their children, servants, and inferiors whatsoever, keep the Lord's day.
8. Regard must be had that strangers shall not openly profane the Sabbath.
9. Whosoever desires to live godly, must propose the example of God himself to imitate.
10. God is able to do great things in short space, and by small means.
11. One special means to get true blessedness is to sanctify the Sabbath.

Doctrines out of the fifth commandment

1. All duties are to be performed to our superiors, with such honour as is meet for them.
2. The chief motive to obey superiors must be the particular jurisdiction which God has given them over us; and that special bond whereby he has tied them to us.
3. The way to get a prosperous and long life is to be obedient to parents and superiors, and to honour them.
4. All good things are gifts of God.

Doctrines out of the sixth commandment

Doctrines out of the seventh commandment

1. Filthy lusts and desires of the heart consented to, are adultery before God, and most hateful to him.

Doctrines out of the eighth commandment

1. To long after our neighbour's goods is theft.

Doctrines out of the ninth commandment

Doctrines out of the tenth commandment

1. The first motion and inclination of the heart to any sin, though a man never yield to it, nor cast about to bring it to pass, is sin.

2. Sin, the more hurtful, the more damnable.

3. The wife ought to be more dear to the husband, than all their substance.

4. Servants ought to be more accounted of, than riches.

5. The least motion after the least thing of our neighbour's, is sin.

Further Reading

Brook, Benjamin, *The Lives of the Puritans*, 3 vols. London: James Black, 1813,
Clarke, Samuel, Lives of Sundry Modern Divines appended to A General Martyrologie, 1677
Collinson, Patrick, *The Elizabethan Puritan Movement*, London: Jonathan Cape, 1967
Collinson, Patrick, *Godly People*, London: The Hambledon Press, 1983
Dever, Mark, *Richard Sibbes*, Macon, Georgia: Mercer University Press, 2000
Durston, Christopher & Eales, Jacqueline (eds), *The Culture of English Puritanism 1560-1700*, London: Macmillan, 1996
Haller, William, *The Rise of Puritanism*, New York: Columbia University Press, 1938
Hulse, Erroll, *Who were the Puritans?*, Darhngton: Evangelical Press, 2000
Kevan, Ernest F., *The Grace of Law*, Grand Rapids: Baker Book House, 1976
Kishlanksy, Mark, *A Monarchy Transformed: Britain 1603-1714*, London: Penguin Books, 1997
Knappen, M.M., *Tudor Puritanism*, Chicago: University of Chicago Press, 1939, 1966
Lake, Peter, *Moderate Puritans and the Elizabethan Church*, Cambridge: Cambridge University Press, 1982
Morgan, Irvonwy, *Prince Charles's Puritan Chaplain*, London: George Allen & Unwin, 1957
Packer, J.I., *A Quest for Godliness*, Wheaton, Illinois: Crossway, 1990
Parker, Kenneth L., and Carlson, Eric J., *'Practical Divinity': The Works and Life of Revd Richard Greenham*, Aldershot: Ashgate 1998
Seaver, Paul, *The Puritan Lectureships*, Stanford: Stanford University Press, 1970
Shapiro, Barbara J., *John Wilkins: An Intellectual Biography*, Berkeley: University of California Press, 1969
Spurr, John, *English Puritanism, 1603-90*, Basingstoke: MacMillan, 1998
Stephen, Sir Leslie, and Lee, Sir Sidney, *Dictionary of National Biography*, 22 vols, 1908-9
Webster, Tom, *Godly Clergy in Early Stuart England*, Cambridge: Cambridge University Press, 1997

A Puritan Theology of Preaching

Chad B Van Dixhoorn

1. Introduction 207
2. Background to the Westminster Assembly: the importance of preaching 210
3. Debates over preaching in the Westminster Assembly ... 213
   - 3.1 The eight debates 213
   - 3.2 The debate behind the Directory for Public Worship 217
4. Comments on preaching in published works 221
   - 4.1 The Works of the Westminster Assembly 221
   - 4.2 The Works of the Westminster divines: the making of a pulpit theology 227
5. Conclusion 256
6. Epilogue. 257

CHAD B VAN DIXHOORN is a Canadian by birth and studied at the University of Western Ontario before gaining both MDiv and ThM from Westminster Seminary, Philadelphia (USA). After completing a PhD in the history and theology of the Westminster Assembly at Cambridge (UK), he served as Associate Minister of Cambridge Presbyterian Church and as a British Academy Post-doctoral fellow in the history department of the University of Cambridge. Since 2008, he has been Associate Pastor at Grace Orthodox Presbyterian Church in Vienna, Virginia (USA) and a visiting professor at Westminster Seminary in California, Westminster Seminary in Philadelphia, and Reformed Theological Seminary in Washington DC as well as a Senior Research Fellow of Wolfson College, Cambridge. His current research project is a major edition of the minutes and papers of the Westminster Assembly with Oxford University Press, and his Westminster Assembly project provides access to rare manuscripts and books by the Assembly and its members at www.westminsterassembly.org.

Preface

Douglas McCallum, Jason Rampelt and Mark Burkill read drafts of this study and I am thankful for their helpful comments and corrections.

I dedicate this lecture to my parents, because they made me listen to sermons.

Chad B. Van Dixhoorn

1. Introduction

The history of preaching has not been ignored in recent years on any level. Hughes Oliphant Old has written a magisterial study of the subject from the biblical period to the present.[1] Scholarly monographs on the preaching of specific persons and narrower subjects are also being produced. Early seventeenth-century preaching has received a fresh and thorough coverage in the doctoral work of Arnold C. Hunt,[2] and the preaching of puritans has earned an almost endless number of historical treatments, too many to mention here.[3] These studies of Christian preaching are profoundly useful, and yet there are still gaps in our understanding of the history of preaching. Even treatments of so narrow a subject as Puritanism tend to be wide-ranging. This lecture proposes something distinct from previous studies in that it narrows the scope from Puritanism in general to the Puritans of the Westminster Assembly in particular. The Westminster Assembly is of particular historical importance because of the influence the Assembly had on the pulpit ministry of later Puritan and Reformed ministers.

The Westminster Assembly is especially pertinent to a study of Puritan preaching because the gathering issued a definitive statement on how to preach and why. In fact the gathering found a great variety of ways to stress the importance of the pulpit. It underlines the importance of preaching and preachers implicitly by mentioning them an astonishing thirty-two times in its Confession and Catechisms. The Assembly highlights the preacher's importance most unusually by giving preaching tips in the Directory for Public Worship. The Assembly-men stress preaching again in the Larger Catechism, reminding the pastor that he is preaching the Word of God,[4] and telling the parishioners that 'it is required of those that hear the word

---

[1] Seven volumes have appeared under the general title of *The Reading and Preaching of the Scriptures in the Worship of the Christian Church* (Grand Rapids: Eerdmans, 1998-2004).
[2] Arnold C. Hunt, "The Art of Hearing: English Preachers and their Audiences, 1590-1640" (PhD diss., University of Cambridge, 2001).
[3] For the best modern bibliography on Puritan preaching and other forms of preaching, see Hunt, "The Art of Hearing."
[4] *Westminster Larger Catechism* (WLC), Q&A 158, 159.

preached, that they attend upon it with diligence, preparation, and prayer; examine what they hear. . . [and] receive the truth with faith, love, meekness, and readiness of mind, as the word of God.'[5] Perhaps the Westminster divines drive home their message most explicitly when they say that 'the spirit of God maketh the reading, but especially the preaching of the word an effectual means of enlightening, convincing, and humbling sinners.'[6]

Of course it was hardly unique for the Assembly to stress the importance of preaching or to announce that biblical preaching was the word of God.[7] But to hear their statements aright, it is useful to recall that these statements were considered controversial by many of the Assembly's contemporaries. Arnold Hunt argues that the popularity of preaching began to slip in the 1620s and 1630s with the increased publication of godly literature and the correlative rise in literacy. Hunt stops his study at 1640, but students of the early-modern period will know that certain trends which began in the early decades of the seventeenth-century did not fall out of fashion during the Civil War. This was true of views about preaching. As is the case in many parts of the world today, the fifth decade of the seventeenth century was a turbulent one for the church as well as the state. In 1644, Robert Baillie, one of the Scottish commissioners to the Westminster Assembly, wrote about the 'democratick annarchie' plaguing the English churches. Though Baillie was apt to exaggerate and fond of vivid language, in 1644 'democratick annarchie' was not far off the mark. Literate Englishmen were increasingly unclear as to why the Bible had to be expounded when it was so clear to begin with. Illiterate Englishmen were unsure why, if preaching were needed at all, the preacher had to be trained and ordained. Anti-clericalism tended to accompany anti-Royalism in a manner that neither the Westminster divines nor the Parliamentarians across the street had anticipated.

The major objective of this study is to outline specifically what the Assembly as a whole had to say about preaching. Certainly Westminster's divines were not promoting preaching in the abstract; some preachers and preaching they liked, some they opposed. But to stop with a bare outline would only serve to state more fully what others

---

[5] WLC, Q&A 160
[6] WLC, 155. Cf., *Westminster Shorter Catechism* (WSC), Q&A 89.
[7] See Hunt, "The Art of Hearing," chapter one.

have commented on previously.[8] Thus this chapter not only outlines the pulpit theology of the Assembly as a whole, but it also canvasses the views of the Assembly's members. By way of orientation, I will briefly trace earlier English conflicts about the pulpit and then outline the Assembly's debates over preaching, delving into one of them. I then turn to a study of published works. Here I first provide a discussion of the works of the Assembly (organised chronologically), and then the works of individual divines (organized topically). The latter part of this study outlines the biblical and intellectual foundations of a Puritan pulpit theology, something which most histories of Puritan preaching have not treated and which the Westminster divines themselves would have considered essential. This may serve a second (perhaps auxiliary) purpose and enable us to make some assessment of the role preaching played in uniting or dividing the Assembly. Thus, beyond looking at the

---

[8] For studies of the Directory for Public Worship which have some discussion of its section on preaching see B. D. Spinks, 'Brief and Perspicuous Text; Plain and Pertinent Doctrine: Behind "Of the Preaching of the Word" in the Westminster Directory,' in *Like a Two-edged Sword: the Word of God in Liturgy and History*, ed. M. Dudley (Norwich: Canterbury Press, 1995), pp 91-111; R. S. Paul, *The Assembly of the Lord: Politics and Religion in the Westminster Assembly and the 'Grand Debate'* (London: T&T Clark, 1985), pp 359-374, esp. pp 364-365; A. F. Mitchell, *The Westminster Assembly: its History and Standards* (London: James Nisbet, 1884), pp 212-245, esp. pp 238-241; and H. Davies, *Worship and Theology in England: from Andrewes to Baxter and Fox*, 1603-1690 (Princeton: Princeton University Press, 1975), pp 412-413. C. P. Venema has contributed an article in which he notes the particular emphasis that the Westminster Catechism and Larger Catechism place on preaching: "The Doctrine of Preaching in the Reformed Confessions," *Mid-America Journal of Theology* 10 (1999), pp 135-183. A similar point is made by A. D. Strange in "Comments on the Centrality of Preaching in the Westminster Standards," *Mid-America Journal of Theology* 10 (1999), pp 185-238. Strange includes an excursus on eighteenth-century preaching (pp 205-212) and appends the text of the Assembly's Directory for Public Worship (pp 233-238). For a discussion of the preaching of the Assembly itself, see R. M. Norris, 'The Preaching of the Assembly,' in *To Glorify and Enjoy God: A Commemoration of the Westminster Assembly*, eds. J. L. Carson and D. W. Hall (Edinburgh: Banner of Truth, 1994), pp 63-81. Norris mostly restates the fuller argument of J. F. Wilson in *Pulpit in Parliament: Puritanism during the English Civil Wars* (Princeton: Princeton University Press, 1969), pp 137-165. For further discussion of preaching before Parliament, most of which was done by Westminster divines, see E. W. Kirby, 'Sermons Before the Commons, 1640-42,' *American Historical Review* 44, no. 3 (1939), pp 528-548; C. Hill, *The English Bible and the Seventeenth-Century Revolution* (London: Penguin Books, 1994), pp 79-108; H. R. Trevor-Roper presents a fascinating study of the fast sermons in *Religion, Reformation and Social Change* (London: Macmillan, 1967), pp 294-344.

preaching theology of the Westminster Assembly, this study will also view the Assembly through the lens of preaching.

2. Background to the Westminster Assembly: the importance of preaching

A study of the Westminster Assembly requires a brief statement of the context in which the divines wrote. Prior to the Assembly, public debate tended to focus on the relative effectiveness of different types of preaching (reading homilies or fresh expositions of Scripture), the merits of the preached word and the inscripturated word, and the importance of preaching compared to the administration of the sacraments.

Older treatments of preaching (such as Paul Seaver's) and modern studies (such as Hunt's) see English conflicts about preaching beginning in the Elizabethan Church. Seaver argues that an increased reading of prefabricated homilies under Queen Elizabeth and threats of ejection levelled at nonconforming Puritans led to more vigorous assertions on the part of Puritans regarding the cardinal place of preaching in the church.[9] These assertions were in turn met with ever stronger responses from the Queen, who reportedly once said 'that it was good for the church to have few preachers.' Archbishop Grindal, the recipient of the Queen's reported comment, wrote back to the Queen and informed her that the 'public and continual preaching of God's word is the ordinary mean and instrument of the salvation of mankind. St. Paul calleth it the *ministry of reconciliation* of man unto God. By preaching of God's word the glory of God is enlarged, faith is nourished, and charity is increased. By it the ignorant is instructed, the negligent exhorted and incited, the stubborn rebuked, the weak conscience comforted.'[10] The Queen forced Grindal, who had also requested that she leave church matters to the church, to resign his archiepiscopal post.

---

[9] Paul Seaver, *The Puritan Lectureships: The Politics of Religious Dissent, 1560-1662* (Stanford: Stanford University Press, 1970), p 17.

[10] Letter of December 20, 1576, cited in Seaver, *The Puritan Lectureships*, p 18.

While Grindal had been the highest ranking clergyman to tell the Queen about the importance of preaching, he was not the first. In 1571, a petition was sent to the Queen informing her that 'an infinite number of your Majesty's subjects, for want of preaching of the word (the only ordinary means of salvation of souls ...)' are perishing.[11] A dozen years later the Puritans were still saying the same thing. One Puritan said that 'the word of God preached' brought life, and since the people needed the word of God applied to them, the minister's 'absence from his flock [is] a dangerous and perilous thing.'[12] No one missed his point. This tendency to tether salvation to preaching and preaching to residency was not well-received by the Queen or by the then Archbishop, John Whitgift. John Penry told the Court of High Commission that non-resident ministers were 'odious in the sight of God and man,' as they keep the people from 'the ordinary means of salvation, which was the word preached.'[13] Whitgift was neither slow nor ambiguous in his response: 'I tell thee it is an heresy, and thou shalt recant it as an heresy.'[14]

After Whitgift, Puritans and their preachers had a quieter time under Richard Bancroft (1604-33). But though there may be fewer references to the unimportance or importance of preaching during Bancroft's tenure in Canterbury, the debate continued. William Bradshaw argued that the greatest work done by Christ and his apostles, and the greatest work done in the church, was preaching. Thomas Cartwright concurred.[15] Others objected. In 1626, Henry Valentine protested at what he saw as an ongoing tendency on the part of Puritans to 'shrink up all religion into preaching.'[16] His concerns may have been fed by the opinions of preachers like Ralph Kirk, the Manchester curate who is alleged to have said in 1604 that 'no man was ever saved but by preaching,'[17] or by Nicholas Byfield, who in two separate works argued

---

[11] Ibid., p 18.
[12] Ibid.
[13] Ibid., p 19.
[14] Ibid.
[15] Horton Davies, *The Worship of the English Puritans* (Morgan, Pa.: Soli Deo Gloria, 1997), pp 183, 186.
[16] Seaver, *The Puritan Lectureships*, p 20.
[17] R. C. Richardson, *Puritanism in North West England: A Regional Study of the Diocese of Chester to 1642* (Manchester: Manchester University Press, 1972), p 41.

that people could not enter heaven without preaching.[18] He might also have heard of Puritan-induced nightmares, like the wedding of Lady Russell's son, where yet another sermon was substituted for the customary dance.[19] Valentine more likely would have read the works of Puritans such as William Ames and James Ussher, both of whom wrote and preached about the importance of proclaiming the Word.[20]

With the enthronement of Archbishop William Laud in Canterbury the debate shifted from the efficacy of the Word read and preached to the efficacy of Word and sacrament. In the previous century John Jewel had emphasized a balance between preaching and the sacraments. Later Puritans tipped the scales by throwing a few more pounds on the side of preaching, but Laud placed his full weight on sacraments, completely removing any vestiges of moderation from the debate.[21] Where Ussher was accused of devaluing the Eucharist over against the sermon,[22] Laud elevated the sacraments at the expense of preaching. As Seaver writes,

> Archbishop Laud ... never one to equivocate, ... reversed the Puritan position. Reverence is properly accorded to the altar, in his view, because it is 'the greatest place of God's residence upon earth. I say the greatest, yea greater than the pulpit, for there it is 'Hoc est Corpus meum,' This is my body; but in the pulpit, it is at most but 'Hoc est Verbum meum,' This is my word. And a greater reverence, no doubt, is due to the Body than to the Word of our Lord.'[23]

Horton Davies wryly observes that 'Laud insisted that all altars should be railed: he never thought of railing off the pulpit.'[24] It was in reaction to Laudianism that the (soon to be) Westminster divine, Richard

---

[18] Ibid.
[19] Seaver, *The Puritan Lectureships*, p 39.
[20] William Ames, *The Marrow of Theology*, trans. J. D. Eusden (Grand Rapids: Baker, 1997), XXXIII-XXXIV (pp 182-189). For Ussher's views of preaching see *The Whole Works*, ed. Charles Richard Elrington (Hodges, Smith, 1864), vol. 1:284-87; for preaching as the 'Word of God' see vol 13:558, 562-66; see also important comments in vol 11:215, 216.
[21] Seaver, *The Puritan Lectureships*, p 20.
[22] For comment on Ussher's view of the Eucharist, see his *Works*, 1:289, n.i.
[23] Seaver, *The Puritan Lectureships*, p 20 (citing Laud).
[24] Horton Davies, *Worship and Theology in England: From Andrewes to Baxter and Fox*, p 138.

Heyrick, modestly told his parishioners that 'heaven itself cannot show forth a more excellent creature than a faithful preacher.'[25] And it was also in reaction to the Archbishop and his policies that on November 17, 1640, Cornelius Burges and Stephen Marshall preached to the House of Commons, each of them bemoaning the lack of preaching in the land.[26] The House of Commons itself in 1641, presumably with much frowning from Canterbury, encouragement from preachers, and a few dissenting votes among the members, declared that preaching 'is even the way to bring People into a state of Salvation; it is the way to save their souls.' The agreed upon text for the declaration was Romans 10:13-14; the agreed upon metaphor was the minister 'as an ambassador, [sent] to publish and spread abroad the mind and message of God touching Man's duty, and salvation, and to instruct the Church of God.'[27] That these laymen took such an interest in preaching is curious, but as Seaver points out, 'If salvation depended on preaching, all laymen had a legitimate interest in the minister's ability to preach' and, we could add, the Church's ability to find preachers.[28] The Commons' declaration leaves us virtually on the eve of the Assembly with a functional sketch of the Assembly's context, at least with respect to preaching. That sketch reveals an established tradition which values preaching as central to the church and ordinary for salvation. The Assembly's debates and the statements of individual divines need to be heard in this context – a context where the importance of preaching and preachers might have been taken for granted by the disputants at the Assembly but not, as they would well know, by the Church at large.

3. Debates over preaching in the Westminster Assembly

3.1. *The eight debates*

That the Assembly-men cared deeply about preaching and preachers is witnessed in their daily routine during their years at Westminster. Each

---

[25] Richardson, *Puritanism in North West England*, p 71.
[26] Christopher Hill, *The English Bible and the Seventeenth-Century Revolution*, pp 84-86.
[27] Seaver, *The Puritan Lectureships*, p 20.
[28] Ibid., p 46.

day the Assembly began with a morning lecture preached at St Margaret's from 6:00 to 8:00 AM,[29] followed 'almost everie morning' by the preaching of a probationer before 'a little committee' of the Assembly itself.[30] At times the sermon could run on a little too long, finally leading the Assembly to decide that preaching may not extend beyond 9:00 AM,[31] for at that hour the Assembly formally began.[32]

However much the members of the Assembly valued preaching, it is unsurprising that with one hundred preachers gathered in one room there were conflicting ideas about preaching. While there are a multitude of comments about preaching in the records of the Assembly (the extant minutes mention preaching over 400 times), I identify eight clusters of comments about preaching that are sufficiently concentrated and focussed to be labelled debates. These debates give us behind-the-scenes information since divines would sometimes make statements in the Assembly that they declined to make in the pulpit or in print. These debates also point to areas of unity and conflict among puritans about, the nature of preaching and related topics and are worthy of an extended study. Here I simply catalogue the eight debates, lingering a little longer on one.

The first debate was occasional: Parliament and the Assembly saw a desperate need for godly preachers, and the Assembly was asked to entertain the idea of unordained preachers. Many in the Assembly were opposed to the idea of giving bishops the sole power or even a special role in ordination. But there were no uncontroverted alternatives. When it was suggested that a step forward would involve Presbyterian ordination, it brought the Assembly two steps backward:

---

[29] Matthew Henry, 'The Life of Mr Philip Henry,' in Matthew Henry, *Works* (Fullarton, 1848), 2: p 607.

[30] Robert Baillie, *Letters and Journals* (A Lawrie, 1841), 2: p 111. John Lightfoot's account of Lords arriving during a probationer's sermon in order not to miss the start of the Assembly indicates that the official opening of the plenary session followed immediately after the sermon (John Lightfoot, *Works*, ed. John Rogers Pitman (London: J F Dove, 1824), 13: p 127.

[31] Minutes L386v. I cite the text of the minutes as transcribed in Chad B. Van Dixhoorn, *Reforming the Reformation: Theological Debate at the Westminster Assembly, 1643-1652* (PhD diss., University of Cambridge, 2004), vols. 3-7. Rather than citing the pagination of the thesis, I cite the volumes and foliation of the original minutes as recorded in the thesis simply as 'Minutes'. See also Lightfoot, *Journal*, p 215.

[32] For the 9:00 AM starting time, see, for example, Cambridge University Library Dd XIV.28 (4), fos. 3v, 56r. Minutes 1 :83v, 242r; 3:70r, 92r, 11 3v, 216r.

the Independents did not want to give the power of ordination to presbyteries. The dispute came to centre on the necessity of ordination for preaching, and the reasons why a man could be eligible to preach but not to administer the sacraments.[33]

The second debate was formally introduced when in November 1643 the Assembly began to discuss the office of the pastor. Here the distinctiveness of preaching is distinguished from other pastoral tasks: what is the difference between preaching and reading, preaching and catechizing, or preaching and praying?[34]

The third debate had simmered for two months. From one perspective, it was the debate over ordination revisited. Who could preach? Comments in the minutes indicate that the question of the preacher gained its urgency from contextual factors: an increasing number of sectarians began to preach without ordination. The debate gained its focus when the Assembly was discussing the office of the deacon: does the New Testament know of such a thing as a preaching deacon? As in the case of the previous debates, interesting and informative comments about preaching are made in the flow of the debate.[35]

There was another reason why the debate over lay preaching and diaconal preaching was so intense. Certainly the divines wanted to stop untrained men from preaching confused or erroneous sermons. But in addition to these theological concerns, there were also ecclesiological ones. This became abundantly clear in the debate over the 'Church of Jerusalem,' which was the fourth debate that related to preaching.[36] Briefly, the debate centered on the size of the church in Jerusalem during the period following Pentecost. The Presbyterians argued for a large number of converts in Jerusalem. Acts 2:41 mentioned 3000 Christians and Acts 4:4 mentioned that the number of converts grew to 5000. The Presbyterians argued that there were two days on which there were conversions on a grand scale, thus totaling at least 8000 Christians in Jerusalem. This was significant, since such a large

---

[33] See Minutes 1:106v-120v.
[34] Minutes 1:154r and following.
[35] Minutes 1:275r; where the account in the Minutes is cut off by a missing gathering, see Lightfoot, p 91 and following. For information on the extant and missing minutes, see Van Dixhoorn, *Reforming the Reformation*, 2:xxv-xxviii.
[36] Minutes 1:327r and following.

number of converts surely met in more than one congregation, and yet the New Testament refers to these many congregations as one Church. Thus the number of converts revealed the idea of a visible plurality in the Church, an idea crucial to Presbyterianism and Episcopalianism alike. A concomitant to this is the idea that there were multiple preachers in the area, including the Apostles. The Independents saw danger in this historical construction and thus tried to limit the total number of converts in Acts, and argue for the plausibility of one large meeting place (the Temple) and a minimum of preaching pastors. Then who was doing all the preaching? It was during this debate that the Independents were forced to state explicitly that the references to preaching in the Bible referred to the laity spreading the word and preaching informally. This debate begins to explain Thomas Goodwin's surprising comment that 'those nobles & commons that sit here, they may speak their mind in divinity & I count it a prophesying & preaching.'[37] This broad definition of preaching is to my knowledge not mentioned, or at least not frequently articulated, in the works of the Independents prior to the Civil War.

The other four debates can be mentioned more briefly. Preaching understandably became the subject of discussion when the Assembly was drafting the doctrinal part of the Directory for Ordination. Ultimately Parliament opted to not print the document, but a copy of the original manuscript submitted to the House of Lords was discovered in recent research.[38] In spite of the frequency with which preaching was mentioned during the debate it is only mentioned in passing in the Directory.

Preaching was the focus of discussion for the sixth time during debates over the Directory for Public Worship, which contained a subdirectory on preaching.[39] Although the record of the debate is

---

[37] Minutes 1:120r.

[38] This is a significant point which I did not make explicit in an earlier bibliography of works by the Assembly: the difference between the MS which the Assembly entitled "The doctrinal part of ordination" and the MS directory for ordination as Document 33. (see Van Dixhoorn, *Reforming the Reformation*, 1:61, 367), The documents were submitted together on 20 April 1644 and catalogued together, but it would have added clarity to my account to have numbered them separately. For the text of the document see the House of Lords Record Office, Main Papers 4 Oct 1644. For mention of the document, see Commons Journals iii.466; Lords Journals vi.525; and Minutes 2:20r.

[39] See Minutes 2:89r and following.

complicated by sections of shorthand, I think it gives a flavour of some of the issues related to preaching which were discussed in the Assembly, and thus I treat the debate in greater detail below.

The penultimate discussion of preaching was occasioned by a second discussion of the pastoral office, again relating to the Directory for Public Worship.[40] The debate included quibbles about the age of the minister, necessity of ordination (again), and disagreements about some of the examination questions to be asked of men seeking ordination.[41]

Finally, the Assembly had a brief debate about who may hear the Word of God.[42] The Erastian, Thomas Coleman, disliked any disjunction between Word and sacrament. Probably viewing the sacraments in a completely objective sense, Coleman argued that the function of the sacraments and the preached word was identical, as should be the recipients. The relationship between the word and sacraments was teased out in debate, but little of the discussion is accessible to us. A thorough study of these eight debates is a real desideratum for historians of practical theology and Puritanism.

3.2. *The debate behind the Directory for Public Worship*

The Assembly's collective statements on preaching and preachers are first published in its Directory for Public Worship, submitted for Parliament's approval in November 1644. An examination of the Assembly's theology of preaching as expressed in its public documents can appropriately begin here.

The Directory for Public Worship has a few features worthy of notice, three of which I will mention. In the first place, the Directory is not always very clear, as Horton Davies and others have noted, about whether it is giving directives as suggestions, or directives as commands. Sometimes the Directory says a minister may do something, in other places it says he shall. Practices are variously termed 'necessary' or 'requisite,' but also 'expedient,' 'convenient' or 'sufficient.' In the second

---

[40] See Minutes 2:95r and following, and Lightfoot, *Journal*, p 284.
[41] This includes the necessity of inquiring about grace in the life of the minister (Wrathband), the necessity of knowing the chronology of scripture, the inclusion of fasting and prayer in the ordination process, and the necessity of two full days of examination (Lightfoot).
[42] Minutes 3:23r and following.

place, the Directory is really a compilation of directories. After the Directory's completion, it was more frequently spoken of as a whole; but while it was being crafted, the minutes of the Assembly refer to the individual directories that make up that whole; a directory for prayer, a directory for visiting the sick, a directory for administering the sacraments, etc.[43] In the third place, the Directory is most unusual for including directives for preaching within a Directory for Worship. Alexander Mitchell points this out in his history of the Assembly,[44] but he is not the first to do so; Jeremiah Whitaker noted the same thing on the floor of the Westminster Assembly. More importantly, Whitaker added that the directory was also unsolicited by Parliament.

On the second day of the Assembly's deliberations about the Directory, the scribe records 'a motion by Mr. Whitaker to consider whether it be fit to have a directory for preaching' at all.[45] John Lightfoot's journal records that in defence of his motion, 'Mr. Whittacre opposed ... a Directory for preaching, as needless and not expected: and he queried of what use of this Directory should be.'[46] Upon this, Samuel Rutherford immediately took the floor and played the Scottish trump card: the Solemn League and Covenant. Rutherford stated that a directory for preaching was needed for 'uniformity' and held that without it 'a speciall article of the covenant [was] called in question.'[47] From there Rutherford characteristically launched into a three point sermonette on the nature of Christian liberty and its application to the proposed Directory for Public Worship.[48] Cornelius Burges's response is lost, but John Arrowsmith's rejoinder is not. Arrowsmith empathised with Whitaker, who may have been concerned about a lack of liberty in preaching, and noted that 'ther is difference betwixt uniformity in praying & in preaching. The one is possible, the other is not.' But this did not mean that there should be no directory, for, Arrowsmith adds,

---

[43] The final form of the Directory for Public Worship begins with one section on the assembling and behaviour of worshippers, and then devotes a section to the public reading of the Word of God. The following three sections are all connected to preaching: one each on prayer before and after the sermon, and one section on the sermon itself.
[44] Alexander F Mitchell, *The Westminster Assembly, its History and Standards*, p 238.
[45] Minutes 2:89v.
[46] Lightfoot, *Journal*, p 277.
[47] Minutes 2:89v.
[48] Minutes 2:89v-90r.

'this [matter] of preaching directs only for the pastors work.'[49] Herbert Palmer, without adding any clarity to the discussion, did add that 'the generality of the godly ministers in this kingdome have been uniform in their preaching.'[50] Eventually the directory was passed; presumably there were enough ungodly preachers needing the Assembly's advice.

The point raised by Whitaker is useful for understanding the divines. There is no evidence that the Parliament required such a Directory for preaching, and the divines were not (in spite of Rutherford's claim) under any obligation to prepare such a work under the Solemn League and Covenant. The Covenant mentions a 'confession of faith, form of church-government, directory for worship' and a directory for 'catechising'; it says nothing of a Directory for preaching.[51] No previous communication between the Church of Scotland and the Westminster Assembly mentions preaching either.[52] Yet the Assembly, in a rare display of initiative, determined that preaching was important enough and bad preaching common enough that some directives were necessary. This came at a price. In spite of initial hopes for the speedy passage of the Directory, it was only passed

---

[49] Minutes 2:90r. Arrowsmith seems to hold out a softer understanding of the directory, one which provided suggestions, not demands.
[50] Ibid.
[51] *A Solemn League and Covenant, for Reformation, and Defence of Religion* (1643).
[52] The various acts of the Scots' own General Assembly which considered making its own directory for worship, and later correspondence with the English frequently mention the need for a common confession, form of church-government, catechism and directory for worship, but from 1641 to 1644 no specific mention is ever made of a directory for preaching, or preaching as one element within a directory for worship. See *The Acts of the Assemblies of the Church of Scotland, From the Year 1638, to the Year 1649, Inclusive* (1682), 107, 131, 142, 147, 172-73, 177, 196. Significantly for understanding Rutherford's response to Whitaker, however, the June letter of the Scottish Commissioners to the Scots Assembly does mention that, among other things, 'the method of Preaching' has been discussed, but is not far enough along for the Assembly's perusal (Ibid., 226-227). The General Assembly in its response does not register any surprise about the preaching directory, and comments instead on the need for a directory for the ordination of ministers (Ibid., 237-239). This may indicate an assumption on the part of the Scots that a directory for worship would as a matter of course say something about preaching, except that, as Mitchell has pointed out, this had never been done before.

after, in Baillie's words, 'a world of debate'; the Directory occupied the Assembly as a whole for the space of six days and some part days.[53]

The debates occupying the Assembly and its committees revolved around the basis, structure and content of the sermon, not the importance of preaching itself. For example, in a burst of compassion, the committee attempted to shorten sermons by stating that 'the preacher shall handle so much for each time, as may be kept in memory by the hearers.' This brief suggestion 'cost large debate, about long sermons' since many, and in the end most, of the divines did not want 'the people's memory' to 'be the stint of sermons.'[54] The committee also suggested that the truth preached in the sermons be 'principally intended in the place [i.e., a biblical text].'[55] Lightfoot and others found this to be objectionable and cited the New Testament's use of the Old as proof that one can move beyond the 'principal intent' of the author.[56] The committee also spoke of 'the several parts of the text' from which the sermon would be preached. Again Lightfoot protested: he held that a sermon text could consist of one word, such as 'Amen.' The Assembly complied and changed the wording to the singular.[57]

While most of the preaching debates can easily be understood, at times little can be determined beyond the fact that there were two sides. This is the case on Monday, June 3, when the divines discussed whether preachers should expound a 'text or argument.' Some opposed the idea of preaching from an argument (i.e., a doctrinal statement) 'because it gives liberty to preach without a text.'[58] The result of the discussion is known: the Directory explicitly states that the sermon is to

---

[53] Baillie, *Letters*, 2: p 191. In a 31 May letter Robert Baillie writes, 'We trust, in one or two sessions, to through also our draught of preaching: if we continue this race, we will amend our former infamous slowness' (Ibid., p 187).
[54] Lightfoot, *Works*, 13: p 277.
[55] Ibid., p 278.
[56] Ibid.
[57] Ibid.
[58] Minutes 2:89r.

come from a text.⁵⁹ The Assembly may have been concerned to combat the recent legacy of King Charles I, who had required that preachers devote one sermon to an exposition of the Church's catechism rather than an exposition of Scripture.⁶⁰ Or perhaps they may have been unhappy with the Independents who tended to expound one biblical text and then preach a series of sermons on the doctrine(s) of that text.

4. Comments on preaching in published works

4.1. *The Works of the Westminster Assembly*

1. The Directory for Public Worship

Throughout the debates on the Directory, the evident concern was to preach the Scriptures faithfully and authoritatively or, as Arrowsmith put it, 'as the oracles of [G]od.'⁶¹ The same concern is visible in the Directory itself where the importance of preaching is highlighted. 'Preaching of the word,' the reader is told in one place, is 'the power of God unto salvation, and one of the most excellent works belonging to the ministry of the gospel.'⁶² Again, after the customary decencies and formalities, the Directory's preface informs the reader of preaching's importance when it states that the 'Prelates, and their faction,' have considered the prayer book the only way of worshipping God 'to the great hindrance of the preaching of the word, and (in some places, especially of late) to the justling of it out as unnecessary, or at best inferior to the reading of common prayer.'⁶³ The reader is also presented

---

[59] Directory for Public Worship (DW), p 379 (I cite the popular Glasgow edition by Free Presbyterian Publications, 1976). This comment in the minutes informs another discussion where Godfrey asserts (contra Phillip Schaff) that the Larger Catechism was not intended as a document for preaching in the churches, as was the practice of continental churches with the Heidelberg Catechism (see Robert Godfrey, 'The Westminster Larger Catechism,' in *To Glorify and Enjoy God*, p 131). The minutes here support Godfrey: if the Assembly deliberately voted against preaching from doctrinal propositions then it is most unlikely that they would intend the Larger Catechism for this purpose.

[60] Tom Webster, *Godly Clergy in Early Stuart England* (Cambridge: Cambridge University Press, 1997), p 144.

[61] Minutes 2:92v.

[62] DW, p 379.

[63] DW, p 373.

with a list of preaching instructions in the Directory itself.

As Packer, Davies, and others have noted, the body of the Directory's practical instructions is Perkinsian in colour, holding closely to the three part sermon structure of exegesis, doctrinal extraction, and application found in *The Art of Prophesying*. The conclusion of the preaching portion of the Directory echoes many of Archbishop Ussher's nine exhortations to his ordinands.[64] But throughout the Directory a theology of preaching is not vocalised; the Directory is more practical than theological. For a theological analysis of preaching one has to turn to the Assembly's Confession and Catechisms.[65]

2. The Confession of Faith and Catechisms

In December of 1646 the Confession of Faith was sent to Parliament. At first glance it appears that the Confession has little to say about preaching and preachers. The role of the minister (the Assembly's preferred term for the preacher or pastor) in the Confession is not advertised in its table of contents. While the Scriptures receive the longest chapter in the Confession and three chapters are devoted to the sacraments, preaching has no chapter at all. That is not to say that preachers and preaching are not mentioned or have an unimportant role. On the contrary, the Confession states that along with the Scriptures ('oracles') and sacraments ('ordinances'), the ministry is a gift of Christ himself to the 'catholic visible Church . . . for the gathering and perfecting of the saints, in this life to the end of the world' and that Christ promises 'by His own presence and Spirit' to make these gifts effectual.[66]

The same holds true for the Larger Catechism. The Catechism catalogues 'the ministry of the gospel' among 'the special privileges of the visible church' and finds that among 'the duties required in the second commandment' are 'the receiving, observing, and keeping pure and entire, all such religious worship and ordinances as God hath instituted in his word,' prominent of which are 'the reading, preaching,

---

[64] DW, p 381.
[65] While acclaimed in Scotland, the Directory was not well distributed or received in England. John Morrill, 'The Church in England, 1642-1649,' in his *The Nature of the English Revolution*, (London: Longman, 1993), p 164.
[66] *Westminster Confession of Faith* (WCF), 25:3.

and hearing of the word.'[67] Perhaps this sheds light on the Confession's insistence that, outside the church, there is no ordinary possibility of salvation.[68] This emphasis certainly corresponds with the Confession's high view of the minister.

Throughout the Confession and particularly the Larger Catechism there are frequent references to the minister.[69] Ministers, along with magistrates, are the people the church is particularly to pray for.[70] Ministers are the sole persons able to administer or dispense the sacraments;[71] and, with other church officers, administer discipline.[72] Ministers are the ones who are to assemble in synods and, 'If magistrates be open enemies to the church, the ministers of Christ, of themselves, by virtue of their office, ... may meet together in such assemblies.'[73] But while the minister had all of these duties (and many more), his chief task was preaching.

At the top of the list is the fact that 'under the gospel Christ the substance [is] exhibited, [and] the ordinances in which this covenant is dispensed are the preaching of the Word, and the administration of the sacraments ... While Christ is preached both in sermon and sacrament, 'repentance unto life' and 'faith in Christ,' is 'preached by every minister of the Gospel,' particularly in the sermon.[74] It is one way in which the covenant of grace is administered under the New Testament.[75] For this reason, the Larger Catechism provides parishioners with a how-to manual for listening to sermons.[76]

---

[67] WLC, 63, 108. The Confession's chapter on 'Religious Worship and the Sabbath Day' also lists, in section five, 'sound preaching, and conscionable hearing of the Word, in obedience unto God, with understanding, faith, and reverence' as one part of religious worship (WCF, 21:5).
[68] WCF, 25:2.
[69] The following are the observations of the author. Additionally, Godfrey also notes a greater emphasis on the ministry in the Larger Catechism than the Shorter in his essay, 'The Westminster Larger Catechism,' p 138.
[70] WLC, 183.
[71] WLC, 169, 176; WCF 27.4; 28.2; 29:3.
[72] WCF, 30:2.
[73] WCF, 31:2.
[74] WCF, 15:1.
[75] WLC, 35.
[76] WLC, 160: 'It is required of those that hear the word preached, that they attend upon it with diligence, preparation, and prayer; examine what they hear by the scriptures; receive the truth with faith, love, meekness, and readiness of mind, as the word of God; meditate, and confer of it; hide it in their hearts, and bring forth the fruit of it in their lives.'

The Assembly stressed to its readers that it is not only by overt censures but also by the regular 'ministry of the Gospel' that 'the keys of the kingdom of heaven' are exercised in the church 'to retain, and remit sins; to shut that kingdom against the impenitent, and to open it unto penitent sinners.'[77] The hope that preaching offers to the lost is a recurring theme in the Assembly's writing. Through preaching the elect are called out of their sin and into a state of grace. Of course not every hearer is saved,[78] and some who are mentally unable to understand the preaching may still be saved,[79] but, as the chapter on 'Saving Faith' says, 'The grace of faith, whereby the elect are enabled to believe to the saving of their souls, is the work of the Spirit of Christ in their hearts, and is ordinarily wrought by the ministry of the Word: by which also [the Word preached], and by the administration of the sacraments, and prayer, it [i.e., faith] is increased and strengthened.'[80]

The emphasis on the efficacy of preaching is underlined again and again by the Assembly. Not only is it stated in the Confession, as above, but it is found again in the Shorter Catechism[81] and is particularly stressed in the Larger Catechism's 155th Q & A:

> How is the word made effectual to salvation? A. The spirit of God maketh the reading, but especially the preaching of the word an effectual means of enlightening, convincing, and humbling sinners; of driving them out of themselves, and drawing them unto Christ; of conforming them to his image, and subduing them to his will; of strengthening them against

---

[77] WCF 30:2. The connection between preaching and the exercising of the keys of the Kingdom is also present in the Heidelberg Catechism, Q & A's 83-84. In addition to these two questions, the Heidelberg also states that 'the Holy Ghost ... works faith in our hearts by the preaching of the gospel, and confirms it by the use of the sacraments' (Q & A 65).

[78] WLC, 68; WCF, 10:4.

[79] WCF, 10:3.

[80] WCF, 14:1. Emphasis added.

[81] WSC, 89: 'How is the word made effectual to salvation? A. The Spirit of God maketh the reading, but especially the preaching of the word, an effectual means of convincing and converting sinners, and of building them up in holiness and comfort, through faith, unto salvation.' Robert Godfrey notes that the Shorter Catechism has little to say about the church, unlike the Larger Catechism which is more church oriented and is occupied with the means of grace in general. See 'The Westminster Larger Catechism,' 135-138. One might add that the Shorter Catechism has a particular dearth when it comes to preaching, where the Larger Catechism is much more ministerially minded.

temptations and corruptions; of building them up in grace, and establishing their hearts in holiness and comfort through faith unto salvation.

While all of these citations are of use in showing the centrality of preaching in the minds of the divines, nothing spells it out more clearly than the above question and answer. Preaching is the one thing of use to any person prior to and during the whole of the Christian life. Yes, Scripture and sermon are effectual through the Spirit's work, for the same spiritual purposes. Yes, while the above list states what preaching 'especially' does, it implies that the reading of the Word is able to do the same. But the difference between them is in the degree of effectiveness. Scripture, as Chapter One of the Confession states, has many qualities that are useful and unique, and is 'sufficient to give that knowledge of God and of His will, which is necessary unto salvation.'[82] According to the Assembly, preaching is the most powerful tool in the church's arsenal. Perhaps the reason for this is to be found in the instructions for hearers, where sermon-attendees are told that 'it is required of those that hear the word preached, that they . . . receive the truth with faith, love, meekness, and readiness of mind, as the word of God.'[83] Here again, the Westminster Assembly echoes those who went before them.

Of course, not everything preached was the 'Word of God' and not everyone was supposed to preach. Only when the Word is properly interpreted is it God's Word that is brought to the people. And while the directory stressed that all should read their Bibles, the Larger Catechism stresses that 'the word of God is to be preached only by such as are sufficiently gifted' and, they add, 'also duly approved and called to that office.'[84] At first and even second glance, such a statement may look a little presumptuous; it sounds as if it could be decoded as an elongated plea for job security. After all, Robert Norris points out, there is something unsurprising about a group of preachers stressing preaching.[85] But when one reflects again on the statements about preaching thus far, these requirements make sense.

---

[82] WCF, 1:1.
[83] WLC, 160. Emphasis added.
[84] DW, p 376; WLC, 158.
[85] Robert M. Norris, 'The Preaching of the Assembly' in *To Glorify and Enjoy God*, p 65. It should be noted that the divines themselves were hardly in a lucrative position: the parliament was invariably behind in paying them their already small allowance for their enormous task.

Preaching is special. The Assembly-men believed the exalted Christ sits at the right hand of God, and 'furnisheth ministers and people with gifts and graces, and maketh intercession for them.'[86] Christ gives his people gifts – some the gift of preaching – and commissions the preacher[87] and makes the preaching effective by His Spirit.[88] An emphasis on preaching and preachers, for the Westminster divines and for those before them, was an emphasis on the grace of Christ and the power of the Spirit. The emphasis on preaching in the Spirit's power and 'not in the enticing words of man's wisdom,' surfaces again in the seventeen point directive given in the Larger Catechism's question on preaching. There, in answer to the question, 'How is the word of God to be preached by those that are called thereunto?' the divines state that,

> They that are called to labour in the ministry of the word, are to preach sound doctrine, diligently, in season and out of season; plainly, not in the enticing words of man's wisdom, but in demonstration of the Spirit, and of power; faithfully, making known the whole counsel of God; wisely, applying themselves to the necessities and capacities of the hearers; zealously, with fervent love to God and the souls of his people; sincerely, aiming at his glory, and their conversion, edification, and salvation.[89]

While this question and answer hardly seems exceptionable, even to the Assembly's loudest critics, most of the other statements of the gathering would be. In particular, there are six assertions that would likely have sounded shrill in the ears of Westminster's opponents. First, preaching is to be restricted to ordained ministers alone. Second, these ministers are to be properly trained prior to their preaching ministry and studious while engaged in preaching. Third, when preaching is in accord with the Scriptures, it is to be heard and received as the Word of God. Fourth, when ordained men preach faithfully, preaching is the most effectual of the ordinary means of grace, more so than Bible reading or the administration of the sacraments; public means of grace are more effective than private. Fifth, and closely connected with the former assertions, the sermon was to be centred on the gospel; it was to be Christ-centred preaching. Sixth, no preaching, however clever and

---

[86] WLC, 54.
[87] WLC, 53.
[88] WLC, 155, etc.
[89] WLC, 159.

persuasive it may be, would be efficacious without God's working, by his Spirit, in the hearer.

To what degree were the divines themselves agreed on these six points? If an argument can be based on silence, it may be significant that, to use an earlier standard, no dissenting votes are recorded. It may also be noteworthy that there are no lengthy debates on these themes at the Assembly, except for the opposition of Tuckney, Gouge, and Gataker to the Directory's recommendation of the Perkinsian tripartite sermon structure.[90]

Why did the Westminster divines hold to these unpopular tenets? Certainly the answer will be tied up in their intellectual heritage, and their historical context. But at the end of the day, the Assembly's key source of authority for all things, theology in particular, was the Bible. The following discussion attempts to trace each of these six conclusions reached by the Assembly back to their exegetical roots, while seeking to determine the degree of unity which obtained among the divines on these points.

4.2. *The works of the Westminster divines: the making of a pulpit theology*

Over a century ago A. F. Mitchell complained that historians were constantly seeking to discover the opinions of the Westminster divines by means of near-contemporaries like Owen or Baxter. He pointed out that this was hardly necessary as Westminster's divines were themselves prolific writers.[91] Heeding Mitchell's complaint and wishing to illustrate the usefulness of the writings of the Assembly-men, I scrutinise the

---

[90] Some Assembly-men, notably Anthony Tuckney, were opposed to one style of sermon – particularly the traditional 'Plain style' of preaching. Tuckney objected to those who were 'considering the tying of a preacher to the forme of doctrine, reason and use'(Minutes 2:901). Lightfoot records that both Thomas Gataker and William Gouge joined in Tuckney's protest 'concerning the prescription of preaching by doctrine, reason, and use, as to strait for the variety of gifts, and occasion doth claim liberty.' Their arguments had some effect as the Assembly decided on 'an addition in the close or preface, – that this method is not to be prescribed to every man, nor upon every occasion, but is recommended upon the experience of the benefit that hath accrued by it.' Lightfoot adds that 'it cost a good deal of time before we could find terms for it' (Lightfoot, *Journal*, p 278).

[91] Mitchell, *History*, p 381, n. 1.

works of the divines on six topics related to preaching. Although I am not perfectly consistent in doing so, in this chapter I frequently cite modern editions in order to illustrate not only the usefulness of the works of the Westminster divines, but the ease with which they can be obtained.

1. God's ambassadors: ordained preachers

The Assembly was divided on the importance of ordination. The most vocal advocates of ordination at the Westminster Assembly were the Presbyterians, and of all the Presbyterians the Scots had the most to say. In his posthumously published Treatise of Miscellany Questions, George Gillespie underscores the need for an ordained ministry by taking up the challenge of a 'fierce furious Erastian' who was teaching that 'neither is there any such thing now to be acknowledged, as a speciall distinct sacred calling, or solemn setting apart of men to the ministrie of the Word and Sacraments.'[92] To Gillespie, such a view contradicted Scripture. First, seeking to establish the perpetuity of word and sacrament administration in general, Gillespie appeals to the special tasks given to the apostles, and later to other teachers in both the Great Commission (Matthew 28) and Ephesians 4:11-13.[93] The Great Commission emphasizes the duration of teaching and baptising till Christ returns.[94] Ephesians 4:13 stresses the same truth but with respect to the recipients of preaching. The work of the Church is to continue 'till we all come in the unity of the faith, and of the knowledge of the Son of God, unto a perfect man, unto the measure of the stature of the fulness of Christ.'[95] Since Christ has not returned and the saints are far from perfect, teaching and baptising must still continue.

Second, Gillespie points out the importance of preaching in particular: 'The preaching of the Gospell is the meane and way ordained of God to save them that beleeve.'[96] For this he appeals to Romans 10:14

---

[92] George Gillespie, *A Treatise of Miscellany Questions* (1649), 1, pp 24-25.
[93] Ibid., p 2.
[94] Thomas Goodwin understands the text in the same way. See his *Works* (Tanski, 1996), 11: p 361.
[95] William Bridge derives an identical lesson from the same text. See his *Works* (Morgan, Pa.: Soli Deo Gloria, 1989), 4:135. Anthony Burgess concludes similarly in *Spiritual Refining* (1658), p 495.
[96] Gillespie, *Miscellany Questions*, p 2.

where the Apostle Paul asks his readers, 'How then shall they call on him in whom they have not believed? and how shall they believe in him of whom they have not heard? and how shall they hear without a preacher?'

Third, the Scot makes several qualifications. He is not equating ordination with the rite Presbyterians use in ordination: the laying on of hands. Luther and Calvin distinguish between ordination and the laying on of hands, Gillespie says, and so does he.[97] Nor is he advocating the necessity of ordination in extraordinary cases, such as in persecuted France.[98] But Gillespie argues that even if sheep have to take the part of a shepherd for a while, there is no need to continue with extraordinary practices ordinarily.[99] He also makes clear that he is not suggesting that ordination is necessary for private Christian fellowship and is not arguing that 'expectants or probationers' need be ordained before preaching.[100] He holds that since they are occasional preachers who are (in the Scottish system at least) approved and licensed, they have a probational calling and approval.[101] What Gillespie does want to establish is that normally preachers are set apart. They are given a special call and a special office. They are ambassadors; they are sent.

It is the metaphor of ambassador that most seems to grip the divines when they think about preaching and preachers. In a sermon on Jeremiah 23:22, Anthony Burgess paused to remind his hearers that ministers are to preach the Word of God as ambassadors.[102] While the divines were able to find references to ambassadors in the book of Jeremiah, they more readily turned to 2 Corinthians 5:20. There the Apostle Paul says, 'Now then we are ambassadors for Christ, as though God did beseech you by us: we pray you in Christ's stead, be ye reconciled to God.' The divines took note of the you-us dichotomy in the text and assumed that God's ambassadors were given a unique and important role. William Gouge, reflecting on this passage writes, 'Preaching is a clear revelation of the mystery of salvation by a lawful minister.' Such a minister is one set apart by God 'according to the rule

---

[97] Ibid., pp 33-34.
[98] Ibid., pp 34-35.
[99] Ibid., pp 55, 61.
[100] Ibid., p 35.
[101] Ibid., p 43.
[102] Burgess, *Spiritual Refining*, p 495.

of God's word, to be a minister of the gospel, doth himself understand the mysteries thereof, and is enabled to make them known to others; he also standeth in God's room, and in God's name makes offer of salvation, 2 Corinthians 5:20. [T]his moves men to believe and be saved. This is the ordinary way appointed of God for attaining salvation.'[103] If this is the case, Gouge concludes, ministers ought to preach earnestly, and neglectful ministers ought to fear God.[104]

Of course the divines were not limited to 2 Corinthians 5:20 in their argument for a divine warrant for ordination. Gillespie follows Paul's argument in Romans 10, where the Apostle says in verse fifteen, 'And how shall they preach, except they be sent?'[105] Sending, for Gillespie, denotes a sender, and therefore the text implies, or at least the Scot infers, a King and an ambassador. For Gillespie, the metaphor of ambassador is important as it is not possible for every Christian to be an ambassador in Christ's Kingdom without total chaos.[106] It goes without saying that chaos, for Presbyterians, is *a priori* unbiblical. Turning to 2 Timothy 2, Gillespie makes a similar point in a different way. He notes the commands for Timothy to teach, to take care in teaching, and to appoint successors in teaching, and then notes the obvious: 'Teachers are distinguished from those who are taught: Every man may not be a Teacher ... it is no part of the general calling of Christians.'[107] This is a pivotal point for Gillespie and he dwells on it: 'The Apostle sayeth not, 'the things that thou heard of me, the same I will that faithfull and able men, who ever shall be willing to the work, teach others also' [;] faithfulnesse, and fitnesse, or ability cannot make a significant calling, but qualifie a man for that which he shall be called unto. Aptitude is one thing: to be cloathed with a calling, power and authority is another thing.'[108] Members of the church have a legitimate reason for skepticism

---

[103] William Gouge, *Commentary on Hebrews* (Grand Rapids: Kregel, 1980), chapter 2, section 23.

[104] Ibid., 2.23, vol. 1, p 102.

[105] Oliver Bowles relies on a similar variety of Scripture texts in defense of ordination: *De Pastore Evangelico Tractatus* (1649), 1-3. P. G. Ryken and J. B. Rockey are producing a translation of this work.

[106] Gillespie, *Miscellany Questions*, pp 36-38.

[107] Ibid., p 52. Citing Galatians 6:6, Gillespie almost lets the text speak for itself: 'Let him that is taught in the word communicate unto him that teacheth in all good things.' His comment is simply that 'some are Teachers, some are taught,' and he adds, 'in the Word.'

[108] Ibid., p 53.

about self-styled ministries. 'Without a clear calling, and lawfull Ordination, how shall people receave the word from the mouths of ministers, as Gods word, or as those who are sent from God[?]'[109] Gillespie also notes that Paul expressly instructs the church to supply the preachers with all their needs (1 Corinthians 9:13-14). If this instruction is not setting apart a particular class of preachers, i.e., lawful ones, then, he laughs, 'its like enough that People shall have good store of Preachers, and their purses shall pay well for it.'[110] Although the Scots wrote more on the preacher's special commission than most Presbyterians, other Presbyterians did speak on the topic. In expounding Romans 10:13-35, John Arrowsmith (to mention only one) tightly tied the effectiveness of preaching to a proper commissioning and sending.[111]

Even then, Presbyterians at the Assembly held no monopoly on the topic of ordination. Both Erastians and Independents speak on the matter, at least obliquely. Throughout his discussion, Gillespie is debating an anonymous Erastian who is an opponent of ordination.[112] It is unlikely that the opponent is Thomas Coleman, a fellow divine with whom Gillespie was forever debating and who has a distinctive method of argumentation. Further, Coleman was not against ordination, though he held that it pertained only to the teaching function of the minister.[113] Likewise, John Lightfoot, the Assembly's other Erastian, states that since the Apostles there is a 'peculiar order and function for the ministry of the gospel.'[114] Neither hold strongly to ordination, but each allows that the preacher has a special role.

The Independents also assign the preacher a special role but, according to Gillespie and Rutherford, sometimes they equate

---

[109] Ibid., p 54.
[110] Ibid., pp 54-55.
[111] John Arrowsmith, *Tactica Sacra* (1657), 2.2.6 (114). '*Ubi necessaria statuitur ad salutem Dei invocatio, ad Dei invocationem fides, ad fidem verbi auditio, ad verbi auditionem praedicatio, & ad praedicationem missio; in via scilicet ordinaria. Alias enim extra ordinem fieri potest, ut cum fructu praedicet qui non est missus; sicut interdum ex providentia singulari surdus creadit absque auditu.*'
[112] Gillespie, *Miscellany Questions*, p 36. Gillespie reports that the work he is referring to throughout was published at Franeker (1).
[113] Thomas Coleman, *Male dicis Maledicis* (1646), 10. 'For ordination of Ministers, I say it is within the commission of teaching, and so appertains to the doctrinal part.'
[114] Lightfoot, *Works*, 2:68.

ordination with the popular election of a pastor by a particular congregation.[115] Certainly their comments on a minister's calling are not univocally in favour of ordination. When William Greenhill preached about the watchman in Ezekiel 3:17, he simply stated that 'Christ himself is the great Watchman of the church, he is the Head, and appoints who shall be in his stead. 2 Corinthians 5:20, the apostles were in his stead; so the prophet here; so all the faithful ministers of the gospel, who are called mediately by the church according to his will.'[116] On the other hand, in his treatise on 2 Corinthians 5:19-20, Jeremiah Burroughs observes that 'the ministers of the gospel are ambassadors of Christ,' but has nothing to say of ordination.[117] According to Burroughs, Christ's ministerial ambassadors are a greater privilege for the church than mere messengers or stewards. He notes that ambassadors are not sent on trivial missions, thus indicating the importance of the message. He cautions that ambassadors are not to go beyond the words of commission that they receive, indicating a need to preach the gospel.[118] And just as the King is represented by his ambassadors, so 'there is a kind of a representation even of the person of Christ in them.'[119] Burroughs also warns his hearers that 'an ambassador must give an account of His employment,' which means that he reports back on the parishioners' response to the preaching, presumably by means of prayer.[120] But he does not explicitly mention the process by which one is made an ambassador.[121] Thus while neither group stresses ordination to the degree of the Presbyterians, both agree that the preacher is set apart for God's service in a way and for a function not common with all believers.

2. Trained Preachers

While the non-Presbyterians were not outspoken about the need for

---

[115] Gillespie attributes this position to most sectaries and some Independents (Gillespie, *Miscellany Questions*, p 25); see also Samuel Rutherford, *The Due Right of Presbyteries* (1644).
[116] William Greenhill, *An Exposition of Ezekiel* (Edinburgh: Banner of Truth, 1994), p 110.
[117] Jeremiah Burroughs, *Gospel-Reconciliation* (Morgan, Pa.: Soli Deo Gloria, 1997), p 258.
[118] Ibid., pp 258-260.
[119] Ibid., p 260.
[120] Ibid., pp 260-263.
[121] Burroughs does make it clear that he wishes to hurry by such matters to address the reconciliation offered in the gospel itself (Ibid., p 257).

ordination, they were unambiguous about the need for an educated clergy. Lightfoot argued that study was important for anyone to be a preacher since it was necessary even for the Apostles. They engaged in 'hearing, study, conference, and meditation,' and they were with Christ himself for a full year before being sent out to preach.[122] Negatively, Thomas Goodwin opposes 'those who decry learning and study.'[123] He takes note of Paul's instruction to Timothy to study (2 Timothy 2:15) and argues that extempore preaching only, without study, is contrary to Scripture. He also comments (perceptively) those who argue against study still rely much on what they have heard and discussed.[124] No one comes into the pulpit with a blank slate.

John Arrowsmith discusses the need not only for training but also for ability. The three things necessary for a 'lawfull calling' are ability, inclination, and separation (ordination). In Arrowsmith's mind, 'He that is Un-gifted, I dare be bold to say, he is Un-sent.'[125] This follows from another of Paul's instructions to Timothy that 'the things that thou hast heard of me among many witnesses, the same commit thou to faithful men, who shall be able to teach others also' (2 Timothy 2:2). Not everyone is an able teacher.

Training for the preacher did not merely consist in thorough Bible instruction, though it could be nothing less than that. Obadiah Sedgwick leaves no doubt of his opinion when he says, 'I am not of his mind who would have preachers study no book but the Bible.'[126] Robert Harris, in a milder tone, apologised to the readers of his *The Way to True Happiness* for not properly citing the authors he quotes:

> 'Once for all, let me tell you, I reverence Antiquity as much as [those] who doth most, and make use of as many Ancients and Moderns as my purse can buy, and strength will bear: If I rather read than name them, it is for your sake, and so I pray you take it.'[127]

---

[122] Lightfoot, *Works*, 3:67.
[123] Goodwin, *Works*, 11:379.
[124] Ibid., pp 378-379.
[125] John Arrowsmith, *Theanthropos, or God-Man: being an exposition upon the first eighteen verses of the first chapter of the Gospel according to John* (1660), p 99.
[126] Obadiah Sedgwick, *Christ's Counsell to his Languishing Church of Sardis* (Morgan, Pa.: Soli Deo Gloria, 1996), viii.
[127] Robert Harris, *The Way to True Happiness* (1653), p 98.

Anthony Burgess, drawing the customary distinction between extraordinary and ordinary ministers, notes that even those 'with extraordinary gifts, did make use of study, and labour, and diligent paines.' Placing both Paul and Timothy in that category, he notes that 'Paul exhorts Timothy, to give himself to reading, that his profiting may appear to all men, 1 Timothy 4:13, 15,' and 'Paul himself made use of his Parchments.' Burgess concludes from this 'that those Lamps which were inlightened by God himself, did yet need the continuall oyl of their labour and paines. And if this is true of the extraordinary gifted persons, how much more of the ordinary? The Nurse that feeds not, cannot long give milk; so neither the Minister that studieth not.'[128]

When considering the divines' stress on learning, the Assembly's debate about displays of scholarship in the pulpit illustrates their ideals, if not the realities of the church.[129] The debate involved an assumption, a worry and a proposed resolution. All assumed that the preacher would be familiar with scholarly and biblical languages, along with standard Reformation and patristic works. This, along with other forms of learning, was actually required in the Directory for Ordination, framed the year before. The worry seemed to have been about ostentatious displays of scholarship in preaching. The proposal of the committee on preaching was to prohibit or warn against citing Calvin or Augustine as authorities in sermons, and quoting Latin, Greek, and Hebrew words or phrases from the pulpit.

Edmund Calamy was quick to inveigh against the committee's proposal. According to the debates in the minutes, Calamy reasoned that 'if I must use my owne deductions & make use of my owne parts why may not I make use of Calvin?' He suggests that he might profitably 'use the name of Calvin and Austin' (Augustine) and, in fact, here were 'many reasons to prove the lawful use of it.' For example, 'Sometimes it is to good edification as to show it is noe new opinion.' Mentioning 'the author doth show it is not my opinion alone, & then it doth secretly put a Reverence upon their opinion.'[130] John Arrowsmith completely agrees. Displays of learning are permissible and he cites Augustine (in Latin) to show that this is not a new opinion in the

---

[128] Anthony Burgess, *The Scripture Directory for Church Officers and People* (1659), pp 75-76.
[129] See Minutes 2:90v-94r.
[130] Minutes 2:92r.

church.¹³¹ The aging Herbert Palmer is on the other side of the fence from Arrowsmith and announces that he is 'not convinced but that it is unlawfull' to cite other names in the pulpit. He reminds his brothers 'that we may make use of humane learning, farre be it from me to contradict it.' But 'whether necessary or fitting to quote the names of those whom we may make the use of. I conceive we may not doe it. It is not according to the patterne of the scriptures; Paul did not doe it. Consider in what case he useth these; if we will follow the apostle, it must be in the like case.' He did not need to add that the name of Paul did give an argument authority. Before sitting down, Palmer stated once more that 'for that reason doe I thinke it unlawfull,' and with some rhetorical flourish asks, 'Doe I preach to gaine authority by man or by the authority of the word of God in their hearts? If the authority of Mr. Calvin shall make my people believe my word, I had rather have had my mouth stoped [caulked] for that time.'¹³² At the end of the day it was the early utterance of Joshua Hoyle that prevailed: 'it should be done sparingly, but it would go ill under the name of the Assembly if we should wholy put it off.'¹³³

It is evident from the debate that those arguing against citations of authors and foreign languages were still advocates of learning, were themselves learned, and took care to make both of those facts clear to the others. Lively debate in the Assembly during the examination of ministers reveals that these sentiments were backed up in practice. While exceptions were occasionally permitted, hopeful preachers that came before the Assembly had to be conversant in Hebrew, Greek, and Latin, in addition to being able to evidence a firm grasp of Scripture and theology. Intense debates over candidates who came before the Assembly's examination committee, wanted to preach, but had 'forgot their Greeke,' highlight the importance of learning to the divines.¹³⁴ Was there to be a different standard of language examination for those already in the ministry than for those wishing to enter? What if the person could read and understand Latin, but not speak it? Did it matter where the person was to preach? The context of some of these debates

---

[131] Minutes 2:92v.
[132] Minutes 2:92v-93r.
[133] Minutes 2:91r.
[134] Minutes 1:126v.

also highlights the fact that these were not ivory-tower discussions. A real person was pacing about the Abbey, waiting for an answer.[135]

3. The Word of God

The third plank of the Assembly's pulpit theology is frequently found in exhortations to hearers of sermons, and not simply to preachers. The reason why ministers needed to be ordained and learned was because (quoting Gillespie again) hearers were to 'receave the word from the mouths of ministers, as Gods word.' According to the Presbyterian William Gouge, this is the message of Hebrews 13:7, which reads, 'Remember them which have the rule over you, who have spoken unto you the word of God.' Gouge told his Blackfriars audience that 'though that which is uttered by men as ministers be properly the sound of a man's voice, yet that which true ministers of God in exercising their ministerial function preach, is the word of God.'[136] Lest his auditors, and later his readers, think he has overstated the point of the text, Gouge asks how the words that 'ministers do or ought to speak' can be 'styled the word of God.' The answer is found in the old distinction between extraordinary and ordinary ministers: 'God did immediately inspire extraordinary ministers, and thereby informed them in his will. 'For the prophecy came not in old time by the will of man, but holy men of God spake as they were moved by the Holy Ghost,' 2 Peter 1:21. Therefore they were wont to use these prefaces, 'The Word of the Lord,' Hosea 1:1; 'Thus saith the Lord,' Isaiah 7:7; and an apostle thus, 'I have received of the Lord, that which also I delivered unto you,' 1 Corinthians 11:23.'[137] A similar case obtains 'for ordinary ministers' as 'they have God's word written and left upon record for their use ... They therefore[,] that ground what they preach upon the Scripture, and deliver nothing but what is agreeable thereunto, preach the word of God.'[138] A few lines later Gouge returns to this point and states again, 'So close ought ministers to hold to God's word in their preaching, as not to dare to swerve in anything from it. The apostle,' he says, 'denounceth a curse against him, whosoever he be, that shall preach any other word' (Galatians 1:8-9).[139]

---

[135] For this entire debate, see Minutes 1:126v-128r.
[136] Gouge, *Hebrews*, chapter 13 section 98.
[137] Ibid., 13:98 (2:316).
[138] Ibid.
[139] Ibid., 13:98 (2:317).

The Erastians of the Assembly wrote little or nothing about preaching as the Word of God. The Independent Jeremiah Burroughs, on the other hand, may have more to say on the subject than any other Assembly-man. On 19 November 1643, Burroughs made use of a fragmentary quote from Isaiah 66:2, 'and that trembleth at My Word,' to cultivate a little reverence among his hearers. His sermon does not tell his hearers to fear God; instead, he paints a verbal picture of a God-fearer and allows his auditors to determine whether they fit that picture. A God-fearing man or woman, he says, does not come 'to hear the Word in an ordinary way, merely to spend so much time, or to hear what a man could say.' Rather, the Word, 'either read or preached,' is attended to 'with all reverence.'[140] Such a one examines the preaching, but 'dares not cavil against it.'[141] Burroughs holds up Moab's King Eglon as an example to be followed by the saints, not, of course, in his 'heathenish' ways, nor in his untimely and disgusting death, but as one who rose to receive Ehud as an ambassador with 'a message from God' (Judges 3:20).[142] Burroughs then pushes the knife in a little deeper, questioning whether their 'hearts . . . swell against' preaching, asking them what they really think about preaching, and pointing out the irony of those who think they have escaped the world but still show the worst pride in rebelling against the Word.[143]

Underlying this discussion of irreverence and pride is the assumption, obvious for Burroughs, that the faithful preaching of the Word of God is the Word of God. Because preaching is the Word of God, irreverence and pride are scandalous. This doctrine of preaching as the Word of God lies under Burroughs's entire first sermon and surfaces in various places, such as his discussion of the power of the Word. Reflecting on the Great Commission, Burroughs asks about the relevance of Christ's assertion, 'All power in heaven and earth is given unto me.' 'What follows?' Burroughs asks. 'Go therefore and preach.' What may we observe from this connection? It is as if He should say, 'Know that all the power in heaven and earth that is given to Me shall go along with you while you are preaching My Word, to make good that

---

[140] Jeremiah Burroughs, *Gospel-Fear* (Morgan, Pa.: Soli Deo Gloria, 1991), p 6.
[141] Ibid.
[142] Ibid., p 8.
[143] Ibid., pp 8-9.

Word of mine that you preach.'[144] The power of God in preaching is so great that 'every sermon I come to hear, I must expect to be nearer heaven or nearer hell.'[145] Few in Burroughs's experience attend to preaching with such seriousness. 'When they come to hear the Word, they come with carnal and vain hearts.' But again, the Word is powerful and 'when they have found that the Word comes to ransack them, and gets into them and grapples with them, and meets with all the inward and secret distemper of their spirits, they are made to fall down before this Word and say, 'Verily, God is in this Word.'[146]

Of course, not every sermon is to be viewed as God's Word and the Reformation rule for testing sermons is Scripture. Burroughs encourages hearers to compare what is heard from the preacher with the Bible in their homes, but he gives a caution: when you hear preaching, 'do not slightly cast it off.' If you hope that what you hear 'out of the Word is not the Word,' you are coming to sermons with an unwilling, unyielding, unprayerful heart.[147] He ends his sermon by pleading, 'When you come to sermons to hear the Word of God, O labor to keep your hearts in a constant trembling frame, and the Word that you do now tremble at will forever hereafter comfort your heart.'[148]

Burroughs's exegetical work supporting such exhortations is expressed in a sermon series on Leviticus 10:3 and in particular his three sermons entitled, 'Of Sanctifying the Name of God in The Hearing of the Word.'[149] The passage that Burroughs uses to support his high view of preaching comes from 1 Thessalonians 2:13: 'For this cause also thank we God without ceasing, because, when ye received the word of God which ye heard of us, ye received it not as the word of men, but as it is in truth, the word of God, which effectually worketh also in you that believe.' Noting that the Thessalonians were commended on this point, Burroughs notes that the Apostle's sermon 'came effectually to work because they [the Thessalonians] received it as the Word of God.'[150] This same principle that worked for the Apostle is at work when a

---

[144] Ibid., p 14.
[145] Ibid., p 20.
[146] Ibid., p 22.
[147] Ibid., pp 27-28.
[148] Ibid., p 29.
[149] Jeremiah Burroughs, *Gospel-Worship* (Morgan, Pa.: Soli Deo Gloria, 1990), pp 192-281.
[150] Ibid., p 200. It may be significant that in commenting on this passage Lightfoot sees a connection to Scripture, but does not mention preaching (Lightfoot, *Works*, 6:56).

minister preaches from the Bible: 'Many times you will say, 'Come, let us go hear a man preach.' Oh no, let us go hear Christ preach, for as it concerns the ministers of God that they preach not themselves, but that Christ should preach in them, so it concerns you that hear not to come to hear this man or that man, but to come to hear Jesus Christ.' Burroughs then quotes 2 Corinthians 5:20 and reminds his hearers again that ministers are ambassadors of Christ.[151] In his treatise *Gospel Reconciliation*, Burroughs uses the same two texts but cites 1 Thessalonians 2:13 only in passing, while exhaustively discussing 2 Corinthians 5:20.[152] He takes explicit note of the fact that the text says 'we are ambassadors for Christ, as though God did beseech you by us.'[153] The latter text is cited again in another sermon Burroughs preaches that 'it is as certain God speaks thus by his ministers as if you heard God speaking by himself.'[154] Thus the metaphor of the ambassador implies not only commissioning but also the authority, even the identity of the preacher. Though relying on different portions of the Bible, it is clear that both Presbyterians and Independents at the Assembly believed that God's words, if they were delivered faithfully by God's ambassadors, remained God's words. And thus in a very real and proper sense, the preaching of the Word of God is the Word of God.

4. The Outward and Ordinary Means of Grace: Preaching

If the preaching of the Word of God is the Word of God, then what is its place in the Christian life and worship? Unsurprisingly, the divines answer that preaching is the ordinary means of grace for Christians. In his *Thesis & Praelectiones Theologicae*, Anthony Tuckney argues that the 'Verbum Dei externum est ordinarium medium conversionis ad salutem' (the eternal word of God is the ordinary means of conversion to salvation).[155] Tuckney makes clear from the start that by 'the external word' he does not simply mean Christ, the one preached, but the means

---

[151] Ibid., pp 200-1. Thus William Bridge can say that 'Christ teacheth by the public ministry of the Word.' (Bridge, *Works*, 4:144).

[152] For the reference to 1 Thessalonians 2:13 see Burroughs, *Gospel Reconciliation*, pp 265-266. For the full treatment of 2 Corinthians 5:20, see pp 256-305.

[153] Ibid., p 256 (emphasis added).

[154] Jeremiah Burroughs, *Gospel-Remission* (Morgan, Pa.: Soli Deo Gloria, 1995), p 305.

[155] Anthony Tuckney, *Prælectiones Theologicae* (1679), part 2, p 258; see pp 258-264.

itself, preaching.[156] Stated differently, people are not only saved by Christ, they are saved by Christ through the means of the preaching of Christ. This position is a commonplace among the preachers at the Assembly. Anthony Burgess states that the faithful ministry of the Word is 'the sure and ordinary way for conversion of men from their evil waies.'[157] He states this more strongly in his exposition of 1 Corinthians 3: 'The Ministry is the only ordinary way that God hath appointed, either for the beginnings or encrease of grace.' After all, 'Faith is said to come by hearing' (Romans 10:17), and his own text informs the Corinthians that Paul and Apollos were the 'ministers by whom ye believed' (1 Corinthians 3:5).[158] Burgess goes even further and argues that 'because it's the ordinary meanes, therefore it's the necessary meanes to which all are tied. We cannot be without it; if a man enjoy it not, his soul becomes like a barren wilderness, yea like a noisome dunghill.'[159]

The Independents at the Assembly were equally vocal in their advocacy of preaching as the primary means of grace. Jeremiah Burroughs once said that 'the great standing ordinance in the church of God is the ministry of the Gospel,'[160] and he esteemed preaching as a 'great gift,' even a 'glorious gift' of Christ.[161] Thomas Goodwin notes that whenever churches were founded in the book of Acts, it was done by preaching. He draws attention to the fact that the preaching of the gospel in 1 Corinthians 2:4 is called a 'demonstration of the Spirit' and in 2 Corinthians 3:8 a 'ministration of the Spirit.'[162]

In 1649, William Greenhill dedicated a preface to a portion of his Ezekiel commentary to a defence of preaching's primacy. In a prophetic tone, he announces that 'where the Word of God is not expounded, preached, and applied to the several conditions of the people, there they perish. . . [L]ay aside preaching and expounding the Scriptures, the people will be scattered, run into errors, wander up and

---

[156] Ibid., p 258 Tuckney guards himself against the charge of '*enthusiasmis*' because he says conversion is possible without preaching (p 259).
[157] Burgess, *Spiritual Refining*, p 500; see also p 494.
[158] Burgess, *Scripture Directory*, p 69.
[159] Ibid.
[160] Burroughs, *Gospel Reconciliation*, p 233; see pp 230-305.
[161] Burroughs, *Gospel Remission*, p 111; see also Jeremiah Burroughs, *Saints' Happiness* (Morgan, Pa.: Soli Deo Gloria, 1996), pp 254-255, 260.
[162] Goodwin, *Works*, II: pp 360-361.

down as sheep without a shepherd.'[163] He appeals, of course, to the Bible, in order to stress the need for preaching.[164] He also appeals to history and cites at length Archbishop Edmund Grindal's letter of protest to Queen Elizabeth after the monarch 'was instigated . . . to abridge the number of preachers.'[165]

Greenhill is well aware of the fact that not everyone agrees with his lofty view of preaching, and he is upset that 'some there be that thrust hard at it, and endeavour to throw it down.'[166] One contemporary objection to Greenhill's view of preaching rested upon the fallibility of the preacher. Were not the Apostles, unlike seventeenth century preachers, infallible? Could they then legitimately stress preaching in a way that England's preachers could not? In response to this, Greenhill readily admits the difference, but points out that the Apostles and prophets did, at times, fail. The reliability of the Apostles rested not in their infallibility, but in the Spirit: 'That which was needful to be the rule and standard, was given out by an infallible Spirit.' Greenhill moves easily from this doctrine to the importance of preaching more broadly: 'The Spirit of truth took of Christ's, showed it to them, and led them in all truth. And,' he says in the strongest terms used by any divine, 'while the ministers now do bring that truth to you, they are infallible.'[167]

Preaching and Reading

At times the sacraments received more reverence from parishioners than did preaching or preachers. Burroughs is both chagrined and perturbed as he comments on how people treat the sacraments so seriously but give preaching second shrift: 'It is an easy matter to convince men and women that they are bound to sanctify the name of

---

[163] William Greenhill, *Ezekiel*, v.
[164] Greenhill notes that 'the infinite and only wise God hath annexed to the ministry conversion, Acts 26:18; regeneration, 1 Corinthians 4:15; the addition of sinners to the church and to himself, Acts 2:41, 47; 11:24; faith, Romans 10:14; 1 Corinthians 3:5; the perfecting of the saints, and edification of the body of Christ, Ephesians 4:12; collation of the Spirit, Galatians 3:2; Acts 10:44; yea, salvation, Acts 11:14; 1 Corinthians 1:21; 1 Timothy 4:16' (Ibid., v).
[165] Ibid., See v-vi.
[166] Ibid., v.
[167] Ibid., vii.

God when they come to receive the holy communion more than for the hearing of the Word.'[168] But it was a foregone conclusion for the divines themselves that preaching would win out over the sacraments since the preached Word could be used for the conversion and the strengthening of the Christian, while the sacraments only for the latter.[169]

However, both of the Assembly's catechisms also give preaching an edge over the reading of the Word.[170] The reason for placing the efficacy of preaching over Bible reading is not evident at first glance. If the Bible is as good as the Assembly says it is, and if a sermon must always be judged by the Bible anyway, why not simply read the Bible? Or perhaps the Bible and Christian literature? Indeed, the divines emphasised preaching in a day when most could not read; perhaps they were addressing these statements to an illiterate or poorly literate audience, and would suggest something different in a more literate society.

At the very least it should be mentioned that every assertion (that historians can access) of the primacy of preaching over reading was delivered to a significantly literate audience – after all, much of our knowledge of these utterances comes through published sermons and treatises. Fortunately, it is also the case that the divines address the matter of reading versus preaching directly. Burroughs is typical: 'You will say, 'Cannot we sit at home and read a sermon?' No. 'The great ordinance is the preaching of the Word. Faith comes by hearing, the Scriptures say, and never by reading.'[171] He softens this somewhat when he admits that his readers 'may think that this or the other means may do the deed as well,' but expects that 'because God hath appointed this to be his ordinance, therefore, in obedience to Him ... [they] will attend upon this means rather than upon the other means.'[172]

Goodwin suggests that good books and conversations are helpful, particularly in times of spiritual drought, that a steady use of these in the absence of preaching is akin to a reliance on 'watering-pots' in the place of rain.[173] Goodwin may have the illiterate in mind when he

---

[168] Burroughs, *Gospel-Worship*, p 249.
[169] See Burroughs, *Gospel-Fear*, pp 248-249.
[170] WSC 89, WLC 155.
[171] Burroughs, *Gospel-Fear*, pp 201-202.
[172] Ibid., p 202.
[173] Goodwin, *Works*, 11:p 360.

suggests that God chose preaching so that rich and poor could both be called into the kingdom.[174] He might have been less persuasive to his contemporaries when he preached that the 'reading [of the Word] alone by ourselves' is inappropriate since 'our first parents took their infidelity in by the ear, and therefore God thought good to let faith in the same way.'[175]

Nor is the reading of the Word aloud a proper substitute for sermons. In the first place, people are dull and would miss things that the trained reader should not. Second, Ephesians 4:8 teaches that Jesus Christ ascended to give gifts to men. Goodwin argues that since so many people can read, it would be 'a derogation from Christ to make a faculty of bare reading to be one of the utmost fruits of his ascension.'[176] Lastly, it is not the letter but the 'spiritual meaning of it, as revealed and expounded,' that 'ordinarilly doth convert.' Even the Devil can quote Scripture. It often takes a preacher to bring out the sense of a passage.[177] He ends by reminding his hearers that Christ died to give gifts to the Church and among those gifts are preachers. Christ emptied himself so the Christian might be filled.[178]

Other treatments of the subject highlight different reasons for the importance of preaching. Burgess's explanation of the necessity of preaching is threefold. First, sermons recast the Word and present old things in new ways, making difficult truths digestible and allowing important doctrines to be more clearly settled. Second, there are old things in God's word that are new to his people and need to be brought out in sermons. And third, preaching is necessary for the pointed and 'powerfull application of necessary truths, to the hearts and consciences of men.'[179] Gouge draws a parallel conclusion from a different starting point when he asks how a person can understand the Bible. His answer is that one must read it, meditate on it, but also be sure to 'attend to the Preaching of Gods Word.'[180] Commenting on Mark 2:1-5, Gouge commends the sick man and his friends for their extraordinary effort in

---

[174] Ibid., p 363.
[175] Ibid.
[176] Ibid., pp 363-364.
[177] Ibid., p 364.
[178] Ibid., p 368.
[179] Burgess, *Scripture Directory*, 140.
[180] William Gouge, *The Whole Armour of God* in *Works* (1627), p 156.

trying to reach the ordinary means of grace.[181] Greenhill admits that 'some would have the word only read, and that there should be no preaching or expounding of it.' But he points out that the eunuch of Acts 8 could read the Bible but did not understand until it was expounded. Ezra and others read the law and gave its sense (Nehemiah 8:8), and Paul told Timothy to divide the word aright (2 Timothy 2:15).[182] The Bible assumed that God's people needed preaching.

Departing from exegetical arguments for the primacy of preaching, Arrow smith suggests that since Eve was deceived through hearing false words it is appropriate that we should be saved by hearing true words, and then says, 'We by hearing of the ministry of the Gospel, are brought home to God. As Calvin saith, sweetly, That we who were deceived by the subtlety of the Serpent might be saved by the foolishness of God' (1 Corinthians 1:21).[183] On another level, Gataker suggests in a prefatory epistle to Thomas Chapman that the difference between the preaching and reading of the Word is connected to the mode of communicating: the 'vivacitie and efficacie' of the 'lifelesse letter. . . cometh farre short of the living voice.'[184] And in a letter to his parishioners at Blackfriars, Gouge writes that he values preaching on the one hand simply because of 'Christ's charge, Goe Preach the Gospell.' In his mind, 'This is that Ordinance wherein and whereby God doth ordinarily, and most especially manifest his owne power, and bestow his blessing.' He also notes that 'preaching is of power especially to worke upon the affections. . . . Printing,' because it can be read multiple times, 'may be one especiall meanes to inform the

---

[181] William Gouge, *An Exposition on the whole fifth chapter of S. Johns Gospell* (1631), Part 1:143. Gouge's conclusion is an odd one, since it seems that the men were coming for miraculous healing, not preaching. Healing, in Gouge's own view, is hardly an ordinary means of grace.

[182] Greenhill sees Ezra preaching, not translating, as some argue. But it would matter little to his argument, as he brings translation in: 'If we may not expound the word because we are fallible, then why should we translate the word out of the original tongue into others, seeing they are fallible, and may, yea have, mistakes therein, as well as others in expounding and preaching' (Greenhill, *Ezekiel*, vii).

[183] Arrowsmith, *God-Man*, p 108.

[184] Thomas Gataker, *An Anniversarie Memoriall of England's delivery from the Spanish* (1637), Part 2:28.

judgements.'[185] Gataker would likely concur with this opinion as he mentions in another preface that he includes notations and scholarly references in his printed sermons that would never be appropriate when preaching in the pulpit.[186] Thus in the divines' opinion, preaching is distinct from reading, and better.

Preachers and Preaching

But what makes a preacher's preaching so special? Cannot anyone at any time expound God's Word? The answer, as Gouge provides it, comes back to a familiar text and metaphor: 2 Corinthians 5:20 and ministers as ambassadors. Gouge argues that there is one 'maine difference between [the exposition] of a minister and a private man. A Private ma[nI may have great knowledge of the mystery of the Gospell, and be able to open and declare the sense and meaning of it, but a Minister by vertue of his office hath this prerogative and preheminence above others, that in God's steede he declareth reconciliation.' This holds a lesson for the man or woman in the pew: 'When a Minister preacheth and applieth the promises of the Gospell, he doth not onely declare and make knowne Gods mercy and goodnesse to poor sinners, but also is an especiall meanes to move those sinners to believe those Promises, and to imbrace reconciliation with God.'[187] There is something special about public preaching.

Samuel Rutherford, preaching around the time that complaints were received about disruptive prayer meetings and Bible studies in the Army, also pointed out the difference between private and ministerial expositions of Scripture. 'There is a very great difference,' he says, 'between private exhortation and private preaching; even as a common sojour [soldier] gives warning to the army that the enemy is coming on them, and he who is appointed watchman, he gives also warning of the

---

[185] Gouge, 'To ... my beloved Parishioners,' in *Works* (emphasis added). Obadiah Sedgwick also brings up the enduring aspect of print when he tells his readers that 'this [book] may Preach to you when I cannot' (in the 'Epistle Dedicatory' of his *The Fountain Opened* (1657), [i].

[186] Thomas Gataker, *A Just Defence of Certain Passages in a Former Treatise concerning the Nature and Use of Lots* (1623), [iv].

[187] Gouge, *Whole Armour*, in *Works*, p 262. Emphasis his.

same.'[188] Ignoring either is foolish, but to ignore the watchman is a double sin. So, too, there is a difference 'between a master, who is clad with public authority for teaching scholars, and one of the condisciples [who] teaches another on the same lesson that he teaches.' Rutherford, who was in favour of such Bible studies and defended them at the 1640 General Assembly of the Scottish Church, argued that 'none . . . will say that either one usurps the watchman's place or the other the master's charge; but the one does what he does by a special designation for that affect, and the other as he is a member of that body.'[189] In Rutherford's view, 'A private Christian he ought to help others in the way to heaven; but he ought not to make that his study – to study divinity for that effect.'[190]

But what if preaching is not building up the Christian? What if people are not benefiting from the sermons? The divines were well aware of this problem. Alexander Henderson once admitted in a sermon, 'I know many of you who has said, when ye came out from the preaching . . . that your souls has been nothing bettered by it.'[191] One question the divines were sure to ask when this complaint was made was whether the person came with a believing heart, ready to hear God's Word. After all, the preached Word is not automatically effective; it must be received by faith. That was the essence of Henderson's response to his own people's complaints. The other question the divines would ask when the problem arose was put to the preachers: were they preaching Christ?[192] It is worth noting that this section, in contrast with the others, contains fewer prescriptive arguments. The majority of the arguments are not exegetical, but theological.

5. Christ-Centred Preaching

When he read about Ezekiel's practice of proclaiming all that the Lord had shown him, William Greenhill, an Independent, had little difficulty transferring the prophet's example into an imperative for ministers:

---

[188] Samuel Rutherford, *Quaint Sermons of Samuel Rutherford* (Morgan, Pa.: Soli Deo Gloria, 1999), p 167.
[189] Ibid., pp 1, 167-168.
[190] Ibid., p 168.
[191] Alexander Henderson, *Sermons, Prayers, and Pulpit Addresses* (1867), p 6.
[192] See Burroughs, *Gospel-Remission*, pp 112-113. He tells the ministers that if they lack the esteem and honour of the people, they had better 'take pains' to preach Christ.

they are to preach only and preach all that they learn at Christ's school (Ezekiel 11:25).[193] Burgess puts forth the same standard when he says that preachers 'must dresse every Sermon at the glasse [mirror] of the Word; they must preach as they read in Scripture.'[194] He gives three reasons for why the preacher is to preach only (and all of) what the Bible has to say, all built off Paul's exhortation in 1 Corinthians 3:10 that ministers take care how they lay their foundations.[195] The first reason to take care in preaching is God. It is his Word that ministers are purporting to preach; his honour is at stake and he does not approve of man's thoughts being substituted for his. Preaching faithfully calls for much humility, prayer and, of course, study on the part of the preacher who must be careful to speak biblical thoughts.[196] The second reason to take care in preaching is for man's sake. If God's words are not preached, the sermon loses all its use and effect. At best, it is hay and stubble – useless for spiritual nourishment, certainly not life-giving. At worst, parishioners come to drink at the fountain and are given poison. 'Foolish and unwarrantable opinions and doctrines of men' are not 'able to produce . . . gracious effects.'[197] The third reason is closest to home: preach the whole Bible for the preacher's sake. Burgess points out that the preacher is given a ministry, not a 'magistery.' God and not the preacher can best determine what Christians need. The minister 'may not be a Master to dictate and affirm what he pleaseth.' Rather, he must imitate Paul and deliver to the people what he receives from the Lord (1 Corinthians 11:23). If not, Burgess says, we 'endanger our own selvs' and others.'[198] This, he says, would make the preacher 'a snare to, or a murderer of other mens souls' and 'the blood of the soul will cry more terribly, than the blood of the body.'[199]

The divines were completely convinced of the truth of what Greenhill and Burgess were teaching: the minister must teach only and all of what God has said in his written Word. But they would never have

---

[193] Greenhill, *Ezekiel*, p 287.
[194] Burgess, *Scripture Directory*, p 141.
[195] The context of the Apostle's extended metaphor makes it clear that he has preaching ministries in view.
[196] Burgess, *Scripture Directory*, p 142. Burgess is equally careful in noting that the preacher is not to subtract from God's Word.
[197] Ibid., p 143; pp 142-43.
[198] Ibid., p 143.
[199] Ibid., p 144.

considered such instruction sufficient for the preacher. Preachers must also heed the biblical counsel of William Perkins, uttered at the conclusion of his *Art of Prophesying*. 'Preach one Christ, by Christ, to the praise of Christ.'[200] Of course, the divines would not have driven a wedge between preaching what the Bible says and preaching about the person and work of Jesus Christ. Their point was rather that the whole Bible was about the Messiah, and therefore proper exegesis demanded Christ-centred preaching. Thus Burgess argues that 'it's the main end and scope of the Scriptures only to exalt Christ, and the end of the Ministry should be the same with the end of the Scripture.'[201] Burgess backs up his claim at length: 'All the Prophets before Christ, they witnessed of the Messiah. Abraham, though [he lived] so long before Christ's Incarnation, yet it's said, 'He saw Christ's day.' The same was true in the Mosaic administration of the covenant: 'All those Rammes, those Bullocks, those Goats, they all did typifie a Christ.'[202]

It is not surprising, then, that following his exhortations to preach the whole Word of God that Burgess expounds the next verse in 1 Corinthians 3 in a Christological fashion: 'for other foundation can no man lay, then that is laid, which is Jesus Christ.'[203] Burgess has much to say about preaching Christ, the Church's one foundation. Christ is the 'only foundation, in respect of knowledge and instruction.'[204] Then moving from epistemology to ethics, he argues that 'we must preach Christ the foundation of all strength and power, from whom we receive all ability to do any thing that is good.'[205] The same applies for ecclesiology and kingdom theology, a Christ is 'head of the Church,' and 'governeth all things.'[206] Furthermore, 'Christ is to be set up the only foundation, in respect of mediation and intercession with God.'[207] Our 'persons and duties' are accepted only through him. No inheritance or blessing comes without his 'imputed righteousnesse.'[208] Burgess is only beginning! 'Christ is to be preached as the foundation of all fulnesse, for

---

[200] William Perkins, *The Art of Prophesying* (Edinburgh: Banner of Truth, 1996), p 79.
[201] Ibid., p 150.
[202] Ibid.
[203] Ibid., pp 145-156.
[204] Ibid., p 145.
[205] Ibid., p 146.
[206] Ibid.
[207] Ibid., p 147.
[208] Ibid.

all our necessities and spiritual wants.'[209] Christ is 'the Fountain of all the happiness, joy and spiritual content the godly hearer can have. We are to preach Christ as the centre in whom all the lines of your hope, love, and desire are to meet. Thus Paul himself, 'I determined to know nothing but Christ crucified,' 1 Corinthians 2:2.'[210] Christ is the one whom we are to expect to meet in the sacraments, prayer and the preaching of the Word.[211] And 'lastly, We are to preach Christ, not only as the foundation of our approaches to God, but of all Gods gracious actions and visitations to us.' By that Burgess means that 'we are not only to come to God in Christs name, but to expect that God will come to us through Christ.' For 'God is in Christ, reconciling the world to himself' (2 Corinthians 5:19).[212]

Echoing similar sentiments, Obadiah Sedgwick states that it is 'but labour lost to set up anything but Christ.' Ministers are 'to bee much in preaching Christ.' Again, 'your labours in preaching, will come to little, perhaps to nothing, if it not be Christ, or some thing in reference to Christ, on which you so laboriously insist in preaching; 'My Kingdom,' said Christ, is not of this world,' John 18:36. So your business is not the business of the world; Go then and preach the Kingdom of God.'[213] The preaching of Christ, he argues in outline, is the preacher's (1) proper work, (2) sufficient and full work, (3) honourable work, (4) excellent work, and (5) comfort. The preacher must be able to know on the Judgement day that he has preached Christ.[214]

William Gouge preached on Ephesians 6:19 where the Apostle Paul requests the saints to pray 'that utterance may be given unto me, that I may open my mouth boldly, to make known the mystery of the gospel.' Gouge deduced from the Apostle's example that 'the Gospell is the proper object of preaching.' He tells his hearers that the Great Commission was a commission to preach the Gospel. He appeals to the letter to the Romans and notes that those who are called beautiful are the ones who preach the Gospel (Romans 10:15), and he quotes Romans

---

[209] Ibid., p 148.
[210] Ibid., p 149.
[211] Ibid., pp 149-150.
[212] Ibid., p 150. The text is erroneously cited as 2 Corinthians 1:19
[213] Sedgwick, *The Fountain Opened*, p 371.
[214] Ibid., pp 371-372.

1:16 which states that 'the Gospell is the power of God unto Salvation.'[215] This does not mean that there is no place for the Law; rather, it means that the Law has a subservient place 'as a preparative unto the Gospell'; the Law is a 'schoole-master to bring us unto Christ' (Galatians 3:24).[216]

The Law was a delicate topic at and around the time of the Assembly. Antinomians were always announcing that Christians needed no laws under the gospel. In the midst of the debates over preaching, the entire Assembly ground to a halt when it considered the Preaching committee's over-zealous suggestion that sermon applications challenge Antinomians without 'the disheartening of weak Christians' by indiscrete ministers.[217] Comments by Burroughs indicate that the worry about 'indiscrete ministers' was well-founded. On more than one occasion he indicates that preaching was at times getting moralistic. A mere preaching 'against the vanities and profits of this world is neither the main thing nor the right method of preaching.'[218] Elsewhere he complains that 'it is common now to preach morality.' Of course, morality is in the sphere of preaching, but is not a replacement for the gospel. 'The great point that all ministers ought to aim at is the great point of reconciliation, and that is to be preached.'[219] Goodwin concurs. Alluding to Romans 10:15, he submits that preachers would 'add more beauty to their own feet' if they would preach more of the gospel and less of 'truths of less moment.'[220]

In the end, the reason for all the emphasis on Jesus Christ rested on the fact that they were his ambassadors and not another's. Christ came into the world saying 'I am the way, the truth and the life.' He said he was the 'bread of life' that 'came down from heaven.' He preached himself as good news to the world. His ambassadors were given the same commission. This was, as Burgess notes, no new thing for 'all the Prophets were Prophets of Christ' and 'all the Officers in the New Testament, are the Officers of Christ.'[221] Burroughs also highlights the fact that it is not only the main task of the preacher to preach 'gospel

---

[215] Gouge, *Whole Armour*, in *Works*, p 255.
[216] Ibid., p 254.
[217] Lightfoot, *Works*, 13: p 280. The motion was sent back to the committee for further work.
[218] Burroughs, *Gospel-Remission*, pp 112-13.
[219] Burroughs, *Gospel-Reconciliation*, p 246.
[220] Goodwin, *Works*, 11: p 228.
[221] Burgess, *Scripture Directory*, p 145.

reconciliation,' but that 'it is their commission to preach that especially.'[222] It is little wonder, then, that after studying John 1:6-9, John Arrowsmith found his ideal model in John the Baptist, the last prophet of the old era whom the Apostle John commends as one who bore witness to the Light, always emphasising that Christ must increase while he must decrease.[223] True ministers, Arrowsmith writes, 'set up Christ in their ministry; they are content themselves to stand in the crowd, and to lift up Christ upon their shoulders; content, not to be seen themselves, so Christ be exalted.'[224]

6. 'The Spirit's working'

In an afternoon communion sermon at Anwoth, in April of 1647, Samuel Rutherford told his auditors that the 'Word's working and the Spirit's working is not tied to the hour of the sand-glass,' neither is the Spirit tied to a pulpit, and a gown, and a minister's tongue.'[225] Elsewhere he asks, 'What can preaching of men or angel doe without God[;] is it not God and God only who can open the heart?'[226] Rutherford did not intend to devalue preaching; he warns explicitly that 'this doctrine should be right understood, for it warrants not the conventicles and unwarrantable meetings of Separatists and Brownists, who despise public meetings.'[227] But Rutherford does raise an important aspect of the divines' theology of preaching, which, if left unmentioned, would leave their portrait of the preacher incomplete.

In contending that preaching is 'the only ordinary Way that God hath appointed, either for the beginnings or encrease of grace,' the Westminster divines were always ready to admit that preaching did not appear to be a sensible means of advancing the gospel.[228] Burgess states quite openly that 'this instituted means [preaching] is very unlikely for such glorious effects to a carnal eie.'[229] Even in the seventeenth century,

---

[222] Burroughs, *Gospel-Reconciliation*, p 246.
[223] Arrowsmith, *God-Man*, p 103.
[224] Ibid., p 104; see also pp 112-113.
[225] Rutherford, *Quaint Sermons*, p 125.
[226] Samuel Rutherford, *A Free Disputation against Pretended Liberty of Conscience* (1649), p 351.
[227] Rutherford, *Quaint Sermons*, p 125.
[228] Burgess, *Scripture Directory*, p 69.
[229] Ibid., p 69.

preaching was 'very despicable and contemptible to human reason.' And citing 1 Corinthians 1:21, Burgess italicises (literally) the fact that Paul refers to 'the foolishness of preaching.' This is not, the divine is quick to say, 'that it is so indeed, for it's the wisdome of God to salvation; but the Apostle calls it so according to the principles of human wisdom.' This applies both to the 'matter' and 'manner of preaching'; both are 'very unlikely ever to produce such effects: The matter is high, paradoxical, incredible to flesh and blood; The manner of delivering is plain, without the affected wisdom of the world, without either miraculous signes' to please the old world 'or scientifical demonstrations' to please the new, 'either of which would persuade men.'[230] Certainly it was not without reason that in his *Treatise of Original Sin* Burgess gives a stern warning to the sophisticated in the audience not to despise preaching, as Augustine once had.[231]

The problem with preaching, then, is partly with the matter preached, partly with the plain style of the Word itself. Burgess points out 'that Preachers of the Word, differ from all the humane Oratours, Greek and Latin,' for orators might 'by their eloquence and affections, perswade their Hearers; for it was about Civil and Moral matters, about which men had understandings naturally able to perceive, and wils, naturally able to choose the things perswaded.'[232] Thus persuasion, for Burgess, is readily possible under normal circumstances. But nothing is normal with preaching. 'Preaching is about those things, to which man hath no understanding to believe, nor no heart to receive. But God must give the hearing ear, and the seeing eye, else we miscarry.' He concludes, slipping into doxology. that 'all is of God, both the Word to be heard, and the Ear to hear. Both the Word to be believed, and the heart to believe.'[233]

If men and women are so unwilling to hear the gospel, and if preaching is ineffectual without God, 'What use is there of Preaching? What need of the ministry?'[234] The answer always offered is that God has appointed both the ends and the means of salvation. He has determined both the message of the Gospel and the method by which it is to be

---

[230] Ibid.
[231] Anthony Burgess, *A Treatise of Original Sin* (1658), pp 364-365.
[232] Burgess, *Scripture Directory*, p 87.
[233] Ibid.
[234] Ibid., p 86.

heard. As Burgess says, 'Though God only gives the encrease, yet it is only in and through the Ministery.'[235] While the Assembly's Erastians have little or nothing to say about the whole matter, the Independents also feel the same tension and give the same answer: 'You will say,' Burroughs predicts, 'What need do we have, then, for so much preaching, and for such arguments to work upon our hearts?' The answer: 'We are bound to do what befits creatures to do and to leave God to do what pleases Him.'[236]

But Westminster's theologians, being the inquisitive type, push the matter further. Why did God appoint means? Why preaching? Two main reasons are supplied, and Arrowsmith, in his exposition of John 1:6-7, points out both of them. Arrowsmith opens by underlining the fact 'that God hath appointed the ministry of men to be used among men.'[237] The first reason for preaching is that humankind is unable to bear the ministry of angels and certainly cannot endure direct contact with God. Manoah and his wife, Zachariah, and the virgin Mary herself were all quite overcome by the angels that visited them; the people of Israel were completely unable to endure the glorious presence of God at Mount Sinai, begging Moses to speak with God in their place. Thus out of necessity, Arrowsmith says, men are sent to preach to men and women. The second reason Arrowsmith supplies is found in the New Testament, where Paul speaks about preaching in 2 Corinthians 4:7 and says, 'We have this treasure in earthen vessels' so that (and Arrowsmith highlights this) 'the excellency of the power may be of God, and not of us.'[238]

Thus the 'problem' with preaching is itself the answer. The reliance upon God and the work of his Spirit is not a reason to abandon preaching, but is the reason for preaching. God deliberately chose a humble means that would amplify his own greatness. Burgess derives an identical lesson from 2 Corinthians 4:7 but also harks back to the metaphor of 1 Corinthians 3 where Paul reminds his readers that the preacher may sow and water, but God gives the increase.[239] And though preachers are described as co-workers with God (2 Corinthians 6:1),[240]

---

[235] Ibid.
[236] Burroughs, *Gospel-Fear*, p 92.
[237] Arrowsmith, *God-Man*, p 96.
[238] Ibid., pp 97-98.
[239] Burgess, *Spiritual Refining*, pp 497, 495.
[240] Ibid., p 495.

Burgess is quick to say that a minister may be faithful but have no success since 'successe is Gods work, not the Ministers duty.'[241]

The Independents agree again. 'It is not the means that work,' Burroughs says, 'but God in the means.' Again, 'Suppose one came and preached the most powerful sermon that ever was. Yet unless God was pleased to go out with the Word, it would never work savingly to humble your souls.'[242] Coming full circle, this does not make the training and study of the minister irrelevant or unimportant. Burgess writes, 'It's true (indeed) that the Parts and Abilities of one Minister, may be objectively better for Conversion, and more likely for profiting then another: They may propound stronger Arguments to convince the Conscience: They may set those Arguments home with greater life and vigour,' but 'God only is the efficient Cause of every good and perfect Gift.'[243] Goodwin points out that this dependence on God gives God all the glory: 'He hath chosen preaching of the word, because it is the weakest means of all others, and therefore his power would the more appear unto his glory in it.'[244]

God is therefore to receive the glory at every point in the preaching of the Gospel. He sent his Son; he sends the preachers. His word is spoken, and his power awakens sinners. He is glorified in the preaching of Jesus Christ, the Saviour of the world. And he is glorified in awaking dead sinners. 'God only giveth the increase,' says Burgess, 'because of the deep pollution that is in every man, who is not only blind and deaf, but dead.'[245] Again, 'God only can give the encrease, because he only hath a soveraignty [sic] and power over the heart. Others may speak to the ear, propound Arguments to perswade; but to change the heart, to perswade the heart indeed, that God only can who

---

[241] Ibid., p 503; see pp 500-503.
[242] Burroughs, *Gospel-Fear*, p 92.
[243] Burgess, *Scripture Directory*, p 87.
[244] Goodwin, *Works*, 11: p 362.
[245] Burgess, *Scripture Directory*, p 87

made the heart.... And so, we Ministers are to look up to God, and you people, that God may be glorified.'[246]

To quote Burgess again, 'successe is Gods work, not the Ministers duty.'[247] Or as Rutherford put it, the benefit of the preaching rests in 'the Spirit's working.

In summing up these six emphases in the Assembly-men's pulpit theology, two main patterns can be noted, one historical, the other theological. The first pattern is the unity regarding these six characteristics of preachers and preaching. The Presbyterian Scots and England's Presbyterians and Independents alike provide a similar portrayal of the pulpit. However much the Scots might argue that the Independents were like the sectaries in their church government and had tendencies toward radicalism, the published works of the Independents themselves reject individualism, anti-clericalism and moralism, and insist on correct doctrine and the preaching of Christ by the power of the Holy Spirit. The egalitarianism and anti-intellectualism of the sects does not appear to obtain among Westminster's Independents. Rather, the picture of the trained, ordained preacher as God's ambassador dominates their attention and governs their understanding of the pulpit. Only in the privacy of the Assembly's debates could it be seen that the Independents were actually driven to accept lay-preaching to a very significant extent, thus giving credence to some Presbyterian concerns.

The second aspect of the Assembly's thought, and one evidenced by all parties, is a concern for a biblical theology of preaching. The divines rarely, if ever, appeal for their form of preaching on the basis of 'reasonableness.' Nor do they heap up proof-texts like stones without mortar. True to their insistence on the proper exposition of the word in preaching, only infrequently do they cite a text in passing without providing some explication. The fault is probably in the other

---

[246] Ibid., pp 86-87. Similar sentiments are stated explicitly by other divines. Reynolds, for example, quotes 1 Peter 1:12 as proof that the Holy Spirit is needed for effective preaching (Edward Reynolds, *Works* (Published 1999), 2:148). But often God's help for faithful ministers is not discussed but merely assumed, though not ungratefully. In the preface of a popular work, Gouge mentions that it was difficult for him to find the time to 'set down distinctly such points as by Gods assistance were uttered [from] Out of the Pulpet.' William Gouge, *A Guide to Goe to God* (1636), [iii].

[247] Burgess, *Spiritual Refining*, p 502.

direction; occasionally the divines are found dwelling on a biblical metaphor or truth for so many pages that they ultimately over-stay their welcome.

5. Conclusion

This brief study does not constitute a reconstruction of a Puritan pastoral theology. Hopefully such a work will eventually appear, and perhaps it could take the Assembly as its focus. Nor is this an exhaustive study even of the Assembly's theology of preaching. I have only scratched the surface of the Assembly's debates and the writings of its members. Hopefully a monograph on the subject will appear one day. Yet even with its limitations, many of which I am surely unaware of, I think we can draw some preliminary conclusions. One purpose of this study was to outline the intellectual prehistory of the Assembly in order to discover historical precedents to the Assembly's theology of preaching. Looking back, it appears that the Westminster Assembly evidences an historical reliance on, or at least an historical continuity with, previous Puritan and Reformed views of the pulpit.

Tentatively, I think we can also posit a shift of focus on the part of the Westminster divines during the civil war. Before the war, Archbishop Laud and his alleged popery were enemy number one, in part because of Laud's opposition to Reformed preaching. Once the war began, a myriad of religious fanatics and self-appointed preachers began to appear. The rise of the radical lay-preachers appears to have only intensified the divines' insistence on a proper pulpit theology and the ordinary means of grace. Although there may have been varying degrees of antipathy to these sects, and while the Presbyterians appear the busiest apologists of the Assembly, all the parties at the Assembly opposed religious radicalism. This social sketch of the Assembly's history indicates that the Assembly was aware of the religious currents around them, but refused to change their vision of the preacher and his preaching.

The reason for this refusal is undoubtedly rooted in the conviction, at least among the Presbyterians and Independents, that the Bible provided an unambiguous theology of the pulpit. God appointed extraordinary ambassadors in the form of the Apostles and continues to appoint ordinary ambassadors in the church in the form of ministers or preachers. These men are set aside, trained and ordained for a special function. The only settings where an every-member ministry was allowable was at an Assembly such as Westminster's, where aside from a small bevy of politicians, every member was in fact a minister. Thus, though the radical sects wanted every sheep to be a shepherd, the divines, like their forebears, insisted that God appointed some to be teachers and some to be taught. The divines did not always express this felicitously, as they occasionally divided up the church, without flattering either group, into 'ministers and people' or 'ministers and Christians.'[248] They were, however, always clear that God had given the Church preachers, and she was to be thankful for them.

While Westminster's Erastians were usually quiet about preaching, the Presbyterian and Independents were both outspoken and unified about preaching, aside from a differing conception of the preacher's ordination. They all agreed that a preacher must be trained, must not vary from the Word of God, and must preach Christ, relying on God's Spirit for blessing. The Presbyterians and Independents were also agreed about how their parishioners were to receive the preaching: they are to hear faithful sermons as the Word of God, and depend on preaching as the most ordinary and effective means of grace, provided it is heard with faith and blessed by God. But if preaching is so important, then the preacher's troubles have just begun. In a special sermon delivered by Edward Reynolds to his fellow divines, he warned them that if they were correct about the preacher's duties, then life will be hard work. The fact is, there are 'noe conditions of life which are not subject to temptations of selfe-seeking.' Thus if there is to be 'soe much preaching . . . we must resolve to live a tedious life. Therfore pray that God would power out a large spirit of selfe denyall.'[249]

6. Epilogue.

What was true of pulpit theology at the Assembly was true for Presbyterians and Independents for the next two centuries. Preaching was central in worship and central in piety, and provided a unifying dynamic for both Presbyterians and Congregationalists. Even during the First Great Awakening, most of the revival preachers of Britain and

---

[248] See, for example, WLC, answer 54; Burroughs, *Saints' Happiness*, p 260.
[249] Minutes 3:97r-v.

America were trained, ordained preachers – Welsh-born Howell Harris is the prominent exception. At the very least, preaching was regarded as central to Christian life and worship. The preaching of God's ambassadors was still the ordinary means which God extraordinarily blessed.

It seems to me that this all changed with the Second Great Awakening. During this Awakening Charles Finney introduced new measures and means with his anxious bench, and D. L. Moody, who was admirably gifted, saw no need for the church to train, ordain, or send him. Moody sent himself. Of course, similar things happened during and after the Westminster Assembly. The difference was that during the Assembly, Presbyterians and Independents considered such measures radical; during the middle of the nineteenth century, these measures became mainstream.

The history of preaching in the 1640s and in subsequent centuries presents something of a challenge for the church today. Church members sometimes prefer simply to read their Bibles at home and not trouble with the commute to a corporate worship service. Some people do not like being 'preached at' and have bad memories of rowdy street preachers or unsavoury televangelists. Perhaps the time has come to change the means used to present the message. Pastors have taken up the challenge and consider eliminating the evening worship service (and sermon) and opting for the easier route of home Bible studies. Pastoral practice may at times collate with seminary curricula, as some centres for pastoral training have been known to provide courses on the content of the gospel, followed by courses on the technique of communicating the gospel, without ever telling the student why he should preach. Some Christians, by-passing pastors and seminaries altogether, feel a personal call to preach but feel no desire to seek the approval of the Church.

But perhaps the time has not come to change the means. A great theme of the Reformation was *semper reformanda* or 'always being reformed.'[250] Calvin and his contemporaries held that a healthy church would always be continuously reformed by the Word of God. In their historical context, a step forward involved a look backward. While

---

[250] The participle is passive, and does not allow the more progressive sounding, 'always reforming.'

the Reformers were familiar with the medieval church and learned from the Schoolmen where possible, they most frequently harked back to the sources: the Church Fathers and ultimately, to the Bible itself. Maybe the largest step forward that the Church could take today would also involve a look backward. From Calvin to the Westminster Assembly and, arguably, for two hundred years following the Assembly, Church members centred their worship and their lives around the words of God's ambassadors. Whether the ambassadors were extraordinary or ordinary, in any usage of these words, preaching was seen to be the ordinary means of grace for the believer, to be used by God in extraordinary ways.

The same understanding of preaching was held by a one-time scorner of the institution, Augustine of Hippo, who in the opening lines of his *Confessions* echoes the questions of Romans 10:14 '*sed quis te invocat nesciens te?... An potius invocaris, ut sciaris? Quomodo autem invocabunt, in quem non crediderunt? Aut quomodo credent sine praedicante?*'[251] It would serve the Church well to ask these questions once again: How shall we call on him in whom we have not believed? And how shall we believe in him of whom we have not heard? And how shall we hear without a preacher? And how will they preach, except they be sent? These are not, of course, only Augustine's questions, Calvin's questions, or the Assembly's questions. If they were only that, we could dismiss them, or say with Herbert Palmer that 'if the authority of Mr. Calvin shall make my people believe my word I would rather have had my mouth stoped [caulked].' But these are the questions of the Apostle Paul himself and, as Palmer rightly assumed, the name of such a man does give authority.

---

[251] Augustine, *Confessions*, Book I, section i. "Who is there that calls upon you without knowing you?... Perhaps we call on you that we may know you. 'But how shall they call on him in whom they have not believed? Or how shall they believe without a preacher?'"

'To Bring Men to Heaven by Preaching': John Donne's Evangelistic Sermons

Peter Adam

1. Was John Donne also among the Puritans?...................264
2. An Anatomy of John Donne's evangelistic preaching... 269
   - 2.1 The Bible..269
   - 2.2 The Gospel of Jesus Christ and his atoning death.........273
   - 2.3 Preaching..277
   - 2.4 Effective Preaching..281
3. Donne's evangelistic sermon on 1 Timothy 1:15..............286
4. Conclusion 290
   BIBLIOGRAPHY... 291

PETER J. H. ADAM served several curacies in Melbourne, Australia and studied in England at both London and Durham Universities, gaining a PhD from the latter on the practice of the imitation of Christ with special reference to the theology of Dietrich Bonhoeffer in 1981. After several years as a tutor at St. John's College, Durham he returned to Australia and was minister of St. Jude's, Carlton for 20 years and Anglican Chaplain to Melbourne University. He became Principal of Ridley Mission and Ministry College, Melbourne in 2002 and has published several books on biblical spirituality and exposition including *Hearing God's Words* and *Written for Us*.

This lecture is dedicated to Donne's descendants, the evangelistic preachers of the Anglican Communion

Væ mihi est si non euangelizavero
Woe to me if I do not preach the gospel

I thank the St Antholin's Lectureship Trustees for their invitation to prepare this lecture. I have wanted to work on Donne's sermons for many years, so I am grateful for this opportunity to do so. I thank Kanishka Raffel for his encouragement, and Ruth Millard and Peter Angelovski for their practical assistance. My thanks also to Andrew Atherstone and Margaret Hobbs of the Latimer Trust..

I am also grateful to those who have written on John Donne's preaching, and whose labour has been so helpful to me.

Quotations retain original spelling, and are from *The Sermons of John Donne*, Volumes 1 – 10, [1953-1962], eds., Potter, M. R. and Simpson, E. M., Berkeley: University of California Press, and from his trial sermons, Donne, John, [1952], *John Donne: Essays in Divinity*, ed., Simpson, Evelyn M., Oxford: Clarendon Press.

John Donne in Brief

1572	Born
1615	Ordained, and made a royal Chaplain
1616–1621	Rector of Keyston, Huntingdonshire
1616–1622	Divinity Reader at Lincoln's Inn
1616–1631	Rector of Sevenoaks, Kent
1621–1631	Dean of St Paul's Cathedral
1622–1631	Rector of Blunham, Bedfordshire
1624–1631	Vicar of St Dunstan's, Fleet Street, London
1631	Died

1. Was John Donne also among the Puritans?

What justification can there be for including a study of John Donne's sermons in a Lectureship dedicated to Puritan Divinity? Here are some brief answers to that question.

1. We should not fall into the trap of thinking that in Donne's lifetime, Puritans could not be Anglicans, and Anglicans could not be Puritans. One sign of success of any reform movement is the number and influence of its ordained and lay leaders: another equally important sign is its success in changing the culture of the church to which it belongs. Though Donne did not identify with the Puritans,[1] his theology of the gospel and his commitment to preaching reflected the triumph of Reformed and Puritan ideals within the Church of England. The Jacobean Church[2] was Reformed in theology,[3] so debate was often about Reformed theology and practice, and the right application of Calvin's thought.[4] Here the *via media* was a mid point between varied Reformed ideas and practices. In the words of Patrick Collinson, Calvinism was the 'theological cement of the Jacobean church,' which bound together conformists and moderate puritans.[5] It was anachronistic and inaccurate for Potter and Simpson to describe Donne as 'Anglo-Catholic.'[6] Donne was a good example of a pre-Laudian and pre-Caroline Reformation Anglican of the Jacobean Church.[7]

---

[1] Though see Daniel W. Doerksen, '"Saint Paul's Puritan": Donne's Puritan Imagination in the Sermons' in Raymond-Jean Frontain and Frances Malpezzie, *John Donne's Religious Imagination: Essays in Honor of John T. Shawcross* (Conway: UCA Press, 1995).

[2] James I reigned from 1603-1625.

[3] Leonard J. Trinterud, ed., *Elizabethan Puritanism* (New York: Oxford University Press, 1971), p 11.

[4] Daniel W. Doerksen, *Conforming to the Word: Herbert, Donne and the English Church before Laud* (Lewisburg: Bucknell University Press, 1997), chapter 1.

[5] Patrick Collinson, *The Religion of Protestants: The Church in English Society 1559-1625* (Oxford: Clarendon, 1982), p 83.

[6] John Donne, *The Sermons of John Donne*, (Vols. I – X; eds., M. R. Potter and E. M. Simpson; Berkeley: University of California Press, 1953-1962), I, p 113.

[7] William Laud, Bishop of London 1628, then Canterbury 1633, promoted and enforced anti-Puritan policies, Arminian theology, and pre-Reformation liturgy. Charles I became King in 1625, and the Caroline Divines were High Church leaders [including Laud], whose ideas and policies he promoted.

2. 'Puritan' could refer to mainstream Anglicans who hoped for and worked for the continuing reformation of the Church of England [Tyacke's 'the mainstream of Calvinistic episcopalianism'[8]], as it could also refer to 'separatists,' and to Presbyterians, who wanted Bishops to be replaced.[9] Donne was content with the reformation that had already taken place in the Church of England, and regarded it as superior to the more drastic changes in some continental churches. He also had a great respect for the monarch as the magistrate.[10] He expected conformity to the established patterns of ministry and liturgy, not because they were all commanded by the Bible, but because they were the patterns of his ordered Church. He distanced himself from any movement that imposed repressive liturgical practices as if they had divine authority, including some Puritans, Roman Catholics, and Laudians. He also distanced himself from separatists, from extreme Reformed doctrines of predestination and the incapacity of the human will,[11] from Puritan preaching that focussed too closely on words within texts and missed their significance in their context, and from illiterate and unprepared extemporary preaching. He also criticised some Puritans when their theology and practice was merely a reaction against Rome.[12] He was also aware of the dangers of excessive disputation and division: 'The more disputing, the lesse believing,'[13] and also criticised those who wrote negative books: 'we see more books written by these men against one another, then by them both, for Christ.'[14] However, he himself used the language of Reformed piety, followed Puritan patterns of personal holiness,[15] and held a

---

[8] Nicholas Tyacke, as quoted in Collinson, *Protestants*, p 82. See Wallace Benn, *Ussher on Bishops* pp 97ff in this volume.

[9] See Mark E. Dever, *Richard Sibbes: Puritanism and Calvinism in Late Elizabethan and Early Stuart England* (Macon: Mercer University Press, 2000), chapters 2 and 7, for an example of contemporary Puritan Anglicanism.

[10] His belief in 'the godly prince,' despite the personal idiosyncrasies of the monarch, had a profound effect on his theology and practice.

[11] King James had instructed all preachers to avoid disputes in sermons on these issues in 1622. Donne's sermon to mark these 'Directions to Preachers' is found in Donne, *Sermons* IV, sermon 7.

[12] Donne, *Sermons* II, p 175.

[13] Donne, *Sermons* III, p 240.

[14] Donne, *Sermons* IV, p 246.

[15] 'So I say, let me live the life of a Puritan, let the zeal of the house of the Lord consume, me, let a holy life, and an humble obedience to the Law testify me reverence to God in his Church and in his Magistrate...this is a Saint *Paul's Puritan...a pure heart..pure hands...pure consciences.*' Donne, *Sermons* I, p 188. See also Donne, *Sermons* IX, p 166 where he claims to be both Papist ['I fast and pray'], and Puritan ['I will endeauvour to be pure'].

Reformed view of the gospel and the Bible.[16] David Edwards wrote of Donne:

> He belonged to the sizeable group in the Church under James I which was in important ways Puritan without being fully Calvinist.[17]

Furthermore, he held together these convictions with the belief that he conformed to the true 'Catholique Church.'[18] He valued traditions, and also knew the early church fathers should be followed as 'Guides, not as Lords of our understandings.'[19] For Donne, there was no incompatibility between being a member of the Catholic Church and his Reformed identity and model of ministry. The Church of England had many moderate Puritans in leadership, and many more in ministry, in Donne's time. Among the former were Archbishop Abbot, Toby Matthew of Durham then York, Thomas Morton of Durham, John Davenant of Salisbury, Joseph Hall of Exeter then Norwich,[20] and John King of London.[21] Among the latter were Richard Sibbes, William Gouge, Thomas Adams, Jeremiah Burroughs, William Whitaker, and Thomas Mountford.[22] Donne's comment on Lady Danvers, the mother of George Herbert, is illuminating: she 'never diverted towards the *Papist*, in undervaluing the *Scripture*, nor towards the *Separatist*, in undervaluing the *Church*.'[23] Izaac Walton records that as Donne faced death, he said,

> I am to be judged by a mercifull God, who hath given me [even at this time] some testimonies by his holy Spirit, that I am of the number of His Elect. I am ful of joy, and shall die in peace.[24]

And he spoke of 'that holy confidence, which belongs to a true

---

[16] For example, he believed in 'conditional election.'
[17] David L. Edwards, *John Donne, Man of Flesh and Spirit* (London and New York: Continuum, 2001), p 319.
[18] Donne, *Sermons* VII, p 61.
[19] Donne, *Sermons* IX, p 161.
[20] Frank Livingstone Huntley, *Bishop Joseph Hall 1574-1656: A Biographical and Critical Study* (Cambridge: D. S. Brewer, 1979).
[21] To these we could add Archbishop Ussher of Ireland, and Archbishop Leighton of Glasgow.
[22] For Mountford see Doerksen, *Conforming*, ch. 4.
[23] As quoted in Doerksen, *Conforming*, p 42.
[24] H. W. Garrod, *John Donne, Poetry and Prose: with Izaac Walton's life, etc* (Oxford: Clarendon Press, 1946), p xlii.

convert.'[25]

Donne disliked labels in an age when labels were a political necessity. However in his early life he worked with John Morton, later Bishop of Durham, in an apologetic appealing to Roman Catholics to join the Church of England. He rejoiced in the Reformation, and described it as 'a deliverance, a victory, a glorious ascent, a miracle, one of the mercies of God.'[26] He criticised the Council of Trent, for example, for its tendency 'to make Problematical Things, Dogmatical; and matter of Disputation, matter of Faith.'[27] He valued Augustine as a theologian,[28] and Calvin and Luther as Bible commentators.[29] However, he also preached that Antichrist and idolatry were found in all churches, not just in Rome: Antichrist is, 'all supplanters, and all seducers, all opposers of the kingdome of Christ, in us,'[30] and, 'As many habituall sins as we embrace, so many Idols we worship.'[31]

3. He shared with other Puritans the belief that preaching was the heart of ordained ministry. Many Puritans followed a plain style of preaching,[32] a style that was appropriate when, as in the case of Richard Greenham, serving in the parish of Dry Drayton, even the churchwardens could not write.[33] Other Puritans used a more ornate style, comparable to that of Donne. These included Thomas Adams ['the prose Shakespeare of Puritan theologians'[34]], Preacher at St Gregory's in the crypt of St Paul's Cathedral,[35] Joseph Hall ['the English Seneca'[36]],

---

[25] Donne, *Sermons* VI, p347.
[26] Doerksen, *Conforming*, p 23.
[27] Donne, *Sermons* IV, p 144, see also I, pp 252, 253; II, pp 203, 204, 302, 303.
[28] Donne, *Sermons* X, pp 376-386 [Appendix A], and [more positively] Mary Ashagouni Papazian, ed., *John Donne and the Protestant Reformation: New Perspectives* (Detroit: Wayne State University Press, 2003), chapter 3.
[29] Donne, *Sermons* X, pp 375, 390, and see III, p 177; VI, p 301; X, p 128. He also received a Dort Medal when he travelled to The Hague, and mentioned it in his Will. R. C. Bald, *John Donne: A Life* (London: Oxford University Press, 1970), p 563.
[30] Donne, *Sermons* VI, p 150.
[31] Donne, *Sermons* V, p 203.
[32] William Perkins, *The Art of Prophesying* (Edinburgh: Banner of Truth, [1562] 1996).
[33] John H. Primus, *Richard Greenham: Portrait of an Elizabethan pastor* (Macon, Georgia: Mercer University Press, 1998), p 32.
[34] David L. Larsen, *The Company of the Preachers: A History of Biblical Preaching* (Grand Rapids: Kregel, 1998), p 265.
[35] 'Thomas Adams and John Donne,' *Notes and Queries*, May-June, 1976, pp 229, 230, and John Chandos, ed., *In God's Name: Examples of Preaching in England 1534-1662* (London: Hutchinson, 1971), pp 155-196.

Henry Smith and John Prideaux.[37] Donne shared his great commitment to preaching with his colleagues in the Jacobean Church. The Canon forbidding 'prophesyings' [popular sermons and training in preaching] was repealed in 1604, the new translation of the Bible requested by Puritans was published in 1611, and it was King James who predicted that Donne would be a great preacher:

> I know Mr. Donne is a learned man, has the abilities of learned Divine; and will prove a powerful Preacher.[38]

For Donne, preaching was the heart of ministry.

> It hath been my desire [and God may be pleased to grant it to me] that I might die in the pulpit.[39]

He also knew that preaching must be based on the Bible, and criticised those who 'make the emergent affaires of the time, their *Text*, and the humours of their hearers their *Bible*.[40] In Donne's time, as after the Restoration, in the words of Margaret Whinney, 'Exposition rather than the mysteries of religion was the major concern of the Anglican Church.'[41]

---

[36] Larsen, *The Company*, p 221.

[37] Hughes Oliphant Old, *The Reading and Preaching of the Scriptures in the Worship of the Christian Church*, Volume 4, *The Age of the Reformation* (Grand Rapids: Eerdmans, 1999), p 333. Some Puritans were opposed to the use of just one [plain] style of preaching: See Chad B. Van Dixhoorn, *A Puritan Theology of Preaching* in this volume, p 227 note 90

[38] William R. Mueller, *John Donne: Preacher* (Princeton: Princeton University Press, 1962), pp 24, 25. James was so committed to preaching that in Chapel the service would be interrupted and the sermon begun on his arrival! Larsen, *The Company*, p 210.

[39] Mueller, *John Donne*, p 3.

[40] Donne, *Sermons* IV, p 276.

[41] Quoted in Horton Davies, *Worship and Theology in England* (3 vols. (6 parts); Grand Rapids: Eerdmans, 1996), Part II, p 44. See also the words of Christopher Wren, quoted on that same page: 'in our reformed Religion, it should seem vain to make a parish church larger than that all who are present can both see and hear...The Romanists, indeed, may build larger churches, it is enough if they hear the murmur of the Mass, and see the Elevation of the Host, but ours are to be fitted for Auditories ... To hear the service, and both to hear distinctly, and see, the Preacher.'

In summary, I am not claiming that Donne was a Puritan, but that he was a true servant of a Reformed Church.[42] The success of the Puritan movement was demonstrated in the theology of John Donne, and in his focus on the priority of preaching and evangelism. In these things he was a 'mainline' Anglican of the Jacobean Church.

2. An Anatomy of John Donne's evangelistic preaching

There are four foundations and ingredients of Donne's evangelistic preaching, each essential, and each powerfully present in many of his sermons, but especially in his preaching of the Gospel, whether at St Paul's, to the King, in parish churches, or on special occasions. They form not only the foundation of his preaching, but are also vividly present in the content and presentation of the sermons. They are: the Bible, the gospel of Jesus Christ and his atoning death, Preaching, and more especially, Effective Preaching.

2.1. *The Bible*

'The Scriptures are God's Voyce; The Church is his Eccho.'[43]

John Donne describes and treats the Scriptures as the word and 'Voyce' of God. So the material of his preaching was the exposition of the words of Scripture, and the strength, passion, and urgency of his preaching comes from his awareness of his great responsibility to project God's eloquent words.

The Scriptures are God voice, God's words: so those who hear and obey those words then communicate them to others, and communicate with God's accent:

> The Scriptures are God's Voyce; The Church is his Eccho; a redoubling, a repeating of some particular syllables, and accents

---

[42] I am aware of the danger of making Donne in my own image! See Jeanne Shami, 'Labels, Controversy, and the Language of Inclusion in Donne's Sermons,' chapter 7 in David Colclough, ed., *John Donne's Professional Lives* (Cambridge: D. S. Brewer, 2003), pp 135-157.
[43] Donne, *Sermons* VI, p 223.

of the same voice.⁴⁴

Donne wrote his 'Essays in Divinity' as trial sermons to test his vocation to ordained ministry. Here we see his belief that the Bible was the work of the Holy Spirit.

> God hath two Books of life, that in the *Revelation*, and else where, which is an eternall Register of his Elect; and this Bible. For of this, it is therefore said, *Search the Scriptures, because in them ye hope to have eternall life.*⁴⁵

According to Donne, the Bible was written 'by Gods own finger,'⁴⁶ he wrote of 'the author of all the book, the Holy Ghost.'⁴⁷ So the Bible is, 'Gods fairest Temple, his Word,'⁴⁸ and so, 'No garment is so neer God as his word: which is so much his, as it is *he.*'⁴⁹ The worst judgement of God is a famine of the word of God.

> God choses that comparison to express his greatest affliction of all, which is a famine of his word...It is a Rack, without either Engine or Executioner; a devouring poison, and yet be substraction; and a way to make a man kill himself by doing nothing.⁵⁰

As the Bible is God's word, so God's 'flock [are those] which hearken together of his voice, his Word.'⁵¹ He spoke in the highest terms of the Bible:

> As much as Paradise exceeded all the places of the earth, doe the Scriptures of God exceed Paradise. In the midst of Paradise grew the *Tree of knowledge*, and the *Tree of life*: in this Paradise, the Scripture, every word is both these Trees; there is Life and Knowledge in every word of the Word of God.⁵²

Donne preached his first sermon at Greenwich in 1615 on the text from

---

⁴⁴ Ibid., *Sermons* VI, p 223.
⁴⁵ John Donne, *John Donne: Essays in Divinity*, (ed., Evelyn M. Simpson; Oxford: Clarendon Press, 1952), p 6.
⁴⁶ Donne, *Essays*, p 9.
⁴⁷ Ibid., p 48.
⁴⁸ Ibid., pp 40, 41.
⁴⁹ Ibid., p 39.
⁵⁰ Ibid., pp 68, 69.
⁵¹ Ibid., p 49.
⁵² Donne, *Sermons* VIII, p 131.

Isaiah 52:3, 'Ye have sold your selves for nought, and ye shall be redeemed without money.'[53] He said that these words conveyed both the miserable condition of man, and the abundant mercy of Christ Jesus, 'which the holy Ghost hath been pleased to express both these in the text.'[54]

The Bible is also a means by which the Bible writers express their humanity:

> As the prophets, and the other Secretaries of the holy Ghost in penning the books of Scriptures, do for the most part retain, and express in their writings some impressions, and some air of their former professions.[55]

So it is the product of human as well as divine activity:

> [A]s Christ is God too, so as that he is Man too; so the Scriptures are from God so, as that they are from Man too: the Gospel is a faithful word essentially, as it is the word of God, derived from him, and it is a faithful word too.[56]

We dare not add to the Bible:

> The body of the Scriptures hath in it limbs taken from other bodies; and in the word of God, are the words of other men, other authors, inlaid and inserted. But, this work is only where the Holy Ghost is the Workman: It is not for man to insert, to inlay other words into the word of God.[57]

Donne saw the unity of Scripture not only in its divine origin but also in its one message: 'Salvation was ever from a faith in the promise of the *Messias*.'[58] Yet he also saw the distinction between Old and New Testaments:

> though their and our Law differ not as diverse in species; but as a perfect and grown thing from an unperfect and growing.[59]

---

[53] Donne, *Sermons* I, pp 151-167.
[54] Ibid., p 152.
[55] Ibid., p 236.
[56] Ibid., p 298.
[57] Ibid., p 252.
[58] Donne, *Essays*, p 92.
[59] Ibid., pp 92, 93.

He was aware of the danger of taking so few words for the text of a sermon, as to lose the meaning. So he criticised preachers who took only two or three incoherent words of a sentence of Scripture:

> So do they demolish Gods fairest temple, his Word, which pick out such stones, and deface the integrity of it, so much, as neither that which they take, nor that which they leave, is the word of God.[60]

He also asserted the sufficiency of Scripture. So the miracles of the Bible do not need to be supplemented by miracles today.

> God at first possest his Church...by conquest of Miracles; but he governs it now...like an indulgent King, by a law which he hath let us know...God forbid I should discredit the great works he hath done...But to set her up a Banke almost in every good Town, and make her keep a shop of Miracles...is fearfull and dangerous to admit.[61]

Donne warned against adding to Scripture, and commends those churches 'which have not by any additions destroyed the foundation and possibility of salvation in Jesus Christ.'[62] He condemned the additions made by the church of Rome, and wrote of,

> the spacious and specious super-edifications which the Church of *Rome* had built therupon...Additions [that] were of so dangerous a construction, and appearance, and misapplyeableness, that to tender consciences they seem'd Idolatrous, and are certainly scandalous and very slippery, and declinable into Idolatry.[63]

Sola Scriptura was not only a fundamental theological principle, but also shaped Donne's ministry, in which the chief instrument of ministry was the Bible. In this he followed the Reformed tradition of the Church of England, demonstrated in the 1552 Ordinal in which the newly ordained priests were not given a chalice and patten as the symbol of their ministry, but instead a Bible. This tradition was retained in the 1662 Ordinal.

---

[60] Ibid., pp 40, 41.
[61] Ibid., pp 84, 85.
[62] Ibid., p 52.
[63] Ibid., p 49, see also Donne, *Sermons* VII, p 402.

Donne claimed that Christ and the Bible had the same formal content, the self-revelation of God. 'God...hath given us security enough; He hath given us his Word; His Written Word, the Scriptures; His Essentiall Word, his Son.'[64] So God speaks of his Son in his written word. 'He speaks in his musique, in the harmonious promises of the Gospel.'[65]

2.2. The Gospel of Jesus Christ and his atoning death

'[We] preach, **Christ Jesus, and him crucified**; and whosoever preaches any other Gospell, or any other thing for Gospell, let him be accursed.[66]

The person and work of Christ is central to Donne's theology and ministry.[67]

> [God] hath decreed my salvation, but that salvation in Christ; he had decreed Christ's coming into this world, but a coming to save sinners.[68]

He showed the significance of Christ when he spoke of 'that eternall kingdom which thy Sonne our Saviour hath purchased for us, with the inestimable price of his incorruptible blood.'[69] The work of Christ necessitated the incarnation.

> He came so to us, as that he became us, not only by a new and more powerful working in us, but by assuming our nature upon himself.[70]

In this theology of the Cross, Donne expressed the Reformed theology of his day, the doctrines of Anselm, the early church, and the Bible. It was Christ, both God and man, who won salvation, by his death. The divine and human person of Christ was necessary because of the work he had to do.

---

[64] Donne, *Sermons* VI, p 216.
[65] Ibid., p 217.
[66] Donne, *Sermons* IV, p 231.
[67] 'The cross of Christ was at the centre of his religion,' Evelyn Simpson, in John Donne, *John Donne's Sermons on the Psalms and Gospels* (ed., Simpson, Evelyn M., Berkeley; University of California Press, 2003), p 9.
[68] Donne, *Sermons* I, p 304.
[69] Ibid., p 251.
[70] Ibid., p 303.

> [T]o make Christ able to pay this debt, there was something to be added to him. First, he must pay it in such money as it was lent; in the nature and flesh of man; for man had sinned, and man must pay. And then it was lent in such money as was coyned even with the Image of God; man was made according to his Image: That Image being defaced, in a new Mint, in the wombe of the blessed Virgin, there was new money coyned; the Image of the invisible God, the second person in the Trinity, was imprimed into the human nature...his person fulfilled all righteousnesse, and satisfied the Justice of God by his suffering.[71]

To claim that the centre of Donne's theology was the incarnation is incorrect,[72] and reflects an anachronistic reading of his writings and sermons. It represents a desire to claim him as a representative of the *Lux Mundi* tradition, which moved the saving death and resurrection of Christ, sin and repentance, from the centre of Anglican theology, and replaced it with incarnation and affirmation. Donne's robust biblical theology of humanity, sin, death and judgment and wrath, and of the atoning death of Jesus Christ as a sacrificial satisfaction for sin, places him at some distance from this tradition, which has tried to claim the Anglican middle ground over the last 100 years. The theologians of the *Lux Mundi* tradition were rightly criticized because, in the words of A. M. Ramsey,

> in their intense concentration upon the Incarnation as the key to the understanding of the world, these writers and their subsequent followers were minimizing the Cross, the divine judgement and the eschatological element in the Gospel.[73]

Donne expressed the theology of the atonement found in the *Book of Common Prayer* Holy Communion Prayer of Consecration.

> Jesus Christ...made there [that is, on the cross] [by his one oblation of himself once offered] a full, perfect, and sufficient sacrifice, oblation, and satisfaction, for the sins of the whole world.

---

[71] Donne, *Sermons* IV, p 288.
[72] John Donne, *John Donne: Selections from Divine Poems, Sermons, Devotions and Prayers* (ed. John Booty; New York: Paulist Press, 1990), p 3.
[73] Arthur Michael Ramsey, *From Gore to Temple* (London: Longmans, 1960), p 9. *Lux Mundi* was published in 1889.

According to Donne, we need to be saved not only because of the sins we commit, but also because of our original sin.

> In the first minute that my soul is infus'd, the image of God is imprinted in my soul...But yet *Originall* Sin is there, as soon as that image of God is there...So swift is this arrow, *Originall Sin*...as that God, who comes to my first minute of life, cannot come before death.[74]

Donne was fascinated by the idea of death.[75] However for Donne physical death carried with it the themes of God's judgement on human sinfulness and human sin. So Christ's death satisfied God.

> But in oure case it was God, that was to be satisfied; and therefore we were not redeemed with corruptible things, such as silver and gold, but with the precious blood of Christ.[76]

This atoning death was necessary because of our great sin, and God's great wrath.

> [W]hen mans measure was full of sin, and Gods measure full of wrath, then was the fulnesse of time...It pleased the Father, that there should be another fulnesse to overflow all these, in Christ Jesus.[77]

In that atoning death Christ endured the curse of God, making peace by the blood of the cross.

> The Crosse, to which a bitter curse was nailed by Moses, from the beginning, he that is hanged is, [not onely accursed of God as our Translation hath it], but he is the curse of God, [as it is in the Originall] not accursed, but a curse; not a simple curse, but a curse of God.[78]

So if anyone rejects the atoning death of Christ, 'he makes Christ Jesus, who is the propitiation of the all the world, his damnation.'[79]

Christ's death demonstrated and conveyed God's love. 'I cannot

---

[74] Donne, *Sermons* II, p 59.
[75] See especially his last sermon, "Death's Duel", Donne, *Sermons* X. pp. 229-248.
[76] Donne, *Sermons* I, p 166.
[77] Donne, *Sermons* IV, p 287.
[78] Ibid., p 296.
[79] Donne, *Sermons* VII, p 321.

name a time, when God's love, began, it is eternal, I cannot imagine a time, when his mercy will end, it is perpetual.'[80] This was God's initiative:

> [H]ow early did he seek thee, when he sought thee in *Adam's* confused loynes, and out of that leavened and sowre loaf in which we were all kneaded up out of that *massa damnata*...he sought and sever'd out that grain which thou shouldst be; yea millions and millions of generations before all this he sought thee in his own eternal Decree; And in that first Scripture of his, which is as old as himself, in the book of life he wrote thy name in the blood of the Lamb which was slain for thee, not only from the beginning of this world, but from the writing of that eternal Decree of thy Salvation.[81]

Donne summarised the gospel for the plain man, and for the greatest theologian.

> The simplest man, as well as the greatest Doctor, is bound to know, that there is one God in three persons, That the second of those, the Sonne of God, tooke our nature, and dyed for mankinde; And that there is a Holy Ghost, which in the Communion of Saints, the Church established by Christ, applies to every particular soule the benefit of Christs universall redemption.[82]

Donne was also concerned that the Gospel be preached throughout the world. In his sermon to the Honourable Company of the Virginia Plantation on 13th November 1622 he reminded his congregation that,

> the *Acts* of the *Apostles* were to convay that name of *Christ Jesus*, and to propagate his *Gospell*, over all the world: beloved, you are *Actors* upon the same Stage too.[83]

He wanted them to be as urgent about conversions to Christ among the native Indians as they were about their profit.

> O, if you would be as ready to hearken at the returne of a *Ship*, how many *Indians* were converted to *Christ Jesus*, as what

---

[80] Donne, *Sermons* I, p 167.
[81] Ibid., p 249.
[82] Donne, *Sermons* V, p 276.
[83] Donne, *Sermons* IV, p 265.

Trees, or drugs, or Dyes that Ship had brought.[84]

Donne also taught the responsibility of Bishops for Gospel progress. For Paul, in 1 Timothy,

> undertakes to instruct a Bishop in his Episcopall function, which is, to propagate the Gospell; for, he is but an ill Bishop that leaves Christ where he found him, in whose time the Gospell is no farther than it was; how much worse is he, in whose time the Gospel loses ground?[85]

For the followers of Christ, called to catch people, 'the world must be their sea, and their net must be the Gospel.'[86]

Donne's concern was for Gospel truth, proclamation, and fruitfulness, the conversion of many to Jesus Christ. No wonder his constant cry was *Væ mihi est si non euangelizavero,* Woe to me if I do not preach the Gospel (1 Cor. 9:16).[87]

2.3. *Preaching*

'To bring men[88] to heaven by preaching.'[89]

If the Bible is the word of God about his Son and his Gospel, then how is this message to be communicated? 'By preaching.'

> Preaching is a miracle, the direct work of God:
>
> But to doe great works by small means, to bring men to heaven by Preaching in the Church, this is a miracle.[90]

For preaching is the means by which we learn of Christ.

> Preaching must be a continuall application of all that Christ Jesus said and did, and suffered, to thee.[91]

How then does God value preaching?

---

[84] Ibid., p 269.
[85] Donne, *Sermons* I, p 286.
[86] Donne, *Sermons* II, p 302.
[87] E.g. Donne, *Sermons* II, pp 164, 308; IV, pp 192, 195, 374; VI, p 93; IX, p 285; X, p 126.
[88] Of course inclusive of women and children, as well as males.
[89] Donne, *Sermons* VII, p 301.
[90] Ibid., pp 300, 301.
[91] Ibid., p 232.

> There is no salvation but by faith, nor faith but by hearing, nor hearing but by preaching; and they that thinke meanliest of the Keyes of the Church, and speak faintliest of the Absolution of the Church, will yet allow, That those Keyes lock, and unlock in Preaching, That Absolution is conferred, or withheld in Preaching, That the proposing of the promises of the Gospel in Preaching, is that binding and loosing on earth, which bindes and looses in heaven.[92]

He reproached those who despised preaching, or who regarded it as merely a human activity.

> [H]ence is it, that you take so much liberty in censuring and comparing Preacher and Preacher, nay sermon and Sermon from the same Preacher...You measure all be persons; and yet...you give not so much reverence to God's Ordinance [Preaching], as he does.[93]

So God judges those who reject the preacher and the sermon. All the judgments found in the Bible will come on those who 'trample upon the pearles, that is, undervalue the Doctrine, and the Ordinance [Preaching] it selfe.'[94]

> God's use of preaching works against our natural intuition:

> Man has a natural way to come to God, by the eye. But God has a super-induced and super-natural way, by the ear. For though hearing be natural, yet that faith in God should come by hearing a man preach is supernatural. God shut up the natural way in Saul, seeing: he struck him blind; but he opened the supernatural way.[95]

So the ministry of preaching has priority over sacraments.

> [For Sacraments were instituted by Christ, as subsidiary things, in a greater part, for our infirmity, who stand in need of such visible and sensible assistances.] Christ preached the Christian

---

[92] Ibid., p 320.
[93] Donne, *Sermons* VII, p 319.
[94] Ibid., p 320.
[95] Donne, *Sermons* VI, p 217.

Doctrine, long before he instituted the Sacraments.[96]

Donne had a high view of the work of God in the sacraments instituted by Christ,[97] but an even higher view of preaching.

> As there lies always upon God's Minister a *væ si non,* Wo be unto me, if I preach not the Gospel, if I apply not the comfortable promises of the Gospel, to all that grone under the burden of their sins.[98]

So the sin of the people of God in the days of Ezekiel, was this:

> The greatest sin of all, treason within doors, contemning of God in his own house, and in his presence; that is, a coming to Church to hear the word of God preached, a pretence of cheerfulness and alacrity, in the outward service of God, yea a true sense and feeling of delight in hearing of the word; and yet for all this, an unprofitable barrenness, and...a despiteful and a contumelious neglecting of Gods purpose and in intention, in his Ordinance.[99]

Donne was aware of the frailty of preachers, but trusted in the plan and power of God. He commented on Peter and Andrew:

> Christ needed not man's sufficiency, he took insufficient men; Christ excuses no man's insufficiency, he made them sufficient.[100]

The conversion of the penitent thief showed 'the powerfulness and the despatch' of the grace of God at work in him even as he was dying on his cross next to Jesus.[101] For he was a great sinner: a thief and murderer, and he had reviled Christ.[102] What were the words of Christ's promise? 'Today you will be with me in paradise.' As Donne said,

> So soon did [Christ] bring this thief...that had a good bargain of death, that scap'd by being condemned, and was the better, and longer liv'd for being hang'd...He came to know those Wounds which were in Christ's Body...then he began to love him

---

[96] Donne, *Sermons* X, p 69.
[97] See Donne, *Sermons* VII, p 321.
[98] Donne, *Sermons* II, p 164.
[99] Ibid., p 166.
[100] Ibid., p 274.
[101] Donne, *Sermons* I, p 255.
[102] Ibid., p 257.

perfectly, when he found his own wounds in the body of his Saviour.[103]

So 'his desire to convert others' was the sign of his conversion to Christ.[104] On his words, 'Do you not fear God?' Donne commented,

> Here was an extemporal Sermon, but a short one: he preaches nothing but the fear of God...And what's his Auditory?...it is but a poor Parish that he hath...and there he visits the poorest, the sickest, the wretchedest person, the [other] Thief.[105]

God addresses his people now in the words of ancient texts.

> God continues his speech, and speaks to us every day; still we must hear *Evangelium in sermone*, the Gospel in the Word.[106]

He pointed to Christ's command:

> *Go ye, and preach.* Because I [Christ] have all power, for preaching, take yee part of my power, and preach too...Preaching then being *God's Ordinance*, to beget Faith, to take away preaching, were to disarme *God*, and to quench the spirit.[107]

Preachers need hearers, and so Donne was concerned that his congregation hear his words, and receive them with humility.

> And the holy Scriptures... have these properties of a well provided Castle, that they are easily defensible, and safely defend others. So they have also this, that to strangers they open but a litle wicket [gate], and he that will enter, must stoop and humble himself.[108]

So to lose preaching is to risk losing Christ:

> [S]o how long soever Christ have dwelt in any State, or any Church, if he grows speechless, he is departing: if there be a discontinuing, or slackening of preaching, there is a danger of losing Christ.[109]

---

[103] Ibid., p 259.
[104] Ibid., p 259.
[105] Ibid., pp 261, 262.
[106] Ibid., p 291.
[107] Donne, *Sermons* IV, p 195.
[108] Donne, *Essays* p 5.
[109] Donne, *Sermons* VII, p 157.

2.4. Effective Preaching

'A good measure of thy Word, and an effectuall preaching thereof.'[110]

Before John Donne preached at Lincoln's Inn at the dedication of a new Chapel on Ascension Day 1622, he prayed in these words:

> And let a full pot of thy Manna, a good measure of thy Word, and an effectuall Preaching thereof, bee evermore preserved, and evermore distributed in this place.[111]

What was 'effectuall preaching'?

Donne did not make the common mistake of educated preachers in confusing an academic lecture with a sermon. We are 'here, not in the School, but in the Pulpit; not in Disputation, but in Application.'[112] For education and information serve a greater purpose, namely exhortation for edification:

> a sermon intends *Exhortation* principally and *Edification,* and a holy stirring of the religious affections, and then *matters of Doctrine*, and points of *Divinity*.[113]

How did Donne work to stir affections, to exhort, convert, challenge, and comfort his congregations? Here are some of the ways by which he made his own preaching 'effectual.'

a) He thought of the task of preaching in active and energetic images. In his sermon on Ezekiel, Donne developed various descriptions of preaching:

- His minister shall be Tuba...a Trumpet, to awaken with terror.[114]
- But then, he shall become *Carmen musicum*, a musical and harmonious charmer, to settle and compose the soul again in a resposed confidence, and in a delight in God.[115]

---

[110] Donne, *Sermons* IV, p 363.
[111] Ibid., p 363. The Chapel still stands, and the pulpit from which Donne preached is still in place.
[112] Donne, *Sermons* I, p 234.
[113] Donne, *Sermons* VII, p 95.
[114] Donne, *Sermons* II, p 166.
[115] Ibid., pp 166, 167.

- The same Trumpet that sounds the alarm [that is, that awakens us from our security] and that sounds the Battail...sounds the Parle too, calls us to hearken to God in his word, and speak to God in our prayers...and the same trumpet sounds a retreat too, that is, a safe resposing of our souls in the merit, and in the wounds of our Saviour Jesus Christ.[116]
- There are not so eloquent books in the world, as the Scriptures...So the Holy Ghost hath spoken in those Instruments, whom he chose for the penning of his Scripture, and so he would in those whom he sends for the preaching thereof...then are we *Musicum Carmen in modo*, musick to the soul, in the manner of our preaching...we content ourselves with that language, and that phrase of speech, which the Holy Ghost hath expressed himself in, in the Scriptures.[117]

Mueller summarised the varied images that Donne used to describe preachers:

> Not only is the preacher a husband to the congregation: he is an archer, a watchman, a trumpeter, a harmonious charmer; he possesses the most desirable qualities of a lion, an ox, an eagle, and a man; he is an earthquake, a son of thunder, the fall of waters, the roaring of a lion.[118]

He also prepared and crafted his sermons to make them easy to hear. He did not preach to be read, he preached to be heard: he understood the need for 'orality' in preaching.[119] Donne preached from notes, and then wrote down his sermons for publication. However we still see plentiful signs of their original 'orality' in his published sermons.

b) To aid effective hearing he used a simple structure, repetition of words and of short key sentences, short memorable sayings, powerful metaphors and symbols, ingenious comparisons and contrasts, and alliteration.[120] He had the self-discipline not to drown his hearers in too

---

[116] Ibid., pp 169, 170.
[117] Ibid., pp 170, 171.
[118] Mueller, *John Donne*, p 43.
[119] 'Orality' is the use of *spoken* rather than *written* language. It is 'orality' for 'aurality,' that is, language that is spoken to be heard, rather than written to be read.
[120] 'The Hypocrite is the miserablest of all other; he does God service, and yet is damned.' Donne, *Sermons* I, p 189.

much background information of little importance. He used all his poetic gifts in the choice of words, in the crafting of sentences and sections, and in the overall dramatic shape of his sermons. Sometimes his strengths became his weaknesses, as when a powerful metaphor dominated a sermon, or when conceits sounded conceited. However, his poetic imagination helped his 'effectual preaching.' He showed us how poetic power can be used to convey the verbal revelation of God in the Scriptures, and to communicate definite theological notions, for example the atoning death of Christ.

c) He engaged his hearers in their every aspect. He addressed their minds, their intellects, their feelings, their consciences, their observation of the world around them, their daily interests and concerns, their work and their relationships, the structure of their society, and the world in which they lived. He used paradox, irony, and similes and examples from law, science, politics, nature, history, literature and daily life. He also engaged the ordinary lives of his hearers, not just their religious consciousness. He did this by using the language of his audience, and images and rhetoric from their ordinary daily non-church lives, to shock them into feeling the connections between God's message in the Bible and every aspect of their existence.

d) He had a deep knowledge of human behaviour. This came from his careful and attentive study of the Bible, in which all aspects of human motives and actions are clearly laid bare. It also came from his own powers of observation, his sympathy with humanity, and the difficulties and frustrations of his own life. For easy lives breed superficiality, and trials enable deeper understanding.

e) Donne also made his preaching 'effectuall' by his detailed knowledge of the Bible, by the unexpected intra-biblical connections that he made in his sermons, and by the ways in which he heightened the contrasts and comparisons found in the Bible text. He projected the eloquence of the Scriptures, the words and accents of God's own voice. At his best, he did not let his own agenda replace, confuse, or interrupt the message of the text. Even in using his eloquence, he knew that: 'Eloquence is not our net...onely the Gospel is.'[121] So Donne used his poetic gifts to serve the clear message of the Bible, the Gospel of Christ.

---

[121] Donne, *Sermons* II, p 307.

f)   Donne also kept the meta-narrative, the Gospel, the big story, in sight for himself and for his hearers, so that careful attention to an individual text did not obscure the central truths of the Bible. In the words of Northrop Frye,

> In the sermons of John Donne, for example, we can see how the text leads us, like a guide with a candle, into the vast labyrinth of Scripture, which to Donne was an infinitely bigger structure than the cathedral he was preaching in.[122]

g)   He preached personally, made himself personally and publicly present in his sermons. They were not abstract and impersonal statements of truth, but deeply personal expressions of God's grace in the life of John Donne, yet without being tediously self-referential.[123]

h)   He was aware of his own weakness and sin, but trusted God to use him and to use his preaching.

i)   He was aware that God was present, and spoke to his people, addressing them by the words of Scripture.[124]

j)   Donne's strengths as a preacher came from his constant and careful Biblical study, and not only of the text of the Bible, but also the

---

[122] Northrop Frye, *The Great Code: The Bible and Literature* (San Diego: Harvest/HBJ, 1983), p 209.

[123] There are studies of Donne's preaching style in Mueller, *John Donne*, chapter 3, Frederick A Rowe, *Launch at Paradise: A Consideration of John Donne, Poet and Preacher* (London: The Epworth Press, 1964), chapter 8, and Colclough, *John Donne's Professional Lives*, chapters 7-10. T. S. Eliot objected to Donne's emotionalism: 'He is a little of the religious spell-binder, the Reverend Billy Sunday of his time, the flesh-creeper, the sorcerer of emotional energy.' T. S. Eliot, *Essays Ancient and Modern* (London: Faber and Faber, 1936), p 17.

[124] His meditative and intuitive approach to the Bible matches that of his Puritan contemporary, Joseph Hall, whose 'The Arte of Divine Meditation' helped individual readers do what Donne did in his sermons. See Huntley, *Bishop Joseph Hall*, chapter 6. See also the accounts of Richard Sibbes' Puritan 'affectionate' theology in Dever, *Richard Sibbes*, chapter 6, and of his preaching in John R. Knott, Jr., *The Sword of the Spirit* (Chicago: University of Chicago Press, 1980), chapter 2.

best commentators of the early church, and contemporary Protestant and Roman writers.[125]

k) He had a remarkable combination of intellectual intelligence, emotional intelligence, pastoral intelligence, powers of observation, and self-discipline in preparation. All of these helped to make him a great preacher.

One of his advantages was that he could assume biblical literacy. This meant that he could make references to many Bible texts without needing to explain each one. However this was also a weakness, as his preaching style would not have educated his hearers in the content of the Bible. His practice of preaching on one or two verses serves his purpose well, in focussing on memorable words. As a long-term policy it would be deficient, as he would not have trained his people to read the Bible for themselves, but would have kept them dependent on his ministry.[126]

Donne's style of preaching was perfectly crafted for his audiences, and for his time. His rhetoric served his purpose of 'effectuall' preaching. By the end of the 17th Century, it was out of date.[127] Of course his style is dated, but that is because it was so carefully crafted

---

[125] Donne had some knowledge of Hebrew, and little of Greek. He read Latin. From the early church he used mainly Augustine, Jerome, Chrysostom, Ambrose, Tertullian, and Gregory the Great. His favourite Protestant commentators were Calvin and Luther. Roman writers included Aquinas, Scotus, Nicholas of Lyra, and Cornelius à Lapide. See Donne, *Sermons X*, Part Two, Chapters 1 & 2.

[126] Donne rightly valued the corporate hearing of the Bible in the congregation, and valued it more highly than individual study of the Scriptures. However if people will read and study the Bible themselves, they need help in understanding it, and good models of exegesis and use. Donne did not provide this training.

[127] Bishop Burnet noted its passing and its replacement by 'plain Notions of simple and genuine Rhetorick':
'Pert Wit and Luscious Eloquence have lost their Relish. So that Sermons are reduced to the plain opening of the meaning of the Text, a few short illustrations of its Coherence, with what goes before and after, and of the Parts of which it is composed; to that is joined the clear Stating of such Propositions as arise out if it, their Nature, Truth, and Reasonabless; be which, the Hearers may form clear Notions of the several Parts of Religion, such as are best suited to their Capacities and Apprehensions: In all which Applications are added, tending to the Reproving, Directing, Encouraging or Comforting the Hearers, according to the several Occasions which are offered.'
From Bishop Burnet's 'Discourse of Pastoral Care' of 1692, in Davies, *Worship and Theology*, Part II, p 136.

to entice, attract, and win the people to whom he preached. However, it was enough for Donne to serve his own age and social context: this is the mark of 'effectuall' ministry of any and every age.

Izaac Walton described him:

> [P]reaching the Word so, as shewed he was possest with those joyes that he laboured to distill into others: A Preacher in earnest, weeping sometimes for his Auditory, sometimes with them, always preaching to himselfe, like an Angel from a cloud, though in none: carrying some [as St Paul was] to heaven, in holy raptures: enticing other by sacred art and courtship, to amend their lives; and all this with a most particular grace, and un-imitable fashion of speaking.[128]

John Donne had a gospel to preach, because he had the Scriptures, which were inspired by the Holy Spirit of God, contained the sure promises of the faithful God, and revealed the Lord Jesus Christ. He invited men and women to hear those Scriptures, and turn to Christ and be faithful to him.[129]

We now turn to an example of Donne's evangelistic preaching. Observe the four grounds and ingredients of his preaching, in which his beliefs shape his practice: the Bible, the gospel of Christ's atoning death, the ministry of preaching, and the need for effective preaching.

3. Donne's evangelistic sermon on 1 Timothy 1:15

'This is a faithful saying, and worthy of all acceptation, that Christ Jesus came into the world to save sinners; of which I am the chiefest.'

Donne preached this sermon at Whitehall on 19th April 1618. As he began he aroused the expectation that his hearers would feel the force and vehemence of God in the words of the Bible:

---

[128] Walton, in Garrod, *John Donne*, p xxviii.
[129] Some may suggest that it is impossible to retrieve Donne's presuppositions or theology. However if we will not allow ourselves to be challenged by the past, we remain trapped in a 'fundamentalism of the present.' Oliver O'Donovan commends the value of such a conversation with the past. See Oliver O'Donovan, *On the Thirty Nine Articles: A Conversation with Tudor Christianity* (Exeter: Paternoster Press, 1986), pp 7, 8.

> Now the holy-Ghost was in all the Authors, of all the books of the Bible, but in Saint *Paul's* Epistles, there is, sayes *Irenaus, Impetus Spiritus Sancti,* the vehemence the force of the holy-Ghost.[130]

Then he showed the three parts of the text, and of his sermon.

> Here then we shall have these three parts; First *Radicem,* The Roote of the Gospel, from whence it springs; it is *fidelis sermo,* a faithful Word, which cannot erre: and secondly, we have *Arborem, Corpus,* the Tree, the Body, the substance of the Gospell, That *Christ Jesus came into the worlds to save sinners;* and then lastly, *fructum evangelii,* the fruit of the Gospel, *Humility,* that it brings them who embrace it, to acknowledge themselves to be the greatest sinners.[131]

He wanted them to hear:

> a faithful word, which cannot err, the substance of the Gospell, that Christ Jesus came into the world to save sinners, the fruit of the Gospel, humility that it brings those who embrace it to acknowledge themselves to be the greatest sinners.[132]

In the *first part,* based on *'This is a faithful saying, and worthy of all acceptation,'* he showed that the reliability of God's 'faithful saying' is essential to the Gospel.

- The Gospell is founded and rooted...in the Word... Christ is the subject of the Word of God, of all the Scriptures, of all that was shadowed in the Types[133]
- Christ is the foundation of all those Scriptures, Christ is the burden of all those Songs; Christ was *in sermone,* then he was in the Word...so then there never was, there never must be any other Gospel then is *in sermone,* in the written word of God in the Scriptures.[134]
- All the word of God then conduces to the Gospel: the Old Testament is a preparation and a pædagogie to the New. All the

---

[130] Donne, *Sermons* I, p 286.
[131] Ibid., p 286.
[132] Ibid., p 286.
[133] Ibid., p 287.
[134] Ibid., p 288.

- word belongs to the Gospell, and all the Gospell is in the word; nothing is to be obtruded to our faith as necessary to salvation, except it be rooted in the Word.[135]
- The Gospell then, that which is the Gospell to thee... is grounded *in sermone*, upon the word; not upon imaginations of thine owne, not upon fancies of others, nor pretended inspirations, nor obtruded Miracles, but upon the word; and not upon a suspicious and questionable, not upon an uncertain or variable word, but upon this, that is *fidelis sermo, This is a faithful saying.*[136]
- Now the Truth, and Faithfulnesse of the Word, consists not only in this, *quod verax*, that it is true in itselfe, but in this also, *quod testificatus*, that it is established by good testimony to be so.[137]
- [I]t is upon a faithful word, upon that which is cleerly and without the encumbrance of disputation, the infallible word of God; no traditionall word, no apocryphall word, but the cleere and faithful word.[138]

In the *second part*, based on *'Christ Jesus came into the world to save sinners,'* he preached the substance of the gospel, Christ and his atoning death.

- [T]he Reason why hee came, Hee came to Save; and whom hee came to Save; to save Sinners.[139]
- God could have saved the world by his word...God having purposed to himself the way of Justice, then could none be capable of that employment but a mixt person; for God could not dye, nor man could not satisfie by death; and both these were required in the way of Justice, a satisfaction and that by death.[140]
- It is not only his person, but it is his very righteousness that saves us.[141]
- Christ is truly both, both the Physitian and the Physick.[142]

---

[135] Ibid., p 291.
[136] Ibid., p 294.
[137] Ibid., p 297.
[138] Ibid., p 294.
[139] Ibid., p 287.
[140] Ibid., p 309.
[141] Ibid., p 310.
[142] Ibid., p 312.

- [O]ther Physitians draw our blood, He makes physick of blood, and of his own blood.[143]
- [N]ot only a bringer, and applier, a worker of our salvation, but he is the author of the very decree of our salvation, as well as of the execution of that Decree: there was no salvation before him, there was no salvation intended in the book of Life, but in him.[144]
- He sav'd us from his killing, by dying himself for us; for being dead, and having taken us into his wounds, and being risen, and having taken us into his glory...And so he was *Agnus occisus ab origine mundi*, the Lamb slain from the beginning of the world.[145]
- [S]o when I looke faithfully upon my Saviour, all my unholinesse falls of as rags, and I shall be invested in his Righteousnesse, in his Holynesse; so that in that lies my comfort, that he is a Holy and a Faithfull God.[146]

In the *third part*, based on, *'of which I am the chiefest,'* Donne pointed to that humility which is the fruit of the Gospel.

- He saves us who acknowledge that we could not be saved without him, and desire, and that with a faithful assurance to be saved by him.[147]
- In the way to heaven, the lower you go, the nearer and highest and best end you are.[148]
- [T]ruly every man is truly dust...[W]e are truly dry ashes...so we have no good in us naturally, neither can we nourish any good that is infus'd by God into us, except God the same Grace that sow'd it, water it, and weed it, and cherish, it, and foment it after.[149]
- [S]in is the wealth of the sinner, and he treasures up the wrath of God.[150]

---

[143] Ibid., p 313.
[144] Ibid., p 310.
[145] Ibid., p 305.
[146] Ibid., p 296.
[147] Ibid., p 314.
[148] Ibid., p 315.
[149] Ibid., p 315.
[150] Ibid., p 318.

- [T]he greatest sinner, because he remained still in his infirmity, and aptness to relapse into former sins... [is] still in a slippery state, and in an evident danger of being the greatest sinner.[151]

Here then is one fine example of Donne's evangelistic preaching.[152]

4. Conclusion

We have seen that Donne, that mainstream Reformed Anglican, was a passionate evangelist, that he used his knowledge of the Bible, his knowledge of Jesus Christ and his atoning death, his wide reading, his observation of the world and of humanity, and all his poetic gifts, in his preaching of the gospel.

Donne challenges contemporary Anglicans, and our sense of Anglican identity and practice. He was an Anglican who believed in and used the Holy Scriptures as the verbal revelation of God, preached the atoning death of Christ, practised faith and piety that was both Reformed and Anglican, viewed preaching as the centre of his ministry, worked hard in preparing and crafting his sermons, used his 'poetic imagination' to communicate the Gospel with doctrinal clarity and power, was a passionate evangelist, and was committed to the evangelisation of the world.

May all our churches and ministers feel his passionate cry, *Væ mihi est si non euangelizavero*, 'Woe to me if I do not preach the Gospel!'.

May God raise up a great army of evangelists, whose passion is 'to bring men, women and children to heaven' by the effective preaching of the gospel of the atoning death of Jesus Christ.

---

[151] Ibid., p 318.
[152] For others see Donne, *Sermons* I, sermons 1, 6; II, sermons 12 –14; III, sermon 15; IV, sermons 3, 11, 13, 14; V, sermons 12, 13; VI, sermons 8, 13, 18; VII, sermons 2,10; VIII, sermon 13; IX, sermons 6, 7; and X, sermons 5, 11.

BIBLIOGRAPHY

Donne's sermons:

Donne, John, [1952], *John Donne: Essays in Divinity*, ed., Simpson, Evelyn M., Oxford: Clarendon Press.

Donne, John, [1953-1962], *The Sermons of John Donne*, Volumes I – X, eds., Potter, M. R. and Simpson, E. M., Berkeley: University of California Press.

Donne, John, [1990], *John Donne: Selections from Divine Poems, Sermons, Devotions and Prayers*, ed., Booty, John, New York: Paulist Press.

Donne, John, [2003], *John Donne's Sermons on the Psalms and Gospels*, ed., Simpson, Evelyn M., Berkeley: University of California Press.

Biographies of Donne:

Bald, R. C., [1970], *John Donne: A Life*, London: Oxford University Press.

Carey, John, ed., [1990], *John Donne*, The Oxford Authors, Oxford: Oxford University Press.

Edwards, David L., [2001], *John Donne, Man of Flesh and Spirit*, London and New York: Continuum.

Garrod, H. W., [1946], *John Donne, Poetry and Prose: with Izaac Walton's Life, etc*, Oxford: Clarendon Press.

Donne's preaching:

Carrithers, Gale H. Jr., [1972], *Donne at Sermons*, Albany: State University of New York Press.

Colclough, David, ed., [2003], *John Donne's Professional Lives*, Cambridge: D. S. Brewer.

Doerksen, Daniel W., "Saint Paul's Puritan': Donne's Puritan Imagination in the Sermons' in Frontain, Raymond-Jean and Malpezzie, Frances, [1995], *John Donne's Religious Imagination: Essays in Honor of John T. Shawcross*, Conway: UCA Press.

Mueller, William R. [1962], *John Donne: Preacher*, Princeton: Princeton University Press.

Rose, Lucy A., [1995], 'Donne, John,' in Willimon, William H. and Lischer, Richard, eds., *Concise Encyclopedia of Preaching*, Louisville: Westminster John Knox Press, pp. 106-108.

Rowe, Frederick A., [1964], *Launch at Paradise: A Consideration of John Donne, Poet and Preacher*, London: The Epworth Press.

Schleiner, Winfried, [1970], *The Imagery of John Donne's Sermons*, Providence: Brown University.

Background to preaching in Donne's day:

Blench, J. W., [1964], *Preaching in England in the late fifteenth and sixteenth centuries*, Oxford: Blackwell.

Chandos, John, ed., [1971], *In God's Name: Examples of Preaching in England 1534-1662*, London: Hutchinson.

Countryman, William, [1999], *The Poetic Imagination: An Anglican Spiritual Tradition*, London: Dartman, Longman and Todd.

Edwards, O. C. Jr., [2004], *A History of Preaching*, Nashville: Abingdon Press.

Hunt, Arnold, [1998], *The Art of Hearing: English Preachers and their Audiences, 1590-1640*, unpublished Ph.D. dissertation, University of Cambridge.
Knott, J. R. Jr., [1980], *The Sword of the Spirit*, Chicago: University of Chicago Press.
Larsen, David L., [1998], *The Company of the Preachers: A History of Biblical Preaching*, Grand Rapids: Kregel.
Old, Hughes Oliphant, [1999], *The Reading and Preaching of the Scriptures in the Worship of the Christian Church*, Volume 3, *The Medieval Church*, and [2002], Volume 4, *The Age of the Reformation*, Grand Rapids: Eerdmans.
Perkins, William, [[1592] 1996], *The Art of Prophesying*, Edinburgh: Banner of Truth.
Smyth, Charles, [1940], *The Art of Preaching 747-1939*, London: SPCK.
Van Dixhoorn, Chad B., [2005], *A Puritan Theology of Preaching*, London: St Antholin's Lectureship.

Background studies to Donne's church and ministry:

Collinson, Patrick, [1982], *The Religion of Protestants: The Church in English Society 1559-1625* Oxford: Clarendon.
Davies, Horton [1996], *Worship and Theology in England*, 3 volumes (6 parts), Grand Rapids: Eerdmans.
Dever, Mark E., [2000], *Richard Sibbes: Puritanism and Calvinism in Late Elizabethan and Early Stuart England*, Macon: Mercer University Press.
Doerksen, Daniel W. [1997], *Conforming to the Word: Herbert, Donne and the English Church before Laud*, Lewisburg: Bucknell University Press.
Frye, Northrop, [1983], *The Great Code: The Bible and Literature*, SanDiego: Harvest/HBJ.
Hill, Christopher, [1994], *The English Bible and the Seventeenth Century Revolution*, London: Penguin Books.
Huntley, Frank Livingstone, [1979], *Bishop Joseph Hall 1574-1656: A Biographical and critical study*, Cambridge: D. S. Brewer.
Hylson-Smith, Kenneth, [1996], *The Churches in England from Elizabeth I to Elizabeth II*, Volume I, 1558-1688, London: SCM Press.
Johnson, Jeffrey, [1999], *The Theology of John Donne*, Cambridge: D. S. Brewer.
O'Donovan, Oliver [1986], *On the Thirty Nine Articles: A Conversation with Tudor Christianity*, Exeter: Paternoster Press.
Papazian, Mary Ashagouni, ed., [2003], *John Donne and the Protestant Reformation: New Perspectives*, Detroit: Wayne State University Press.
Primus, John H. [1998], *Richard Greenham: Portrait of an Elizabethan Pastor*, Macon: Mercer University Press.
Samuel, D. N., ed., [1979], *The Evangelical Succession in the Church of England*, Cambridge: James Clarke.
Trevor-Roper, Hugh [2000], *Archbishop Laud: 1573-1645*, Second Edition, London: Phoenix Press.
Trinterud, Leonard J. ed., [1971], *Elizabethan Puritanism*, New York: Oxford University Press.
Zahl, Paul F. M., [1998], *The Protestant Face of Anglicanism*, Grand Rapids: Eerdmans.

1807-2007: John Newton and the Twenty-first Century

Tony Baker

Preface 294

Introduction..295

1. Newton's conversion.. 296
2. Newton's theology...300
3. Newton's call to the ministry and attitude to denominations 302
4. Newton's preaching and praying..................................... 305
5. Newton's pastoral and evangelistic work........................309
6. Newton's letter-writing 312
7. Newton's hymns 314
8. Newton's attitude to the slave trade................................316
9. Newton's marriage...319
10. Newton's leadership... 321
11. Conclusion 322

Bibliography 323

TONY P BAKER retired from parish ministry in 2003, having served in five churches over 40 years. His final appointment was as Vicar of Bishop Hannington Memorial Church, Hove. He and his wife Margaret have two married sons (one a minister, one a history teacher), and four grandchildren. He is a Trustee of the John Newton Project, and lectures in Biblical Theology on the Sussex Coast Ministry Course.

Preface

When John Newton was Rector of St. Mary Woolnoth, he was aware that in the heart of London, as well as outside it, there was a kind of Anglican Evangelical 'underworld,'[1] which sought the spread of the gospel by all possible means, sometimes novel and sometimes maybe irregular.

Two hundred years later I thank the St. Antholin's Trustees for the privilege of popping my two little feet into the stalwart shoes of Foster, Newton, and many other faithful men. I hope this lecture may show Newton's considerable significance for our own times, and introduce readers to the man, to his own writings, and to those who have written about him.

Tony Baker

---

[1] Bruce Hindmarsh, *John Newton and the English Evangelical Tradition* (New York: Oxford University Press, 1996), p 291.

Introduction

John Newton died 200 years ago on 21st December 1807. Fourteen months earlier his pulpit ministry had finally concluded when he preached in St. Mary Woolnoth at a charity service in aid of those injured and bereaved through the Battle of Trafalgar. His memory, as well as his sight and hearing, had now almost gone – although even when over 80, 'it was remarked', says Josiah Bull, 'he was nowhere more collected or more lively than in the pulpit.'[2] But on this final occasion as the elderly Newton more or less wandered to a halt, his curate had to remind him what he was preaching about.

In an extraordinary way, Newton's ministry had come full circle. It was almost half a century earlier in September 1758 that he had preached his first sermon in the Presbyterian church in Leeds. In spite of initial hesitancy in accepting the invitation, when offered a room for quiet and final preparation after tea, he responded 'O I am prepared.' His text was Psalm 16:8 ('I have set the Lord always before me; because he is at my right hand, I shall not be moved'). However, perhaps there was an element of over-confidence and he had not in fact set the Lord quite so definitely before him, for he simply dried up and had to move out of the pulpit! John Edwards, the minister, took over with an appropriate address on the Spirit's help in our weakness.

This is what Newton experienced down the years that followed. The amazing grace that saved him also called and equipped him for ministry, enabling him to proclaim and practise the grace of our Lord Jesus Christ according to the Scriptures. 'Newton's whole ministry' says Alec Motyer, 'bore the marks so evident in his lovely hymns: it was consistently *biblical* (to share the Word of God), *spiritual* (to promote walking with God), *simple* (to make biblical truth and principles plain), and *practical* (to inculcate personal holiness and sound relationships in church and society).'[3] One of Newton's more recent biographers, Brian Edwards, summarizes Newton's ongoing significance: 'The flame of his example as a Christian, husband, preacher, correspondent, counsellor

---

[2] Josiah Bull, *But Now I See* (1868, reprinted Edinburgh: Banner of Truth 1998), p 356.
[3] Foreword to Marylynn Rouse ed., *365 Days with Newton, from his unpublished sermons and writings* (Leominster: Day One, 2006).

and hymn-writer has never dimmed, even two hundred years after his death.'[4]

What Brian Edwards says expresses the aim of this lecture: rather than simply retelling Newton's story, it is to show his significance in ten areas for the 21st century. Indeed, in summary form Newton's biography can appear deceptively straightforward: born on 21st July 1725, Newton had a godly mother who died just before he was seven. He had only two years formal education. He then gradually rejected his Christian roots but God met with him during a storm at sea in March 1748. There were four further voyages on slave-ships (one as First Mate, three as Captain). Between the first and second, he married a distant relative, Mary (Polly) Catlett, whom he had first met when he was seventeen and she was thirteen. After some years as Tide Surveyor at Liverpool, he was ordained as curate to an absentee vicar at Olney in Bucks in 1764, later becoming Rector of St. Mary Woolnoth in 1779.

To see the biographical bones fleshed out with high drama at sea, tear-jerking romance, and a developing 'all-round' ministry, read one or more of the biographies, from the first by Richard Cecil (1808) to the latest by Jonathan Aitken (2007). But begin if possible with Newton's own *Authentic Narrative* of his early life, published in 1764.

To read this is to be confronted immediately with the first reason for Newton's continuing significance for our own century:

1. Newton's conversion

It was Newton's contention that some conversions are so ordered that 'sovereign, efficacious grace' (Newton's phrase)[5] is particularly evident:

> ... the wise and good providence of God watches over his people from the earliest moment of their life, over-rules and guards them through all their wanderings in a state of ignorance, leads them in a way they know not, till at length his providence and grace concur in those events and impressions, which bring

---

[4] Brian Edwards, *Through Many Dangers* (second edition, Darlington: Evangelical Press, 2001), p 350.
[5] Bruce Hindmarsh, introduction to *An Authentic Narrative* in *The Life and Spirituality of John Newton* (Vancouver: Regent College Publishing: 1998), p 14.

them to the knowledge of him and themselves.

> ... The outward circumstances of many have been uniform: they have known but little variety in life: and with respect to their inward change, it has been effected in a secret way, unnoticed by others, and almost unperceived by themselves. The Lord has spoken to them, not in thunder and tempest, but with a still small voice he has drawn them gradually to himself; so that, though they have a happy assurance of the thing, that they know and love him, and are passed from death unto life; yet of the precise time and manner, they can give little account. Others he seems to select, in order to shew the exceeding riches of his grace, and the greatness of his mighty power: he suffers the natural rebellion and wickedness of their hearts to have full scope; while sinners of less note are cut off with little warning, these are spared, though sinning with a high hand, and, as it were, studying their own destruction. At length, when all that knew them are perhaps expecting to hear, that they are made signal instances of divine vengeance, the Lord (whose thoughts are high above ours, as the heavens are higher than the earth) is pleased to pluck them as brands out of the fire, and to make them monuments of his mercy, for the encouragement of others; they are, beyond expectation, convinced, pardoned, and changed. A case of this sort indicates a divine power no less than the creation of a world: it is evidently the Lord's doing, and it is marvellous in the eyes of all those, who are not blinded by prejudice and unbelief.[6]

Newton cites the example of Saul of Tarsus, to which we might well add Manasseh (2 Chronicles 33). Essentially, coming to faith in our Lord Jesus Christ is always the same: the sovereign regenerating work of the Spirit (see Titus 3:5 ESV) which draws forth the human response shown in conversion.

Following the early death of his mother and the swift remarriage of his somewhat aloof and severe father, Newton had not immediately thrown Elizabeth Newton's Christian faith overboard (so to speak) when first taken to sea by his father at the age of eleven. Indeed, 'I took up and laid aside a religious profession three or four different times before

---

[6] Ibid., p 12.

I was sixteen ... but I loved sin and was unwilling to forsake it.'[7] His religion, unlike his mother's, was at this stage never vital. A temporary reformation is not the same as spiritual regeneration and repentance. Newton's spiritual journey teaches us caution: his superficial religion fell away, and was replaced by profanity, blasphemy and immorality. Conscience vanished: 'I was possessed of so strong a spirit of delusion, that I believed my own lie, and was firmly persuaded that after death I should cease to be.'[8] In the mid eighteenth century, as in the twenty-first, atheism and annihilationism are very convenient beliefs.

After his remarkable rescue from the West African coast in February 1747 where he had become 'servant of slaves' (his own description in his epitaph), his conscience was awakened during a very severe storm on board the 'Greyhound' in March 1748, and he started to pray, a key sign of the conversion of both Manasseh and Saul of Tarsus, and to read the New Testament. By the time – against all human odds – the ship limped into Lough Swilly on the west coast of Ireland, Newton says 'I saw God might declare not his mercy only, but his justice also, in the pardon of sin, on the account of the obedience and sufferings of Jesus Christ. I stood in need of an Almighty Saviour, and such a one I found described in the New Testament.'[9]

Newton's conversion is a great encouragement to keep praying for even cynical unbelievers – and to pray that on occasions there may be dramatic conversions in a way that exalts and proclaims the sovereign grace of God. It is an encouragement for every parent and grandparent to pray and keep praying for their children: Newton clearly remembered his mother – surely an eighteenth century Hannah – praying with tears over his infant head. She taught him the Shorter Catechism and, above all, Scriptures which the Holy Spirit brought to mind in his hour of need. No wonder Newton was so keen on teaching the gospel to the children of Olney every Thursday afternoon, before even the Sunday School movement associated with Robert Raikes

---

[7] Ibid., p 20.
[8] Ibid., p 33.
[9] Ibid., p 63.

clearly got under way.[10] Midweek or after school clubs (as we now call them) meeting on similar lines are wisely renewing a Newton innovation.

But, wonderful though Newton's encounter with God had been, the years that follow are a reminder of the indispensable need to receive God's Word proclaimed, taught and shared by other believers. This he lacked: 'I had no Christian friend or faithful minister to advise me ... I was not brought in the way of evangelical preaching or conversation (except a few times ...) for six years after this period.'[11]

As First Mate on board the slaver 'Brownlow' (1748-9), he backslid: prayer and Bible reading slipped. 'The enemy' said Newton, 'prepared a train of temptations and I became his easy prey; and, for about a month, he lulled me asleep in a course of evil ...'[12] – including, it seems, raping some of the female slaves on board the 'Brownlow.' Severe fever was used to restore him to his spiritual senses. 'From that time, I trust, I have been delivered from the power and dominion of sin: though as to the effects and conflicts of sin dwelling in me, I still "groan, being burdened."'[13]

It was not until 1754 that Newton met a committed, instructed captain, Alexander Clunie at St. Kitts, who discipled him: 'I received an increase of knowledge; my conceptions became clearer and more evangelical ... I began to understand the security of the covenant of grace.'[14] The need for 21st century Clunies to be active for Christ in every area is undiminished. What would have happened to Newton if Clunie's Independent congregation in Stepney had told him that the navy was no place for a spiritual man? One wonders if Newton finding Clunie in the right place at the right time was one factor that years later led to his encouraging the newly converted Wilberforce to stay in Parliament?

---

[10] Pollock quotes Newton as saying his aim was to 'talk, preach and reason with them, and explain the Scriptures to them in their own little way.' Pollock continues: 'He taught them plenty of hymns; he shrewdly instituted a system of rewards for knowledge and good behaviour; but it was his manner and affection, and not least his sea stories which drew them.' John Pollock, *Amazing Grace: John Newton's Story* (London: Hodder, 1981), p 154.
[11] Hindmarsh, "Introduction," p 64.
[12] Ibid., p 69.
[13] Ibid., p 71.
[14] Ibid., p 88.

2. Newton's theology

It was with his heart freshly warmed and his mind newly alerted by Clunie's instruction in the Word of God that Newton began to find much more of a framework to his Christian faith. We need to realise that he already had a profound awareness of God's sovereign and merciful providence, through his own experience of saving grace. He had known that providence remarkably preserving his life on many extraordinary occasions: his rescue from the West African coast depended on split second timing as the vessel captained by the man Newton's father had asked to look for his son, passed by Kittam. Later as the 'Greyhound' lurched in the storm of March 1748, Newton was within a hair's breadth of being washed overboard. Staying in Londonderry while the 'Greyhound' was refitted, he managed almost to kill himself in a shooting accident: 'My fowling-piece ... went off so near my face, as to burn away the corner of my hat.'[15]

Five years before these events he had experienced in God's providence an extraordinary dream that spoke of God's knowledge of what lay ahead. It concerned a ring symbolizing the mercy of God which Newton in his dream threw away, but which he was assured could be restored to him. Newton's view of such 'monitory and supernatural dreams' was that, although he never encouraged any Christian to seek such occurrences 'those who are acquainted with the history and experience of the people of God are well assured, that such intimations have not been totally withheld in any period down to the present time.'[16]

Newton therefore already had a deep awareness of God as both truly sovereign and irresistibly gracious when he encountered again the Old Dissent Calvinistic theology of his mother and early childhood. By the end of 1754 Newton reckoned himself theologically a Calvinist: 'I should have much to answer for had I invented it myself or taken it upon trust from Calvin', he wrote later, 'but as I find it in the Scripture I cheerfully embrace it.'[17]

Soon after, Newton became much more aware of the Revival and the whole Methodist movement, and before long 'Whitefield fast

---

[15] Ibid., p 65.
[16] Ibid., p 25.
[17] Introduction to *Letters (selection)* (Edinburgh: Banner of Truth, 1960).

became Newton's supreme ideal.'[18] The Calvinistic wing of Methodism shared Old Dissent's theology, but was more aware of the eighteenth than the seventeenth century: it was in no sense antiquarian. It quarried the Puritan mines, but was too busy preaching the ospel and discipling new believers to spend all day down them, or to write with the prolixity of an Owen, Gurnall, or Charnock.

Newton's own eclectic reading thus included *Calvin's Institutes*, the Puritans Baxter, Owen, Leighton, and Flavel (an especially pastoral Puritan and a special favourite), as well as Reformed contemporaries such as Watts, Doddridge, and the Erskines.

Newton's Calvinism was a pastoral Calvinism (as shown in Flavel's ministry) and an evangelistic Calvinism as winsomely seen and powerfully heard in Whitefield. It was (in the seventeenth and eighteenth century sense of the word) an 'experimental' Calvinism. So when Newton described himself as a 'moderate Calvinist,' he was referring to the eirenic way he sought to hold his beliefs, rather than being lukewarm about his Reformed theological convictions. He sought to recognise the goodness and grace of God wherever he found it – in John Wesley, for example, though he differed from him, not surprisingly, on a number of doctrinal issues. Of any minister who was essentially orthodox but for some reason did not identify entirely with 'Mr N' (as Richard Cecil called him), he would say 'let him alone: he that is not against us is on our side. Make no man an offender for a word. He is doing good according to his views. Let us pray for him, and by no means weaken his hands. Who knows but God may one day put him far above our heads, both in knowledge and usefulness.'[19]

Again, Newton said:

> ... though a man does not accord with my views of election, yet if he gives me good evidence that *he* is *effectually called of God*, he is my brother; though he seems afraid of the doctrine of final perseverance; yet, if grace enables him to persevere, he is my brother still. If he loves Jesus, I will love him, whatever hard name he may be called by, and whatever incidental mistakes I may think he holds. His differing from me will not always prove

---

[18] Hindmarsh, *John Newton and the English Evangelical Tradition*, p 72.
[19] Richard Cecil, *The Life of John Newton* (1808, new edition ed. Marylynn Rouse; Fearn, Ross-Shire: Christian Focus, 2000), p 237.

him to be wrong, except I am infallible myself.[20]

We should not minimize Newton's theological acumen: he was increasingly suspicious of theological systematizing which went beyond Scripture, and successfully weaned John Ryland Jr. from the High (we would say 'hyper') Calvinism and supralapsarianism prevalent in some Baptist circles, which produced acute spiritual introspection and cut the nerve of the free offer of the Gospel.

In content, style, and spirit here is theology for today. Our evangelical colleges need those who will teach it, live it, and show how to apply it wisely and pastorally.

3. Newton's call to the ministry and attitude to denominations

Initially, Newton was so tongue-tied in public speaking that he assumed that he was not called to full-time ministry. However, as he continued to share his testimony, he became an increasingly articulate and attractive speaker. In 1758, friends in Yorkshire suggested ordination. 'My first thought was to join the Dissenters' Newton wrote,[21] amongst whom he had by now frequently ministered. This is important to note, for never in his life did Newton show any prejudice against their ministers or congregations. Many such nonconformist ministers were his close friends – for example, William Jay, who ministered in Bath from 1789-1853 and who said of Newton: 'I deem Mr Newton the most perfect instance of the spirit and temper of Christianity I ever knew ...'[22]

Early on, in Liverpool, in a rare anonymous pamphlet, *Some Thoughts on the Advantages and Expediency of Religious Associations*,[23] Newton argued against 'the unhappy prevalence of a spirit of bigotry on all sides; an undue attachment to systems and denominations, or a fondness for our own experiences.' Rather, he argued for associations where 'we are led into a clear acquaintance with the work of the Holy

---

[20] John Newton, *Works* (1820, reprinted Edinburgh: Banner of Truth, 1985), Vol 6, p 199.
[21] Newton's theological pastoring of John Ryland is unfolded by Hindmarsh, *John Newton and the English Evangelical Tradition*, pp 142-159.
[22] Hindmarsh, "Introduction," p 94.
[23] William Jay, *Autobiography* (reprinted Edinburgh: Banner of Truth, 1974), p 285.

Spirit, and the nature of the divine life ... when ... we observe with wonder and delight, that it is the same God that worketh all in all in his children, amidst the great variety of talents, tempers, dispositions and circumstances he has assigned them.'

In a day when boundaries between Anglicans and Dissenters, between Independents and Presbyterians and Methodists could be high, to Newton they were very low. He believed each minister or church member should be where God wanted him to be, and that they should work together for the Gospel. He would undoubtedly have rejoiced in conferences, training courses and church planting across the denominations today.

But we jump ahead: Newton took his possible call to the ministry with extreme seriousness. Between 23rd June and 4th August 1758 (his 33rd birthday) he wrote down his 'Miscellaneous Thoughts and enquiries on an important subject.'[24] The contents are most significant and reveal how much he had grown in the four years since he had met Alexander Clunie and in the three since he had met George Whitefield. 'I am willing' wrote Newton 'to take the apostle's resolution to know nothing but Jesus Christ and him crucified, that I may declare his unsearchable riches to sinners.'[25] He clearly saw the ministerial calling as one of proclaiming and teaching the Word of God.

Newton goes on to speak of 'the necessity of divine assistance ... To enable a person to preach the Gospel with *purity*, free from essential errors, *propriety* according to the state and circumstances of the audience and with *power* so as to be able to enforce his message and to give evidence that it is indeed the Word of God.'[26] In the final section, written on his birthday, he said:

> It is my prayer that I may not be permitted to keep back any part of the counsel of God. Yet I resolve and would endeavour always to bear in mind the Scripture distinction of babes and men, milk and strong meat, and remember the practice of my Dear Lord and Master who taught his disciples as they were able to bear.[27]

---

[24] Printed for the John Newton Project from the ms. in Lambeth Palace Library by Marylynn Rouse, 2001.
[25] Newton, *Miscellaneous Thoughts* (A5 edition), p 9.
[26] Ibid., p 12.
[27] Ibid., p 28.

For Newton, 'the three great branches of divine truth' were

1. The Doctrine of Jesus Christ crucified ...

2. The great doctrine of love which is the life and soul of the gospel, and which seems too much to be left unnoticed amidst the general strife there is for and against other doctrines;

3. The doctrine, or rather, the practice of Gospel holiness.[28]

The whole of *Miscellaneous Thoughts*, which makes no more than a booklet of thirty-two pages, is a largely unknown gem which could continue to fire the hearts of those moving towards ordination today.

From then on, Newton knew ministry was right for him – and in the Church of England (though he was offered Independent charges in 1759-60). Henry Crook, Vicar of Hunslett 'moderated my scruples' and offered him a curacy.[29] There is no doubt that Newton saw the Church of England as 'the best boat to fish from' (although he did not use that phrase!) and he spoke even in 1764 of 'preferring the established church in some other respects.'[30]

One might have thought that, on interview, any bishop would have been glad to ordain a man with Newton's spiritual experience, now evident gifts, and clear potential. However, the Bishop of Chester ('rich and proud' – so Pollock)[31] simply forwarded him to the Archbishop of York ('elderly, idle' – so Pollock)[32], who did not want to meet him. Those tainted with Methodism were scarcely welcome ordination candidates, as (it has been alleged) conservative evangelicals are not always welcome today. It was not till 29th April 1764, after tortuous twists and turns, that Newton was finally ordained by the Bishop of Lincoln through the influence of the evangelical Earl of Dartmouth, sometime President of the Board of Trade and Colonial Secretary. The lesson is still that, if God is indeed calling to preaching and pastoral ministry, keep prayerfully pushing every door, and do not despise those in high places who can pull strings!

---

[28] Ibid., p 29.
[29] Hindmarsh, "Introduction," p 64.
[30] Ibid., p 94.
[31] Pollock, *Amazing Grace*, p 32.
[32] Ibid., p 33.

Twenty years later, Newton wrote four letters to the minister of an Independent church as an apologia for his serving in the Church of England. Anglican Evangelical ministers who wish to explain their denominational allegiance today to free church friends could well find their arguments strengthened by reading it. Negatively, Newton found disputes amongst the Independents unattractive; and he found the Regulative Principle impossible to implement. He was also unconvinced by Baptist distinctives. However, says Newton, he can exercise a gospel ministry with liberty in the Church of England, and he says 'I approve of parochial order.' Of the *Book of Common Prayer* he writes 'I approve the service and therefore it is no burden to me to use it.' I do not know that we could always echo his comment, 'I have reason to acknowledge that the administration of our church government is gentle and liberal' (sadly, today it is sometimes liberal in another sense!). 'Indeed,' Newton continues, 'I have often thought I have as good a right to the name of Independent as yourself.'[33]

4. Newton's preaching and praying

(I link these, as for Newton they were two sides of the one coin).

People flocked to hear Newton when he settled in Olney and later at St. Mary Woolnoth. Yet we cannot call him one of the really great preachers of the church, either because of fresh insight into the Word or because of an outstanding delivery. Whitefield was his hero, but Newton must have known he could never preach quite like him, and that he would be wiser not to try.

Under God, Newton was his own man, and God honoured that. In his first winter at Olney he wrote to Alex Clunie: 'Neither short days, uncertain weather or dirty roads make any considerable diminution in our assemblies, and their attention and seriousness give me hope they do not all come in vain.'[34]

What then were his strengths? Newton sought always to expound and apply the Scriptures as the Word of God, and to glorify Christ. 'Effect, I believe has been produced in my preaching by a solemn

---

[33] Newton, *Works*, Vol. 5, pp 3-58.
[34] Pollock, *Amazing Grace*, p 155.

determination to bring forth Jesus Christ as the great subject in all my discourses.'³⁵ He sought 'to break a hard heart, and to heal a broken heart.'³⁶ Newton said in a letter to a friend in America, Dr Robbins, that his aims were:

> First, to set forth the glory and grace of God in the person of the Saviour. Second, to show the danger and folly of a form of godliness without the power, of a mere talking, speculative profession. Third, to persuade, if possible, those that love the Lord Jesus Christ to love one another, to lay much stress upon the things in which we are agreed, and but little upon those in which we differ.³⁷

It was because Newton wanted to be both eirenic and effective that he preached his Calvinism as he did. William Jay records a breakfast conversation with a 'high' (or 'hyper') Calvinist who was querying Newton's doctrinal credentials, and who, says Jay, 'required some moderating':

> 'I am more of a Calvinist than anything else: but I use my Calvinism in my writings and my preaching as I use this sugar' – taking a lump, and putting it into his tea-cup, and stirring it, adding, 'I do not give it alone, and whole; but mixed, and diluted.'³⁸

'So,' says John Piper, 'Newton did not serve up the "five points" by themselves, but blended them in with everything he taught. This way of flavouring life was essential to his pattern of tenderness that developed in dealing with people's doctrinal differences.'³⁹

Of Newton's preaching in London, Brian Edwards writes: 'Newton continued to preach, as he had always done, not to create dissension, but for disseminating the truth. He aimed to lead his hearers to a deeper knowledge of, and personal relationship to, the Son of God, and to live a life of faith in him. Consequently John avoided

---

[35] John H. Pratt, *The Thought of the Evangelical Leaders* (reprinted Edinburgh: Banner of Truth, 1978), p 20.
[36] Pollock, *Amazing Grace*, p 155.
[37] Cecil, *The Life of John Newton*, p 201.
[38] Jay, *Autobiography*, p 272.
[39] John Piper, Chapter one in *The Roots of Endurance* (Leicester: IVP, 2002), p 64.

issues that were not essential but would only antagonize ... However, it must not be imagined that Newton sat loosely to vital doctrine'[40].

His preaching was practical; he was down to earth; he could illustrate from his own experience (not least when preaching the Book of Jonah!). He did not preach over long (not more than an hour). He communicated love for the Lord Jesus and love for his hearers.

Newton had his weaknesses. Perhaps surprisingly, in view of his appreciative hearers, Richard Cecil says 'His utterance was far from clear, and his attitudes ungraceful.' Was Cecil referring to diction and mannerisms? But who was really bothered, even at St. Mary Woolnoth, that their minister did not have the polish or sophistication of many of the preachers of the day? Newton's preaching was real preaching by a man whose university had been on the high seas and as 'a servant of slaves' on the west coast of Africa.

However, two particular charges must be faced. One is that in desiring to be 'patient, tender-hearted, non-controversial' (so Piper) he failed to attack error as he should have done. But Piper concludes that pastors 'cannot be faulted that they mainly have flocks to love and hearts to change. Defending the truth is a crucial part of that, but it is not the main part. *Holding* the truth and *permeating* all our ministry with the greatness and sweetness of truth for the transformation of our people's lives is the main part of our ministry.'[41]

The other charge relates to Newton's extempore preaching. In spite of the experience of his first sermon, he went back to this to give him more freedom in delivery, and more eye-contact with his hearers. By extempore is meant his lack of notes in the pulpit – but certainly in Olney years he filled notebooks with his advance preparation. I think we have to admit that as life wore on and in London pressures increased, and as eyesight weakened, fresh detailed preparation in advance decreased.

I am not excusing this, but because Newton was full of the Word and of the Spirit, and had over the years studied it and meditated upon it so fully, faithfully and fruitfully, God continued greatly to use and own his preaching ministry. True, he had admitted in 1766

---

[40] Edwards, *Through Many Dangers*, p 287.
[41] Piper, *The Roots of Endurance*, p 67.

'coldness in prayer and darkness and formality in reading the Word are almost my continual burden,'[42] but who has not known such battles? The sign of true life is that such times bother us. Hundreds owed their conversion to him, and the Lord's strength was perfected in his servant's weakness.

Read Newton's preaching for yourself: for example, the fifty sermons based on the texts used in Handel's *Messiah*;[43] or, very accessibly, in the previously unpublished material from his sermon preparation notebooks in *365 Days with John Newton*.[44] You will not be disappointed, and may well find yourself praying for preachers in our century with the knowledge and application of the Word, with the Christ-centredness, and with the experience of life that marks his ministry.

My comments about Newton and prayer are much briefer, but this is not because it was unimportant to him. Josiah Bull asks, 'What ... was the great secret of Mr Newton's power and steadfastness?' He answers: 'unquestionably it was his *spirit of prayer*. From the commencement of his religious history we find him cultivating this holy habit.'[45]

Newton wrote to 'a Student in Divinity':

> The chief means for attaining wisdom ... are the holy Scriptures and prayer. The one is the fountain of living water, the other the bucket with which we are to draw. And I believe you will find that the man who is most frequent and fervent in prayer, and most devoted to the Word of God, will shine and flourish above his fellows.[46]

Read Hindmarsh for invaluable insight into Newton's prayer and communion with God.[47]

It is not surprising that this priority was reflected in church life. In 1765 in Olney Newton began regular prayer meetings: he selected

---

[42] See Newton's letter to Henry Venn in Cecil, *The Life of John Newton*, p 199.
[43] Newton, *Works*, Vol. 4.
[44] Extracts from the notebooks are very helpfully combined with Newton's hymns and extracts from his letters.
[45] Bull, *But Now I See*, p 368.
[46] Newton, *Works*, Vol. 1, p 141.
[47] Hindmarsh, *John Newton and the English Evangelical Tradition*, pp 221-239.

those who would pray, but he was delighted when he could add another name to his list of extempore pray-ers. He must have been delighted too that other lay-initiated prayer meetings sprang up at Olney – one at 6am on Sunday to pray for Newton and the services; one amongst young people; and one 'on account of the present appearances of the times.'[48]

The priority of prayer, with the priority of the Word, must be kept right at the centre for every minister, every believer, and every church in every century.

5. Newton's pastoral and evangelistic work

All things being equal, Newton at Olney studied, prepared and wrote in the mornings and visited in the afternoons. His visits were of course always pastoral in intent. To such pastoral visits he aimed to add Baxter's Kidderminster pattern of spending an hour with each member of the congregation as a time for spiritual check-up and encouragement.[49]

Newton came across as warm, genuine, caring, accepting, and of course discerning. He was certainly not formal in either dress or manner. William Cole, from the same archdeaconry as Newton, described him as 'a little odd-looking man of the Methodistical order, and without any clerical habit' (i.e. dress).[50] Evidently evangelicals in the latter part of the 20th century were not the first to start dispensing with the accoutrements of clericalism! We should take courage from his example. Nor was Newton an advocate of clerical exclusivism. He involved others in visiting the sick and needy – like Richard Stamford, one of his early converts;[51] and Betty Abraham (d.1774) was what we would call an honorary 'pastoral assistant,' a 'Mother in Israel ... exceedingly useful, especially to the lambs of the flock.' However, Newton's encouragement of lay leadership in different spheres – unusual for the times in the Church of England – did lead to a loss of ministerial authority and to tensions in the church and beyond, which

---

[48] Ibid., p 198; Cecil, *The Life of John Newton*, p 132.
[49] See Wallace Benn, *The Baxter Model*, Orthos booklet 13 (Hartford: Fellowship of Word and Spirit, 1993).
[50] Hindmarsh, *John Newton and the English Evangelical Tradition*, p 206.
[51] Ibid., p 203.

contributed to his leaving Olney. But surely it was a risk it was right to take.

I want to comment also on Newton's detailed and invaluable pastoral ministry to those who were to have a wider influence. First is Thomas Scott, curate-in-charge of Ravenstone and Weston Underwood, who was chagrined by Newton visiting dying parishioners, whom Scott had neglected. Doctrinally, Scott 'was the opposite of all that evangelicalism stood for.'[52] He was in the ministry to earn a living and hopefully become a literary man. He was ordained in 1772 with he says, 'a heart full of pride and wickedness: my life polluted with many unrepented, unforsaken sins.'[53] Convinced of his theological correctness ('I was nearly a Socinian and Pelagian, and wholly an Arminian')[54], he spoiled for a fight with Newton.

An initial discussion at a clergy meeting was handled with great wisdom by Newton, who refused to be confrontational in public, but sent him a note and a book – and prayed. More letters followed, with Newton seeing as his priority building up the friendship but dropping hints about the nature of and need for true faith. Scott's reading began to take him in a more orthodox direction. After a gap of fifteen months, friendship was resumed and Scott started attending Newton's lectures. Slowly, gradually 'I began ... to perceive our Lord's meaning when he says 'except ye receive the Kingdom of God as a little child, ye shall in no wise enter therein.'"[55] Scott was won by friendship, earnest prayer, and by the right word at the right time, with Newton convinced that the Lord was at work. Scott became a noted preacher and commentator.[56]

The second example is the famous friendship with William Cowper, the poet. A highly-strung depressive, bullied at boarding school, he had like Newton lost his mother when he was six. But, unlike Newton, he was not allowed to marry the woman he loved, his cousin Theodora. Overwhelmed finally by the pressures of his work in the House of Lords, he had a bad breakdown. While in hospital, he was

---

[52] Edwards, *Through Many Dangers*, p 210.
[53] Thomas Scott, *The Force of Truth* (reprinted Edinburgh: Banner of Truth, 1984), p 28.
[54] Ibid., p 27.
[55] Ibid., p 87.
[56] See J. E. Marshall, introduction to Scott, *The Force of Truth*, and biographical summary in Cecil, *The Life of John Newton*, p 324.

converted mainly through his cousin, Martin Madan. Later, he moved to Olney, cared for by a clergyman's widow, Mary Unwin.

Cowper and Newton became firm friends. Newton drew the best out of Cowper, especially his poetic and hymn writing gifts. Cowper was involved in sick visiting and leading church prayer meetings, but his mental illness returned and he attempted suicide. Although in large measure he recovered, a sense of rejection by God never left him.

Newton showed to Cowper true Christian love, friendship and support, and shared with him the grace of the gospel. But to be on the receiving end of such ministry is no necessary guarantee against mental illness. Newton has been blamed for this by many – including Lord David Cecil in his 1930 biography of Cowper, *The Stricken Deer*, which openly despises Newton and all that he stood for. Of Cowper's mental state, Cecil says 'Of course, it was partly the fault of the evangelical creed, which ... made an emotional condition into a moral virtue.'[57] This is answered in the study on Cowper by Dr Gaius Davies, who speaks of 'the immense credit Newton deserves.'[58] Cowper himself said of Newton 'a sincerer or more affectionate friend no man ever had.'[59]

The third example is that of Hannah More, who arrived in London in 1773 at the age of twenty-eight as successful playwright and poet. She was one of five sisters who had started a girls' boarding school in Bristol. Mixing with the mighty in London (including Dr Johnson and David Garrick) failed to satisfy her any more than her conventional religion.

However, encounters with Thornton and Wilberforce of the Clapham Sect impressed her with their zeal. A copy of Newton's *Cardiphonia* both gave her a spiritual hunger and pointed to how it could be satisfied. In response to her letter to Newton, Newton offered spiritual counsel and Christian friendship. Newton's letters were supplemented by visits from him and Wilberforce. Rather than force the spiritual pace, Newton trusted (as with Scott) the Holy Spirit to be about his work. Encouraging her to seek the Lord, he identified with her by

---

[57] Lord David Cecil, *The Stricken Deer* (London: Constable, reprinted 1933), p 133.
[58] Dr. Gaius Davies, *Genius, Grief and Grace* (2nd ed; Fearn, Ross-shire: Christian Focus, 2001), ch. 3 "Darkness into Light: William Cowper."
[59] John Piper, *Tested by Fire* (Leicester: IVP, 2001), ch. 2 "Insanity and Spiritual Songs in the life of William Cowper", p 95.

saying 'I have stood upon that ground myself.'[60] Hannah More was converted, and her Christian educational work and her writing, including popular Christian tracts for the poor and downtrodden had far-reaching influence for the gospel.

Newton remains not only an example for our day of a conscientious pastor in the Baxter tradition (though he never saw as much fruit at Olney as Baxter at Kidderminster), but of one who was led alongside those whose gifts and service would in turn have a wide impact. We need to be praying that Newton will have his successors in this sphere today.

6. Newton's letter-writing

Newton's letters are one of two areas where he is chiefly remembered, although, as we are seeing, he was under God a man of many parts. We have noted already his ministry of letter-writing to Thomas Scott and Hannah More. Newton's use of letters for pastoral counselling fitted the eighteenth century way of life, when the development of the post office, as well as a more relaxed English prose style, made letters increasingly significant for both general and spiritual communication. It was the chief way evangelicals 'networked' – hence the significance of Wesley's and Whitefield's correspondence. But it was Newton who made letter-writing such a significant conduit of spiritual advice. He was, says Hindmarsh, 'the gentle casuist of the Revival';[61] and says G. R. Balleine 'the St. Francis de Sales of the evangelical movement, the great spiritual director of souls through the post.'[62] The six volume *Works* contain the main collections *by Omicron and Vigil, Cardiphonia, Letters to a Wife* and a *Sequel to Cardiphonia*; but there are very many more. Newton saw it as a priority: 'it is the Lord's will I should do most by my letters.'[63]

Running one's eye down the subjects covered by *Omicron* indicates their range, e.g. 'on the inward witness to the ground and reality of faith,' 'on the doctrines of Election and Final Perseverance,'

---

[60] Edwards, *Through Many Dangers*, p 323.
[61] Hindmarsh, *John Newton and the English Evangelical Tradition*, pp 243-256.
[62] George R. Balleine, *A History of the Evangelical Party in the Church of England* (new edition, London: Church Book Room Press, 1951), p 84.
[63] Ibid., p 84.

'on Union with Christ,' 'of the Lord's promised Guidance.' 'Such gentle sympathy, combined with such sturdy commonsense, made him a friend in whom it was indeed good to confide.'[64] The letters were popularised Puritan theology – equally experimental but appropriate to Newton's ministry.

Of particular interest are Letters X, XI, and XII from the *Omicron* selection, which Hindmarsh adds to the *Authentic Narrative* in his *Life and Spirituality of John Newton*.[65] 'I sit down to give you my general views of a progressive work of grace, in the several stages of a believer's experience' wrote Newton to John Thornton. 'It will be needful ... to set aside such things as may be personal and occasional ... and to collect those only which, in a greater or less degree, are common to them all.'

Newton summarized the three stages he observed from Scripture and experience as 'A: Grace in the Blade'; 'B: Grace in the Ear' and 'C: Grace in the Full Corn in the Ear,' drawing the imagery from Mark 4:28. Hindmarsh's four page introduction is as worth reading as the Letters. 'A' says Hindmarsh, is 'characterised by *desire* and ... sharp feelings of contrition and spiritual comfort and longing.' In 'B,' 'conflict is the dominating characteristic.' In 'C,' 'his or her will is united to the will of God so far as is possible in this life.'[66] Hindmarsh says of this outline of pastoral theology 'Its genius was its simplicity,'[67] and adds 'it is a unique contribution to evangelical theology.'[68]

Moving from the eighteenth to the twenty-first century, it is clearly an often neglected key to pastoral ministry to understand spiritual development with Newton's spiritual perceptiveness. Further, is the letter format outmoded as many assume? May there not be value in ministers still producing focussed pastoral letters for their congregations (remember Newton's letters were often written with an eye to later publication)? The congregational letter was developed by William Still and other evangelical ministers in the Church of Scotland in the second half of the twentieth century.[69] The individual pastoral letter was a key

---

[64] Ibid., p 84.
[65] Hindmarsh, "Introduction," pp 95-111; Newton, *Works*, Vol. 1, pp 197-217.
[66] Ibid., p 7.
[67] Ibid., p 8.
[68] Ibid., p 9.
[69] William Still, *Letters of William Still* (Edinburgh: Banner of Truth, 1984).

element in the extraordinary ministry of the Rev. E. J. H. Nash ('Bash') (1898-1982).[70] His letter-writing was a key part of discipling public schoolboys who had been helped spiritually at his camps. John Stott wrote: 'I do not know any Christian leader of modern days who shared, as he did, the apostle Paul's convictions of the value of letter-writing.'[71] I do not think that the style of Mr N and of Bash would have been very similar; but they wrote of the same Lord and under the authority of the same Scriptures. It encourages us to wonder whether there may indeed be a future for a letter-writing ministry in some shape or form.

7. Newton's hymns[72]

The eighteenth century was also the key time for the writing, development and use of hymns amongst evangelicals as the Awakening spread. Isaac Watts was the first significant figure, and his hymns would have been familiar to Newton from his early background in Old Dissent, a background he picked up again (as we have seen) in the early years of his own spiritual awakening.

Not all evangelicals approved of introducing hymns in addition to the metrical Psalms: William Romaine (1714-95), for example, of St. Andrew-by-the-Wardrobe, said of his exclusive Psalm-singing policy: 'This should silence every objection – It is the Word of God.'[73] However, it did not silence every objection: Newton and many others could see no intrinsic difficulty with hymn-singing.

He started writing them – sometimes at the rate of almost one a week – when he went to Olney, although chiefly for non-liturgical prayer meetings. For Newton, there was the closest of links between hymns and the Word of God. Robin Leaver writes:

> Most of Newton's hymns are linked with his preaching ... Either the hymn grew out of the Biblical text or subject he was preaching on, or his sermon grew out of the hymn he had

---

[70] John Eddison, ed., *"Bash": A Study in Spiritual Power* (Basingstoke: Marshalls, 1983).
[71] Ibid., p 58.
[72] Newton's hymns are discussed by Robin Leaver in *Churchman* 1979/4 and 1980/1, and in Hindmarsh, *John Newton and the English Evangelical Tradition,* ch. 7.
[73] Hindmarsh, *John Newton and the English Evangelical Tradition,* p 264; and Tim Shenton, *The Iron Pillar: William Romaine* (Darlington, Evangelical Press, 2004).

written.[74]

For example, the celebrated *Amazing Grace* was almost certainly written for Newton's New Year sermon in 1773 on 1 Chronicles 17:16-17.[75] Others were written with a sharp eye to the contemporary scene – e.g. 'On the commencement of hostilities in America' in 1775.[76]

Newton wrote in no detached way, but conscious of his own spiritual experience and that of others. He is the representative 'I' in many of the hymns.

> As the workings of the heart of man, and of the Spirit of God, are in general the same, in all who are the subjects of grace, I hope most of the hymns, being the fruit and expression of my own experience, will coincide with the views of real Christians of all denominations.[77]

That is why one whole section (Book 3) of *Olney Hymns* is devoted to 'the Rise, Progress, Changes and Comforts of the Spiritual Life.' Newton thus aimed to be both biblical and 'experimental.'

Further, Newton wrote conscious of his unsophisticated parishioners who would first sing them. His hymns are

> for the use of plain people. Perspicuity, simplicity and ease, should be chiefly attended to; and the imagery and colouring of poetry, if admitted at all, should be indulged very sparingly and with great judgement.[78]

Hindmarsh is right in saying 'Newton saw himself as a journeyman in the trade ... a skilled versifier, not a sophisticated poet'[79]. Newton's aims and principles guide us to a correct evaluation of his hymns. Of course, with such a number they are variable as verse; but there is nothing wrong with doggerel (understood as simple rhyming verse), and some are that, if it is good doggerel and achieves its purpose. Another outstanding example is found in Bunyan's verse in *Pilgrim's Progress*.

---

[74] Leaver, *Churchman*, 1979/4, p 332.
[75] See *365 Days with Newton*, Jan. 1-4.
[76] *Olney Hymns* (facsimile reprint, Cowper and Newton Museum, 1984), Book 2, 64. (Also in Newton, *Works*, Vol 3).
[77] Ibid., Preface, p viii.
[78] Ibid., Preface, p vii.
[79] Hindmarsh, *John Newton and the English Evangelical Tradition*, p 268.

What is remarkable is that so many of Newton's hymns are of such very high quality in terms of wording, theology and the sense of personal involvement. *How sweet the name of Jesus sounds, One there is above all others, Day of judgement, day of wonders, Glorious things of Thee are spoken, Approach, my soul, the mercy seat*, are a few amongst the large number which appear in twentieth century hymn books. Such hymns place Newton, with his near contemporaries Isaac Watts and Charles Wesley as surely amongst the greatest hymn writers.

Today, the principles that guided Newton are equally indispensable for twenty-first century hymn and song writers. We are also foolish beyond measure if we see the hymns of Newton and other great hymn writers of the past as simply 'golden oldies' to be only occasionally taken from the shelf and dusted down (*Amazing Grace* being the almost too frequent exception!).

8. Newton's attitude to the slave trade

Some may be surprised that it is only now that this subject is introduced, but this is where it belongs. The fact is that Newton did not begin his four voyages as a slave-trader (one as First Mate and three as Captain) until after God had met with him in the great storm while on the 'Greyhound' in March 1748.

The fact also is that slave-trading and slavery was an almost complete blind spot amongst Europeans at this stage: this included most committed Christians, some Quakers excepted. It was almost universally viewed as economically essential, and it is feared that most Europeans scarcely thought of Africans as their equals as human beings. Tragically, as we know, Africans were also ready to enslave fellow Africans and to aid Europeans to do the same. As we shall see, when we jump to the twenty-first century, blind spots can be very blind indeed.

It would be thirty to fourty years before Hannah More wrote with reference to *Rule Britannia*:

> Cease, ye British Sons of murder!
> Ye that boast 'ye rule the waves'
> Cease from forging Afric's chain,
> Bid no slave ship soil the sea,
> Mock your Saviour's name no further,
> Ye that 'never will be slaves,'

> Cease you savage lust of gain.
> Bid poor Afric's land be free.[80]

From 1748-1754, when involved in the slave trade, Newton's own spiritual light, let alone knowledge of God's Word, was limited. He did not meet Clunie, who was not a slave-trader, until almost at the end of his slave trading career. He certainly endeavoured to make conditions less inhumane than on many other ships. Nor was Newton wrong to write of his consciousness of the providential hand of God closely on him personally even while slaves suffered and died in the holds below. Amazing saving grace draws alongside us in Jesus as we are and where we are, and insists on loving us as that grace gradually begins to change us into the likeness of the one who himself became a slave.

There are indications Newton's conscience was troubled earlier than some suppose. Ten years after he left the slave trade, he wrote in the *Authentic Narrative* in 1764:

> During the time I was engaged in the slave trade, I never had the least scruple as to its lawfulness. I was, upon the whole, satisfied with it, as the appointment Providence had marked out for me ... I considered myself as a sort of gaoler or turnkey: and I was sometimes shocked with an employment that was perpetually conversant with chains, bolts, and shackles. In this view I had often petitioned, that the Lord, in his own time, would be pleased to fix me in a more humane calling ... [81]

This indicates that by or before 1764 he *was* having scruples. None of this is to excuse Newton, but it is to set him in the context of his times.

Eventually, in 1784, in his poem *The Task,* Cowper denounced slavery, clearly with Newton's approval:

> Here's padlocks and bolts, and screws for the thumbs,
> That squeeze them so lovingly till the blood comes,
> They sweeten the temper like comfits or plums
> Which nobody can deny.[82]

The following year, the twenty-six year old spiritually searching William

---

[80] John Wolffe, *The Expansion of Evangelicalism* (Nottingham: IVP, 2006), p 130.
[81] Hindmarsh, "Introduction," p 88.
[82] Bernard Martin, *An Ancient Mariner* (revised edition, London: Epworth Press, 1960), p 207.

Wilberforce, sought 'some serious conversation' with the man he remembered as his boyhood hero and referred to as 'Old Newton.' Newton not only spoke of the Gospel, but crucially 'urged him not to cut himself from his present circles or to retire from public life.'[83] Wilberforce heeded all the advice he was given.

As he grew as a Christian, and as his campaign against the slave trade got under way, Wilberforce stayed in close contact with Newton and Hannah More. In 1788 Newton's *Thoughts Upon the African Slave Trade* was published.[84] It is a cogently argued tract depicting the horrors of the trade for black people, and its dehumanising effect on the whites. He concludes that the slave trade is 'a commerce so iniquitous, so cruel, so oppressive, so destructive.'[85]

Newton both discipled Wilberforce as a believer and encouraged him in his campaign by his letters to him. These letters to Wilberforce and his wife total 79 and were written between 1785 and 1804.[86] They must have been a continuing source of stimulus and encouragement to Wilberforce in the opposition he faced:

> Oh, my Dear Sir, how much do you owe to the mercy and grace, which snatched you out of that whirlpool in which so many are daily swallowed up! My heart congratulates you. May the Lord be your sun and shield, make you as a watered garden yourself and a spring of water for the benefit of many.[87]

No wonder Newton was a key witness before the Committee of the Privy Council which Pitt set up in 1788.

In our generation we desperately need committed evangelical Christians in every area of public life. We need those who will tackle long term the anti-Christian morality now being written into our legislation whereby heterosexual and homosexual lifestyles are viewed

---

[83] John Pollock, *Wilberforce* (London: Constable, 1977), p 38. Pollock has also produced a summary account of Newton's and Wilberforce's roles in the abolition of the slave trade in *Abolition!* (Leominster: Day One, 2007).
[84] Newton, *Works*, Vol. 6, pp 519-548.
[85] Newton, *Works*, Vol. 6, p 548.
[86] Printed for the John Newton Project from the mss. in the Bodleian library, Oxford, by M. Rouse, 2002.
[87] Letter 49, 3rd October 1795.

as equally valid.[88] We need Christians who will tackle the blind spots that seem amongst many to be about as total as the eighteenth century attitude to slavery, especially the scandal of the abortion of unborn human beings. Since the 1967 Abortion Act as many or more have been killed by abortion as died in the Nazi Holocaust. And unborn children have no successors to call for apologies and reparation.

In an article in *The Church of England Newspaper*,[89] Catherine Fox asked of Newton and the slave trade: 'How could Newton not have noticed the shocking truth? The Lord had promised good to him while people were rotting in chains just yards beneath his feet. Surely the implications of the Gospel must have been plain to him?' To Catherine Fox 'this makes singing *Amazing Grace* a very tricky business.' (She thinks, surely incorrectly, that Newton wrote that hymn *before* becoming a slave trader). Her conscience is eased by adapting Anglican Article XXVI: 'The grace of Christ isn't rendered any less effective by the sinfulness of the hymn writer.' But in each generation, blind spots are just that, and they can affect Christians unless minds are more fully enlightened by the Word of God.

To be fair, Catherine Fox continues: 'It occurred to me ... that Newton holding services on deck was a good metaphor for us in the affluent West. We sail on, while just below our feet is the poverty and enforced labour of millions, yet we manage to edit it out.' This is an entirely fair and significant point; but I return to the stark and tragic parallel between the slave trade and abortion. Many, including Christians, will daily work within or travel close to hospitals or clinics, where – also daily – unborn life is terminated. And perhaps with never a thought.

9. Newton's marriage

With the marriage of Richard Baxter and Margaret Charlton in the seventeenth century, Hudson Taylor and Maria Dyer in the nineteenth, and C.S. Lewis and Joy Davidman Gresham in the twentieth, the marriage of John Newton and Mary Catlett in the eighteenth has its

---

[88] Our debt to organisations such as The Christian Institute is enormous.
[89] 30th March 2007.

rightful place in the romantic annals of the people of God. We shall never know exactly what it was that caused 17 year old John to fall head over heels in love with 13 year old Mary (Polly) when Newton called for the first time on the Catletts, old family friends, on 12th December 1742. Perhaps in some way, young though she was, she reminded him of his mother. For love of her, Newton became a naval deserter, but love of her almost certainly kept him alive when 'all at sea' in the seven years before they married.

No doubt they worked at their marriage, as all need to do. Interestingly, it was Polly who first suggested they should pray aloud together – with John of course taking the lead!⁹⁰ Newton's chief complaint was his fear that the strength of his love for her would usurp the primacy of his love for the Lord. 'Newton's extreme and undisguised attachment used to puzzle some of his friends, "as she seemed to have few or any attractions." They were obvious enough to him, for she was a dream wife and he had never woken from the dream.'⁹¹

They cherished one another through good health and bad. They practised hospitality. Having no children of their own, they gladly adopted two orphaned nieces, Eliza Cunningham and Betsy Catlett. Along with the joy of having children to care for, there was a spiritual concern: Newton wrote in his diary concerning Betsy 'Oh may He by His grace adopt her into His chosen family.'⁹² He did, and Betsy cared for Newton in old age.

He suffered with Polly during her two final years of illness before she died on 15th December 1790, and he preached at her funeral on Habakkuk 3:17-18. Newton shows us that unselfish self-giving Christian love in marriage can bring spiritual maturity and can spill over into a particular richness in Christian service that our generation may not often see or experience. Jonathan Aitken describes it as 'a union of romance, prayer, service and joy.' He continues 'Household servants were also regarded as part of the Newton family. It was a Christian home and marriage which set an outstanding example in its time and to posterity.'⁹³

---

[90] Pollock, *Amazing Grace*, p 114.
[91] Pollock, *Amazing Grace*, p 178.
[92] Cecil, *The Life of John Newton*, p 273.
[93] Jonathan Aitken, *From Disgrace to Amazing Grace* (London: Continuum, 2007), p 272.

10. Newton's leadership

Leadership in the church of God is made in heaven and sadly not always reflected in so-called ecclesiastical hierarchies on earth. Newton spent his entire ministry as curate of one parish and then rector of another, but he was undoubtedly the most significant leader amongst Anglican evangelicals and beyond in the final part of the eighteenth century. Others saw in him a leader raised up by God.

It was not his dramatic early years, but the man God in his grace made of him, that led to Newton becoming a recognised leader. 'My connections have enlarged – my little name is spread' he wrote soon after arriving at St. Mary Woolnoth. Despite only two years' formal education, Newton comes across as someone with a sharp if not always original mind. He was seen as a man with clear biblical and theological convictions, but one who held his views eirenically, who reached out to all who shared his gospel priorities. He was an able and in some areas a quite exceptional all-rounder.

His godly influence was further forwarded in London through the Eclectic Society. Founded in 1783, the Society was 'for discussion of religious truths and mutual improvement.' Note that from the start this included 'clergy from the established church, dissenting ministers and laymen.'[94] An example of Newton's ongoing influence is John Stott's revival of the Eclectics in the early years of his own ministry.[95]

His influence on the next generation of evangelicals was considerable (on Simeon for example[96]) and on pioneer missionaries, such as William Carey and Henry Martyn.

Behind the scenes, remember Newton the leader was ever a man of personal prayer. Jonathan Aitken's verdict is: 'The secret of Newton's relationship with God was his prayer life ... The theology of his prayer life – giving glory to the sovereign God; struggling to obey and suffer with the crucified Christ; and confiding in his Heavenly

---

[94] Cecil, *The Life of John Newton*, p 200; and see Pratt, *The Thought of the Evangelical Leaders*.
[95] Timothy Dudley-Smith, *John Stott: The Making of a Leader* (Leicester: IVP, 1999), pp 305-308.
[96] See Hugh Evan Hopkins, *Charles Simeon of Cambridge* (London: Hodder, 1977).

Father with the heartfelt penitence of a sinner, combined to create a holy relationship between the giver and hearer of prayer.'[97]

Evangelical historians agree on Newton's significance. For example, Skevington Wood: 'For 28 years Newton delivered the evangelical message from this strategic pulpit (St. Mary Woolnoth) and did perhaps more than any other to commend the cause.'[98] Kenneth Hylson-Smith: 'John Newton was not only one of the most remarkable evangelical leaders: but arguably one of the most remarkable men in the whole history of the Church of England.'[99]

11. Conclusion

As he grew old with his powers declining, Newton could not contemplate ceasing from ministry unless compelled to do so. To Richard Cecil he said: 'Shall the old African blasphemer stop while he can speak?'[100]

Josiah Bull said: 'It was his *goodness* rather than his *greatness* that rendered him so especially attractive – the abundance of the grace of God that was in him ... Some men excel in one virtue more than another; but Mr Newton's character was beautiful in its entireness.'[101] Hagiography is never in place and disputes over words inappropriate; but the grace that saved Newton and worked goodness into his character, surely also made him great – great in ministry and leadership in his own generation, and great in example and inspiration for the centuries to come.

---

[97] Aitken, *From Disgrace to Amazing Grace*, p 273.
[98] A. Skevington Wood, *The Inextinguishable Blaze* (London: Paternoster, 1960), p 208.
[99] Kenneth Hylson-Smith, *Evangelicals in the Church of England 1734-1984* (Edinburgh: T & T Clark, 1989), p 37.
[100] Cecil, *The Life of John Newton*, p 164.
[101] Bull, *But Now I See*, p 363.

Bibliography

Newton's writings
Works, 6 Vols. 1820, reprinted Banner of Truth 1985

An Authentic Narrative is one of two items in *The Life and Spirituality of John Newton*, introduction by Bruce Hindmarsh, Regent College Publishing 1998

The Searcher of Hearts, Sermon Notes on Romans 8, ed. Marylynn Rouse, Christian Focus 1997

365 Days with Newton, from his unpublished sermons and writings, compiled and edited by Marylynn Rouse, Day One 2006

Letters (selection), Banner of Truth 1960

Letters of John Newton, edited by Josiah Bull, reprinted Banner of Truth 2007

Olney Hymns, facsimile reprint, Cowper and Newton Museum, 1984 (also in Works, Vol.3)

The complete works will be appearing on www.johnnewton.org

Biographies and studies of Newton
Aitken, Jonathan, *From Disgrace to Amazing Grace*, Continuum 2007

Bull, Josiah, *But Now I See*, 1868, reprinted Banner of Truth 1998

Cecil, Richard, *The Life of John Newton*, 1808, new edition with much additional material and edited by Marylynn Rouse, Christian Focus 2000

Edwards, Brian, *Through Many Dangers*, second edition, Evangelical Press 2001

Hindmarsh, Bruce, *John Newton and the English Evangelical Tradition*, Oxford University Press 1996. Indispensable in any study of Newton.

Martin, Bernard, *An Ancient Mariner*, revised edition, Epworth Press 1960

Piper, John, Chapter one in *The Roots of Endurance*, (also features Simeon and Wilberforce), IVP 2002

Pollock, John, *Amazing Grace: John Newton's Story*, Hodder 1981

Turner, Steve, *Amazing Grace: John Newton, Slavery and the World's Most Enduring Song*, Lion 2002

General histories
Balleine, G.R: *A History of the Fvangelical Party in the Church of England*, new edition, Church Book Room Press, 1951

Bebbington, D.W: *Evangelicalism in Modern Britain*, Unwin Hyman, 1989

Hylson-Smith, Kenneth: *The Churches in England from Elizabeth I to Elizabeth II*, Vol.2, SCM Press, 1997

Hylson-Smith, Kenneth: *Evangelicals in the Church of England 1734-1994*, T & T Clark, 1989

Noll, Mark: *The Rise of Evangelicalism*, IVP 2004

Wolffe, John: *The Expansion of Evangelicalism*, IVP 2006

Wood, A. Skevington: *The Inextinguishable Blaze*, Paternoster 1960

The John Newton Project
For further details, write to: Marylynn Rouse, The Hill Lodge, Warwick Road, Stratford-on-Avon, CV37 ONP. Email: admin@johnnewton.org

From Life's First Cry: John Owen on infant baptism and infant salvation

Lee Gatiss

Setting the Scene 327
1. What is the question? 329
2. Why not baptise infants? 333
3. Making things worse for children 336
4. Infant regeneration and salvation 343
5. Children and parents go together 350
6. Final arguments 353
Conclusion 355
Appendix 1: John Owen's *Of Infant Baptism* 357
Appendix 2: Owen's letter to Lady Hartopp 363
Appendix 3: A liturgical introduction to infant baptism 365
For further reading: 366

LEE GATISS read Modern History at New College, Oxford before training for Anglican ministry at Oak Hill Theological College in London. He served a curacy in Northamptonshire before becoming Associate Minister of St. Helen's, Bishopsgate in the City of London in 2004. He holds a ThM in Historical and Systematic Theology from Westminster Theological Seminary in Philadelphia (USA) and his PhD at Cambridge University is on seventeenth century biblical interpretation. He is the Editor of *Theologian* (www.theologian.org.uk), Review Editor of *Churchman*, and Series Editor of the *Reformed Evangelical Anglican Library* as well as author of *The True Profession of the Gospel*.

No guilt in life, no fear in death;
this is the power of Christ in me;
from life's first cry to final breath
Jesus commands my destiny.
No power of Hell, no scheme of man
can ever pluck me from his hand:
till he returns or calls me home,
here in the power of Christ I'll stand!

From 'In Christ Alone' by Keith Getty and Stuart Townend,
© Copyright 2001 Kingsway's Thankyou Music.

Setting the Scene

With the great Assembly of puritan Divines sitting in Westminster, a sermon was preached each morning in Westminster Abbey. One such sermon from 1644 by Mr. Stephen Marshall, minister of Finchingfield in Essex, sparked something of a controversy when another minister chose to publish a long and weighty response to it. The sermon, itself somewhat longer than usual, was part of a series on the Ten Commandments, the Lord's Prayer, the Creed, and the Sacraments and took as its subject the doctrine of infant baptism. Marshall outlined the basic historical, theological, and biblical case for the practice.[1] Mr. John Tombes, who was fast gaining a reputation as one who was against infant baptism, read Marshall's printed sermon and decided it must be answered.

Tombes had already been turned down for a prestigious preaching post[2], by a committee on which the influential Marshall sat, because of his views on this subject. As 'the archetypal Anglican Antipaedobaptist'[3] he was particularly concerned to justify his own position in a church and nation which had long accepted the practice of baptising the children of believers. Tombes' response was about three times the length of Marshall's sermon, and was bound along with some of his other polemical writing on the subject, the first of many such published works to come from his pen over the next few years.[4] Marshall replied to Tombes's response, and soon others weighed in too. Thus began a long and spirited exchange of views amongst the English

---

[1] Stephen Marshall, *A Sermon of the Baptizing of Infants* (London, 1644). On Marshall's reputation and influence as a preacher, see W. Barker, *Puritan Profiles* (Fearn, Ross-shire: Mentor, 1999), pp 120-127.
[2] Preacher for the Honourable Societies of the Temples, in London.
[3] Michael T. Renihan, *Antipaedobaptism in the Thought of John Tombes: An untold story from Puritan England* (Auburn, MA: B&R Press, 2001), p 47.
[4] John Tombes, *An Examen of the Sermon of Mr. Stephen Marshal about Infant Baptisme* (London, 1645). In total he wrote at least 14 books touching on the issue of baptism according to Renihan, *Antipaedobaptism*, p 66. His paper on the issue presented to the Westminster Assembly probably accounts for Marshall's verbosity in outlining the case for infant baptism in his sermon; as Renihan, p 142 comments, 'Polemicising with Tombes brought about tedious work for all parties involved'!

Puritans of the mid-seventeenth century concerning the place and privileges of children in the church.

This debate over infant baptism certainly made waves in Oxford, where John Owen, 'Prince of Puritans' was Dean of Christ Church (1651-1660) and Vice-Chancellor (1652-58). At the annual academic convocation in 1652, for example, Henry Savage delivered a dissertation specifically against John Tombes's views. Moreover, in 1654, Tombes was appointed as a 'Trier,' charged with the examination and approval of ministers. This was a high profile role, and would naturally have drawn attention to Tombes and his distinctive theological convictions from the universities where new clergy were being trained by men such as Owen (also a Trier).[5] It is into this rhetorical and theological context that we can place Owen's own work on infant baptism, which is (unfortunately) undated.[6] Whether it originates from the 1640s, perhaps as a position paper sent to the Westminster Assembly,[7] from the 1650s when the debate was evidently current in Oxford, or from the post-Restoration period when Richard Baxter also continued to wield his prolific pen against Tombes,[8] we cannot say with certainty. Yet his only work devoted to the sacrament of baptism, a short treatise of about 2400 words simply called *Of Infant Baptism*, is a classic example of Puritan theological exegesis and polemical argumentation.

---

[5] See Renihan, *Antipaedobaptism*, pp 44-45.

[6] The text in *The Works of John Owen* (Edinburgh: Banner of Truth, 1968) is reprinted from an edition of his 'Sermons and Tracts' only published posthumously in 1721 and perhaps never intended for publication at all. The next treatise in the *Works*, 'A vindication of two passages in Irenæus against the exceptions of Mr. Tombs' (pp 263-265 of Volume 16), is a direct reply to Tombes's *Antipaedobaptism* Part 3, section 89, pp 760-762 which was published in 1657. If this 'vindication' was originally appended to *Of Infant Baptism*, as seems possible judging from the final point made there about 'particular testimonies may be pleaded and *vindicated* if need be' (emphasis mine), then it is not unlikely that he completed both around 1657-1658.

[7] Tombes had sent a short *Exercitation* on the subject to a committee of the Assembly. Owen himself was not a member of the Westminster Assembly, but may well have been asked by members for his opinion.

[8] Tombes moved to a chapel-at-ease in Bewdley, where he would not be required to baptise anyone, in 1649 (Renihan, *Antipaedobaptism*, p 52 footnote 44). According to *Reliquiae Baxterianae* (London: Matthew Sylvester, 1696), Part 1, p 96, Tombes vigorously pursued Baxter, his near neighbour, for a public debate which finally took place in January 1649/50. Baxter's first work dedicated to the issue was *Plain Scripture Proof of Infants Church-Membership and Baptism being the arguments prepared for... the publick Dispute with Mr. Tombes at Bewdley* (1650).

The doctrine of infant baptism, especially its denial by Anabaptists, was a major catalyst for the development of covenant theology in the 16th and 17th centuries, a movement in which Owen was very much involved. Yet it was not merely a scholastic exercise that led the greatest mind amongst the puritans to consider the related subjects of infant baptism and infant salvation. Owen and his first wife had 11 children together, only one of whom survived past infancy.[9] Sadly, such immense tragedy was not unusual or exceptional for his time,[10] which meant that the puritans generally gave more thought than perhaps we do today to issues of infant salvation. They did not always have the luxury of time to consider whether to baptise their children or not.

We turn our attention then to the pithy and tightly woven argument which Owen makes for infant baptism. He has four sections to his argument, but in true puritan fashion the fourth section has eight major sub-points and several sub-points have sub-sub-points! So I will try to clarify how it all fits together as we proceed. My first point deals with Owen's first three sections, lines of argument I-III.

1. What is the question?

Owen begins in the style of an Oxford disputation by defining very carefully the question to be debated. He clears the ground for his more positive arguments by denying three things. First, he says, the issue is not 'whether professing believers... not baptised in infancy, ought to be baptised.' This, he states, is an uncontroversial truth, confessed by all Christians.

---

[9] Two of his sons died in a plague in 1655, just before the date I have suggested Owen wrote *Of Infant Baptism*, according to P. Toon, *God's Statesman: The Life and Work of John Owen* (Exeter: Paternoster, 1971), p 63. His daughter Mary had died in July 1647 aged only three weeks (Toon, p 38 footnote 3).

[10] For example, in Arnold G. Matthews, *Calamy Revised* (Oxford: Clarendon Press, 1988 [1934]), pp 13-14 records that Samuel Annesley had 24 children, only three of which survived him. One of these was Susanna, the mother of John and Charles Wesley (and 16 others!). David M. Thompson, *Baptism, Church and Society in Modern Britain* (Milton Keynes: Paternoster, 2005), p 1 narrates something of the story of the 17th century Revd Isaac Archer who lost eight of his nine children in infancy, and as many as three out of ten children in Puritan New England did not reach their first birthday according to Catherine A. Brekus, ('Children of Wrath, Children of Grace: Jonathan Edwards and the Puritan Culture of Child Rearing') in Marcia J. Bunge (ed.), *The Child in Christian Thought* (Cambridge: Eerdmans, 2001), p 316.

Presumably the wording of the Great Commission in Matthew 28:18-20 was clear enough in its insistence that disciples of Jesus ought to be baptised, even if in actual fact that is not universally the case.[11]

Second, Owen continues, neither is the debate about whether faith and repentance should precede baptism in such disciples. It obviously should, and Owen would insist on pastors taking great care over this, so as not to baptise adult converts without being sure their profession of faith is genuine. He claims to be more assiduous and careful about this than most antipaedobaptists, for whom admission to baptism was something to be extremely scrupulous about. By clarifying that this is not the main issue, he rules out any simplistic appeal to verses (such as Acts 8:12) which speak of repentance or faith coming before baptism as if they settled the issue of baptizing infants. To pile up quotations, from either the Bible or great theologians of the past, showing that faith did or should precede baptism *in adults* is not pertinent to the question of infant baptism, since it is perfectly consistent with the paedobaptist position.[12]

---

[11] I have met some Christians, converted and nurtured through the Salvation Army for example, who have never been baptised, and there are always others who have 'not gotten around to it yet.' Whilst it is gloriously true that baptism is not strictly necessary for salvation, it is clearly abnormal in New Testament terms to neglect baptism altogether (see *Westminster Confession* 28.5). After all, there are many things which are 'not strictly necessary for salvation' but which are either beneficial to growth in faith, or matters of simple obedience to God's word (e.g. Bible reading, prayer, the Lord's Supper).

[12] Owen possibly has Tombes in his sights here since he argued thus in *An Examen of the Sermon of Mr. Stephen Marshal*, p 153, making much of a list of several verses in which either John the Baptiser or the Apostles baptised adults after a profession of faith and/or repentance. For a modern example of this kind of argument, see Robert H. Stein, 'Baptism in Luke-Acts' in Thomas R. Schreiner & Shawn D. Wright (eds.), *Believer's Baptism: Sign of the New Covenant in Christ* (Nashville: B&H Academic, 2006), pp 35-66. Since the context of Luke-Acts must be the whole of Scripture (breathed out by the same divine author), to consider a doctrinal question settled by appeal to narrative examples in only a section of the whole would be premature, even if the examples *were* directly relevant to the issue at hand. Whilst this kind of 'biblical theology' description of what a particular corpus of biblical material says can be useful, unless we move from 'what does Luke-Acts say' to a consideration of how that coheres with the rest of the Bible and how it is relevant to the systematic question being asked, it is ultimately misleading and cannot be normative. The rest of the Schreiner-Wright volume does attempt this. However, it is to be feared that many would simply conclude that 'if in Luke-Acts baptism is for adults who have heard the gospel and professed faith, then infant baptism cannot be right.' It is that logical fallacy which Owen is here addressing.

Third, Owen denies that all infants should be baptised. In other words, he and his fellow paedobaptists do not wish to argue that every child born into the world without exception ought to be baptised. Some children, he says, ought not to be baptised, i.e. those 'whose parents are strangers from the covenant.' This is the first mention in the argument of that important concept of 'the covenant,' to which we will return again as Owen develops his case. It is sufficient to note at this stage that Owen was not in favour of indiscriminate baptism nor would he have approved of a policy of baptising the children of anyone who happens to live in the parish (whether they are committed to Christ and his covenant people or not). As we will see later, Owen was of the view that some of those born outside the covenant who died in infancy were actually elect and saved; yet that did not mean they should be baptised (since God alone knows those who are his) or that any child could be baptised simply in the hope that they might be one of the elect. Baptism was, then, part of the outward administration of the covenant, a sign to be given only to those whose profession of saving faith and repentance was judged sincere, and to their children.[13]

So, Owen has cleared away three false definitions of the question he has chosen to discuss, in order to focus the dispute more precisely. The issue for him is not whether believers who weren't baptised in infancy should be baptised – they should. It is not whether faith and repentance should come before baptism in such converts – it should. And it is not whether all infants are to be baptised indiscriminately – they should not. Therefore he concludes that 'the question is only concerning the children or infant seed of professing believers who are themselves baptized.' And the question is, should *they* be baptised?

---

[13] See *A Declaration of the Faith and Order Owned and Practised in the Congregational Churches in England, Agreed upon and Consented unto By their Elders and Messengers in Their Meeting at the Savoy, October 12, 1658* (London, 1658) section 29.4. This is identical to *Westminster Confession* 28.4 except that it strengthens the limitations on who can be baptised: believers and their children, 'and those only' (the last three words being added at the Savoy). Owen was instrumental in drawing up this 'Savoy Declaration,' which is a lightly edited version of the *Westminster Confession*, and so the revisions made are significant when considering Owen's own views, especially if my view (above, footnote 6) of the date of *Of Infant Baptism* is correct.

It is not pedantic or 'scholastic' to narrow the question down in the way Owen did. Clarity is vital in such debates, especially where passions can often run high. It is also important not to forget at the beginning of his argument that Owen believes in adult 'believer's baptism' (or credobaptism) as much as any antipaedobaptist.[14] Indeed, as a keen supporter of missions to the un-reached people groups of Great Britain and Ireland who worked and prayed for the propagation of the gospel, he would have taken great joy in the baptism of such new converts.[15] This is a healthy reminder that a firm belief in infant baptism need not involve neglecting the evangelisation of the nation, or indeed replacing such a vision with the potentially more parochial concern of breeding the next generation.

Many Christians now and in Owen's day were baptised as babies but came to a living faith only later in life. It is perhaps natural for such people to question the validity of what could appear from their position of new-found vibrancy to have been merely an empty ritual. Yet just because a practice may have been abused in the past does not mean there is no right and proper, biblically-mandated use for it. For Owen to make it clear from the start that non-covenantal, indiscriminate baptism is not what paedobaptism is meant to be about could be incredibly helpful in preventing such people from (if I may put it like this) throwing out the baby of the biblical doctrine with the font water of nominal faith. We may be rightly skeptical about the policy of certain churches because they seem to have failed in their duty to preach the gospel clearly and nurture faith in those they initiate into baptism. Yet this should make us passionate not to abolish infant baptism but to see it reformed according to a more biblical pattern, administered and followed-up correctly. That, I believe, was Owen's concern in the face of radical antipaedobaptism in his day, when much that had been merely 'traditional' was reassessed and abandoned.

---

[14] The official statistics show that the number of adult baptisms in the Church of England in 2006 was 9,300, an increase of 11% since 2002, demonstrating that a paedobaptist denomination can also in a sense be a credobaptist one. So where I use the term 'antipaedobaptist' (Tombes's designation of choice in the title of his magnum opus) this is not meant as a slur, but merely as a convenient designation in this context.

[15] The theme of Owen's heart for gospel propagation is brought out in Toon, *God's Statesman*, e.g. pp 41, 80.

We must now turn to the substantive part of his argument to see if he was able to put the doctrine of infant baptism on a sufficiently secure foundation to make its retention viable. We are dealing now, then, with the eight major sub-points of section IV.

2. Why not baptise infants?

Owen's first major point in effect throws back a question to those who would deny infant baptism. Where, he asks, does Scripture forbid such a thing? Which Bible text says that the children of believers should not be baptised? Opponents of infant baptism 'can produce no testimony of Scripture wherein their negation is formally or in terms included, nor any one asserting what is inconsistent with the affirmative.' That is, there is no verse forbidding infant baptism and no verse inconsistent with infant baptism. We have already noted above that some non-paedobaptists would point to a pattern in Acts where baptism follows the reception of preaching and a profession of faith. Tombes, for example, has a list of such verses, from which he logically concludes 'in which places, profession of repentance and faith is still made the antecedent to baptism: but this does not agree to infants, therefore they are not to be baptised.'[16] Yet Owen replies in a withering manner that, 'it is weak beneath consideration to suppose that the requiring of the baptism of believers is inconsistent with that of their seed.' That is, if one is going to oppose this practice, then one needs to produce clear arguments from Scripture which address it and oppose it directly. To assert that believers must be baptised is not a logical argument against baptising their children as well, since the two things are by no means mutually exclusive.

Owen's second major point is a similarly aggressive rhetorical thrust against what he perceives as the structural flaws in the antipaedobaptist case. Not only are there no verses against infant baptism, his opponents also have no examples in Scripture or in early

---

[16] Tombes, *Examen*, p 153 cf. Renihan, *Antipaedobaptism*, pp 132-135. As with all quotations made out of 17th century sources here, I have updated the spelling and punctuation. American readers will be delighted to learn that 'to baptise' and its cognates was often spelled with a 'z' in seventeenth century English. I have corrected this indelicacy.

church history where the children of believers were not given 'the same sign and seal of the covenant' as their parents. There were no examples of circumcised fathers with uncircumcised sons or baptised parents with un-baptised children — if they were being brought up in the knowledge of God, then they received the same sign as their parents. There was no counterexample in Scripture or 'the approved practice of the primitive church.'[17] There was significant debate about the historical evidence from the early church,[18] but Owen's point is undeniable regarding the lack of evidence in Scripture. There were, Owen implies, serious and significant silences when it came to assessing the evidence for the non-paedobaptist case.

Owen was of course not alone in pointing to such gaps in the opposition's argument. Stephen Marshall had done the same thing in his Westminster Abbey sermon which sparked off the initial publishing war with Anglican antipaedobaptist John Tombes. Like Owen, Marshall points out that nowhere in the New Testament is there a command 'that the children of believers when they are grown, should be instructed and baptised, though instructed by their parents... nor any example where ever that was done.' But he confessed that non-paedobaptists had their own spin regarding arguments from silence when they pointed out that 'there is no command, no express institution, or clear example in all the New Testament of baptising of infants.' To this he freely admitted, and yet he denied the legitimacy of the logical leap then made: to say 'that Christians are not tied to observe that which is not expressly and in so many words set down in the New Testament' was 'not true divinity.' Why not? Because there were several areas in which Christians did not require a specific word in the New Testament to bind them: there was no express law against polygamy, for example, and no reiteration of the

---

[17] By which Owen means the early church of the first few centuries after Christ. See Renihan, *Antipaedobaptism*, p 145 where Tombes casts doubt on infant baptism in the early church saying, 'it is a wonder to me, that if it were so manifest as you speak, you should find nothing in Eusebius for it, nor in Ignatius, nor in Clemens Alexandrinus, or in Athanasius, not in Epiphanius.' Silences in historical remains could be taken either way it seems.

[18] One contemporary defence of a paedobaptist reading of the historical texts was Robert Ram's *Paedo-Baptisme or, The Baptising of Infants Justified* (London, 1645). The debate continued in the exchange between Joachim Jeremias, *Infant Baptism in the First Four Centuries* (London: SCM, 1960) and Kurt Aland, *Did the Early Church Baptize Infants?* (London: SCM, 1961).

forbidden degrees of marriage (as in Leviticus 18).[19] Did that mean that Christians could take multiple wives or have sexual intercourse with their siblings? Surely not! There was no express command or example in the New Testament to justify women receiving the Lord's Supper either, but that did not mean they were not fit to partake of that sacrament. Should the children of believers be denied access to the other sacrament on the same grounds?[20]

Arguments from silence cannot be compelling on their own. They must be part of a larger case, as indeed they are for both Owen and Marshall. But it is significant that Owen begins here with a challenge to non-paedobaptists. It is common experience in many conservative evangelical circles today to find that the burden of proof on this issue is simply assumed to lie with paedobaptists. It is they who must justify what is sometimes considered to be their pragmatic continuance of a Roman Catholic practice, as if the case for not baptising infants was so patently obvious from Scripture as to not require justification.[21] Owen reminds us that there is a burden of proof on both sides of the divide here, and a heavy burden at that for antipaedobaptists. It is not an issue which can be easily and straightforwardly settled by brandishing a few proof-texts; it is more like trying to piece together a complex jigsaw in which some of the key pieces seem to be missing, and there is legitimate debate over how the gaps might be filled in a manner most in keeping with their surroundings.

---

[19] Though Marshall acknowledges Paul's horror regarding the specific incestuous relationship in 1 Corinthians 5.
[20] Marshall, *A Sermon of the Baptizing of Infants*, pp 34-35.
[21] For a provocative exposure of and answer to this sort of thinking see Peter J. Leithart's, "The Sociology of Infant Baptism" in *The Baptized Body* (Moscow, Idaho: Canon Press, 2007), pp 113-136 where he concludes (pp 135-136) that "Baptist theology and baptismal practice seem reasonable and natural only because our definitions of 'reasonable and natural' are thoroughly infected with the modern notion that consent is the alpha and omega of social, moral, and religious life." Indeed, early Anabaptists were committed theologically to 'free will' according to Keith G. Miller, "Complex Innocence, Obligatory Nurturance, and Parental Vigilance: 'The Child' in the Work of Menno Simons" in Bunge, *The Child in Christian Thought*, p 207 and David C. Steinmetz, *Luther in Context* (Bloomington: Indiana University Press, 1986), p 59 (on Hubmaier). More recently the case against paedobaptism has been argued differently, sometimes with more Reformed views of theological anthropology.

So first, Owen challenges those against infant baptism to be more rigorous in their methodology and to admit the weaknesses in their case. Some of the pieces they would no doubt like to see are missing. Then once it is clear that this debate is not simply over the interpretation of a few isolated verses but over how the Bible as a whole is structured and put together it should be easier to proceed with a certain level of charity and patience born of humility. Inference and implication will have to play an important part in any answer to the question of infant baptism. So Owen will challenge us in subsequent arguments to recover confidence in a Reformed hermeneutic that sees the Bible as the one unfolding story of God's unchanging plan of salvation, a hermeneutic which provides the big picture into which infant baptism fits harmoniously, comfortably, and securely.

3. Making things worse for children

Owen's third major argument concerns the revocation of spiritual privileges given by God. The essence of his argument here is that if the non-paedobaptists are right, God has made things worse for the children of believers now that Christ has come. What he says is this: 'A spiritual privilege once granted by God unto any cannot be changed, disannulled, or abrogated, without an especial divine revocation of it, or the substitution of a greater privilege and mercy in the room of it.'

The spiritual privilege he refers to is that in Genesis 17 God granted the infant seed of believing Abraham a right to participate in the covenant, including its initial seal. The covenant was cut with Abraham and his children, and as part of it Abraham and his male children were all to receive the covenant sign.[22] To deny the children of believers that right to the initial seal of the covenant (though the sign may have been changed) cannot be appropriate unless God has expressly changed his instructions. As Marshall said in his sermon, speaking of the first disciples as they went about baptising and teaching,

---

[22] Owen does not make the rather obvious paedobaptist point here that Abraham (a 'believer' since at least Genesis 15:6) was definitely *not* told to wait until his children shared his faith before he circumcised them. Whilst it is true that it is those who believe who are sons of Abraham (Galatians 3:7) this cannot function as an argument against infant baptism since it evidently did not function as an argument against infant circumcision.

'it behoved the Lord to give them a caution for the leaving out of infants in this new administration, that they might know his mind, if that he intends to have them left out – which that ever he did in word or deed, cannot be found in the Scriptures.'[23] Besides, God would only do that, Owen says, if he was replacing the privilege those children enjoyed with something greater for them, which antipaedobaptists do not think he has. Therefore, now that Christ has come, the children of believers are apparently in a worse situation spiritually than they were before, if the antipaedobaptists are correct.[24]

Owen traces out several implications of adopting this view. First, if the privilege given to the children of believers in Genesis 17 is now to be revoked, then the lordship of Christ over the church is being overruled. For he himself has not spoken to remove the right of children to receive the seal of the covenant, as Owen has already established: the New Testament says nothing about children now being excluded from the outward sign of covenant membership. So then, 'To abolish or take away any grant of privilege made by him to the church, without his own express revocation of it, is to deny his sovereign authority.'

Second, if a spiritual privilege given by God to his people is revoked then we should expect a greater privilege to have been granted in its place.[25] Otherwise it appears contrary to his goodness, love, and care for the church, which Owen does not wish to see impugned. It is one thing to remove, for example, the Jerusalem Temple and its glories but God clearly substituted in its place 'a more glorious spiritual temple and worship' in Christ.

John Tombes had at least two answers to this sort of argument. First, he said that some individuals in the former dispensation did have greater privileges than those in the new; for example, 'no man besides Abraham is called the father of the Faithful; no woman besides one, The

---

[23] Marshall, *A Sermon of the Baptizing of Infants*, p 39.
[24] Antipaedobaptist Robert Barrow, *A Briefe Answer to A Discourse Lately Written by one P.B... Wherein is Declared... That the Baptizing of Infants hath no Authority from the Scriptures* (London: 1642), p 13 declares simply that 'although infants were of the church before Christ yet the Lord hath manifestly declared, that they should not be so now,' basing his argument on Galatians 4:22-31.
[25] Owen is not speaking here about the granting of spiritual gifts to individuals, which he may or may not decide to take away from time to time, as he wills.

mother of Christ."[26] This does not quite answer Owen here, since he clearly has in mind privileges of the covenant people in general, rather than individual privileges and blessings as part of salvation history.

Tombes's best answer to this type of argument was to throw back at paedobaptists what he saw as an inconsistency: if things cannot be worse for children under the new covenant then why not include infants in the Lord's Supper, since they were part of the Passover? He pointed to this inconsistency on many occasions.[27] Needless to say this aroused strong opposition from Marshall and other Puritans[28], who were not in favour of paedocommunion, partly on the grounds that whether children participated in the Passover or not was a contentious point, and partly on the grounds that 1 Corinthians 11:28-29 seemed to them to lay down that participants should be capable of examining themselves spiritually and discerning the body, which infants could not.[29] Both the *Book of Common Prayer* and the *Westminster Directory of Public Worship* found no place for infants in the Lord's Supper, although it is now permitted and widely practiced in the Church of England, something which divides conservative evangelicals.[30] It may be that Jewett (no paedobaptist!) was right to say that, 'the argument from the covenant for infant baptism, when managed with adroitness, has about it an aura of plausibility; but the more convincingly it is pressed, the more embarrassed is the defense [*sic*] of believer communion.'[31]

---

[26] Renihan, *Antipaedobaptism*, p 125.

[27] See Renihan, *Antipaedobaptism*, pp 123-124. Augustus H. Strong used this same argument in the 19th century and was answered by Benjamin B. Warfield in "The Polemics of Infant Baptism" in *Studies in Theology, The Works of Benjamin B. Warfield: Volume 9* (Grand Rapids: Baker, reprinted 2003), pp 401-402.

[28] Marshall, *A Sermon of the Baptizing of Infants*, pp 51-52.

[29] Calvin had addressed the issue this way in *Institutes* 4.16.30. Some might argue on the basis of 1 Corinthians 10:1-5 that Paul envisages infants as being involved in both sacraments because they were involved in the Old Testament events Paul compares them to - baptism into Moses at the Red Sea, and partaking of the spiritual food of manna and water from the rock in the desert. I am grateful to Martin Foord for this insight.

[30] For discussion amongst conservative evangelical Anglicans on this issue, see Roger Beckwith and Andrew Daunton-Fear, *The Water and the Wine: A Contribution to the Debate on Children and Holy Communion* (London: Latimer Trust, 2005) for an argument against paedocommunion, and Matthew Mason, "Covenant Children and Covenant Meals: Biblical Evidence for Infant Communion" in *Churchman* 121/2 (2007), pp 127-138 for an argument in favour.

[31] Paul K. Jewett, *Infant Baptism and the Covenant of Grace* (Grand Rapids: Eerdmans, 1978), p 207.

Sadly, Owen does not address this tangential but significant question. He is, however, very concerned that if God were to make things worse for covenant children, to take away a spiritual privilege once solemnly granted, it would be particularly contrary to 'his constant course of proceeding with it [the church] from the foundation of the world, wherein he went on in the enlargement and increase of its privileges until the coming of Christ.' In other words, having a right to the seal of the covenant is a spiritual privilege, and things have always been improving and getting better for the church in terms of its spiritual privileges. There has been a progression in redemptive history. God's people were better off after Abraham than before; they were more blessed after Sinai, then with the replacement of the tabernacle for the more permanent Temple and its worship. The spiritual privileges of God's people were constantly being enlarged – with the grant of kingship, the sending of the prophets, and then with the coming of Christ and the Spirit. Owen's argument, then, is this: if this is how God works, why with the great and final revelation of his Son would he remove and revoke completely such an immense spiritual privilege as believers' children had previously enjoyed?[32]

To suppose that this is actually what God has done (which was the non-paedobaptist position) seemed to Owen to take away from the glory and honour of Christ and the gospel, the great culmination of all

---

[32] We might mention here the sometimes controversial question of how much the Old Testament saints knew about God. Even just a glance at volume 1 of his works shows that Owen is very clear on this. Speaking of the Old Testament and God revealing himself to Moses in Exodus 33:18-23 he says: 'This is all that God would grant, viz., such external representations of himself, in the proclamation of his name, and created appearances of his glory, as we have of a man whose back parts only we behold as he passeth by us. But as to the being of God, and his subsistence in the Trinity of persons, we have no direct intuition into them, much less comprehension of them [that is, in the Old Testament].' See *Christologia: On the Person of Christ* in *The Works of John Owen: Volume 1* (Edinburgh: T&T Clark, 1862), p 67. Again, it is true of Old Testament saints that, 'Neither they nor the angels knew clearly either the sufferings of Christ or the glory that should ensue.' *Christologia*, p 263. And yet, 'The meanest believer may now find out more of the work of Christ in the types of the Old Testament, than any prophets or wise men could have done of old.' *Christologia*, p 101. This is because, '*when the Son of God 'appeared in the flesh,'* and in the discharge of his office, – God himself, as unto his being, and manner of existence in three distinct persons, – with all the glorious properties of the divine nature, was illustriously manifested unto them that did believe' – *Meditations and Discourses on the Glory of Christ* (also in volume 1), p 298 [emphasis mine].

God's dealings with his people. He states that it would be contrary 'to all his promises, the honour of Christ, and a multitude of express testimonies of Scripture.' He does not at this stage cite which promises and Scriptures he has in mind, but Stephen Marshall's sermon cites Hebrews 8:6 and 2 Corinthians 3:10 amongst others as showing that the privileges of believers under the new covenant were greater, not less, than those under the old. He also points out that in Christ there is neither male nor female (Galatians 3:28) – so girls as well as boys may now be baptised, a clear enlargement of the privilege.[33] Tombes agreed that privileges had been enlarged, but only in regard to the inclusion of gentiles and the increased clarity of revelation in the new era.[34]

Later in his argument, however, Owen will refer to several Old Testament texts which mention believers and their children as *together* part of the future new order.[35] These texts certainly do not indicate that God will be going back on the inclusion of children within the covenant arrangement as soon as the messiah comes. So God has not left 'the seed of believers, whilst in their infant state, in the same condition with those of pagans and infidels... contrary to God's covenant' as Owen accuses non-paedobaptists of believing. Quite the contrary, God's promises assure believers about the continuing status and importance of their children in God's plan.[36]

There is a powerful pastoral argument here which all those tasked with the spiritual education of children would do well to ponder. Should we think of them as 'pagans and infidels' requiring evangelisation, which Owen points out is the logical conclusion of seeing believers' children as outside the covenant?[37] It is of course agreed by people on both sides of the debate that 'we as Christians

---

[33] See Marshall, *A Sermon of the Baptizing of Infants*, p 30.
[34] Tombes, *Antipaedobaptism: Part 3*, pp 704-705.
[35] He refers to Isaiah 22:24, 44:3, 61:9, and 65:23. We might also add the 'everlasting' covenant prophecies such as Isaiah 59:20-21, Jeremiah 32:38-40, or Ezekiel 37:25.
[36] See also Owen's comments on Hebrews 4:15 in Gould (ed.), *The Works of John Owen: Volume 21* (Volume 20 in the Banner of Truth edition, i.e. volume 4 of the Hebrews commentary), pp 417-418 which are on these same lines.
[37] Peter Leithart, *The Baptised Body*, p 115, speaks in a similar way to Owen about the Baptist view of children: 'The nurture of their early years may indeed involve Christian training – instruction in the Bible, teaching the child to pray, involvement in the church, and so forth – but it is not seen as the nurture of a *Christian* child... it is nurture of a pagan or unbelieving or neutral child.'

should give ourselves to teaching the gospel to our children and praying for them privately and publicly' and that 'children of believing parents do not need baptism to be taught the Ten Commandments, the Lord's Prayer, and the gospel in all its fullness.' Paedobaptists and non-paedobaptists can both pray 'that none of our children ever know any lengthy period of conscious rebellion against God.'[38] Yet the antipaedobaptist position requires a fundamentally different attitude to be adopted towards such children.

For instance, Mark Dever insists that Christians should 'not treat your children as if you presume they are elect' and 'parents should not presume to be certain of their children's faith.'[39] So must they be taught that passages such as Ephesians 1:1-14 are inapplicable to them personally, since they are only allowed to look in at the blessings of the predestined Christian objectively, from the outside? And would it not be inconsistent for children presumed to be un-elect and without faith to be permitted to sing, for example, the verse from 'In Christ Alone' with which this study began, since it puts into their mouths such confident assertions about their eternal security? Other Reformed Baptists would agree that it is presumptuous to nurture our children as if they could be disciples of Christ without a conversion experience or at least mature intellectual capacity.[40] So it seems that although they *may* be converted before they are permitted to drive a car, we must not speak to our children in a way that implies we think they have been, but should instead wait and see how they turn out later.[41]

On the other hand, passages such as Ephesians 6:1-4 do seem to call on Christian parents to treat their children *as Christians*. From their earliest years they are not just to be 'taught about God' but nurtured within the covenant and disciplined according to it (verse 4). In verses 1-3 children are even commanded to obey their parents 'in the Lord' (ἐν κυρίῳ, *en kurio*) and are given a promise to be apprehended by faith.

---

[38] Mark Dever, 'Baptism in the Context of the Local Church' in *Believer's Baptism*, pp 333, 350, and 348 footnote 28.
[39] 'Baptism in the Context of the Local Church', p 343 footnote 17 (sub-point 17) and p 349.
[40] See e.g. Dennis Gundersen, *Your Child's Profession of Faith* (Amityville, N.Y.: Calvary Press, 1994). For a critical paedobaptist review of this, see Rich Lusk, *Paedofaith: A Primer on the Mystery of Infant Salvation and a Handbook for Covenant Parents* (Monroe, LA: Athanasius Press, 2005), pp 154-158.
[41] '"Time will tell" is the point of many of Christ's parables' says Dever, p 333.

Interestingly, they are not commanded here to repent and believe 'just like mummy and daddy did,' but to grow in the family faith as they are nurtured in obedience to it. Presumably if Paul can apply the command and promise of the fifth commandment to the children of believers in Ephesus then some other appropriate scriptural (covenantal) promises, threats, comforts, and assurances might also be held out to them to receive and accept by faith.

In Ephesians 6, Paul chose to emphasise the positive side of the fifth commandment rather than speaking about the sanction children could face if they broke it under the old covenant (e.g. Deuteronomy 21:18-21). Such positive motivations can work exceptionally well, so that we do not need to indulge in 'frightening poor innocent children with talk of hell fire and eternal damnation' as some might, in order to somehow provoke a conversion experience.[42] As Lewis Schenck rightly says, 'It was unfortunate that the Great Awakening made an emotional experience, involving terror, misery, and depression, the only approach to God.'[43] Some may never have such an experience, but grow up knowing and loving Jesus from their earliest days. At some point they will be born again, but it may be an unnoticed, un-dramatic event. Would it be right to presume such children are unregenerate and un-elect?

Moreover, a child's faith may not have the cognitive sophistication of an adult's, but that does not mean they are incapable of relying on and trusting Christ until they have passed through puberty.[44]

---

[42] The great American preacher Jonathan Edwards was accused of this, with some justification it seems, according to Brekus, 'Children of Wrath, Children of Grace', p 321 (see also pp 313-320 on his sermons to children). See the careful remarks of Timothy A. Sisemore, *Of Such is the Kingdom: Nurturing Children in the Light of Scripture* (Fearn, Ross-Shire: Christian Focus, 2000), p 67 on Edwards and his context.

[43] Lewis B. Schenck, *The Presbyterian Doctrine of Children in the Covenant: An Historical Study of the Significance of Infant Baptism in the Presbyterian Church* (Phillipsburg, NJ: P&R, [1940] 2003), p 71.

[44] Jewett, *Infant Baptism and the Covenant of Grace*, p 168 is right to say that 'few have found the courage to rest the weight of their case on so tenuous a foundation' as the idea that very young babies have 'a kind of inchoate faith germinating like a seed in the soul.' Some like Lusk, *Paedofaith* would build a great deal on the idea of 'baby faith' (from Psalm 22:9-10 for example), and it is true that Luther, Calvin, and Turretin spoke about a kind of faith in infants. But the case for infant baptism does not need to include or rest upon this, as Pierre C. Marcel, *The Biblical Doctrine of Infant Baptism: Sacrament of the Covenant of Grace* trans. Philip E. Hughes (London: James Clarke, 1953), pp 209-218 clearly shows.

Nor does it suggest that all we can do is teach them 'law' (to be nice, obedient sinners) until they are old enough to 'grasp the gospel properly' and be saved. Speaking of infants, Jesus said that 'of such is the kingdom of heaven' (Matthew 19:14). He did not just mean that people who are like children in some way are saved, (a point made elsewhere in Matthew 18:3)[45] but that infants themselves would make up a part of his kingdom.[46] Yet as Owen argues it, to see the children of believers as 'young servants of the king'[47] is compatible and consistent only with the paedobaptist position. Since they have that immense privilege, however, the church has a duty towards children: to pray for them, to instruct them 'according unto their capacities,' to advise parents on their upbringing, to visit and encourage them, and to prepare them to come into 'full communion' with the church. Owen therefore advised that not only should parents be taught about their duties and responsibilities towards their children, but each church should have a teacher set aside especially for their instruction.[48]

4. Infant regeneration and salvation

Someone may ask, 'Granted that children may be regenerate (God does not work in adults alone), does that necessarily mean they ought to be

---

[45] The word is τοιούτων (*toiouton*, 'of such') in the Greek of Matthew 19:14, Mark 10:14, and Luke 18:16. Bearing in mind how this adjective is used elsewhere in the Gospels (e.g. Matthew 9:8; Mark 4:33, 6:2, 7:13; Luke 9:9; John 4:23), it simply cannot mean 'those *like* this' while excluding the children themselves. See also Calvin's comments on Matthew 19:14 in *Commentary on a Harmony of the Evangelists*, Calvin's Commentaries Volume XVI (Grand Rapids: Baker, 1993), pp 390-391 (volume 2) and the comments of Spurgeon (a Baptist) quoted in Sisemore, *Of Such is the Kingdom*, p 136.

[46] Charles Hodge, *Systematic Theology: Volume 1* (Hendrickson, reprinted 1999), p 27 says, 'Of such He tells us is the kingdom of heaven, as though heaven was, in great measure, composed of the souls of redeemed infants.' See also the similar thoughts of J. C. Ryle, *Expository Thoughts on Luke: Volume 2* (Edinburgh: Banner of Truth, 1986), p 268 on Luke 18:16. Though it must be noted, as Ryle says in *Expository Thoughts on Mark* (Edinburgh: Banner of Truth, 1985), p 203, 'Of course, it is not pretended that there is any mention of baptism, or even any reference to it in [Mark 10:13-16]. All we mean to say is that the expressions and gestures of our Lord in this passage, are a *strong indirect argument* in favour of infant baptism' (emphasis mine).

[47] R. C. Sproul, 'In Jesus' Name, Amen' in Gregg Strawbridge (ed.), *The Case for Covenantal Infant Baptism* (Phillipsburg, NJ: P&R, 2003), p 310.

[48] *The True Nature of a Gospel Church*, pp 22-24 in *The Works of John Owen: Volume 16*.

baptised?' As a Baptist, for instance, Mark Dever states that 'refusal to baptize is not intended as a statement asserting that the child is not regenerate but simply as a reluctance publicly to affirm that which has not yet been maturely evidenced.'[49] Obviously this line of argument contains something of a Baptistic presupposition that baptism is about affirming the candidate's faith, whereas Reformed paedobaptists like Owen would be happier to say that it was primarily about the promise and covenant of God.[50] Yet even if such an argument could be made without this presupposition, Owen will not accept the core idea that someone can be regenerate and yet denied a right to baptism. The two things go together – 'They that have the thing signified have a right unto the sign of it.' This is the core of Owen's fourth and fifth points in section IV.

The text which undergirds Owen's argument here is Acts 10:47. There we find the apostle Peter and his believing Jewish colleagues amazed at the grace of God shown to the gentiles gathered at Cornelius's house. When they received the Holy Spirit, Peter asked, 'Can anyone withhold water for baptizing these people, who have received the Holy Spirit just as we have?' Owen takes this as a principle, that those who are partakers in the thing signified have a right to the outward sign of it. How can they be denied the lesser if they already possess the greater? Later he cites Acts 2:38-39 as also demonstrating this same principle, and says, 'That unto whom the covenant or promise doth belong, to them belongs the administration of the initial seal of it.' Interestingly, the Ethiopian Eunuch in Acts 8:36 asks, 'What prevents me from being baptised?' which also appears to be consistent with this way of thinking: he believed the good news brought to him by Philip and wondered if there was any reason why he should not therefore receive the sign of baptism. Philip's consequent baptising of him would seem to demonstrate early agreement with this principle.[51]

---

[49] 'Baptism in the Context of the Local Church', p 350. The context is more about young children who profess belief than infants who have just been born, but the point is the same.

[50] Miller, 'Complex Innocence', p 201 avers that 'For Simons, baptism represents the believer's faith, while for Luther and Calvin baptism represents God's promise, a contrast Simons may not fully grasp or appreciate.' Not all Baptists would agree with Menno Simons or Mark Dever of course!

[51] It should be noted that whereas some Baptist exegesis of Acts assumes that the pattern of 'faith then baptism' seen there must be normative for today, Dever and others must argue that the equally prevalent pattern of immediate baptism after conversion 'need not be the normative practice today' ('Baptism in the Context of the Local Church' p 334 footnote 11).

Owen then considers the application of this principle to children. He states that the children of believers are all capable of the grace signified in baptism. That is, they are not angels or animals incapable of regeneration but have the potential to be born again.[52] But then he moves into what might today be considered much more controversial territory when he says that some of those children 'are certainly partakers of [that grace], namely, such as die in their infancy... therefore they may and ought to be baptised.' Owen assumes that the children of believers who die in infancy are partakers of the grace signified in baptism – that is, regeneration, new birth – just as much as those who profess faith as adults are. And he concludes that since that is the case, they ought to be baptised. He is not arguing for the post-mortem baptism of dead children.[53] He is arguing that since believers' children are capable of the grace signified (as evidenced in the salvation of those who die in infancy) they ought to be permitted the sign.[54]

How can Owen base so much on infant regeneration and salvation? It helps to understand that this was not a widely disputed point in his day. Broadly speaking, most Reformed theologians around Owen's time agreed that the infants of believers, dying in infancy, were saved.[55] As Lewis Schenck says, 'The Reformed church has always believed, on the basis of God's immutable promise, that all children of believers dying in infancy were saved... because the promise was "unto us and our children."'[56] Kuyper adds an important qualifier here when

---

[52] They also have *potentia credendi*, the potential to believe, though as with adults the transformation of this into an actual disposition of faith must be a gracious gift of God (see Philippians 1:29; 2 Peter 1:1,3; Ephesians 2:8). God is free to give this to whoever he chooses; a mature intellectual capacity is never made a pre-condition for his gift. Infant salvation, therefore, does not entail a denial of salvation by faith alone – unless faith is thought to be a 'work' which only adults are capable of performing, rather than a gift granted by God to his elect (see Acts 13:48).

[53] This is not his solution to the debate over the meaning of 'baptism for the dead' in 1 Corinthians 15:29!

[54] J. C. Ryle, *Expository Thoughts on Mark* (Edinburgh: Banner of Truth, 1985), page 204 argues in the same vein in comments on Mark 10:16, saying, 'It is allowed on all sides that infants may be elect and chosen of God unto salvation – may be washed in Christ's blood, born again of the Spirit, have grace, be justified, sanctified, and enter heaven. If these things be so, it is hard to see why they may not receive the outward sign of baptism.'

[55] Benjamin B. Warfield, 'The Development of the Doctrine of Infant Salvation' in *Studies in Theology, The Works of Benjamin B. Warfield: Volume 9*, p 429-438.

[56] Schenck, *The Presbyterian Doctrine of Children in the Covenant*, p 118. See Calvin, *Institutes*, 4.16.17-19.

he says that Calvinists 'have never usurped the right to pronounce on the presence or absence of spiritual life in infants. They only stated how God would have us *consider* such infants, and this consideration based on the divine word made it imperative to look upon their infant children as elect and saved, and to treat them accordingly.'[57]

There were, however, some differences of opinion in the Reformed tradition regarding the children of unbelievers. Some, such as Zwingli, Bishop John Hooper, and Augustus Montague Toplady saw death in infancy as a sign of God's election, whoever the child's parents were. Others rejected the idea that any infant dying outside the covenant was saved. Many, like the great Puritan Bible commentator Matthew Henry, were merely agnostic about those born to unbelievers. Owen's own view is that since God is perfectly free to elect anyone there may well be some infants born and dying outside the covenant who are nevertheless saved: he had 'no doubt but that God taketh many unto him in Christ whose parents never knew, or had been despisers of, the gospel.'[58] Yet when it came to the children of believers there was a great consensus that (as the Synod of Dort puts it), 'godly parents ought not to doubt of the election and salvation of their children whom God calls out of this life in their infancy.'[59]

Owen, therefore, seems to be building on an essentially undisputed truth and trying to establish another 'by good and necessary consequence' (as *Westminster Confession* 1.6 says). Marshall had also

---

[57] Quoted in Schenck, *The Presbyterian Doctrine*, p 18. See also the views of Richard Baxter, which accord with this, in *The Nonconformist Advocate* (1679), p 53 (Part 2).
[58] *Display of Arminianism* (1642) in *The Works of John Owen: Volume 10*, p 81. I can find no basis for saying that Owen believes that all who die in infancy are elect as is claimed in Terrance L. Tiessen, *Who Can Be Saved? Reassessing Salvation in Christ and World Religions* (Leicester: IVP, 2004), p 210 (citing Augustus H. Strong), though this is one of the most insignificant of the inadequacies in Tiessen's analysis. I am deeply unconvinced by the analogy he draws between saved infants and unevangelized adults, and unimpressed by the atomistic exegesis he uses to defend it and undermine alternatives.
[59] Article 1.17 in *The Judgement Of The Synode Holden at Dort* (London: John Bill, 1619). The 1662 *Book of Common Prayer* declares that, 'It is certain by God's Word, that children which are baptised, dying before they commit actual sin, are undoubtedly saved.' See Lee Gatiss, *The Tragedy of 1662: The Ejection and Persecution of the Puritans* (London: Latimer Trust, 2007), pp 22-23 for some Puritan objections to this.

done something similar in his sermon.[60] Such an appeal was possible because even many non-paedobaptists believed firmly in the salvation of those who die in infancy. The view of 16th century Anabaptist leader Menno Simons may in fact have been closest to Zwingli's position,[61] as was that of 19th century Baptist Charles Haddon Spurgeon.[62] This may not be entirely consistent[63] and Tombes, it should be said, was much less certain about infant salvation.[64]

Owen does not here elaborate on all the details of the doctrine itself,[65] though it is important to note that he does not affirm that infants are 'innocent' or worthy of salvation: he is quite clear that they are born in sin (Psalm 51:5), spiritually dead, and facing God's curse

---

[60] Marshall, *A Sermon of the Baptizing of Infants*, p 45.

[61] See Miller, 'Complex Innocence', p 203.

[62] In Iain H. Murray (ed.), *Letters of Charles Haddon Spurgeon* (Edinburgh: Banner of Truth, 1992), p 150 (Letter 1869), Spurgeon says, 'I have never, at any time in my life, said, believed, or imagined that any infant, under any circumstances, would be cast into hell. I have always believed in the salvation of all infants... I do not believe that, on this earth, there is a single professing Christian holding the damnation of infants; or, if there be, he must be insane; or utterly ignorant of Christianity.' His Sermon number 411 "Infant Salvation" (available at http://www.spurgeon.org/sermons/0411.htm) is equally emotive, 'If we had a God, whose name was Moloch, if God were an arbitrary tyrant, without benevolence or grace, we could suppose some infants being cast into hell; but our God, who heareth the young ravens when they cry, certainly will find no delight in the shrieks and cries of infants cast away from his presence.'

[63] In his sermon (p 45), Marshall points out that if (on antipaedobaptist assumptions) faith *must* precede baptism for children as well as adults because Scripture says faith is essential for salvation, then that precludes infants from being saved not just from being baptised. Marcel, *The Biblical Doctrine of Infant Baptism*, pp 213-214 makes the same point.

[64] Although he says in *Antipaedobaptism: Part 3* that 'salvation belongs to some infants' (p 562) and 'there is ground for a strong hope of the salvation of infants of Christian believers so dying' (p 557), even a 'strong probability' (p 560), his overall conclusion is that 'there is no certainty concerning the salvation of this or that particular infant of a believer dying, nor is there a sure ground for faith concerning it, nor is the hope of it certain, and we are to suspend our judgement concerning it' (p 555).

[65] For more on this, see Ronald H. Nash, *When a Baby Dies: Answers to Comfort Grieving Parents* (Grand Rapids: Zondervan, 1999) and Robert A. Webb, *The Theology of Infant Salvation* (Harrisonburg, Virginia: Sprinkle Publications, [1907] 2003). Owen would no doubt approve of the insistence by Nash, Webb, and Warfield that confidence in infant salvation is only coherent if one has a Calvinist (monergistic) soteriology, and is not strictly possible in a consistently Arminian or semi-Pelagian theology.

(Ephesians 2:1-3).[66] So, he says, the only way they can be saved is if they are regenerated, born again (John 3:3).[67] He could point to 2 Samuel 12:22-23 as an example of an infant being saved,[68] and Luke 1:15 as an example of an infant (even an embryo) being filled with the Spirit.[69] This is far from proving the salvation or regeneration of every infant of course; yet it does demonstrate that a mature capacity to understand the gospel is not strictly necessary, biblically speaking, for infants to be regenerate or saved. So we cannot infer that they are automatically damned on the basis of original sin or because they are unable to access the means of grace.[70] Owen's conclusion is that 'regeneration is the grace whereof baptism is a sign or token. Wherever this is, there baptism ought to be administered.... infants who die in their infancy have the grace of regeneration, and consequently as good a right unto baptism as believers themselves.'

In his fifth point, Owen makes the case that if God explicitly does not want someone to be baptised then they are eternally damned, since the sign and the grace must go together. This is why impenitent sinners are not to be baptised, because not having the reality they have no right to the sign. But he goes on to say that if the sign is denied to believers' infants then that implies (by the same logic) that God is denying them the reality of salvation too – 'and then all the children of

---

[66] It is important to stress that we are here discussing infants who die in infancy, not all infants. Some infants grow up to reject the gospel, and no-one would say they were saved simply by virtue of having once been infants!

[67] As a contrast to this, and to attempts to root infant salvation in election, see the view of W. H. Griffith-Thomas in Alan H. Hamilton, 'The Doctrine of Infant Salvation: Part 2' in *BSac* 101/404 (October 1944), pp 472-473, who bases it upon a supposed universality in the atonement. The same link can be found in a seventeenth century funeral sermon for an infant by Samuel Acton, *Dying Infants Sav'd by Grace, Proved* (London: 1699), p 9. See Warfield's answer to this contention in 'The Doctrine of Infant Salvation', p 439.

[68] Owen alludes to this text in his letter to Lady Hartopp, on the death of her daughter (see appendix 2). He is equally clear that the child's enjoyment of blessedness is a result of God's grace alone, shown in his covenant promises. Tombes denies this exegesis of the text in *Antipaedobaptism: Part 3*, p 558.

[69] Cf. Luke 1:41, 66. Some have also seen 2 Kings 4:8-37, Job 3:16-17, Ecclesiastes 6:3-6 and Jeremiah 31:15-17 (cf. Matthew 2:18) as important texts to consider here.

[70] *Westminster Confession* 10.3 (Savoy 10.3) says that 'Elect infants, dying in infancy, are regenerated, and saved by Christ, through the Spirit, who worketh when, and where, and how he pleaseth: so also are all other elect persons who are incapable of being outwardly called by the ministry of the Word.'

believing parents dying in infancy must, without hope, be eternally damned.' He does not wish to contemplate such a consequence. It is certainly not that for Owen baptism is essential for salvation, but rather that if God desires the sign of salvation to be withheld it must be because he withholds salvation itself from such infants.[71]

What shall we make of Owen's attempt to use infant regeneration/salvation as part of his case for infant baptism? As a recognition that baptism and the language of regeneration often go together in Scripture (e.g. Galatians 3:26-27, Romans 6:3-4), it could be helpful. As an argument for the baptism of anyone who is regenerate, it has obvious strengths. As an argument for the baptism of those infants of believers who are about to die it has some coherence, if one grants the idea that such infants are saved. However, if Owen is arguing for more (i.e. that all believers' children should be baptised), there seems to be a gap in his logic here, a missing step. Such an argument may be represented like this:

1. Believers' infants are capable of being regenerated (of which baptism is the sign).
2. Some of them definitely are regenerated (i.e. those who die in infancy).
3. Therefore believers' infants should be baptised.

Step 3 does not seem to be a legitimate conclusion, given his premises. What is being left unsaid here? Is he suggesting, as some do, that we presume all believers' infants are in some sense regenerate and therefore have a right to be baptised?[72] If so, he leaves the 'presumed

---

[71] Owen says elsewhere that elect infants are saved even if they die before being baptised. See *A Discourse of Spiritual Gifts*, p 432 of *The Works of John Owen: Volume 4*. William Hubbock, *An Apologie of Infants in a Sermon: Proving by the revealed will of God that children prevented by death of their baptisme, by Gods election, may be saved* (London: 1595), p 9 takes issue especially with the Roman Catholic view that infants dying before baptism are damned.

[72] See Schenck, *The Presbyterian Doctrine*, pp xiv, 11. For an overview of Reformed debates over presumptive regeneration and whether it can be used as a basis for infant baptism, see Richard J. Mouw, 'Baptism and the Salvific Status of Children: An Examination of Some Intra-Reformed Debates' in *CTJ 41* (2006), pp 242-251. Geerhardus Vos, *Redemptive History and Biblical Interpretation* (Phillipsburg, N.J.: P&R, 1980), p 264 points out that many Reformed theologians (including Ursinus, Voetius, and Witsius) use an argument from the regeneration of covenant children who die in infancy in their polemics with Anabaptists.

regeneration' step in the argument un-stated. Or is he merely talking about the capacity to be regenerate? If so, he has left himself open to the suggestion that on his logic anyone who is *capable* of being regenerated should be baptised. And does that not include the children of unbelievers, since he himself held that some of them are undoubtedly elect and so will be regenerated at some point? Yet he has already stated that such should not be baptised.

Has he therefore proved too much with this argument? The solution here does not appear to be straightforward or clearly spelled out in the condensed line of reasoning Owen presents. I do not think he is merely trying to establish that we should baptise all believers' children *in case* they die and prove thereby to have had a right to baptism (because, dying in infancy, they are saved). The evidence Owen brings can, however, be successfully deployed against his opponents' presuppositions in this way: if some children are saved they must be regenerated, and if regenerated then they have a theological right to be baptised; and if at least *some* children have a legitimate right to be baptised, then antipaedobaptists are wrong to say that no child should be baptised.[73]

Certainly to read Owen this way fits his polemical context and makes good logical sense of his otherwise difficult argument. On this reading, it does present a substantial counter to a familiar non-paedobaptist assertion, building on a commonly agreed premise that would be hard (theologically and pastorally) to deny. Yet however we evaluate the success or otherwise of this particular line of reasoning, clearly this argument involving the undeveloped assumption of infant salvation is not sufficient to establish the validity of infant baptism on its own.

5. Children and parents go together

The principle that the sign (the external rite) and the grace (the spiritual reality) of baptism go together may be on firmer ground in Owen's sixth sub-point. Here he contends that children are by nature part of the same covenant as their parents, and are said by Scripture to be associated in it

---

[73] I am grateful to Gert van den Brink for pointing me to this solution.

with them.[74] If true, this would be a strong argument that the sign of the covenant ought to be administered to them, since they already possess the covenant relationship which it seals. This perspective conceives of 'the thing signified' by baptism as at least partly a covenant relationship which can be objectively verified rather than an inner spiritual reality (such as regeneration) which cannot. Hence Owen argues from creation and from Romans 5:14 and 1 Corinthians 7:14 that children are dealt with by God in terms of the same covenant as their parents and 'those who, by God's appointment, and by virtue of the law of their creation, are, and must of necessity be, included in the covenant of their parents, have the same right with them unto the privileges of that covenant.'

This argument is more in keeping with the general thrust of his argument in previous points about the covenant. It argues on the basis of objective covenantal categories rather than from presumed or inferred subjective spiritual realities in the child itself, and is thus able to be focused on a promise of God which is where the Reformed doctrine is always strong. Stephen Marshall had used a similar line of defence, saying 'Thus it is by the laws of almost all nations... children follow the covenant-condition of their parents.'[75] Whether 1 Corinthians 7:14 could be used to prove the 'federal holiness' of the children of believers was of course hotly disputed. Marshall defended against several objections but Tombes summarised the usual rejoinder when he pointed out that on Marshall's exegesis of the passage an unbelieving spouse could legitimately be said to be part of the covenant and therefore be baptised, just as much as the children of such a union, since both were said to be 'holy.'[76]

Marshall and Tombes argued over whether 1 Corinthians 7:14 was referring to matrimonial/civil legitimacy or federal holiness/status.[77] Either way, however, Owen is not using the verse to say children are

---

[74] See also his comments on Hebrews 9:18-22 in *The Works of John Owen: Volume 23* (Volume 6 of Hebrews), p 354.
[75] Marshall, *A Sermon of the Baptizing of Infants*, p 15.
[76] Tombes, *An Examen*, p 79. Marshall in turn responded with further exegesis in *A Defence of Infant-Baptism* (London, 1646), pp 145-164.
[77] William Hubbock, *An Apologie of Infants*, p 22 referred to the view Tombes espoused as a Jesuit argument!

holy and therefore should be baptised, as some would.[78] He is merely using it as an example of how children are accounted to be in the same covenantal state as their parents. Whether the status being referred to is civil or spiritual, the verse does clearly show that the children share that legal standing with their parents, which is all Owen is asking it to prove. If children share the same legal standing within the covenant as their parents then they have a right to the sign and seal of that covenant.

For all its strengths, this argument must also account somehow for the strand of biblical evidence which does see baptism specifically as a sign of regeneration / new life and not merely a covenant relationship e.g. Romans 6:3-4 and Colossians 2:11-12. The Anglican answer is to say that 'Baptism is not only a sign of profession, and mark of difference, whereby Christian men are discerned from others that be not christened, but it is also a sign of Regeneration or New-Birth, whereby, as by an instrument, they that receive Baptism rightly are grafted into the Church' (Article 27). The right reception or efficacious appropriation of baptism may occur in or some time after the sign itself is applied. It is of course the response of faith, which enjoys the benefits granted by the legal 'instrument' of baptism.[79] Owen would agree elsewhere that baptism is linked to the new life spoken of in Romans 6, and is clear that without eventual faith all the privileges and benefits of baptism are lost.[80]

---

[78] *A Directory For The Publique Worship of God* (London, 1645) otherwise known as the *Westminster Directory*, states (p 21) that those baptised 'are Christians, and fœderally holy before baptism, and therefore are they baptised.'

[79] The famous Gorham Judgment delivered by the supreme tribunal of the Church of England in 1850 found that, 'the grace of regeneration does not so necessarily accompany the act of baptism that regeneration invariably takes place in baptism; that the grace may be granted before, in, or after baptism; that baptism is an effectual sign of grace by which God works invisibly in us, but only in such as worthily receive it – in them alone it has a wholesome effect; and that without reference to the qualification of the recipient it is not in itself an effectual sign of grace; that infants baptized and dying before actual sin are undoubtedly saved, but that in no case is baptism unconditional.' See John R. W. Stott, 'The Evangelical Doctrine of Baptism' in *Churchman* 112/1 (1998), p 54. *Westminster Confession* 28.6 (Savoy 29.6) also states that, 'The efficacy of baptism is not tied to that moment of time wherein it is administered.'

[80] See *A Discourse Concerning the Holy Spirit*, pp 560-561 in *The Works of John Owen: Volume 3* and *The True Nature of a Gospel Church*, p 12 (Volume 16).

Again we see then that the case for infant baptism has to be made by way of inference, consequence, and careful deduction. It cannot be decided simply by way of decisive proof-texting. Owen, however, is on clearer ground when he returns to arguments concerned with the covenant, and his logic here is less confusing than in the previous point.

6. Final arguments

Owen's seventh argument revolves again around the covenant which God made with Abraham to be God to him and to his offspring. Elsewhere he argues that whenever God declares that he will be God to someone ('I will be your God...') this is covenant language, by which God engages himself to work on their behalf and for their good.[81] So if God promises to be God to the children of believers, he is taking them into covenant with himself. This is what he explicitly said to Abraham in Genesis 17:7, declares Owen, and Christ has fulfilled that very same covenant: he came to 'confirm the promises given to the patriarchs' (Romans 15:8), and to be 'the messenger of the covenant' (Malachi 3:1).[82] So, he argues, if God is no longer a God unto believers *and their offspring*, if believers' children are no longer to be part of the covenant, then Christ has not faithfully confirmed the truth of God in his promise to Abraham. We can no longer trust God to keep his promises! To get around this, Tombes wanted to deny that the covenant of which Christ was the messenger was the same as the Abrahamic covenant; that was 'not a pure Gospel-covenant' but 'mixed' he claimed, with some spiritual, some temporal and material promises.[83] Owen, however, replies that, 'Let it be named what covenant he was the messenger of, if not of this. Occasional additions of temporal promises do not in the least alter the nature of the covenant.'

---

[81] *The Works of John Owen: Volume 19* (Hebrews, volume 2), p 84. The context is a discussion of the *pactum salutis* or covenant of redemption, whereby the Father and the Son covenanted together in eternity concerning our salvation. I am grateful to Professor Willem van Asselt for pointing me to Owen's exegetical argument here.

[82] Owen also cites Luke 1:72-73 as showing that Christ's coming was explicitly related to God remembering 'his holy covenant, the oath he swore to our father Abraham.'

[83] Renihan, *Antipaedobaptism*, p 72.

According to Owen, Christ has fulfilled 'the covenant with Abraham, enlarged and explained by following promises.' Not only did the original promise include Abraham's children but Owen goes on to list other verses where it is said that 'the promises made unto the fathers were, that their infant seed, their buds and offspring, should have an equal share in the covenant with them' (Isaiah 22:24, 44:3, 61:9, 65:23). So again, to deny that children of believing parents had the same right and interest in the covenant as their parents was 'plainly to deny the fidelity of Christ in the discharge of his office.' If children are not to be accounted a part of the same covenant as their believing parents then Jesus has not done what he promised he would do, and God cannot be trusted. This again is a variant on the covenant arguments that Owen has already presented, but proven from different texts. Importantly, he makes it clear that children were included in God's plans long before the 'old covenant' of Sinai ('the covenant in its legal administration'). Their inclusion predates the now abolished Mosaic law but was part of the more comprehensive and overarching covenant promise to Abraham which endures in Christ.

We are ready now to hear his summary of the case:

> In brief, a participation of the seal of the covenant is a spiritual blessing. This the seed of believers was once solemnly invested in by God himself. This privilege he hath nowhere revoked, though he hath changed the outward sign; nor hath he granted unto our children any privilege or mercy in lieu of it now under the gospel, when all grace and privileges are enlarged to the utmost. His covenant promises concerning them, which are multiplied, were confirmed by Christ as a true messenger and minister; he gives the grace of baptism unto many of them, especially those that die in their infancy, owns children to belong unto his kingdom, esteems them disciples, appoints households to be baptized without exception. And who shall now rise up, and withhold water from them?

Owen adds here the argument often made from the household baptisms in Acts,[84] as part of the overall picture being developed. Like Warfield,

---

[84] Acts 16:15, 16:32-33, 18:8. See also Acts 11:14 and 1 Corinthians 1:16. Marshall also enlists the household baptisms in a minor role in his *Sermon of the Baptizing of Infants*, p 40.

he does realise that 'infant baptism should not be founded solely on these passages alone,'[85] yet they do provide potential evidence at least that where there were children present (other baptisms in Acts were of solitary individuals or groups of adults) they were included in the administration of the seal of the covenant for 'the culture of that day assumed that children were usually part of the family... the preference is for, not against, the inclusion of family members. It had been that way since the time of Noah (Genesis 7:1), Abraham (Genesis 17:12-13), Joshua (Joshua 24:15), and David (2 Samuel 12:10).'[86]

Owen's eighth and last point is to say that more could be said, and arguments from church history could usefully be employed at this stage of the argument. Indeed, he goes on to engage in just such an argument (against Mr. Tombes) on the very next page. It may well be significant that since his brief opening remarks about the silences of church history, he has only put forward biblical and doctrinal evidence, choosing to consign further arguments over church history to the end of the case (and not really developing them to any great extent). It is possible that this could be construed as something of a rebuke or correction to Tombes, Marshall, and others who indulged in extensive historical arguments at the beginning of their works on the subject, prior to biblical exegesis. Whether such a rebuke is intended here, it is certainly safe to say that for Owen we should begin with the Bible and build our doctrine from there. Church history and custom is important but should never be primary when it comes to determining our present practice.

Conclusion

Owen presents a rationale for covenantal infant baptism. He defines the question carefully, and sets about proving his case with biblical and theological arguments designed to interact with and counter the attack

---

[85] Warfield, 'The Polemics of Infant Baptism', p 397. Stein, "Baptism in Luke-Acts", page 62 warns against building too much on them.
[86] Jonathan M. Watt, 'The *Oikos* Formula' in Strawbridge, *The Case for Covenantal Infant Baptism*, p 84.

made on the practice by antipaedobaptists such as John Tombes.[87] He has his eye throughout on the glory and honour of Christ which he perceives to be under threat if the children of believers are not given the sign of the covenant which Christ has confirmed. He seeks to defend not just a doctrine but the loving care God has for the church, which he felt was not always adequately appreciated. He argues by way of inference and consequence, sometimes less successfully, but always with a view to the practical implications not just for baptism but for other areas of theology and practice as well.

It is interesting that Owen does not rest his argument on paedofaith or on a particular reading of the new covenant described in Jeremiah 31, or from a single text such as Colossians 2:11-12 as some might.[88] Significantly, he does not seem to have Roman Catholic errors particularly in mind as he develops this short treatise. Nor does he so anathematise non-paedobaptism that differences over this doctrine become a bar to fellowship or toleration.[89] Owen's respect for non-paedobaptists like John Bunyan is well-known.[90] What Owen is concerned with, however, is expounding the doctrine of infant baptism in a way that pays attention to the whole unified sweep of biblical revelation from creation to consummation, in order to demonstrate that Jesus does indeed secure and command the destiny of his children, from life's first cry until their final breath.

---

[87] As Renihan, *Antipaedobaptism*, p 223 says, 'All of the major works on baptism in the middle thirty years of the seventeenth century were written to interact with Tombes.' He was 'the sharpening agent for the Covenantal Paedobaptistic view' (p 210). Cf. pp 11-12.

[88] *Westminster Confession* 28.1 speaks of baptism as admission into the visible church, and it is perhaps also noteworthy that Owen does not use that language here (cf. its omission from the Savoy Declaration 29:1).

[89] For Owen's views on toleration see *Of Toleration: and the Duty of the Magistrate about Religion* in *The Works of John Owen: Volume 8*, pp 163-206 about which R. Glynne Lloyd, *John Owen: Commonwealth Puritan* (Pontypridd: Modern Welsh Publications, 1972), pp 62-63 comments, 'it was the first work on toleration ever to be published in England while the author's own party was in power.'

[90] See Toon, *God's Statesman*, pp 161-162. See also Bunyan's *Differences in Judgement about Water-Baptism no Bar to Communion* (London, 1673) in which he took an eirenic position towards paedobaptists in contrast to other 'Baptists' such as Kiffin, Paul, and Danvers. A similar debate about whether to allow those only baptised in infancy to be church members or to share in the Lord's Supper is active in baptistic circles today.

Appendix 1: John Owen's *Of Infant Baptism*

Note: Page numbers from *The Works of John Owen: Volume 16* edited by W. H. Goold (Johnstone & Hunter, 1850-1853 // Edinburgh: T&T Clark, 1862 // Edinburgh: Banner of Truth, 1968) are placed in square brackets for ease of reference. I have updated verse references (changing Roman numerals). Footnotes are mine.

[258] I. THE question is not whether professing believers, Jews or Gentiles, not baptized in their infancy, ought to be baptized; for this is by all confessed.

II. Neither is it whether, in such persons, the profession of saving faith and repentance ought not to go before baptism. This we plead for beyond what is the common practice of those who oppose us.

Wherefore, testimonies produced out of authors, ancient or modern, to confirm these things, which consist with[91] the doctrine of infant baptism, are mere tergiversations,[92] that belong not to this cause at all; and so are all arguments produced unto that end out of the Scriptures.

III. The question is not whether all infants are to be baptized or not; for, according to the will of God, some are not to be baptized, even such whose parents are strangers from the covenant, But hence it will follow that some are to be baptized, seeing an exception confirms both rule and right.

IV. The question is only concerning the children or infant seed of professing believers who are themselves baptized. And, —

First, They by whom this is denied can produce no testimony of Scripture wherein their negation is formally or in terms included, nor any one asserting what is inconsistent with the affirmative; for it is weak beneath consideration to suppose that the requiring of the baptism of believers is inconsistent with that of their seed. But this is to be required of them who oppose infant baptism, that they produce such a testimony.

---

[91] i.e. are consistent with.
[92] That is, they evade the real question. Or as we might say, they are red herrings.

Secondly, No instance can be given from the Old or New Testament since the days of Abraham, none from the approved practice of the primitive church, of any person or persons born of professing, believing parents, who were themselves made partakers of the initial seal of the covenant, being then in infancy and designed to be brought up in the knowledge of God, who were not made partakers with them of the same sign and seal of the covenant.

Thirdly, A spiritual privilege once granted by God unto any cannot be changed, disannulled, or abrogated, without an especial divine [259] revocation of it, or the substitution of a greater privilege and mercy in the room of it; for, –

> 1. Who shall disannul what God hath granted? What he hath put together who shall put asunder? To abolish or take away any grant of privilege made by him to the church, without his own express revocation of it, is to deny his sovereign authority.
>
> 2. To say a privilege so granted may be revoked, even by God himself, without the substitution of a greater privilege and mercy in the room of it, is contrary to the goodness of God, his love and care unto his church, [and] contrary to his constant course of proceeding with it from the foundation of the world, wherein he went on in the enlargement and increase of its privileges until the coming of Christ. And to suppose it under the gospel is contrary to all his promises, the honour of Christ, and a multitude of express testimonies of Scripture.

Thus was it with the privileges of the temple and the worship of it granted to the Jews; they were not, they could not be, taken away without an express revocation, and the substitution of a more glorious spiritual temple and worship in their room.

But now the spiritual privilege of a right unto and a participation of the initial seal of the covenant was granted by God unto the infant seed of Abraham, Genesis 17:10, 12.

This grant, therefore, must stand firm for ever, unless men can prove or produce, –

> 1. An express revocation of it by God himself; which none can do either directly or indirectly, in terms or any pretense of consequence.
>
> 2. An instance of a greater privilege or mercy granted unto them

in the room of it; which they do not once pretend unto, but leave the seed of believers, whilst in their infant state, in the same condition with those of pagans and infidels; expressly contrary to God's covenant.

All this contest, therefore, is to deprive the children of believers of a privilege once granted to them by God, never revoked, as to the substance of it, assigning nothing in its room; which is contrary to the goodness, love, and covenant of God, especially derogatory to the honour of Jesus Christ and the gospel.

Fourthly, They that have the thing signified have right unto the sign of it, or those who are partakers of the grace of baptism have a right to the administration of it: so Acts 10:47.

But the children of believers are all of them capable of the grace signified in baptism, and some of them are certainly partakers of it, namely, such as die in their infancy (which is all that can be said of professors): therefore they may and ought to be baptized. For, –

[260] 1. Infants are made for and are capable of eternal glory or misery, and must fall, dying infants, into one of these estates for ever.

2. All infants are born in a state of sin, wherein they are spiritually dead and under the curse.

3. Unless they are regenerated or born again, they must all perish inevitably, John 3:3. Their regeneration is the grace whereof baptism is a sign or token. Wherever this is, there baptism ought to be administered.

Fifthly, God having appointed baptism as the sign and seal of regeneration, unto whom he denies it, he denies the grace signified by it. Why is it the will of God that unbelievers and impenitent sinners should not be baptized? It is because, not granting them the grace, he will not grant them the sign. If, therefore, God denies the sign unto the infant seed of believers, it must be because he denies them the grace of it; and then all the children of believing parents dying in their infancy must, without hope, be eternally damned. I do not say that all must be so who are not baptized, but all must be so whom God would have not baptized.

But this is contrary to the goodness and law [love?] of God, the nature and promises of the covenant, the testimony of Christ reckoning them to the kingdom of God, the faith of godly parents, and the belief of the church in all ages.

It follows hence unavoidably that infants who die in their infancy have the grace of regeneration, and consequently as good a right unto baptism as believers themselves.

Sixthly, All children in their infancy are reckoned unto the covenant of their parents, by virtue of the law of their creation.

For they are all made capable of eternal rewards and punishments, as hath been declared.

But in their own persons they are not capable of doing good or evil.

It is therefore contrary to the justice of God, and the law of the creation of human kind, wherein many die before they can discern between their right hand and their left, to deal with infants any otherwise but in and according to the covenant of their parents; and that he doth so, see Romans 5:14.

Hence I argue, —

Those who, by God's appointment, and by virtue of the law of their creation, are, and must of necessity be, included in the covenant of their parents, have the same right with them unto the privileges of that covenant, no express exception being put in against them. This right it is in the power of none to deprive them of, unless they can change the law of their creation.

Thus it is with the children of believers with respect unto the [261] covenant of their parents, whence alone they are said to be holy, 1 Corinthians 7:14.

Seventhly, Christ is 'the messenger of the covenant,' Malachi 3:1, – that is, of the covenant of God made with Abraham; and he was the 'minister of the circumcision for the truth of God, to confirm the promises made unto the fathers,' Romans 15:8. This covenant was, that he would be 'a God unto Abraham and to his seed.'

Now if this be not so under the new testament, then was not Christ a faithful messenger, nor did confirm the truth of God in his promises.

This argument alone will bear the weight of the whole cause against all objections; for, –

1. Children are still in the same covenant with their parents, or the truth of the promises of God to the fathers was not confirmed by Christ.

2. The right unto the covenant, and interest in its promises, wherever it be, gives right unto the administration of its initial seal, that is, to baptism, as Peter expressly declares, Acts 2:38, 39. Wherefore, —

The right of the infant seed of believers unto baptism, as the initial seal of the covenant, stands on the foundation of the faithfulness of Christ as the messenger of the covenant, and minister of God for the confirmation of the truth of his promises.

In brief, a participation of the seal of the covenant is a spiritual blessing. This, the seed of believers, was once solemnly invested in by God himself. This privilege he hath nowhere revoked, though he hath changed the outward sign; nor hath he granted unto our children any privilege or mercy in lieu of it now under the gospel, when all grace and privileges are enlarged to the utmost. His covenant promises concerning them, which are multiplied, were confirmed by Christ as a true messenger and minister; he gives the grace of baptism unto many of them, especially those that die in their infancy, owns children to belong unto his kingdom, esteems them disciples, appoints households to be baptized without exception. And who shall now rise up, and withhold water from them?

This argument may be thus further cleared and improved: —

Christ is 'the messenger of the covenant,' Malachi 3:1, – that is, the covenant of God with Abraham, Genesis 17:7; for, –

1. That covenant was with and unto Christ mystical, Galatians 3:16; and he was the messenger of no covenant but that which was made with himself and his members.

2. He was sent, or was God's messenger, to perform and accomplish the covenant and oath made with Abraham, Luke 1:72, 73.

3. The end of his message and of his coming was, that those to whom he was sent might be 'blessed with faithful Abraham,' or that **[262]** 'the blessing of Abraham,' promised in the covenant, 'might come upon them,' Galatians 3:9, 14.

To deny this, overthrows the whole relation between the old testament and the new, the veracity of God in his promises, and all the properties of the covenant of grace, mentioned, 2 Samuel 23:5.

It was not the covenant of works, neither originally nor essentially, nor the covenant in its legal administration; for he confirmed and sealed that covenant whereof he was the messenger, but these he abolished.

Let it be named what covenant he was the messenger of, if not of this. Occasional additions of temporal promises do not in the least alter the nature of the covenant.

Herein he was the 'minister of the circumcision for the truth of God, to confirm the promises made unto the fathers,' Romans 15:8; that is, undeniably, the covenant made with Abraham, enlarged and explained by following promises. This covenant was, that God would be 'a God unto Abraham and to his seed;' which God himself explains to be his infant seed, Genesis 17:12, – that is, the infant seed of every one of his posterity who should lay hold on and avouch that covenant as Abraham did, and not else. This the whole church did solemnly for themselves and their posterity; whereon the covenant was confirmed and sealed to them all, Exodus 24:7, 8. And every one was bound to do the same in his own person; which if he did not, he was to be cut off from the congregation, whereby he forfeited all privileges unto himself and his seed.

The covenant, therefore, was not granted in its administrations unto the carnal seed of Abraham as such, but unto his covenanted seed, those who entered into it and professedly stood to its terms.

And the promises made unto the fathers were, that their infant seed, their buds and offspring, should have an equal share in the covenant with them, Isaiah 22:24, 44:3, 61:9. 'They are the seed of the blessed of the LORD, and their offspring with them,' chap. 65:23. Not only themselves, who are the believing, professing seed of those who were blessed of the Lord, by a participation of the covenant, Galatians 3:9, but their offspring also, their brads,[93] their tender little ones, are in the same covenant with them.

---

[93] A variant of brat, which in Owen's day did not necessarily carry the negative overtones it does today.

To deny, therefore, that the children of believing, professing parents, who have avouched God's covenant, as the church of Israel did, Exodus 24:7, 8 have the same right and interest with their parents in the covenant, is plainly to deny the fidelity of Christ in the discharge of his office.

It may be it will be said, that although children have a right to the covenant, or do belong unto it, yet they have no right to the initial seal of it. This will not suffice; for, –

[263] 1. If they have any interest in it, it is either in its grace or in its administration. If they have the former, they have the latter also, as shall be proved at any time. If they have neither, they have no interest in it; – then the truth of the promises of God made unto the fathers was not confirmed by Christ.

2. That unto whom the covenant or promise doth belong, to them belongs the administration of the initial seal of it, is expressly declared by the apostle, Acts 2:38, 39, be they who they will.

3. The truth of God's promises is not confirmed if the sign and seal of them be denied; for that whereon they believed that God was a God unto their seed as well as unto themselves was this, that he granted the token of the covenant unto their seed as well as unto themselves. If this be taken away by Christ, their faith is overthrown, and the promise itself is not confirmed but weakened, as to the virtue it hath to beget faith and obedience.

Eighthly, Particular testimonies may be pleaded and vindicated, if need be, and the practice of the primitive church.

Appendix 2: Owen's letter to Lady Hartopp

Sir John and Lady Hartopp were particular friends of Owen, and for many years members of the small church in which he officiated during the closing years of his life. I include here the following letter from Pastor Owen to Lady Hartopp following the death of her baby daughter (probably Anne, who died in 1674), as an example of his pastoral use of the doctrine of covenant-infant salvation. We may not wish to emulate his style in every respect (encouraging a newly bereaved mother to 'be cheerful' may not always be a wise or effective approach) but his earnest sincerity, compassion, and we might say even empathy (given his own history) do shine through. Can we see here something of his personal mental reasoning after the death of his own children?[94]

To Lady Elizabeth Hartopp,

Dear Madam, —

    Every work of God is good; the Holy One in the midst of us will do no iniquity; and all things shall work together for good unto them that love him, even those things which at present are not joyous, but grievous; only his time is to be waited for, and his way submitted unto, that we seem not to be displeased in our hearts that he is Lord over us.

    Your dear infant is in the eternal enjoyment of the fruits of all our prayers; for the covenant of God is ordered in all things, and sure. We shall go to her; she shall not return to us. Happy she was in this above us, that she had so speedy an issue of sin and misery, being born only to exercise your faith and patience, and to glorify God's grace in her eternal blessedness.

    My trouble would be great on the account of my absence at this time from you both, but that this also is the Lord's doing; and I know my own uselessness wherever I am. But this I will beg of God for you both that you may not faint in this day of trial, – that you may have a clear view of those spiritual and temporal mercies wherewith you are yet entrusted (all undeserved), – that sorrow of the world may not so overtake your hearts as to disenable to any duties, to grieve the Spirit, to prejudice your lives; for it tends to death. God in Christ will be better to you than ten children, and will so preserve your remnant, and to add to them, as shall be for his glory and your comfort. Only consider that sorrow in this case is no duty, it is an effect of sin, whose cure by grace we should endeavour. Shall I say, 'Be cheerful'? I know I may. God help you to honour grace and mercy in a compliance therewith.

    My heart is with you, my prayers shall be for you, and I am, dear madam, your most affectionate friend and unworthy pastor,

    J. Owen

---

[94] I have updated the spelling and introduced paragraphing to aid the modern reader. The text can be found at the end of Andrew Thompson's biography of Owen in Goold (ed.), *The Works of John Owen: Volume 1*, pp cxvi-cxvii or Peter Toon (ed.), *The Correspondence of John Owen (1616-1683)* (London: James Clarke, 1970), pp 157-158.

Appendix 3: A liturgical introduction to infant baptism

To flesh out the practical implications of Owen's doctrine of infant baptism a little, I include below the introductory words that I use in Sunday services whenever an infant baptism takes place. As a pithy opening to that part of the proceedings it no doubt has its shortcomings, and I am not suggesting that it could be simply regurgitated in any context. But it reflects something of Owen's exegesis and approach, and since I have been asked for the wording on more than one occasion in the past I thought it might be a useful and appropriate appendix here.[95]

… Since the time of Abraham about 4000 years ago, God's people have been given an outward sign of admission into his covenant family. In the Old Testament the sign was circumcision; in the New Testament baptism is the sign of being part of God's people.

God said to Abraham in Genesis chapter 17 that the promises he signed and sealed through circumcision were for Abraham *and also for his children* – that he would be their God and they would be his people. Hence the children of believers were circumcised as babies under the Old Covenant.

This privilege has never expressly been taken away from our little ones. So, now that Christ has come to confirm the promises given to Abraham, children of believers under the New Covenant may receive baptism in the same way because again, as the Apostle Peter says, '*the promise is for you and for your children.*'

Baptism is the physical sign of a spiritual reality, which is that *N* here is a part of God's covenant family because she has been born to Christian parents. Her baptism today recognises that covenant reality, the spiritual privilege of being part of the household of faith.

But this does not mean, of course, that she is automatically going to heaven simply because we splash her with some water. As she matures she must believe and trust in the Lord Jesus to 'cash in' (so to speak) on God's promise of eternal life. So we hope and pray that she is

---

[95] See also the useful introductions to the two baptism services in *An English Prayer Book* (Oxford: OUP, 1994).

born again, and grows up to know and love Jesus as her Lord and saviour always.

So, using the words on the sheet, let's all pray for her now...

For further reading:

These works sometimes take very different views on the theology of children, but together they give a sense of where the debate lies and what the major lines of argument have been.

M. J. Bunge (ed.), *The Child in Christian Thought* (Cambridge: Eerdmans, 2001)

J. Calvin, *Institutes of the Christian Religion* Book 4, Chapters 15 and 16.

R. H. Nash, *When a Baby Dies: Answers to Comfort Grieving Parents* (Grand Rapids: Zondervan, 1999)

M. T. Renihan, *Antipaedobaptism in the Thought of John Tombes: An Untold Story from Puritan England* (Auburn, MA: B & R Press, 2001)

L. B. Schenck, *The Presbyterian Doctrine of Children in the Covenant: An Historical Study of the Significance of Infant Baptism in the Presbyterian Church* (Phillipsburg, NJ: P&R, [1940] 2003)

T. R. Schreiner & S. D. Wright (eds.), *Believer's Baptism: Sign of the New Covenant in Christ* (Nashville: B&H Academic, 2006)

T. A. Sizemore, *Of Such is the Kingdom: Nurturing Children in the Light of Scripture* (Fearn, Ross-Shire: Christian Focus, 2000)

G. Strawbridge (ed.), *The Case for Covenantal Infant Baptism* (Phillipsburg, NJ: P&R, 2003)

B. B. Warfield, 'The Polemics of Infant Baptism' and 'The Development of the Doctrine of Infant Salvation' in *Studies in Theology, The Works of Benjamin B. Warfield: Volume 9* (Grand Rapids: Baker, reprinted 2003)

R. A. Webb, *The Theology of Infant Salvation* (Harrisonburg, Virginia: Sprinkle Publications, [1907] 2003)

Evangelical Mission and Anglican Church Order: Charles Simeon Reconsidered

Andrew Atherstone

1. The Dundonald Affair 369
2. The Great White Knight of Evangelical Churchmanship 371
3. Irregular Preaching 376
4. Illegal Conventicles 384
5. Autonomous Societies and Quasi-Episcopal Ministry ... 390
6. Conclusion 394

ANDREW C ATHERSTONE is tutor in history and doctrine, and Latimer Research Fellow, at Wycliffe Hall, Oxford. His publications include *The Martyrs of Mary Tudor* (second edition, 2007), *Oxford's Protestant Spy* (2007), *Oxford* (2008) and, as editor, *The Heart of Faith* (2008) and *Such A Great Salvation* (2008). His major research interest is the history of evangelicalism in the Church of England, and he is preparing a critical edition of the complete correspondence of Charles Simeon for the Church of England Record Society.

1. The Dundonald Affair

In November 2005 three young evangelical preachers were ordained as deacons at Christ Church, Surbiton in the diocese of Southwark, in a bold move which provoked a furore throughout the Church of England. The ordaining bishop was Martin Morrison from the Church of England in South Africa (CESA), not officially part of the Anglican Communion. The ordinations took place without the permission or knowledge of Tom Butler (Bishop of Southwark) who reacted by summarily revoking the licence of Richard Coekin (senior minister of the Co-Mission Initiative), the chief instigator of the event. Coekin appealed to the Archbishop of Canterbury, who eventually ordered that his licence be restored, after legal proceedings presided over by the Bishop of Winchester as the Archbishop's commissary.[1]

This painful episode highlighted once again the perennial question of the relationship between evangelical faith and Anglican church order. What should be done when evangelical priorities and Anglican regulations collide? In turn, that question provoked important arguments about the history of Anglican evangelicalism. In his appeal to the Archbishop, Coekin acknowledged that the Surbiton ordinations were 'irregular,' but pointed to the legacy of Charles Simeon, doyen of the Anglican evangelical movement. He argued that Simeon himself had helped to organize irregular ordinations, two centuries ago, to supply evangelical clergymen for the mission field in the early years of the Church Missionary Society.[2]

Amongst the most outspoken responses to the Surbiton ordinations were those from Fulcrum, claiming to represent the 'evangelical centre' in the Church of England. Fulcrum's theological secretary, Graham Kings (Bishop of Sherborne from June 2009),

---

[1] For Coekin's defence of the ordinations, see Richard Coekin, 'No Option but to Ordain,' *Church of England Newspaper*, 11 November 2005. For a summary of the Archbishop's judgment, see *Ecclesiastical Law Journal* vol. 9 (January 2007), pp 145-147.

[2] Richard Coekin to Archbishop Rowan Williams, 18 November 2005, quoting Eugene Stock, *The History of the Church Missionary Society* (3 vols, London, 1899), vol. 1, p 245.

assailed the action as 'precipitate' and 'schismatic.' In particular, he asserted that it was a 'breathtaking' irony to offer Simeon as a precedent. Kings was keen to emphasise Simeon's 'loyalty to his bishop and concern for church order,' arguing that Simeon would have been 'the last person' to support such irregularity.[3] In vindication of this rival interpretation of Anglican evangelical history, Kings quoted from the standard popular biography, Hugh Evan Hopkins' *Charles Simeon of Cambridge* (1977):

> No one could have been more loyal to his bishop ... No one did more than he to retain within the established church those evangelical enthusiasts whose zeal for preaching the gospel tempted them at times to ignore its rules and regulations. It was his love of his own church, his satisfaction with its liturgy, and his belief that the reformers in the 16th century had faithfully brought it back to the Bible, that led Simeon to pray that his own *magnum opus* [his twenty-one volume *Horae Homileticae*] might be used 'not to strengthen a party in the church, but to promote the good of the whole.' His enthusiastic loyalty was so infectious that most of the 'serious' young men who gathered round him, and who could so easily have been carried away by the extremists of the day, were retained to make their full contribution to the very needy national church.[4]

Elsewhere Hopkins calls Simeon 'the complete Anglican.'[5] The interpretation put forward by Canon Hopkins and Bishop Kings, of Simeon as the archetypal obedient Anglican churchman, has dominated Simeon studies for many decades. Yet this booklet aims to probe that assumption by demonstrating Simeon's subversive flirtation with irregularity and disorder. It will argue that Simeon believed that the spread of the gospel must take priority over obedience to ecclesiastical regulations whenever evangelical mission and Anglican order collide, as sometimes they do.

---

[3] Graham Kings, 'Judicious or Precipitate? Evangelicals and Order in the Church of England' (Fulcrum Newsletter, December 2005).
[4] Hugh Evan Hopkins, *Charles Simeon of Cambridge* (London: Hodder & Stoughton, 1977), pp 213-214.
[5] Ibid., p 181.

2. The Great White Knight of Evangelical Churchmanship

The portrait of Simeon as a diligent defender of Anglican order is almost ubiquitous in the abundant studies of his life and legacy. As John Bennett observes, Simeon often appears in the pages of British ecclesiastical history as the great 'white knight' of evangelical churchmanship.[6] Numerous examples could be given. Alan Munden has recently emphasised Simeon's loyalty to his diocesan bishop and respect for parish boundaries.[7] Paul Carr believes that Simeon would dissuade evangelicals from seeking 'alternative episcopal oversight' because of his commitment to the Church of England.[8] Rudolph Heinze told his evangelical audience at the Islington Conference that although Simeon 'recognized the weaknesses of the Church of England, he loved that Church and did not make the mistake of rejecting her because she was not perfect.'[9] Arthur Pollard calls him 'an unswervingly faithful Anglican.'[10] According to Stephen Neill, it was Simeon's influence which transformed all the Anglican evangelicals of the early nineteenth century into 'convinced and devoted churchmen.'[11] Likewise, James Gordon writes in his study of evangelical spirituality:

> By his loyalty to the Church of England Simeon encouraged other Evangelicals to stay within their spiritual home. Evangelical spirituality, far from being incompatible with firm churchmanship had been shown to flourish in the deep soil of the Anglican tradition.[12]

Archbishop Donald Coggan agrees:

---

[6] John C. Bennett, 'Voluntary Initiative and Church Order: Competing Values in the Missionary Agenda of Charles Simeon,' *Bulletin of the Scottish Institute of Missionary Studies*, new series 6-7 (1990-91), p 2.
[7] Alan Munden, 'Charles Simeon (1759-1836)' in Andrew Atherstone (ed.), *The Heart of Faith: Following Christ in the Church of England* (Cambridge: Lutterworth, 2008), p 84.
[8] Paul A. Carr, 'Are the Priorities and Concerns of Charles Simeon Relevant for Today?,' *Churchman* vol. 114 (Summer 2000), p 160.
[9] Rudolph W. Heinze, 'Charles Simeon – Through the Eyes of an American Lutheran,' *Churchman* vol. 93 (1979), p 248.
[10] Arthur Pollard (ed.), *Let Wisdom Judge: University Addresses and Sermon Outlines by Charles Simeon* (London: IVP, 1959), p 12.
[11] Stephen Neill, *Anglicanism* (Harmondsworth: Penguin, 1958), p 236.
[12] James M. Gordon, *Evangelical Spirituality* (London: SPCK, 1991), p 104.

> Simeon was no weak inter-denominationalist. If a man loved Christ, Simeon grasped hands with him. But he loved the Church of England. He loved its liturgy. And he was content to live and die a son of the Church of England, even though within that Church he suffered so much and saw so much that was weak and unworthy in its priests and people.[13]

Meanwhile Archbishop Marcus Loane declares: 'The English Church can have had few sons and servants more loyal and devoted than Charles Simeon.' It was Simeon who 'proved that the truest Evangelical could and should be loyal to the order of the Church of England.'[14]

The same emphasis is found in a collection of essays published in 1959 to mark the bicentenary of Simeon's birth, written by members of the Evangelical Fellowship for Theological Literature (founded by Max Warren). Secession was a live issue amongst Anglican evangelicals in the 1950s and 60s in the years leading up to the Keele Congress, and Professor Colliss Davies used his essay to emphasize the need for upholding Anglican order. Having noted Simeon's concern for biblical preaching, theological training, missionary expansion and evangelical patronage, Davies nevertheless concluded:

> But perhaps his chief strength and most lasting influence lay in his insistence upon an ordered and disciplined ministry; in refusing to be drawn into irregularities, and by scrupulous care in maintaining the rules of order of the Church. His wisdom and statesmanship saved many enthusiastic young men from drifting into the ranks of non-conformity, so assisting to maintain Evangelicalism within the Church of England at a most formative period of its development. For this above all his memory deserves to be had in honour, as the character of this Evangelical leader is recalled to those who minister in the mid-twentieth century.[15]

A similar motif is apparent in the best-loved of all Simeon biographies,

---

[13] Donald Coggan, *These Were His Gifts* (Exeter: University of Exeter, 1974), p 16.
[14] Marcus Loane, *Cambridge and the Evangelical Succession* (London: Lutterworth, 1952), pp 212-213.
[15] G.C.B. Davies, 'Simeon in the Setting of the Evangelical Revival,' in Arthur Pollard and Michael Hennell (eds), *Charles Simeon (1759-1836): Essays Written in Commemoration of his Bi-Centenary* (London: SPCK, 1959), p 26.

by Handley Moule (first principal of Ridley Hall in Cambridge, and later Bishop of Durham), published in 1892 but often reprinted by Inter-Varsity Press and Christian Focus, and still in print. He writes: 'Perhaps the English Church never had a more loving and devoted son and servant than Simeon. ... Cordial was his loyalty to his ecclesiastical leaders.'[16] Moule drew parallels between Simeon's ecclesiology and that of the early Oxford Movement, in a passage worth quoting at length:

> As regards the Church of England, his dearly beloved Mother Church, he has proved himself one of its truest servants and most effectual defenders. Perhaps more than any other one man who ever arose within her pale, he has been the means of showing, in word and in life, that those Christian truths which at once most abase and most gladden the soul, as it turns (in no conventional sense of the words) from darkness to light, from death to life, from self to Christ, are not the vagaries of a few fanatical minds, careless of order and of the past, but the message of the Church, the tradition of her noblest teachers, the breath and soul of her offices and order. ...
>
> He loved ancient order and solemn ordinances, and he magnified the office of the Christian ministry. He greatly desired to see, not merely more energy in individual Christians, but more life and power in the English Church as such; he was, as we have seen, decidedly and thoughtfully a Churchman. The Evangelical revival of the eighteenth century found a certain defect supplied in the school of Simeon. Its earlier leaders, with really few exceptions, were by no means careless of the essential sacredness of order and cohesion; but they found themselves often in circumstances where at least there seemed to be 'a need of disorder.' Simeon, one with them in main spiritual principles, always in quest, like them, of individual conversions, was led both by his situation and his reflections to a more distinct sense than most of them had felt of the claims of corporate and of national religious life. ... He venerated order and authority.[17]

However, the most influential study of Simeon's churchmanship

---

[16] Handley C. G. Moule, *Charles Simeon* (London, 1892), pp 107, 109.
[17] Moule, *Simeon*, pp 259-261.

remains the Birkbeck Lectures for 1937-38 at Cambridge University, delivered by Canon Charles Smyth one hundred years after Simeon's death, and published under the succinct title, *Simeon and Church Order*. In this ground-breaking analysis based on significant primary research (unlike most studies of Simeon), Smyth concludes:

> For it was Simeon, more than any other single individual, who taught the Evangelicals to believe in the Church of England and to steer clear, not only of the Scylla of academic latitudinarianism, but also of the Charybdis of that pastoral enthusiasm which walks disorderly in its indiscriminate and unthinking zeal. ... It was Simeon who, more than any other single individual, taught the younger Evangelicals to love the Church of England and enabled them to feel that they belonged within her body.[18]

This interpretation of Simeon's attitude to church order was not invented by Bishop Moule or Canon Smyth, but stretches right back to contemporaries who knew the preacher at first hand. For example, Charles Jerram (1770-1853), the influential evangelical rector of Witney in Oxfordshire, had sat at Simeon's feet when an undergraduate at Magdalene College, Cambridge in the 1790s. He recalled that in later life Simeon managed to restrain his youthful zeal and that

> he not only conformed to the strictest regularity in the performance of his ministerial duties, but was the most strenuous adviser to his younger friends not to deviate from the prescribed rules of our Church in the discharge of their clerical functions.[19]

Likewise Daniel Wilson (1778-1858), Bishop of Calcutta from 1832, wrote at Simeon's death that his friend 'never varied throughout a long life, in ardent, marked, and avowed attachment to the doctrine and discipline of our Apostolical Church.'[20] A similar verdict is given by

---

[18] Charles Smyth, *Simeon and Church Order: A Study of the Origins of the Evangelical Revival in Cambridge in the Eighteenth Century* (Cambridge: Cambridge University Press, 1940), pp 250, 311.
[19] James Jerram, *The Memoirs and a Selection from the Letters of the Late Rev. Charles Jerram* (London, 1855), p 126.
[20] William Carus, *Memoirs of the Life of the Rev. Charles Simeon* (third edition, London, 1848), p 597.

Edwin Sidney in his biography of Rowland Hill (1744-1833), the Calvinist preacher at Surrey Chapel in London who had been mentored by George Whitefield and John Berridge. Hill found it almost impossible to obtain ordination in the Church of England because of his passion for itinerant preaching which often led him into other men's parishes or Nonconformist pulpits. Six bishops turned him down, until he was eventually ordained deacon by the Bishop of Bath and Wells in 1773, but his ordination as presbyter was banned by the Archbishop of York due to Hill's notorious law-breaking. He was forced to remain permanently in deacons' orders and so ministered for the next sixty years, as he used humorously to say, 'wearing only one ecclesiastical boot.'[21] His biographer drew an explicit distinction between the attitudes of Hill and Simeon to Anglican ecclesiastical regulations, explaining that Simeon

> disapproved all irregularity in a clergyman's ministrations. Indeed, there is every reason to believe, that the observance of *order*, which has been so judiciously regarded by Mr Simeon and his followers at Cambridge, has tended greatly to promote the influence and numbers of the zealous clergy, who are now so vigilantly and successfully defending the best interests of the church. On one occasion Mr Rowland Hill, with his usual delicacy of feeling, refused to preach in a dissenting place of worship at Cambridge, lest he should appear in any way to interfere with the course so wisely pursued by Mr Simeon.[22]

However, not everyone approved of Simeon's caution. According to Abner Brown, chronicler in the late 1820s of Simeon's famous 'conversation parties' at King's College, some evangelical critics accused the preacher of being 'more of a *Church-man* than a *Gospel-man*,' whose trumpet gave an uncertain sound.[23]

One of the ways in which Simeon strengthened gospel witness within the Church of England was by encouraging young evangelicals to remain within its communion. Many were tempted to flee to Nonconformity due to qualms over Anglican theology, or frustrations

---

[21] William Jones, *Memoir of the Rev. Rowland Hill* (London, 1837), p 76.
[22] Edwin Sidney, *The Life of the Rev. Rowland Hill* (fourth edition, London, 1844), pp 174-5.
[23] Abner W. Brown, *Recollections of the Conversation Parties of the Rev. Charles Simeon* (London, 1863), p 11.

with the restrictions of Anglican order and the obstructionism of Anglican bishops. There was a sensational flurry of departures in the mid-1810s in the south-west of England (the so-called 'Western Schism') and again at Oxford in the early 1830s.[24] Cambridge, by contrast, could boast only one prominent seceder at the same period – Henry Battiscombe (1802-71), fellow of King's College and curate of St Giles' who resigned in 1837, the year after Simeon's death. He founded Zion Baptist Chapel in Cambridge, but returned to Anglican ministry a few years later. Despite these high-profile departures, it was partly due to Simeon's example that so *few* evangelicals left the Church of England in the early nineteenth century. As Smyth concludes, 'I think we may confidently say that, without the steadying influence of Simeon at Cambridge, there would have been many more secessions than in fact occurred.'[25] G.M. Trevelyan agrees that it was Simeon who put an end to the Anglican evangelical drift into Nonconformity.[26]

As this brief historiographical survey indicates, Simeon's defence of Anglican order and ecclesiastical regulations is a dominant theme in the standard literature on the evangelical movement. Indeed this interpretation is so prevalent as to have become a long-established assumption, seldom questioned.[27] However, this booklet will show how Simeon pushed at the boundaries of Anglican order in several ways, through his irregular preaching, illegal meetings and autonomous associations.

3. Irregular Preaching

During the first decades of the Evangelical Revival, in the mid-eighteenth century, irregular preaching was widespread – pioneered by

---

[24] See Grayson Carter, *Anglican Evangelicals: Protestant Secessions from the Via Media, c.1800-1850* (Oxford: Oxford University Press, 2001), chs 4, 7; Timothy Stunt, *From Awakening to Secession: Radical Evangelicals in Switzerland and Britain 1815-35* (Edinburgh: T&T Clark, 2000), chs 10-11.
[25] Smyth, *Simeon and Church Order*, p 255.
[26] George M. Trevelyan, *English Social History: A Survey of Six Centuries, Chaucer to Queen Victoria* (London: Longmans, Green & Co, 1942), p 510.
[27] The scholars swimming against the tide are Bennett, 'Voluntary Initiative and Church Order' and Wesley D. Balda, 'Charles Simeon, Dissent, and Disorder,' *Studia Biblica et Theologica* vol. 8 (October 1978).

early clerical converts like George Whitefield (1714-70) and John Wesley (1703-91). In a deliberate breach of Anglican order, they preached across the country wherever a congregation could be found, whether in fields, market-places, cottages or barns. Wesley defended this irregular ministry in famous words, penned in 1748, with a sense of eschatological urgency:

> in plain terms, wherever I see one or a thousand men running into hell, be it in England, Ireland, or France, yea, in Europe, Asia, Africa, or America, I will stop them if I can: as a minister of Christ, I will beseech them in His name to turn back and be reconciled to God. Were I to do otherwise, were I to let any soul drop into the pit whom I might have saved from everlasting burnings, I am not satisfied God would accept my plea, 'Lord, he was not of my parish.'[28]

Earlier he challenged the same correspondent:

> But methinks I would go deeper. I would inquire, What is the end of all ecclesiastical order? Is it not to bring souls from the power of Satan to God, and to build them up in His fear and love? Order, then, is so far valuable as it answers these ends; and if it answers them not, it is nothing worth.[29]

Elsewhere Wesley declared: 'I would observe every punctilio of order, except where the salvation of souls is at stake. There I prefer the end before the means.'[30] Other Anglican clergymen caught up in the revival adopted similar methods, such as John Berridge (1717-93), rector of Everton in Bedfordshire, and Henry Venn (1725-97), rector of Yelling in Huntingdonshire. Both men were converted in the late 1750s, more than a decade after their Anglican ordinations, and soon began to engage in 'gospel rambles' with little concern for parish boundaries. Indeed, as Smyth observes, it was Berridge who first taught Venn to use barns as 'threshing-floors for Jesus.'[31] John Newton (1725-1807) had the

---

[28] John Wesley to 'John Smith,' 22 March 1748, in John Telford (ed.), *The Letters of the Rev John Wesley* (8 vols, London: Epworth, 1931), vol. 2, p 137.
[29] John Wesley to 'John Smith,' 25 June 1746, in Telford, *Letters of Wesley*, vol. 2, p 77.
[30] John Wesley to George Downing, 6 April 1761, in Telford, *Letters of Wesley*, vol. 4, p 146. For further discussion of Wesley's attitude to Anglican order, see Frank Baker, *John Wesley and the Church of England* (new edition, London: Epworth, 2000); Adrian Burdon, *Order and Authority: John Wesley and his Preachers* (Aldershot: Ashgate, 2005).
[31] Smyth, *Simeon and Church Order*, p 279.

sense to wait until he was converted before he applied for ordination, and he too joined the band of irregular preachers from his base at Olney in Buckinghamshire (though he innocently protested his obedience to canon law).[32]

Berridge, Venn and Newton were Simeon's chief mentors in the early years of his ministry in the 1780s. Their defiance of Anglican order brought inevitable retaliation from the church authorities, as Berridge recalled:

> When I began to itinerate, a multitude of dangers surrounded me, and seemed ready to ingulph me. My relations and friends were up in arms; my college was provoked; my Bishop incensed; the clergy on fire; and the church canons pointing their ghastly mouths at me.[33]

Yet Berridge justified his irregular actions with an emphasis strikingly similar to Wesley before him:

> And sure there is a cause, when souls are perishing for lack of knowledge. Must salvation give place to a fanciful decency, and sinners go flocking to hell through our dread of irregularity? Whilst irregularities in their worst shape traverse the kingdom with impunity, should not irregularity in its best shape pass without censure?[34]

Some thought Berridge was too pessimistic about the Church of England, but he insisted that it was necessary to face facts and to recognize that many Anglican clergymen were unconverted (as he himself had been). He told the Countess of Huntingdon that there was a crying need for true 'gospel labourers' since those who had been awakened by evangelical preaching would not put up with typical Anglican ministry: 'If they have tasted of manna, and hunger for it, they cannot feed on heathen chaff, nor yet on legal crusts, though baked by

---

[32] Bruce Hindmarsh, *John Newton and the English Evangelical Tradition* (Oxford: Clarendon, 1996), pp 205-217.
[33] John Berridge to David Simpson, 8 August 1775, in J.B. Williams, 'The Life of the Rev. David Simpson,' prefixed to David Simpson, *A Plea for Religion and the Sacred Writings* (new edition, London, 1837), p xxiii.
[34] John Berridge to John Thornton, 10 August 1774, in Richard Whittingham, *The Works of the Rev. John Berridge* (London, 1838), p 394.

some staunch Pharisee quite up to perfection.'[35]

Berridge believed that Anglican regulations were restricting evangelical ministry and he acted accordingly, by breaking the rules. This led to predictable recriminations from the diocesan hierarchy. He was summoned by Bishop Thomas of Lincoln who forbade him from itinerant preaching, threatened him with dismissal from his parish, and even warned that he might be thrown in Huntingdon gaol. Berridge recalled the conversation, in which the bishop urged:

> 'Well, and will you promise me, that you will preach no more out of your own parish?' 'It would afford me great pleasure,' said I, 'to comply with your lordship's request, if I could do it with a good conscience. I am satisfied, the Lord has blessed my labours of this kind, and I dare not desist.' 'A good conscience!' said his lordship, 'do you not know it is contrary to the canons of the church?' 'There is one canon, my lord,' I replied, 'which saith, *Go preach the Gospel to* EVERY CREATURE.' 'But why should you wish to interfere with the charge of other men? One man cannot preach the Gospel to all men.' 'If they would preach the Gospel themselves,' said I, 'there would be no need of my preaching it to their people; but as they do not, I cannot desist.'[36]

As Smyth wryly observes, the bishop might well have responded that the Great Commission was not one of the canons of the Church of England.[37] Yet Berridge believed that the commands of Scripture always trump the commands of the church. It is perhaps this clash between Berridge and his bishop that Simeon recounted years later to the Cambridge undergraduates gathered at one of his 'conversation parties.' Berridge was rebuked for preaching too often, at all times of day and on all days of the week, but cheekily replied, 'My Lord, I preach only at two times.' 'Which are they, Mr Berridge?' 'In season and out of season, my Lord.'[38]

In the mid-1780s Berridge sought to recruit Simeon for this irregular preaching ministry, and appealed to his young friend in Cambridge:

---

[35] John Berridge to Countess of Huntingdon, 26 April 1777, in Richard Whittingham, *An Appendix to the Works of the Rev. John Berridge* (London, 1844), p 517.
[36] *Evangelical Magazine* vol. 2 (February 1794), p 75.
[37] Smyth, *Simeon and Church Order*, p 264.
[38] Brown, *Conversation Parties*, p 200.

> If every Parish Church were blessed with a Gospel Minister, there would be little need of Itinerant Preaching; but since those Ministers are thinly scattered about the Country, and neighbouring Pulpits are usually locked up against them; it behoves them to take advantage of fields, or barns, or houses, to cast abroad the Gospel Seed.

Yet Berridge knew that many, even fellow-evangelicals, would try to dissuade Simeon from these acts of disorder. He urged his young charge: 'The chief Block in your way, will be from prudent *Peters*, who will beg and entreat you to avoid irregularity: Give them the same answer that Christ gave Peter ... They savour not the things of God, hear them not.'[39] Perhaps Berridge had his old ally, Henry Venn, in mind when he spoke of 'prudent Peters.' Venn had grown more cautious in his old age, and although an itinerant preacher himself, he tried to dissuade Simeon from following his example in this act of flagrant law-breaking. Smyth paints a picture of 'the battle for Church Order being fought out, like some Homeric context, between Venn and Berridge, with Charles Simeon's future as the prize' – an attractive image, though too polarized.[40] Berridge complained to John Thornton (the evangelical philanthropist in Clapham) that although Venn was 'a vagabond preacher as well as myself, a right gospel hawker and pedlar,' for some reason the rector of Yelling wanted 'to fasten the shackle on Simeon' and to put his feet 'into the stocks.' He exclaimed: 'O worldly prudence, what a prudish foe thou art to grace!' It is significant that he chose an ecclesiastical epithet to sum up Venn's excessive caution, labelling him in good humour 'the Archdeacon of Yelling.'[41]

During the early years of Simeon's ministry, he did engage in itinerant preaching like so many Anglican evangelicals before him, and was often to be found proclaiming the gospel in villages near Cambridge on Mondays, Tuesdays and Wednesdays.[42] He also conducted evangelistic tours through other parts of England and Scotland, even officiating in the Scottish Kirk, a highly irregular activity for an Anglican clergyman. He tried to justify this dubious flirtation

---

[39] John Berridge to Charles Simeon, no date, *Arminian Magazine* vol. 17 (September 1794), pp 496-497.
[40] Smyth, *Simeon and Church Order*, p 270.
[41] John Berridge to John Thornton, 2 July 1785, in Whittingham, *Works of Berridge*, p 445.
[42] Memoir (1813) in Carus, *Memoirs of Simeon*, p 50.

with presbyterianism by arguing, unconvincingly, that although the Church of Scotland lacked bishops it was the established church north of the border.[43]

Nevertheless, by the early nineteenth century Simeon had abandoned his itinerant preaching. Having begun by following Berridge's model, he eventually adopted Venn's advice. This shift in policy occurred for several reasons. It was partly motivated by a widespread British revulsion at political developments in France in the 1790s, where disorder was identified with revolution and Robespierre's 'reign of terror.' Simeon could not afford to compromise his wider ministry by being tarred with the Jacobin brush. His desire for church order was closely linked to his understanding of civic order, and he drew some parallels between the submission of clergy to the episcopate and of the British populace to parliament.[44] Seen in this light, Simeon's disavowal of itinerant preaching had as much to do with his Tory politics as with any theological principle. At the same period evangelicals in the Church of England, most notably the Clapham Sect, began to represent themselves as a movement of stability and respectability, unlike their radical cousins within Methodism. Moreover, evangelicalism began to gather momentum in the Church of England and many doors were opened for regular preaching, so Simeon concluded that irregular preaching was no longer either necessary or expedient. In these changed circumstances, he believed that the disadvantages of breaking the rules now out-weighed the benefits.

By the 1830s, the next generation of Anglican evangelicals had grown embarrassed at the disorderly attitude of their fathers, who put zeal before prudence. John Venn of Clapham wanted to 'draw a veil' over this aspect of his father's ministry and emphasised that Henry Venn had come to repent of his early irregularity.[45] William Carus, Simeon's curate and first biographer in the 1840s, shows a similar embarrassment. He was particularly concerned to present his mentor in

---

[43] Ibid., pp 89-90.
[44] For further discussion of Simeon's attitude to social order, see John C. Bennett, *Charles Simeon and the Evangelical Anglican Missionary Movement: A Study of Voluntaryism and Church-Mission Tensions* (PhD thesis, University of Edinburgh, 1992), ch. 2.
[45] Henry Venn, *The Life and a Selection from the Letters of the Late Rev. Henry Venn* (London, 1834), pp 170-171. See further, Michael Hennell, *John Venn and the Clapham Sect* (London: Lutterworth, 1958), pp 268-271.

a favourable light to his early-Victorian readership and therefore sought to downplay and to excuse any signs of Simeon's evangelical irregularity. Carus admitted that, like other 'earnest and zealous clergy,' Simeon had often engaged in irregular preaching in his youth because he wanted to embrace every opportunity to proclaim 'the glorious Gospel' to any who would listen. Yet Carus explained:

> At that period however it should be remembered, that the notions among all parties, of order and discipline, and even of Church-government, were very different from what they are now. ... In forming our estimate therefore of the acts of Mr Simeon in his earlier days, and of other men who pursued the same course, we must never lose sight of the views, and feelings, and principles of the age. It would scarcely be consistent with candour or justice to judge those men by the maxims or rules of our own times. The very men who were irregular then, would be the first to conform in every particular now. Many indeed lived to give the proof of this; and in the case of Mr Simeon this was remarkably true; for not only in later life was he singularly attentive to order himself, but was wont particularly to enforce upon his younger brethren the importance and duty of not indulging their zeal at the expense of regularity and discretion.[46]

Carus went on to repeat an anecdote from the end of Simeon's life when an old friend reminded him of his habit of irregular preaching in a farmer's barn, early in the mornings before the labourers went to work. Simeon hid his face and exclaimed, 'O spare me! Spare me! I was a young man then.'[47] Simeon's attitude to irregular preaching undoubtedly shifted in the last decades of his life, but Carus' *Memoirs* – which has dominated all subsequent Simeon studies – had a particular agenda to present his hero as a champion of good order, attractive to Victorian churchmen in the late 1840s. A different perspective is offered by another of Simeon's curates, Matthew Preston, who reports that he spoke more positively of his old habit of barn-preaching.[48]

---

[46] Carus, *Memoirs of Simeon*, p 199.
[47] Ibid., p 200.
[48] Matthew M. Preston, *Memoranda of the Rev. Charles Simeon* (London, 1840), p 39.

With the benefit of hindsight, more than thirty years after Berridge's death, Simeon reflected on the wisdom of his mentor's itinerant ministry:

> He was, perhaps, right in preaching from place to place as he did. ... He lived when few Ministers cared about the Gospel, and when disorder was almost needful. I don't think he would do now as he did then; for there are so many means of hearing the Gospel, and a much greater spread of it; a much greater call for order, and a much less need of disorder. To do *now* as he did *then* would do much harm.[49]

The emphasis here is important. Even in his maturity, Simeon's primary concern was not for order but for the spread of the gospel. He opposed disorder when he perceived it to be harmful for evangelical ministry, but also acknowledged that sometimes it was 'needful.' In Simeon's judgment, blatant acts of law-breaking were necessary in the 1780s, but had become inappropriate or unwise by the 1820s. At the age of seventy, he wrote to a young clergyman in Oxford:

> Days are materially altered in two respects: much good is in existence and in progress now, so that the same irregular exertions that were formerly necessary do not appear to be called for in the present day; and our ecclesiastical authorities are more on the alert now, to repress anything which may be deemed irregular. I should be disposed therefore to carry my cup more even than I did in former days: not that I would relax my zeal in the least degree, but I would cut off occasion from those who might be glad to find occasion against me.[50]

When lay members of his own congregation at Holy Trinity in Cambridge began itinerant preaching, Simeon tried to stop them, not because he thought it was wrong *per se* but because he knew he was under scrutiny:

> whether it was evil in itself or not, it was not possible for me as a minister of the Established Church to countenance such proceedings amongst my people, since I should assuredly be

---

[49] Brown, *Conversation Parties*, p 200.
[50] Charles Simeon to R. W. Sibthorp, 9 December 1829, in Carus, *Memoirs of Simeon*, p 449.

represented by my enemies as a patron and encourager of these irregularities.[51]

Simeon understood that if he had a reputation as a law-breaker it would damage his wider ministry. Yet, as can been seen, his attitude to these Anglican regulations was not determined by fixed principle but by expediency. Careful discernment was needed in each situation to determine whether an act of disorder would promote the gospel or hinder it.

4. Illegal Conventicles

As a young minister, Simeon found himself forced into deliberate and premeditated acts of disorder in other ways too. The regular channels for gospel ministry in his parish were initially closed to him by his hostile parishioners. The Sunday morning service was boycotted by many of the congregation who also locked their rented pews to prevent others attending. When Simeon brought in extra benches they were removed by the churchwardens. Many who wanted to hear Simeon preach on a Sunday morning were forced to go elsewhere because there were no seats for them at Holy Trinity. The Sunday afternoon lectureship (a hang-over from Puritan days), which would have provided a good opportunity for gospel preaching, was also blocked to Simeon. In order deliberately to snub their new incumbent, the congregation voted in John Hammond (their former curate) as lecturer. When Simeon tried to start a Sunday evening lecture, the churchwardens locked the doors of the church – and although on one occasion he hired a lock-smith to break into the building, it did not seem wise to persist. One-to-one discipleship through home visiting was also impossible because, as Simeon wrote, the parishioners 'were so imbittered [*sic*] against me, that there was scarcely one that would admit me into his house.'[52]

In that situation, what was Simeon to do? He felt that he had only one option – disorderly innovation. So he began a meeting on Sunday evenings, not inside the church building but in a private room, where he met with sympathetic members of the congregation to pray

---

[51] Ibid., p 111.
[52] Ibid., p 39.

and expound the Scriptures. Since this service took place in unlicensed premises it was equivalent to a 'conventicle,' in deliberate defiance of the law. Yet a more brazen act of disorder was still to come. When the meeting grew too large, and Simeon could not find a bigger room in his own parish, he hired one nearby. This, in effect, was a church-plant from Holy Trinity into another man's parish, uninvited and unwelcome, and Simeon admitted: 'I was sensible that it would be regarded by many as irregular; but what was to be done?'[53] Here again it is clear that his primary concern was not to uphold church order but to further the gospel. He concluded that there was no way to provide evangelical ministry to the people of central Cambridge without disobedience to the canons. His friends were alarmed and Henry Venn again tried to talk him out of this irregular activity, but this time Simeon persisted.

In the mid-1790s Simeon launched a second equally un-Anglican innovation in his parish. In order to provide diligent pastoral care, he divided the core of his congregation at Holy Trinity into six 'societies' of about twenty people each, with whom he met every month. Such 'small groups' or 'home groups' are taken for granted in the Church of England today, but in the eighteenth century they were highly subversive. Simeon admitted that they were 'by many accounted irregular, and that very few of the governors [that is, bishops] of our Church would sanction them.'[54] Nevertheless, he persevered, insisting that the provision of pastoral care in this way was part of his obligation as an Anglican minister, as laid down in the ordination charge. Simeon argued that these irregular activities actually strengthened the Church of England, because if the people of Cambridge could not find gospel ministry in the Established Church they would depart for Nonconformity. As he warned, too often 'the clergyman beats the bush, and the Dissenters catch the game.'[55] Yet at the same period Simeon helped to fund the ministry at Green Street Meeting House in Cambridge of a local preacher, John Stittle (1727-1813), an ill-educated former hedger and thresher who had been converted through Berridge's evangelism. Simeon joked that his financial gifts were to pay Stittle 'for shepherding my stray sheep,' but this was again a highly subversive

---

[53] Ibid., p 40.
[54] Ibid., p 108.
[55] Ibid., p 109.

collaboration.[56] Far from maintaining good Anglican order, Stittle's congregation became Particular Baptists and founded Eden Chapel in 1823 (where Stittle is buried). As Abner Brown notes, Simeon endeavoured 'to promote the good of souls anywhere and everywhere' so he 'sometimes shut his eyes to irregularities.'[57]

Simeon did not go looking for trouble. He was not irregular just to be provocative. Indeed, he advised that when responding to hostile bishops, 'A soft answer turneth away wrath' (Proverbs 15:1).[58] When one fervent clergyman was clashing with his bishop over issues like the introduction of a new hymn book, Simeon counselled him to stay out of trouble, keep his head down in his parish until the storm blew over, and 'avoid everything that can give offence, except the faithful preaching of 'Christ crucified.'"[59] However, Simeon also knew that, in some instances, the benefits of disorder far outweighed the disadvantages. Even his famous 'conversations parties' remained only one step away from irregularity and illegality. They were in effect regular weekly meetings for bible teaching, open to all undergraduates, led by an Anglican clergyman in unlicensed premises (Simeon's rooms at King's College) – not unlike a 'conventicle.' In order to remain just the right side of the law, Simeon deliberately refrained from 'expounding' the Scriptures – he would simply point to relevant Bible texts in answer to questions. He was also careful not to begin or end the meeting in prayer, lest it become a 'religious' gathering and fall under the restrictions of the Conventicle Act.[60]

Remarkably, Simeon's irregular meetings remained 'under the radar' and he was able to continue this ministry unmolested for many years. There were however, occasional attacks upon his contempt for good order. One who questioned Simeon's loyalty to the Church of England was Benjamin Flower (1755-1829), the radical political commentator and editor of the *Cambridge Intelligencer*. In a pamphlet attack in 1796, Flower accused Simeon of undermining Anglican order:

> ... it is well known that he every week, if not oftenener, holds *illegal conventicles*. I hope no one will imagine, that I have any

---

[56] Arthur B. Gray, *Cambridge Revisited* (Cambridge: Heffer, 1921), p 98.
[57] Brown, *Conversation Parties*, p 13.
[58] Charles Simeon to [Henry Budd?], 18 January 1814, in Carus, *Memoirs of Simeon*, p 271.
[59] Charles Simeon to [Henry Budd?], 7 March 1814, in Carus, Ibid., p 272.
[60] Charles Simeon to R. W. Sibthorp, 9 December 1829, in Carus, Ibid., p 449.

objection to the gospel being preached any where. On the contrary, I have heard sermons with equal pleasure, in a cathedral, a meeting-house, a room, a barn and a field. But I certainly think it a very dishonest part in a clergyman of the establishment, who has sworn that he will neither preach nor pray in an unlicensed place of worship, and who prides himself on his loyalty, to whom, as that famous ecclesiastical lawyer Dr Burn [Richard Burn (1709-85), author of *Ecclesiastical Law* (1760)] informs us, the canons are the laws of the land – for such a man, in defiance of his oath of canonical obedience, and of every principle of decency, in the face of one of the Universities, to carry on his illegal practices every week of his life. What is equally surprising and equally to be lamented is, that his hearers, some of whom are persons of sense and piety, should encourage him in so doing.[61]

Flower warned the congregation at Holy Trinity church that one day they would have to give an account to Almighty God for their support of 'the *perjured* services of their minister' – in other words, of a dishonest clergyman who had sworn canonical obedience and yet was frequently in breach of the canons.

Similar accusations were thrown at Simeon a decade later, in Flower's new journal, *The Political Review and Monthly Register*. The main focus of controversy was Francis Stone (rector of Cold Norton in Essex) a seasoned campaigner against clerical subscription to the Thirty-Nine Articles. Stone's rationalist theology had led him to Unitarianism, but he was tolerated in the diocese until July 1806 when he preached at the archdeacon's visitation. Stone's outspoken sermon rejected the doctrine of the Trinity and the Virgin Birth, and proclaimed that the first two chapters of Matthew's Gospel were a forgery.[62] He was taken to trial in the consistory court and deprived of his living by Bishop Porteus of London. His appeal to the court of arches was dismissed and he died in November 1813 in the debtors' prison in Southwark. Yet some of Stone's Unitarian allies argued that he ought to be allowed to keep his

---

[61] Benjamin Flower, *National Sins Considered, in Two Letters to the Rev. Thomas Robinson ... to Which are Added a Letter from the Rev. Robert Hall, to the Rev. Charles Simeon; and Reflections on the War* (Cambridge, 1796), pp 87-88.

[62] Francis Stone, *Jewish Prophecy, the Sole Criterion to Distinguish between Genuine and Spurious Christian Scripture* (London, 1806).

position as an Anglican clergyman, even though he did not believe traditional Christian doctrine. Their counter-offensive was to assail evangelicals like Simeon as equally un-Anglican. They argued that Simeon was also a notorious law-breaker. If Stone was to be dismissed for rejecting Anglican doctrine, then Simeon should also be dismissed for undermining Anglican order. One correspondent to the *Political Register* attacked Simeon and Thomas Haweis (1734-1820), a close associate of the Countess of Huntingdon, as 'schismaticks' who were guilty of preaching 'in unlicensed places.' He continued:

> Now self will in matters of discipline is just as bad as self will in matters of doctrine: but both Mr Haweis and Mr Simeon will justify themselves by saying, that the conversion of sinners is of more importance, than a regard to places and subjection to episcopal rules; and that whilst they do their duty in their respective churches, they shall not quit their charges but upon compulsion. If the bishops do not call upon them on account of their itenerant [sic] preaching, they shall continue in that holy exercise.[63]

Another joined in the assault:

> ... many of the *evangelical* clergy are equally guilty of the falsehood and prevarication which affords so much matter of complaint to every serious, thinking Christian. These gentlemen have taken the oath of canonical obedience, which as their great ecclesiastical lawyer, and oracle, Dr Burn informs us, enjoins them to the observance of every one of the canons. Now Sir, many of this class of the clergy, make a common practice, in direct violation of their oath, of preaching in dissenting meeting houses, where the liturgy of the established church is never used, and what is still more extraordinary, of preaching in unlicensed places of worship, or what the law terms *illegal conventicles!* This I have been assured was the weekly practice for many years, (if it is not still continued), of the Revd. *Charles Simeon, M.A. Fellow of Trinity College, Cambridge* [sic]. To which instance I may add that of his reverend brother, *Rowland Hill, M.A.* who in a late publication with effrontery fully equal to Mr *Stone's*, glories 'in having broken the laws of his church,

---

[63] *Political Review and Monthly Register* vol. 1 (January 1807), p 55.

hundreds of times!'[64]

Simeon was quick to distance himself from the charge of being a law-breaker, blaming the attack on Benjamin Flower's 'Jacobinical malignity.' He was fortunate that he had a good working relationship with the Bishop of Ely, James Yorke, who for twenty-five years had allowed Simeon to work in peace and consistently turned a blind eye to his irregularities. The bishop refused to investigate these new rumours, 'persuaded as I am, that your zeal is regulated with that prudence, which is the best security against malevolent writers.'[65]

This happy relationship with the diocesan hierarchy quickly dissolved when Bishop Yorke died in August 1808, aged 78. Trust was replaced by mutual suspicion when Thomas Dampier (Bishop of Rochester) was translated to Ely. Simeon had often experienced hostility from his parishioners, yet now for the first time in his ministry he was on the receiving end of aggression from his bishop. Dampier made it abundantly obvious in his first Charge that he had no sympathy for the evangelicals in his diocese, and Simeon was thrown on the defensive.[66] He reassured Dampier that if any rumours of disorder emanating from Holy Trinity, Cambridge should reach the bishop's ears they must be false. He also proclaimed his humble submission to episcopal authority, knowing that Dampier had reason to doubt it: 'under divine providence your Lordship is now become my immediate superior in the Church, to whom I owe all possible deference and respect.'[67]

Such protestations could not save Simeon from episcopal interference. With the change in diocesan leadership, his enemies in Cambridge saw their chance and more than forty parishioners wrote to Ely complaining at Simeon's ministry. Whereas Yorke would have ignored the protest, Dampier chose to investigate. He tried to persuade the University Vice-Chancellor and the Heads of Houses to censure Simeon's teaching, which would give the bishop an excuse to close down his evening lectures. There was also the irregular prayer-meeting held each week in Holy Trinity parish, which had been running since the 1780s with Simeon's cognisance though no longer with his close oversight. One of his local opponents

---

[64] *Political Review and Monthly Register* vol. 1 (May 1807), p 376.
[65] Quoted in Charles Simeon to Edward Edwards, 14 March 1807, in Carus, *Memoirs of Simeon*, p 170.
[66] Memoir (1813) in Carus, Ibid., p 234.
[67] Charles Simeon to Thomas Dampier, 10 February 1809, in Carus, Ibid., p 198.

threatened to inform against this 'conventicle,' and Simeon was alarmed that it would provide the excuse the bishop needed to shut down his teaching ministry and perhaps even dismiss him from his post. Simeon had countenanced these disorderly proceedings for twenty-five years, yet because he was now under scrutiny he chose forcibly to shut down the prayer-meeting (despite the resistance of its members). For the sake of his wider ministry, he could not afford to be associated with this act of disorder, as he explained in a private memorandum:

> But was it right, that I should lay myself open to such imputations, when the cause of Religion in Cambridge depended so essentially on my conducting myself with wisdom and prudence? Assuredly not: and therefore, I told the chief of the people [that is, the leader of the prayer-meeting], that if they determined to follow their own ways, I wished them to separate entirely from me and from my ministry, that I might not be involved in their irregularities. If they chose to let off fireworks, they were at liberty to do so; only I desired they would not put them under my thatch, to burn down my house.[68]

Here again it is important to note that Simeon's primary concern was not for Anglican order. He did not close down the prayer-meeting because it was illegal, out of a dislike for irregularity. Indeed, he himself had established the meeting and supported it for many years. Rather, he disbanded it because it was now under scrutiny from a hostile bishop and would put in danger his other more important gospel projects. As with itinerant preaching, his attitude was determined not by fixed principle but by expediency. On this occasion he decided to close down the 'conventicle' in his parish not because of a desire to uphold the ecclesiastical rules (which he had often flouted), but in order to protect wider gospel opportunities.

5. Autonomous Societies and Quasi-Episcopal Ministry

Alongside Simeon's itinerant preaching, his illegal 'conventicle' and his other irregular meetings in Cambridge, he also provoked hostility

---

[68] Memoir (1813) in Carus, Ibid., pp 240-241.

amongst his Anglican opponents by his support of voluntary societies. Simeon was a prominent figure in the work of new evangelical organizations such as the Church Missionary Society (CMS), the British and Foreign Bible Society (BFBS) and the London Society for Propagating Christianity Amongst the Jews (LSPCJ). Although it was not against canon law to support these autonomous societies, their very existence was seen by some as disorderly and un-Anglican.

The Church Missionary Society, for example, was run exclusively by evangelicals and operated independently from the hierarchy of the Church of England, outside the usual church structures and exempt from episcopal jurisdiction. Furthermore, it was seen to be in direct competition with the two 'official' Anglican mission agencies, the Society for Promoting Christian Knowledge (SPCK, founded in 1698) and the Society for the Propagation of the Gospel in Foreign Parts (SPG, founded in 1701). Mark Smith argues that the creation of voluntary associations like CMS represented 'nothing less than the birth of a new model of Anglicanism,' taken for granted today, but a radical departure from the traditional territorial and hierarchical mindset of the late Hanoverian church. He shows how the formation of a local CMS auxiliary at Bath in 1817 provoked outrage in the diocese, where the archdeacon denounced its 'subversion of ecclesiastical order.'[69]

There was similar controversy at Cambridge six years earlier, in December 1811, when Simeon helped to launch a local auxiliary of the Bible Society, a pan-evangelical association – one of his many close collaborations with Nonconformists.[70] The BFBS was opposed by a powerful lobby within the University, led by Herbert Marsh (1757-1839), Lady Margaret Professor of Divinity and future Bishop of Peterborough. In an address to the University Senate Marsh proclaimed that loyal Anglicans should support the SPCK ('the *ancient* Bible Society') whereas to support the BFBS was to undermine the Church of

---

[69] Mark Smith, 'Henry Ryder and the Bath CMS: Evangelical and High Church Controversy in the Later Hanoverian Church' (forthcoming).
[70] For the crisis over the Cambridge auxiliary, see Ford K. Brown, *Fathers of the Victorians: The Age of Wilberforce* (Cambridge: Cambridge University Press, 1961), ch. 8. For the early years of the BFBS, see Roger H. Martin, *Evangelicals United: Ecumenical Stirrings in Pre-Victorian Britain, 1795-1830* (Metuchen, N.J.: Scarecrow, 1983), chs 5-7.

England.⁷¹ This was followed by a lengthy pamphlet attack in which Marsh likened evangelicals to the Puritans of the 1640s who had overthrown the national church.⁷² Simeon mocked the professor's claim that this new voluntary society was somehow subversive of Anglican order:

> we see already, as it were, before our eyes, the *Test Act repealed*, the *Monarchy subverted, Episcopacy banished*, and all the *horrors of former ages renewed*. ... If you *can* produce any proof of it, produce it: if you *cannot*, what becomes of all your eloquent descriptions, all your fine comparisons, all your sad complaints, all your terrible predictions? they will all vanish as the dreams of a disturbed imagination, or as the baseless fabric of a vision.⁷³

Nevertheless, Simeon's bold protestations did not dispel the suspicion that loyal Anglicans should not be involved in these innovative and autonomous voluntary associations.

There were also concerns that Simeon was challenging the authority of the bishops' bench by his deployment of Anglican clergy. Although only a humble parish minister in Cambridge, by the early nineteenth century he was exercising quasi-episcopal functions throughout Britain and indeed the Empire. The historian and essayist, Thomas Babington Macaulay (1800-59), an undergraduate at Trinity College in the early 1820s, famously declared:

> As to Simeon, if you knew what his authority and influence were, and how they extended from Cambridge to the most remote corners of England, you would allow that his real sway in the Church was far greater than that of any primate.⁷⁴

---

[71] Herbert Marsh, *An Address to the Members of the Senate of the University of Cambridge; Occasioned by the Proposal to Introduce in this Place an Auxiliary Bible Society* (Cambridge, 1811).

[72] Herbert Marsh, *An Inquiry into the Consequences of Neglecting to Give the Prayer Book with the Bible, Interspersed with Remarks on Some Late Speeches at Cambridge, and Other Important Matter Relative to the British and Foreign Bible Society* (Cambridge, 1812).

[73] Charles Simeon, *The Excellency of the Liturgy in Four Discourses ... to which is prefixed An Answer to Dr Marsh's Inquiry* (Cambridge, 1812), pp 42-43, 58.

[74] G.O. Trevelyan, *The Life and Letters of Lord Macaulay* (2 vols, London, 1876), vol. 1, p 68.

Through his conversation parties and preaching classes in Cambridge, Simeon recruited and trained numerous evangelical curates, missionaries and chaplains for the nascent Anglican Communion. Young men seeking curacies often looked to Simeon rather than their local bishop. His patronage trust was entirely legal, but was nevertheless viewed by some as an act of disorder, subversive of Anglican unity, because he refused to appoint non-evangelicals to his parishes.[75] Simeon also procured more than twenty chaplains for the East India Company (Henry Martyn, Daniel Corrie, Thomas Thomason and their successors), side-stepping the official Anglican hierarchy and using instead his personal contacts at India House.[76] In his old age, Simeon wrote of India:

> *Almost* all the good men who have gone thither these 40 years have been recommended by me. I used jocosely to call India my *Diocese*. Since there has been a Bishop [of Calcutta, from 1814] I *modestly* call it my *Province*.[77]

Sometimes it was difficult to procure Anglican ordination for these young recruits, but Simeon's personal networks and powers of persuasion usually found a way, in an age when the path to ordination was much more flexible than it later became.[78] Sir James Stephen (1789-1859) observed of one anti-evangelical bishop that

> the splendour of his own mitre waned before that nobler episcopate to which Charles Simeon had been elevated, as in primitive times, by popular acclamation. His *diocese* embraced almost every city of his native land, and extended to many of the remote dependencies which then, as now, she held in subjection. In every ecclesiastical section of the Empire he could point to teachers who revered him as the guide of their youth, and the counsellor of their later years. In his frequent visitations

---

[75] See further, Wesley D. Balda, *'Spheres of Influence': Simeon's Trust and its Implications for Evangelical Patronage* (PhD thesis, University of Cambridge, 1981).

[76] See further, Bennett, *Charles Simeon and the Evangelical Anglican Missionary Movement*, ch. 6.

[77] Note (c.1829), attached to a letter from David Brown, William Chambers, Charles Grant and George Udny to Charles Simeon, September 1787, Ridley Hall Archives, Simeon MSS.

[78] A typical example is Charles Simeon to William Mansel (Bishop of Bristol), 2 December 1818, in Carus, *Memoirs of Simeon*, pp 346-348.

of the churches of which he was the patron or the founder, love and honour waited on him.[79]

Simeon's training and deployment of clergy worldwide, and his support of autonomous mission agencies (sometimes hand-in-hand with Nonconformists), could not be stopped by the Church of England's hierarchy because they broke no rules. Nevertheless, these provocative activities remained a subversive challenge to established Anglican order.

6. Conclusion

Historians of evangelicalism have long portrayed Charles Simeon as the exemplar of loyal Anglican churchmanship, a convinced defender of canonical obedience and submission to episcopal authority. However, as this study has shown, there were several ways in which Simeon pushed at the boundaries of Anglican order. In his early ministry he blatantly disregarded church regulations, as witnessed by his itinerant preaching and his foundation of a 'conventicle' in Cambridge. Although he later distanced himself from these irregularities, Simeon continued to challenge the status quo by his collaboration with Nonconformists, his Cambridge 'conversation parties' and parish 'societies,' his public support of autonomous associations and his quasi-episcopal deployment of Anglican clergy.

Even in his later ministry, Simeon's public protestations of a concern for Anglican order were not consistently put into practice. Indeed, as Wesley Balda observes, Simeon's implacable advocacy of church order was often contradicted 'by surreptitious or quietly executed actions ... He persistently qualified strong statements on church order by transparent acts of disorder.'[80] John Bennett suggests, unpersuasively, that this tension reveals Simeon's 'tolerance for paradox.'[81] Yet Balda is nearer the mark when he argues, as this booklet

---

[79] James Stephen, *Essays in Ecclesiastical Biography* (2 vols, London, 1849), vol. 2, p 374; originally published in James Stephen, 'The Clapham Sect,' *Edinburgh Review* vol. 80 (July 1844).
[80] Balda, 'Charles Simeon, Dissent, and Disorder,' pp 59, 72.
[81] Bennett, 'Voluntary Initiative and Church Order,' p 9.

has done, that Simeon's ecclesiology was 'not based upon a fixed and consistent agenda' but upon 'expediency and the need of the moment.'[82]

As has been shown throughout this study, Simeon's ultimate concern was for the spread of the gospel. In some instances, he distanced himself from acts of irregularity because he believed they would damage gospel ministry and limit his influence elsewhere. However, on other occasions, he was willing to subvert Anglican order if he believed it would help to promote the cause of the gospel. Balda rightly concludes:

> Simeon's lesson is not that church order must be maintained at all costs, but that contemporary circumstances must be respectfully but adroitly exploited. He has left us a conservative ecclesiology which is tempered by the needs of the Gospel and not the demands of strict church order.[83]

Popular portrayals of Charles Simeon as the archetypal obedient Anglican are only half the picture. Like many evangelicals before and since, he was willing to breach Anglican regulations for the sake of the gospel. By his actions, if not always by his words, Simeon demonstrated that evangelical mission always takes priority over the rules of the church.

---

[82] Balda, 'Charles Simeon, Dissent, and Disorder,' pp 56-57.
[83] Balda, Ibid., p 73.

Re-establishing the Christian Faith – and the public theology deficit

David Holloway

1. Introduction 399
2. Public theology 399
3. Making good the deficit 401
4. The Establishment 403
5. Social realities 404
6. The Old Testament 405
7. Divorce and remarriage 407
8. Culture 408
9. Secularism 410
10. Institutions 411
11. De-institutionalization 413
12. Irrationalism 415
13. Adoption, women priests, and sexual health 417
14. Re-establishing the Christian faith 420
15. A new Positivism and new Liberalism 422
16. Conclusion 425

DAVID R J HOLLOWAY is Vicar of Jesmond, Newcastle upon Tyne. Having previously worked in the Sudan, Leeds, and on the staff at Wycliffe Hall Theological College, Oxford, he was for many years a member of the General Synod of the Church of England and on its board for Social Responsibility and Standing Committee. He is also a Trustee of *Reform* and *The Christian Institute.*

1. Introduction

The St Antholin's Lectureship was founded around 1559 for lectures on the 'Puritan School of Divinity.' But in the light of the debate over the precise definition of 'Puritan,' what precisely was the Puritanism being referred to by those founders? At this date it is safest to define a Puritan as someone recently returning from the Continent following Elizabeth I's accession and might parallel modern Evangelicals in that they had a variety of views.

One hundred years later these differences had led to the sad division between conforming and non-conforming Puritans that meant the latter leaving the Church of England in 1662 after the Act of Uniformity. That, indeed, was a great loss to the Church, but to the world a great gain because of subsequent non-conforming Puritan initiatives. In the words of the title of Douglas Kelly's study it resulted in 'the emergence of liberty in the modern world';[1] and 'liberty' must be a fundamental component in any 're-establishing of the Christian faith,' our subject for this lecture.

The Puritans (of whichever sort), however, were not divided over one thing, namely that Jesus Christ is Lord of all – of the whole of life including the things of this age (in Latin, this *saeculum*) and not just the private world of personal spirituality. So they were true secularists being openly theistic secularists. What they would never have understood was how a believer could possibly have a 'public theology *deficit*,' a subject we also are going to be considering.

2. Public theology

But what is public theology? It is wider than a political theology that only focuses on the state, with the state being defined as the one social cohesion that alone is entitled to use force within a wider cohesive society. Public theology sees the public square as more than Parliament Square. It considers men and women in the context of all their social

---

[1] Douglas F Kelly, *The Emergence of Liberty in the Modern World* (New Jersey: P&R, 1992).

relationships and not just their statutory or legal relationships. Its goal is to understand God's activity and purposes for the world in all its complexity. Public theology has as its subject not only God and man, but God, man, *and the world.*

So what is a 'public theology deficit'? It is a deficit due to the wider world always changing and presenting new challenges that Christians have failed to think through. Nor is this something peculiar to the modern age. The fourth century at the time of Constantine is a good example. At that great moment of transition, the Constantinian revolution, for whatever cause the Church lacked a considered view of society and had such a deficit.

Before the time of Constantine and, indeed, in earliest New Testament times when Christians had little, if any, public power or say either in government or policy-making, any questions on how to relate to the wider public world of officialdom would have been answered by a straightforward reading of, or remembering, Proverbs 8:15-16. Those are the Old Testament words of the Divine Wisdom (and identified as the Divine Son, the pre-incarnate *Logos* or Word):

> By me kings reign and rulers make laws that are just; by me princes govern, and all nobles who rule on earth.

It was enough for many to know that all power and politics are under the control of the sovereign Lord. But from their general reading of the Old Testament, not least of the Former Prophets – Old Testament histories – they were also taught two other fundamental lessons: one, that trust in, and obedience to, the one true and living God is vital to societal well-being; and, two, that flirting pluralistically with other gods and religions does not lead to pleasurable prosperity but civilizational collapse.

Of course, as the teaching and records of the activity of Jesus and his apostles became available in written form for those earliest Christians, there was the New Testament as it related to the public world. But it supplemented the Old Testament in terms of fulfilment and a new hope and new power more than in terms of public life.[2]

---

[a] So Max Warren can say, 'The State has to deal with man as he is – essentially self-centred. The Church exists to remind the State that man can be changed, can become what he ought to be. The Church represents the principle of hope – something very different from facile optimism.' *The Functions of a National Church* (Oxford: Latimer House, 1984), p 21.

However, there is more to learn from the New Testament about Christian social responsibility than many are aware,[3] and it supremely witnesses to the basic datum for all public theology, namely the absolute truth of 'the resurrection of Jesus Christ, who has gone into the heavens and is at God's right hand – with angels, authorities and powers in submission to him' (1 Peter 3:21-22).[4]

3. Making good the deficit

But does having all the biblical resources automatically give you an adequate public theology? We know the answer from the Evangelical successors to those Elizabethan returnees. In 1967 at the National Anglican Evangelical Congress at Keele, Sir Norman Anderson addressed the delegates on the lack of Evangelical public and political involvement. This followed his conference paper that spoke of ...

> ... obligations which fall on the Christian, both as a citizen of this world and an ambassador for Christ – and, indeed, on the Church as the Body of Christ resident in the world – in all those aspects of life which lie outside the Church as such. This is a sphere in which the Evangelical has, in recent years, far too often failed. At the time of the Reformation Christians had a deep concern for the total welfare of their fellow men. This also characterized the Puritans, the leaders of the Evangelical Revival and many in the nineteenth century. But during the last hundred years or so we seem to have lost this concern.[5]

This challenge gave rise to new initiatives, but some highlighted a perennial problem. While the intention behind the initiatives was good, a 'social gospel' sometimes emerged that ignored the essential redemptive component of the gospel, the most important social and political contribution the Christian can make.

Given modern failures we should not expect too much, therefore, from the fourth century, when Constantine endorsed the

---

[3] For an excellent summary see chapter 5, 'The Christians' Political Responsibility according to the New Testament' in C.E.B.Cranfield, *The Service of God* (London: The Epworth Press, 1965), p 45ff.
[4] See also, Revelation 1:5; 17:14; 19:16 and Matthew 28:18.
[5] J.N.D. Anderson, *Guidelines* (ed, J.I.Packer, London: Falcon Books, 1967), p 213ff.

Christian faith. Christians were now asked to exercise power and advise on policy but without much theological teaching to help them in analysis or to give guidance on how to act and react.

This deficit, however, was made good by two remarkable Christians, Ambrose and, especially, Augustine. They established a tradition of making use of existing institutions and ideas, but with one caveat. Augustine puts it like this:

> While this Heavenly City ... is on pilgrimage in this world, she calls out citizens from all nations ... She takes no account of any difference in customs, laws, and institutions, by which earthly peace is achieved and preserved – not that she annuls or abolishes any of those, rather she maintains them and follows them (for whatever divergences there are among the diverse nations, those institutions have one single aim – earthly peace), provided that no hindrance is presented thereby to the religion which teaches that the one supreme and true God is to be worshipped (Augustine, *City of God*, Book XIX, chapter 19).[6]

What then followed the fourth century to the present day? The answer is that there has been a series of ups and downs between the Church and the wider society, of course, including the state. It has been something like a less-than-ideal marriage.[7] The current situation is why, among other reasons, we need to consider re-establishing the Christian faith.

---

[6] David Knowles, tr. *City of God* (Middlesex: Penguin Books, 1980), p 878.
[7] We may compare those early first three centuries to the 'going out' phase. From the 'conversion' of Constantine to the end of the 8th century, you have the 'engagement' period. From that date and the coronation of Charlemagne to the fifteenth century you have the marriage but not always a happy one. Then in the 16th and 17th centuries at the time of the Reformation there were explosions in the relationship. However, in the late 17th century there was a patching up of differences, certainly in England. This followed liberal Puritan advice from John Locke with his *Letter of Toleration* and the Toleration Act of 1689 which followed the Glorious Revolution of the previous year. But in France with its revolution at the end of the 18th century in 1789, there was a straight divorce, while in the US there was, following the revolution in America and its Constitutional arrangements of 1788, a legal separation but on friendly terms. In the 19th century the marriage got messy again in England. The 20th century saw more and more living apart with public talk of divorce by some. Then at the end of the 20th century were the beginnings of what today in 21st century England have became outright attacks on individual Church members by the state.

But, first, we need to distinguish the term 'establishment' from 're-establishing the Christian faith.'

4. The Establishment

The last official report on the 'Church and State,' published forty years ago in 1970, made it clear that the word 'established' and 'establishment' meant different things to different people.[8] One common misunderstanding was that it refers to elites in control of 'the political, social, and economic life of the nation' or even 'the church at the centre.'

The words 'by law established' were originally used in the 16th and 17th centuries to refer to the statutory process 'by which the allegiance of the Church of England to the Sovereign (and not the Pope) and the forms of worship and doctrines of the Church were imposed by law.' This distinguished the Church of England from other Churches whose worship was technically 'unlawful' and some of whose doctrines were 'illegal.'

Today, however, this distinction has quite disappeared. All Churches have a basis in law. Their constitutions are enforceable at law as voluntary associations. Their property and endowments can be held under trusts defined by reference to their doctrine and worship. And there are other ways 'the state' has made judgments regarding Churches other than the Church of England.

The main distinguishing mark of the Church of England is, of course, the amount of legislation that has affected it since the Reformation that gives it certain privileges but also imposes certain duties. But that is no longer much of a problem as changes can now be initiated by the Church of England since the inception of the Church Assembly in 1919 and of the General Synod in 1970. The problems, therefore, within the Church of England at the beginning of the 21st century, and any problems it has with the state, seem unlikely to be related either to a surfeit, or lack, of legislation.

---

[8] *Church and State, Report of the Archbishop's Commission*, (London: Church Information Office, 1970), p 1.

That is why it is hard to argue, as some do, that re-establishing the Christian faith in the nation will be better achieved by disestablishing the Church of England to free it for any necessary reforms. Any sensible changes to the establishment are always possible as things stand.

Indeed, it is easier to argue for maintaining the current arrangements. These act as a minimal check at a time of creeping state totalitarianism.[9] If the Christian faith is to be formally and legally privileged in national life, the state has to have some definition of what 'Christian' means. It cannot establish a 'mere' Christianity. It has to take a specific definition of Christian doctrine which, with the current establishment of the Church of England, it has in Canon A5 – the canon of canons according to the *Church of England (Worship and Doctrine) Measure 1974*. Section 5.1 says:

> the doctrine of the Church of England shall be construed in accordance with the statement concerning that doctrine contained in the Canons of the Church of England, which statement is in the following terms: 'The doctrine of the Church of England is grounded in the holy Scriptures, and in such teachings of the ancient Fathers and Councils of the Church as are agreeable to the said Scriptures. In particular such doctrine is to be found in the Thirty-nine Articles of Religion, the Book of Common Prayer, and the Ordinal.'

5. Social realities

At such a time as this, to clarify our thinking we can do worse than go back to Richard Hooker at the end of the 16th century. Hooker importantly argues that the Church must make distinctions within itself. It must, first, distinguish the Church mystical from the Church visible. In Book III.i.9 of the *Laws of Ecclesiastical Polity* he writes:

> For lack of diligent observing the difference, first between the

---

[9] T. S. Eliot was clear: "A Church, once disestablished, cannot easily be re-established, and the very act of disestablishment separates it more definitely and irrevocably from the life of the nation than if it had never been established." *The Idea of a Christian Society* (London: Faber and Faber, 1982), p 72.

Church of God mystical and visible,[10] then between the visible sound and corrupted, sometimes more, sometimes less, the oversights are neither few nor light that have been committed.[11]

Many know of that distinction. But they also need to know about the distinction Hooker made in Book I.xv.2:

> the Church being *both a society and a society supernatural*, although as it is a society it have the selfsame original grounds which other politic societies have ... yet unto the Church as it is a society supernatural this is peculiar, that part of the bond of their association which belongs to the Church of God must be a law supernatural, which God himself hath revealed [italics mine].[12]

So within however 'sound' (or not so sound) a church, there must also be made a distinction between, on the one hand, the church as a 'society' and, on the other hand, the church as a 'society supernatural.'

As a society it shares a similar social nature and similar social possibilities in terms of human functioning as other organizations outside the church of the same size and structure.

Christians when converted do not cease to be human individuals with the laws governing created human existence suddenly suspended. But they should be progressively more human as God intended. Similarly, believers corporately do not suddenly find the basic laws of human association for human societies suddenly suspended. Rather believers forming a society that is also a 'society supernatural' now have new resources for living corporately and socially more as 'God himself hath revealed.' It surely, therefore, is vital that Christians understand how societies and Christian societies work.

6. The Old Testament

This means that after understanding the biblical resources we have to

---

[10] He prefers the word 'mystical' to the word 'invisible,' as some of God's elect are alive and visible in every generation.
[11] Hooker, *Of the Laws of Ecclesiastical Polity Vol 1* (London: J.M. Dent, 1954), p 289.
[12] Ibid., p 221.

come to terms with the natural or created order, and the nature of human society as given. What is given indicates 'natural laws' – regularities in human social behaviour – and those are seen as part of God's general revelation. But as Christians, and as the Puritans argued, we should look at what God reveals through the natural order in the light of his special revelation in scripture. We should view it wearing the spectacles, to use John Calvin's metaphor,[13] of those biblical resources which, for public theology, must include the Old Testament as the Puritans very much recognized.

We must never forget, *one*, that for Jesus and his first followers the Old Testament (their Bible) and the history of Israel taught or underlined that the God of Israel was the one and only ultimate ruler of all nations and that his alone was the kingdom and the power and the glory; and, *two*, that God's revelation is progressive in that the New Testament has fulfilled the Old, but it is also a cumulative revelation as the Old Testament continues to teach us much.

The Old Testament, indeed, has a great deal still to teach about social organization and human culture, as well as the principles God means men and women to follow in their social lives. Oliver O'Donovan puts it well:

> The church exists *vis-à-vis* the social structures of Israel, once the locus of God's self-giving to mankind and still bearing their public witness to his purposes ... The public tradition of Israel carries an unrealised promise for the full socialization of God's believing people, the appearing ... of the New Jerusalem from heaven. This means that any question about social forms and structures must be referred to a normative critical standard: *do they fulfil that will of God for human society to which Israel's forms authoritatively point us* [italics mine].[14]

But we have to handle the Old Testament carefully. Did those first Puritans always do that? Take an important issue for public theology – sex ethics and marriage.

---

[13] John Calvin, *Institutes of the Christian Religion* (tr. Ford Lewis Battles, Philadelphia: Westminster Press, 1960), Bk 1.vi.1, p 70.
[14] Oliver O'Donovan, *The Desire of Nations – Rediscovering the Roots of Political Theology* (Cambridge: Cambridge University Press, 1999), p 25.

Some of the returnees influenced by Calvin, such as the Scottish Puritan leader, John Knox, were arguing for remarriage after divorce, while English Reformers disagreed. The issue related to the use of the Old Testament.

7. Divorce and remarriage

Both Calvin and Knox were not arguing that Jesus was allowing remarriage with a former partner still living.[15] Rather Calvin and Knox argued from the Old Testament and its rule that an adulterer should be executed, which they said was a duty for the magistrate. But if the magistrate did not do his duty, the Church could not wait until he did. So the offending party should be counted 'as dead' and the marriage bond considered dissolved. The New Testament makes clear that death releases from a marriage (Romans 7:3) with the offended party free to remarry. So in the year after the founding of these lectures, 1560, Knox and his fellow reformers were writing as follows:

> Marriage once lawfully contracted, may not be dissolved at man's pleasure, as our Master Christ Jesus doth witness, unless adultery be committed; which, being sufficiently proven in presence of the Civil Magistrate, the innocent (if they so require) ought to be pronounced free, and *the offender ought to suffer the death as God hath commanded.* If the Civil sword foolishly spare the life of the offender, yet may not the Church be negligent in their office, which is to excommunicate the wicked, and to repute them as dead members, and to pronounce the innocent party to be at freedom, be they never so honourable

---

[15] They might, therefore, have agreed with some modern scholars that Matthew is not contradicting Mark or Luke because the exceptive clause in Matthew 19:9 refers (from its position in the sentence) to divorce or separation only and not to remarriage. It does not, however, seem that they had considered, as other modern scholars suggest, that *porneia* (the exceptive sexual wrongdoing) might well refer in Matthew 19 only to nullifying incestuous relationships within the forbidden degrees of marriage (such as the relationships of Herod and Herodias, relevant for Jesus and John the Baptist, and of Henry VIII and Catherine of Aragon, relevant for all the Reformers). For *moicheia* (adultery) is not the word here being used by Jesus, and *porneia* is the only word available for such incestuous relationships (as in Acts 15:19 and 29 and 1 Corinthians 5:1).

before the world [italics mine].[16]

Nearly ninety years later this is plainly spelt out in the Reformed *Westminster Confession* as follows:

> In the case of adultery after marriage, it is lawful for the innocent party to sue out a divorce and, after the divorce, to marry another, as if the offending party were dead (chapter 24:5).

The *Westminster Confession*, as it now stands including this clause, was passed in the General Assembly of the Church of Scotland in 1647. But the English Parliament did not approve the confession until 1648. However, it did so but with some important omissions. These included deleting this very paragraph 5 of chapter 24 on divorce and remarriage.[17] This was of great significance. It helped keep alive in the English Reformed tradition the restraints of the Church of England's Canon 107 of 1603 against a divorce and remarriage culture.[18]

8. Culture

That leads us to ask, what do we mean by 'culture' (but as an aspect of any society, not in terms of 'high culture' as in art, ballet, and drama)? Let me give you a helpful definition from Raymond Johnston:

---

[16] *First Book of Discipline in John Knox's History of the Reformation in Scotland* (ed. William Croft Dickinson), Vol II, London, 1949 p 318) in *Scottish Journal of Theology* Vol.23.No.3, August 1970, p 303ff.

[17] John H. Leith, *Assembly at Westminster: Reformed Theology in the Making* (Richmond, Va.: P&R, 1973), p 62.

[18] The doctrine and practice of the Church of England according to the Canons of 1603 in Canon 106 provided only for 'separation *a thoro et mensa* [from bed and board], or for the annulling of pretended matrimony [nullity].' Canon 107 was entitled *'In all sentences for Divorce, Bond to be taken for not marrying during each other's Life.'* It said this: 'In all sentences pronounced for divorce and separation *a thoro et mensa*, there shall be a caution and restraint inserted in the act of the said sentence, That the parties so separated shall live chastely and continently; neither shall they, during each other's life, contract matrimony with any other person. And, for the better observation of this last clause, the said sentence of divorce shall not be pronounced until the party or parties requiring the same have given good and sufficient caution and security into the court, that they will not any way break or transgress the said restraint or prohibition.'

> [Culture is] a persisting pattern of thinking, feeling, believing and evaluating, socially acquired by learning as distinct from biologically inherited, through which the cumulative heritage and value systems of a society are transmitted, and by virtue of which both individual meanings and social institutions cohere and continue.[19]

So cultures are complex. The task of public theology is not to give blanket judgments on cultures (and institutions within them). It is to help evaluate, in the light of God's revelation, the positive and the negative. The affirmation, therefore, of all of all cultures including Western cultures required by much 'multi-culturalism' is clearly unwise.

Cultures, like the societies in which they are embedded, are made up of many factors including political, economic but also and vitally spiritual factors. The spiritual *are* vital, for without transcendent convictions law and government become based on pure human will, with politics reduced to power struggles and with might being the arbiter of right – a recipe for real social conflict.[20] The Christian faith, which some are now wanting to marginalize, has provided for the West and, since the late 18th century, for many in the rest of the world such a transcendent grounding for what is 'right' and 'wrong' in public life.

Also for a culture (and its society) to cohere there has to be the unity of a worldview. Ultimately there can be no pluralism. Experienced pluralisms in stable surviving societies are subordinate pluralisms under a unifying worldview as a canopy. Of course, that worldview may be for a short time the anarchistic view that 'there is no such thing as a worldview,' or the softer version that 'no society should have a positive world-view.' Neither of those positions, however, are compatible with social survival.

Currently in the West, as the truth regarding the impossibility of a naked public square is being re-discovered, a new controlling worldview is being subtly established, namely materialistic atheistic

---

[19] Quoted in David Holloway, *A Call for Christian Thinking and Action – the Life of Raymond Johnston* (Newcastle upon Tyne: The Christian Institute, 2004), p 18.

[20] When there are conflicts over what is 'good' regarding, for example, beginning and end of life issues, there is no possibility of an external referee without *some* transcendent reference point.

humanism – a view of a minority of people, but with influence. The Office of National Statistics 2010 figures for religious identity in Britain are that 71% are Christian, 8% are of non-Christian religions (with Muslims 4%) while 21% have no religion.[21] With these small proportions of other religions which, indeed, have freedoms and rights, how justified is it to apply the concept of a 'multi-faith' society to Britain? But what is certain is that enforcing a version of atheism on a culture that has a clear Christian identity and roots is difficult and ultimately, if successful, dangerous. The reason is this. To have deep seated conflict over worldviews is socially tolerable so long as the Christian tradition of peaceful non-violent protest remains. But as those Christian roots get destroyed and that tradition gives way to other cultural traditions that legitimate aggression, such as fascism, aggressive socialism and extreme Islam, we have to treat serious social collapse as an actual possibility.

9. Secularism

It is quite undeniable that the Christian faith has created basic Western values that still have some influence and cultural traction after the loss of individual Christian faith.

But what gives rise to the loss of individual Christian faith? One important factor is the separation of the Christian faith from the cultural and social worlds. As Christopher Dawson, the cultural historian, has said:

> Secularization arises not from the loss of faith but from the loss of social interest in the world of faith. It begins the moment men feel that religion is irrelevant to the common way of life and that society as such has nothing to do with the truths of faith.[22]

If that is true, the problem of secularism lies not only with subtle persuasion through secular media and secular education but with the

---

[21] *Office for National Statistics Statistical Bulletin – Integrated Household Survey*, September 2010 (p 4) download from www.statistics.gov.uk.
[22] Christopher Dawson, *The Historic Reality of Christian Culture* (London: Routledge and Kegan Paul Ltd., 1960), p 19.

Christian church and the message it preaches! Christians need to proclaim the whole gospel of the Cross, the Resurrection, the giving of the Holy Spirit, the consequential humanizing Christian lifestyle and, ultimately, the return of Christ for judgment. The preaching of the gospel is not to be as an escape from cultural, social, or political activities. Rather it is to enable people to engage in those activities but with a clear conviction that Christ is Lord and King over all – the sacred and the secular. As he faced the rise of secularism and Hitler, V.A. Demant put it like this:

> It has to be confessed that by neglecting to enthrone the spiritual over the secular in an organic relationship and by attempting to maintain its sovereignty *in vacuo*, contemporary Christianity has largely in fact surrendered to secularism.[23]

10. Institutions

Culture – this social construct – should be able, if healthy, to support a range of social institutions. But what, then, are institutions?

The difference between institutions and other social organizations is this: an institution not only has a relatively stable pattern of rules and structures to meet social needs; it also, and most significantly, takes on a life of its own and has an ability to act upon, and control, those active within it. We do not simply build and control institutions as we do organizations. They also control and act on us, hence the meaning of 'institutionalisation' and being 'institutionalised.' So the Church of England is an institution while a Parish Church is an organization. The BBC Proms are an institution while the individual concerts are organizations (this sentence was written listening to the last night of the Proms in 2010). The Proms are a good illustration of four marks of institutions – heroes, symbols, rituals, and values. Henry Wood is the hero, the symbol is the Royal Albert Hall, a key ritual is that last night concert, and the value is good music.

An institution we have already touched on, and one most important as an essential stabilizer of society, is marriage. Marriage is an institution while the household of the married couple is an

---

[23] V.A. Demant, *Christian Polity* (London: Faber and Faber, 1936), p 123ff.

organization. The great value of marriage as an institution is that it gives stabilizing support to the married couple and also to the children of the marriage-family. The opposite to the institution of marriage is cohabitation as a relationship where external supports have been dissolved.[24] That is why a divorce and remarriage culture is pernicious. It radically undermines marriage by de-institutionalizing it and moving the union towards a pure unsupported relationship. Social science tells us that the result is dire (on average) – for the couple and for any children of the marriage, and all at great cost not only to public morals but also the public purse.[25] The stable family is also a mediating community between the impersonal state and the lonely individual and plays an essential role in social education. The stronger the family the better that education.[26] Nor is the institution of marriage only threatened by a divorce and remarriage culture. It is also threatened by

---

[24] *The Office for National Statistics – Populations Trends 139* – Spring 2010 reports that "of adults aged between 16 and 54 in 1991 around four in five married adults (82 per cent) were still living with the same partner in 2001, compared with around three in five cohabiting adults (61 per cent)." p 54.

[25] The words of Professor A.H. Halsey of Oxford and a former Reith Lecturer from nearly 20 years ago are still relevant as the evidence now is greater: 'No one can deny that divorce, separation, birth outside marriage and one-parent families as well as cohabitation and extra-marital sexual intercourse have increased rapidly. Many applaud these freedoms. But what should be universally acknowledged is that the children of parents who do not follow the traditional norm (i.e. taking on personal active and long-term responsibility for the social upbringing of the children they generate) are thereby disadvantaged in many major aspects of their chances of living a successful life. On the evidence available such children tend to die earlier, to have more illness, to do less well at school, to exist at a lower level of nutrition, comfort and conviviality, to suffer more unemployment, to be more prone to deviance and crime and finally to repeat the cycle of unstable parenting from which they themselves have suffered' (from the Foreword to Dennis and Erdos, *Families without Fatherhood* (London: IEA Health and Welfare Unit, 1993), p xii).

[26] The Christian tradition of marriage was endorsed, strange as it may seem, by D.H. Lawrence who wrote: 'The marriage bond is the fundamental connecting link in ... society. Break it, and you will have to go back to the overwhelming dominance of the State ... Perhaps the greatest contribution to the social life of man made by Christianity is – marriage as we know it ... This little autonomy of the family within the greater rule of the State ... has given man the best of his freedom, given him his little kingdom of his own within the big kingdom of the State.' *Apropos of Lady Chatterley's Lover* (1930, reprint New York: Haskell House, 1973), p 35ff.

its being de-privileged by the state while privileging other relationships such as homosexual relationships.[27]

Given the strength of institutions it is not surprising if others working for social change pursue a policy of de-institutionalizing the institutions they oppose. In the West there has been such an intentional programme.

11. De-institutionalization

The overt and intentional phase goes back to the anarchic 1960s. Its roots, however, go back further to the Italian Communist philosopher and political theorist, Antonio Gramsci (1891-1937). He argued that the failure of Marxism to achieve its objectives was due to a failure to win the war of ideas. Therefore, there needed to be a 'war of position' – a culture war. Only when that war was won could there be a winning of a 'war of movement' – a physical seizing of power. This philosophy led to the idea of controlling the media, education and other mass institutions and organizations and actively subverting them. The new left of the 1960s (remembering Mao Zedong) coined the phrase 'the long march through the institutions.' Undoubtedly some of those ideas still have currency. There is in our culture today a lingering anarchic feeling that institutions are incompatible with true freedom and that a lack of structure and informality is always a virtue.

A weakening of the churches as institutions at a denominational level, and particularly the Church of England, is undeniable. This, however, has gone hand in hand with a self-inflicted increase in bureaucratization through synods and the like. This bureaucratization has then been one contributor to the failure of local churches as organizations; and organizational breakdown is a factor in the weakening of institutions and so of the Christian culture. The resulting

---

[27] The September 2010 figures for sexual identity from the Office for National Statistics and based on a survey of a quarter of a million over 16 year olds show 94.8 per cent "Heterosexual" while 1.0 per cent "Gay/Lesbian". Proposals for homosexual marriage have to face these facts. Freedom in a society requires the balancing of the rights of majorities and minorities. But the majority community has a right not to have its reasonable convictions and practices ignored or undermined by the public acts of others. *Office for National Statistics – Statistical Bulletin* – September 2010, p 2.

de-Christianizing of the culture then makes Christian apologetics and communication difficult. For the social environment powerfully conditions beliefs.

The sociology of knowledge is common sense. It just draws attention to the fact that when post-modern intellectuals or journalists say we must be sensitive to this or that aberrant behaviour or new set of anti-Christian propositions, it is not just reason that dictates new attitudes. There is a 'plausibility structure' in place which means people are *conditioned* to feel that such new morality or beliefs are reasonable. This 'feeling' of reasonableness often has little to do with logic and much to do with conditioning caused by the wider society, not least, by broadcasting and education.

So where are we now? Peter Hitchens, the journalist, describes the current situation within which a new brand of militant atheistic secularism is being given disproportionate promotion by the media and acceptance by politicians:

> It adopts a mocking and high-handed tone of certainty, sneers at its Christian opponents and states, or implies, that they must be stupid. This style of attack conforms with the irreverent spirit of the age and so is not very carefully examined. It is not widely recognised that secularism is a fundamentally political movement, which seeks to remove the remaining Christian restraints on power, and the remaining traces of Christian moral law in the civil and criminal codes of the Western nations. It campaigns with increasing energy against the existence of specifically Christian state schools, not least because such schools are usually superior to their secular equivalents. It employs the cause of 'equality' among sexual orientations to achieve this, allocating the privileges of heterosexual marriage to homosexual civil partnership (and by implication unmarried heterosexual couples) and so making them cease to be privileges. It makes it impossible for Christian churches to operate adoption societies, despite their effectiveness in this task, because it is no longer lawful for them to 'discriminate' against homosexual couples who wish to adopt. It harasses and persecutes government employees who do not wish, on religious grounds, to solemnise homosexual unions. It compels the keepers of guest houses to welcome homosexual couples beneath their roofs, regardless of any moral objections they may

have. It even punishes hospital nurses for offering to pray for their patients. All the above have taken place in Great Britain in recent years.[28]

But it is not only religion but reason that has fled the public square. Such 'unreason' manifests itself often in the law of unintended consequences. But even then rationality seems to be of little value. This is especially the case in these issues of sexuality and sexual health.

12. Irrationalism

The Times newspaper in a leading editorial about the 2010 visit to Britain of the Pope commented on the controversies accompanying the visit:

> Protesters have every right to state their case, which is far from negligible. On many issues – on homosexual equality, including the right of same sex couples to adopt children; on women priests; and on education in safe sex and the use of condoms to counter the spread of sexually transmitted diseases – the position of the Catholic Church is not only out of step with the modern world. It is out of step with many in its own congregation.[29]

But there is little rational basis for these 'modern world' complaints. Reason is on the side of common sense morality not modernism. Let us take these four 'modern' issues identified by the editorial.

First, 'homosexual equality'. Such equality based as it is on claims for homosexual rights is highly questionable as these rights are not morally grounded. A claim, of course, can be made for equality in respect of normal *human* rights for people who engage in homosexual

---

[28] Peter Hitchens, *The Rage against God* (London: Continuum, 2010), p 119.
[29] *The Times*, 13 September 2010.

activity; but *homosexual* rights are in no way like human rights.[30] Also, human rights are only effectively grounded when believed to be God given (as the *American Declaration of Independence* states they are),[31] otherwise they have no moral force.[32] Furthermore, they are rights to join the human world and its moral order for those excluded. So Martin Luther King with total legitimacy could claim the human right for Black people to be included. But they are not rights *to be exempt* from the human world with its moral order to engage in corrupting behaviours.

The 1967 Act that in the UK decriminalized homosexual relationships over 21 did not intend, according to Lord Reid, "to lay down that indulgence in homosexual practices is not corrupting, [but] if people choose to corrupt themselves ... the law will not interfere. But no licence is given to others to encourage the practice" (in *Knuller* v *DPP*).[33]

Indeed, John Locke (one of the architects of modern human rights and a student of the great Puritan leader, John Owen) argued in his famous *Letter of Toleration* that while the state should never enforce beliefs (as had been done), it could proscribe sedition, violence and

---

[30] Homosexual rights have simply been determined by legal enactment and so are more 'accidental' or merely legal than 'essential' or fundamental human rights. Such human rights, for example, we have in the UN Universal Declaration of Human Rights. This also asserted (Article 29) that rights should be limited by 'the just requirements of morality, public order and the general welfare in a democratic society'. The brilliance of the campaign since the 1970s to overturn accepted morality regarding homosexual activity has been the subtle conflation of two different sorts of rights. Of course, once a law is passed there are rights. But these legal rights can be on a spectrum from good (certainly when endorsing genuine human rights and morality) to neutral to quite wicked; this depends on the law makers and the context. My car has a right. It has a right to be parked in our street provided it has a parking permit. This is neutral. Terrifyingly Hitler had rights under Nazi law to imprison and murder millions of Jews and a number of Christians and homosexuals. These were wicked rights. In discussions of rights we must compare like with like.

[31] 'We hold these truths to be self-evident, that all men are created equal, that they are endowed by their Creator with certain unalienable rights, that among these are life, liberty and the pursuit of happiness' (1776) – with 'happiness' being subject to the principles of ordered liberty and morality.

[32] As Pope Benedict XVI said in his address to British leaders in the Westminster Hall, 17 September 2010: 'If the moral principles underpinning the democratic process are themselves determined by nothing more solid than social consensus, then the fragility of the process becomes all too evident.'

[33] *Homosexual Relationships – Contribution to Discussion* published for the General Synod Board of Social Responsibility (Church Information Office, London, 1979), p 59.

gross sexual immorality.³⁴ And the Bible makes clear what is moral. In the words of the House of Bishops of the Church of England:

> There is ... in Scripture an evolving convergence on the ideal of lifelong, monogamous, heterosexual union as the setting intended by God for the proper development of men and women as sexual beings. Sexual activity of any kind outside marriage comes to be seen as sinful, and homosexual practice as especially dishonourable.³⁵

13. Adoption, women priests, and sexual health

Secondly, 'the right of same sex couples to adopt children.' From one of the few genuinely scientific studies an established fact is that one quarter of the children growing up in the homosexual homes studied ended up having homosexual relationships, while none of the children in the control group did. Does the modern world actually think that is in the best interests of the child?³⁶

---

[34] In his letter he referred to people who 'lustfully pollute themselves in promiscuous uncleanness'. Locke's Letters are easily available on-line and are in the public domain.

[35] *Issues in Human Sexuality – A Statement by the House of Bishops* §2.29 (Church House Publishing, London, 1991), p.18. Another bishop needs to be listened to as well, the former Archbishop of Canterbury, Michael Ramsey. He wrote: 'A Christian principle is the equal right of every person created in God's image to the full realization of his powers of mind and body, and this includes full and free citizenship with democracy as a corollary. We should always distinguish carefully a non-Christian conception of the rights of people to do what they like, and a Christian conception of their right to become by God's grace their own truest selves' – which is discovered in being more like Jesus Christ the true man. (*The Christian Priest Today* London, SPCK, 1972), p 37-38.

[36] See Joy S. Holloway, *Lesbian Parenting May Make a Difference* (*British Medical Journal*, 24 August 2002) – a published response to an editorial in the *British Medical Journal*, 15 June 2002: 'In her editorial on adoption by lesbian couples Golombok gave a favourable interpretation of the research findings that is not universally agreed. Even the American Academy of Pediatrics in its technical report about adoption by same sex co-parents sounded a note of caution about the research, saying: 'The small and non-representative samples studied and the relatively young age of most of the children suggests some reserve.' Also, Stacey and Biblartz criticised the way 'researchers frequently down-play findings indicating differences regarding the children's gender and sexual preferences and behaviour.'

Thirdly, 'women priests.' It is probable that as people begin to understand the nature of institutionalisation, more will realize that the jury still has to be out. To 'ordain' a woman is an institutional act that is significantly different from merely endorsing the Holy Spirit's call to a particular woman to the Christian work of teaching or even leadership. The Old Testament priesthood being exclusively male (but with Old Testament judges, like Deborah, and female prophetesses), Jesus' apostolic band being exclusively male (with Matthias having the divine appointment in place of Judas, rather than Mary, despite her having been a prime witness to the Resurrection), and Pauline teaching making sexual difference a fact of creation and paralleling the difference between the first and second persons of the Divine Trinity, all need more explanation before there can be confidence over such institutionalisation.[37]

Then the fourth and last issue for *The Times* editorial writer and allegedly for the modern world, 'education in safe sex and the use of condoms to counter the spread of sexually transmitted diseases.' The problem here is that hard facts are not rationally being faced. There are the facts that users of the condom as a contraceptive have a 'typical use' failure rate in preventing contraception of 15% per year.[38] True, the

---

Golombok quotes her own studies to support her editorial, so I will comment on her main longitudinal study. Lesbian and single heterosexual mothers were recruited in 1976-7. The families were followed up in 1992-3, when the children were young adults. Golombok *et al* found that 14 of the 25 young adults reared in lesbian homes had considered having a lesbian or gay relationship, compared with only three of the 21 of the young adults reared by single heterosexual mothers (Fp = 0·003). In addition six of the 25 of those from lesbian homes had been involved in a sexual relationship with one or more people of the same sex, whereas none of those from heterosexual homes had had a same sex relationship (Fp = 0·022). Thus they did find significant differences of outcome.

Also two of the young adults reared by lesbians identified themselves as lesbian but none of the young adults from heterosexual homes did. This difference was not significant but with the small samples and the low incidence of lesbianism in the general population, it does seem to indicate a trend.

Of course, some may not be concerned if young people choose to have lesbian or homosexual relationships. But surely commentators should be willing to admit that what evidence there is does show significant differences in outcomes in this and in other areas.'

[37] See for further discussion, David Holloway, *A Few Thoughts on Women Bishops – August 2010* (at www.church.org.uk, and Coloured Supplements).

[38] Figures from Contraceptive Technology for 2010 at www.contraceptivetechnology.org.

'perfect use' failure rate is 2%; but most people are not 'perfect users.' So in any given year we must predict that 15% of most women who rely on condoms for contraception will conceive. However, we know that women are fertile for only a small proportion of any given month. Therefore, the failure rate of the condom as a prophylactic against HIV/AIDS and other STI's (sexually transmitted infections) could be considerably higher than 15% for most people (not, of course, for the 'perfect users').

All this should be warning enough. But 'Utopian' politicians and health-workers are refusing to face other and more significant hard facts. We now have the research of David Paton, Professor of Industrial Economics, Nottingham University Business School, with regard to adolescent behaviour. He argues that 'measures aimed at cutting teenage pregnancy and sexual disease among teenagers, such as making condoms more widely available, have had the opposite effect.'[39] All this, of course, is 'on average.' His own words in the conclusion to his paper on *Random Behaviour or Rational Choice* are:

> It is not enough to introduce a measure aimed at a specific outcome without considering the endogenous response of agents to the policy itself. In the case in question, it appears that some measures aimed at reducing adolescent pregnancy rates induced changes in teenage behaviour that were large enough not only to negate the intended impact on pregnancy rates but to have an adverse impact on another important area of adolescent sexual health – sexually transmitted infections.[40]

The point is this: some 'measures' lessen some dangers when 'perfectly' followed, once there is a decision to engage in sexual activity. But the measures themselves increase the amount of sexual activity. The result then is that the overall health outcome is not what was intended, rather the reverse.

The only truly safe sex education is sexual abstinence until marriage and faithfulness within marriage, something not always now clearly taught even in schools with a Christian tradition.

---

[39] *The Journal*, 6 April 2004.
[40] David Paton, *Random Behaviour or Rational Choice? Family Planning, Teenage Pregnancy and STIs*, (Presented at the Royal Economic Society Conference, Swansea, April 2004).

14. Re-establishing the Christian faith

That brings us, finally, to the practical question of how in the West do we work to 're-establish the Christian faith.'[41]

First, we do not stop but continue praying and preaching.[42]

We must pray that God's kingdom comes and God's will is done *on earth* as well as in heaven. And we must preach the whole gospel that includes the Christian worldview of creation, fall, redemption, and final judgment. That gospel alone ensures a true humanism with true liberty, equality, and fraternity, those 18th century Enlightenment ideals. The pursuit of these, however, over recent centuries without God has been disastrous, if not demonic.

Fraternity pursued in defiance of God produced a nationalistic cult based on a racial-blood brotherhood in the form of Nazism, which was defeated in 1945. Equality pursued in defiance of God produced an utterly ruthless Marxist mission for the proletariat in the form of Stalinism, which was finally defeated in 1989. And liberty pursued in defiance of God is with us today in the form of selfish libertarianism, uncontrolled behaviour, and creeping totalitarianism. But the Christian doctrine of the Fatherhood of God ensures a true brotherhood of man world-wide. The doctrine of humankind created in the image of God

---

[41] J.I.Packer's answer is, 'We must aim, with God's help, to do four things together. First, **Recover Vision**, the vision of true humanness under God, the goal towards which Christian action in society must always be directed. Second, **Restore Concern**, and avoid the tolerance trap, by which I mean willing never to tolerate the intolerable. I know that tolerant inaction is a prime virtue in a permissive society, but I also know that all that is needed for evil to triumph in any human situation is for good men to do nothing. Third, **Renew Evangelism**, making it our top priority to win our fellow men and women to faith in Christ. Fourth, **Rebuild Community**, at home in the family and abroad in society, so creating a milieu which helps on the human maturity that flows from Christian faith.' *Knowing Man* (Exeter, Paternoster, 1979) pp 51-52.

[42] Alex Vidler's preaching agenda is helpful: 'A Church to be worthy of the name, however small a minority it may be in any given society, is charged with the responsibility of bearing testimony to God's Sovereignty and God's will before kings and rulers and the whole people. It must declare man's civic duties as well as his ecclesiastical duties. It must teach the law of God, as well as preach the Gospel of God. It must denounce injustice and sin wherever they are to be found, and call upon all men to repent and return unto the Lord their God by obeying his law in their common life.' *The Orb and the Cross* (London, SPCK, 1945), p 133.

and so worthy of respect ensures a true equality for all. And the doctrine of final judgment, presupposing the human freedom even to choose hell, ensures a true liberty now but with a heavenly hope for the future for believers. That is because of forgiveness through the Cross of Christ, the triumph of his Resurrection, his Reign and his gift of the Holy Spirit to enable an ordered liberty.

Secondly, we have to realize that a real problem in re-establishing the Christian faith today is a currently ill thought out secular philosophy of society. This sees the state as a universal community with the Church as just one voluntary association within it (but the state, of course, is not universal but national and limited).

Christian people, however, see the Church as more than a 'visible' community. It is also that truly mystical, supernatural and universal community and not only universal throughout space but also time. The various national states are then seen as limited associations for certain limited ends. But because of Jesus' teaching on the duty to 'Give to Caesar what is Caesar's and to God what is God's,' the Church always believes there is a legitimacy to the state and its rulers, however, inadequate or misguided (until, that is, they are completely demonic). But this is in contrast to extreme secularists who give no credence to God, and some extreme religions (like extreme Islam) that give no credence to Caesar or his equivalent.

So the Christian Church aware that the state with its limitations must have some worldview as to what constitutes the good life, at least as a 'canopy' under which other law-abiding views may co-exist, should see its duty both as a body corporately and as individual members to propose, not impose, an enculturation of the Christian faith in public life.

But cultural formation requires so much. It certainly includes convinced and orthodox Christians a) being more open in public life about their convictions, b) their greater representation on public bodies together with a necessary reduction of unrepresentative, unorthodox and vocal minorities, and c) their continual working to reform when deformed and protect when attacked the key repositories and transmitters of social wisdom, the church, the family, and the school.

Also, where there is unreasonable public imposition of secularism, as in many state schools, in local authorities, and health services and, not least, through the state funded BBC, there needs to be a new positive opposition.

What form should that take? The answer demands another lecture. For the moment let me say this. Public theology always has to keep in mind Jesus' words to Pilate: 'My kingdom is not of this world. If it were, my servants would fight to prevent my arrest by the Jews. But now my kingdom is from another place' (John 18:36). So in an age when Islamic terrorism forces people to concede to Islamic demands, and secular bullying through political manipulation forces through a secularist agenda, Christians must never be tempted to similar methods. Martin Luther King's defence of non-violent resistance is still relevant:

> The alternative to violence is non-violent resistance ... The non-violent resister is just as strongly opposed to the evil against which he protests as is the person who uses violence. His method is passive or non aggressive in the sense that he is not physically aggressive toward his opponent. But his mind and emotions are always active, constantly seeking to persuade the opponent that he is mistaken ... Non violent resistance does not seek to defeat or humiliate the opponent, but to win his friendship and understanding ... The aftermath of non-violence is the creation of the beloved community, while the aftermath of violence is tragedy.[43]

We need to consider a 'PC Christian uprising' – a truly 'politically correct' movement because it is 'peaceful and civilized.' The word 'uprising' calls to mind the role the churches played in the ending of the Soviet Empire and global Marxism in 1989. Of course, the churches were only one factor. They were, however, able to witness to the truth, but in a unique and peaceful way.

15. A new Positivism and new Liberalism

And we need to avoid being negative. The 'law' is necessary but it must lead to Christ and his 'good news.' So there needs to be a new

---

[43] Martin Luther King, Jr., 'Nonviolence and Racial Justice,' *A Testament of Hope: the Essential Writings of Martin Luther King, Jr.*, ed. by James M. Washington (San Francisco: Harper & Row, 1986), pp 7ff.

'positivism.' This word usually refers to a scientism that deifies empirical verification of a very narrow sort as the only way to truth. That is folly. By positivism we mean a positive pro-active attitude that does not only complain about the opposition and difficulties. Rather it has a hopeful attitude that with God nothing is impossible. So we should, in the words of William Carey, a great late 18th century Puritan missionary to India: 'expect great things (from God); attempt great things (for God).'[44] Yes, the Christian must be law-abiding. But when the law orders what God forbids or forbids what God orders, the Christian, like Daniel and his friends in the Old Testament and many believers today, has to respond as the apostle Peter did with the words: 'we must obey God rather than men!' (Acts 5:29).

There still, therefore, needs to be the defending of people who are suffering because of the stand they are taking against current illiberality. But in addition we now, humbly but fearlessly, need positively to work at a new cultural agenda, remembering that the cultural mandate of Genesis has not been repealed.

Humankind should still be 'fruitfully, subduing and ruling' throughout the created order, in so far as we are called to and can (Genesis 1:28-30). But this 'rule' should take place humbly and as servants not 'lording it,' to quote Jesus (Mark 10:42). Helping people understand this cultural mandate is part of Christian discipling, not an optional extra. So we should all be concerned, at least in our praying but many in our actions, with education, the media, the arts, sport, government, finance – the whole of life; and we should work for the adoption of Christian principles and values as much as possible. Do we not all want there to be honesty in the City, genuine care in our health and social services and minds properly exercised, morals taught, and faith in God normalized in our schools and universities? Christians being light by their words and salt by their presence should seek to have a social impact. Clearly that cannot be forced. But such a social impact can be planned.

---

[44] See Iain H. Murray, *The Puritan Hope* (Edinburgh: The Banner of Truth Trust, 1991) of which F.F. Bruce wrote, 'Perhaps the most important practical aspect of this study is its demonstration of the influence which the 'Puritan Hope' had on the beginnings of the modern missionary movement. Carey and others ... were far from giving any place in their thoughts to that pessimism over the future of the Church's work in the world which, here and there, in more recent generations has acquired the status of a new orthodoxy.'

Then we also need a new 'liberalism' as well as a new 'positivism.' By that I mean a new liberality of mind and a new confidence in liberal democracy, instead of the current irrationality, disillusionment with politics which is disturbing, and the erosion of Christian liberties.[45]

The problem goes back to 1958 and Sir Isaiah Berlin's inaugural lecture at Oxford entitled *Two Concepts of Liberty*. In simple terms Berlin argued that political philosophies of 'freedom *for*' result in tyranny; it was, therefore, safest only to have philosophies of 'freedom *from*' (that is, freedom from any ideas of the good life). Such a philosophy is now bankrupt.

In the Cold War it motivated a fight for freedom from Soviet tyranny from 1958-1989. Defeating a common enemy was proxy for a unifying public canopy of a nobler sort. But since victory has been achieved, the naked public square lacking a common enemy is now mutating this philosophy into a freedom *for* an irrational and tyrannical secularism and a state enforced opposition to the majority (certainly in Britain). That majority, if having to choose, would identify the 'good life' as the Christian faith teaches it. It may be a vicarious faith for many – the faith taught in the church they do not attend regularly but think they ought to! This vicarious faith, however, is not secularism.

More, of course, needs to be said about the change process. For the Christian believer and the Church it always involves prayerful trust and costly obedience. There is, indeed, much we can learn about cultural and institutional change, with one thing certain.

To see change we need networks with cultural and institutional clout – like the network of our Puritan and Evangelical forefathers at Clapham around William Wilberforce, the great anti-slave campaigner. These we must be working on to reproduce. But that 'clout' is not

---

[45] At its heart 'ordered liberalism' in healthy liberal democracies, as it has evolved after the 17th Century Wars of Religion, has an inveterate hatred of cruelty and the conviction that beliefs cannot be enforced by the state. For religious liberty is the one most important right and liberty. It underlines that there is a limit to the power of the state. Peter Berger, the Sociologist, claims: "The status of religious liberty in a society is a very good empirical measure of the general condition of rights and liberties in that society." 'The Serendipity of Liberties' in *The Structure of Freedom: Correlations, Causes and Cautions* ed. Richard John Neuhaus (Grand Rapids: Eerdmans, 1991), p 19.

simple political power. Rather, as James Davison Hunter says: 'it is the power to define reality in ways that sustain benevolence and justice.'[46] And the gospel of Jesus Christ alone is the source for such a definition.[47]

16. Conclusion

I must conclude. I do so with three quotations, the first from Wilberforce himself:

> The only solid hopes for the well-being of my country depend not so much on her fleets and armies, not so much on the wisdom of her rulers or the spirit of her people, as on the persuasion that she still contains many who, in a degenerate age, love and obey the Gospel of Christ, [*and*] on the humble trust that the intercession of these may still be prevalent, [*and*] that for the sake of these, Heaven may still look upon us with an eye of favour.[48]

The second quotation is of the words spoken in 1953 by the Archbishop of Canterbury at the Coronation of Elizabeth II as the orb, one of the Crown Jewels, was presented:

> Receive this Orb set under the Cross and remember that the whole world is subject to the Power and Empire of Christ our

---

[46] James Davison Hunter, *To Change the World* in *Briefing*, Vol.3. No.2, 2002 (www.ttf.org).

[47] In response to Hunter, John Seel responds that 'Lasting change doesn't happen unless there is a constructive strategic partnership between academics and activists, between theorists and practitioners, scholars and businessmen. [On a spectrum from] the Most Conceptual to the Most Concrete you have:- Theorists (who discover knowledge), Researchers (who prove knowledge), Academics (who teach knowledge), Popularizers (who simplify knowledge), Consultants (who advise about knowledge), Practitioners (who apply knowledge). Cultural influence thus requires a long-term commitment of intellectual effort and financial resources that are strategically placed. Changing the cultural direction requires reshaping the taken-for-granted assumptions about reality, which necessitates gaining access to the reality-defining spheres of cultural influence and establishing strategic linkages to the channels of cultural diffusion. The aim is to reframe the collective imagination. There are no short cuts or quick fixes to lasting cultural change.'

[48] William Wilberforce, *Practical View of the Prevailing Religious System of Professed Christians, in the Middle and Higher Classes in this Country, Contrasted with Real Christianity* (Dublin, 1797) free on-line at www.hailandfire.org.

Redeemer.[49]

To remember that truth is good public theology; to apply it would be to help re-establish the Christian faith.

The third quotation from St Paul is an urgent and vital reminder:

> I urge, then, first of all, that requests, prayers, intercession and thanksgiving be made for everyone – for kings and all those in authority, that we may live peaceful and quiet lives in all godliness and holiness.[50]

---

[49] From *The Music with the Form and Order of the Service to be Performed at the Coronation of Her Most Excellent Majesty Queen Elizabeth II* (London: Novello, 1953), p 67.
[50] 1 Timothy 2:1-2 (NIV).

St. Antholin's Lectureship Charity Lectures

1991 J.I.Packer, *A Man for All Ministries: Richard Baxter 1651-1691.*

1992 Geoffrey Cox, *The Recovery and Renewal of the Local Church – the Puritan Vision.*

1993 Alister E. McGrath, *Evangelical Spirituality – Past Glories – Present Hopes – Future Possibilities.*

1994 Gavin J. McGrath, *'But We Preach Christ Crucified': The Cross of Christ in the Pastoral Theology of John Owen.*

1995 Peter Jensen, *Using the Shield of Faith – Puritan Attitudes to Combat with Satan.*

1996 J.I.Packer, *An Anglican to Remember – William Perkins: Puritan Popularizer.*

1997 Bruce Winter, *Pilgrim's Progress and Contemporary Evangelical Piety.*

1998 Peter Adam, *A Church 'Halfly Reformed' – the Puritan Dilemma.*

1999 J.I.Packer, *The Pilgrim's Principles: John Bunyan Revisited.*

2000 Ashley Null *Conversion to Communion: Thomas Cranmer on a Favourite Puritan Theme.*

2001 Peter Adam, *Word and Spirit: The Puritan-Quaker Debate.*

2002 Wallace Benn, *Ussher on Bishops: A Reforming Ecclesiology.*

2003 Peter Ackroyd, *Strangers to Correction: Christian Discipline and the English Reformation.*

2004 David Field, *"Decalogue" Dod and his Seventeenth Century Bestseller: A Four Hundredth Anniversary Appreciation.*

2005 Chad B. Van Dixhoorn, *A Puritan Theology of Preaching.*

2006 Peter Adam, *'To Bring Men to Heaven by Preaching' – John Donne's Evangelistic Sermons.*

2007 Tony Baker, *1807 – 2007: John Newton and the Twenty-first Century.*

2008 Lee Gatiss, *From Life's First Cry: John Owen on Infant Baptism and Infant Salvation.*

2009 Andrew Atherstone, *Evangelical Mission and Anglican Church Order: Charles Simeon Reconsidered*

2010 David Holloway, *Re-establishing the Christian Faith – and the Public Theology Deficit.*

adoption, 125, 414, 417

advowson, 7, 12, 21, 24, 35, 36, 44

Anglican, 45, 46, 51, **99-121**, 264-269, 274, 290, 294, 303, 305, 319, 321, 327, 334, 352, **369-372, 375-381, 384-386, 388-395**, 401

Arminianism, 14, 15, 18, 346

assurance, 83, 155, 189, 196, 197, 289, 297, 342

atonement, 65-67, 269, 273-275, 283, 286, 288, 290, 348

baptism, 118, 327-334, 336, 338, 341-345, 347-350, 352-357, 359-361, 365

Baxter, Richard, 14, 15, 51, 54-59, 69-83, 92-95, 103, 160, 209, 212, 227, 301, 309, 312, 319, 328, 346

Beza, Theodore, 105

Bible, *see also Scripture* 20, **52-63, 69, 72-80, 83-94**, 100, 114, 154, 160, 168, 172, **208-216, 226-233, 238-248, 256-259**, 265-278, 283-287, 290, 292, 299, **305-308**, 330, 333, 336, 340, 346, 355, 370, 386, 391, 392, 406, 417

Bishop, 11, 43, 44, **98-120**, 140, 158, 264-267, 277, 284, 285, 292, 304, 346, **369-379, 387-393**

Bucer, Martin, 109, 126, 127, 129, 130-136, 139, 141, 144, 146

Bunyan, John, 54, 67, 94, 315, 356

Calvin, John, 17, 59, 84, 85, 93, 95, 108, 109, 130, 185, 229, 234, 244, 258, 259, 264, 267, 285, 300, 301, 338, 342, 343-345, 366, 406, 407

Calvinism, 10, 36, 115, 264, 265, 292, 301, 302, 306

Cartwright, Thomas, 152, 156, 159-161, 211

catechism, 131, 128, 161, 219, 221

Catholicism, 16, 23, 101, 114, 446

Chaderton, Laurence, 152, 156, 159, 161

children, 24, 53, 82, 151, 152, 165, 170-175, 180, 188, 193, 199-203, 277, 290, 298, 303, 319, 320, **327-366**, 412-418

Christ, 8, 10, 14, 15, 38, 41, 53, 55-57, 60-75, 78, 81, 83-87, 90, **93**, 100, 104-109, 114, 117, 119, 127-138, 143, 144, 153, 160, 166, 171-174, 180, 185-201, 211, **222-224, 226-233, 237-250, 254-257**, 265-283, 286-290, 295-299, 303-308, 313, 319, 321, 328-348, 353-366, 369-373, 377, 380, 386, 399, 401, 407, 411, 417, 420-426

church, 7, 13-26, 32, 33, 38-46, 51-54, 68-74, **100-115, 123-146, 152-175**, 208-225, 231-235, 240, 241, 255-258, 264-268, 272, 273, 283, 285, 292, 295, 303-311, 321, 327, 334-345, 355-363, **369-381, 384-395**, 403-424

Communion, Anglican 262, 369, 375, 393

Communion, Holy 26, 27, 118, 242, 251, 274, 338, 343

conscience, 72, 78, 79, 162, 167, 172, 173, 186-189, 194, 198, 210, 298, 317, 319, 379

conventicle, 385, 386, 390, 394

conversion, 53, 55, 68, 132, 226, 239-242, 277-280, 296-298, 308, 341-344, 388, 402

correction, 126-135, 140-146, 173, 355

Cranmer, Thomas, 125-133, 139-147

cross, 65-67, 175-176, 180, 273-275, 279, 411, 421, 425

Crowley, Robert, 5-8

culture, 94, 152, 264, 329, 355, 406-413

death, 16, 17, 74, 106, 152, 155, 165, 166, 176, 182, 191, 192, 199, 237, 266, 275, 279, 288, 297-298, 346-349, 363, 364, 373, 407

death of Christ, 65-67, 273-275, 283, 286-290

denominations, 293, 302, 303, 315

discipline, 51, 76, 111-115, **125-146**, 156, 223, 282, 285, 374, 382, 388

divinity, 100, 126, 149, 159, 162, 163, 173, 179, 201, 216, 246, 334

divorce, 402, 407, 408, 412
Dod, John, 149-201
Donne, John, 264-292
doubt, 158, 171, 175, 185, 346, 347
duty, 101, 132, 133, 143, 164, 172, 188, 195, 196, 213, 254, 255, 332, 343, 364, 382, 388, 407, 421
ecclesiology, 102, 103, 114, 115, 248, 373, 395
Edwards, Jonathan, 92, 93, 266, 291, 295, 296, 306, 307, 310, 312, 323, 329, 342, 389
election, 232, 266, 301, 346, 348, 349
enlightenment, 86, 420
episcopacy, 33, 43, 97, 104, 106, 107, 110, 111, 114, 117, 118, 367, 390
establishment, 35, 140, 387, 403, 404
eternal life, 80, 365
eternity, 165, 353
Evangelical, 6, 16, 44-46, 87-88, **90-92**, 98, 102-103, 114, 125-128, **133-145**, 299, 302-305, **309-314**, 318, 321-322, 335, 338, **369-395**, 399, 401, 424
evangelism, 14, 15, 20, 68, 269, 286, 385, 420
excommunication, 129-138, 141-145
faith, 5, 53, 54, 58, 60, **66-68**, 73, 76-80, 84, 86, 127, 131, **153**, **169-170**, 175, 183, 187, 210, 223-225, 228, 240-243, 246, 257, 267, **271, 278,** 280, 288-290, **297**, 300, 306, 310, 312, **330-333**, **341-347**, 352, 356-357, 360, 363-365, 369, 399, 402-404, **409-410, 420-424**, 426
- biblical, 89, 91, 92, 128, 132, 208
- confession of, 66, 99, 114, 219, 222
- justification by, 46, 59, 66, 125, 127
family, 13, 29, 32, 320, 342, 355, 365, 412, 420, 421
Family of Love, 76
funeral, 21, 41, 102, 152, 155, 320, 348
future, 26, 65, 67, 130, 314, 340, 380, 391, 421, 423
Geneva Bible, 15, 183

glory, 14, 25, 34, 36, 61, 70, 91, 169, 194, 198, 210, 226, 254, 289, 305, 306, 321, 339, 356, 359, 364, 406
godliness, 76, 99, 306, 426
gospel, 5, 9, 15-17, 20, 23-25, 37, 39, 42, 45, 46, 54, **56**, 67-69, 75, 78, **87-88**, 104-107, 114, 125-127, 144, 221-224, 226, 228, 230-232, 239, 240, 244-245, 249-252, 254, 258, 264, 266, **269-280**, 283-290, **296-311**, 312, 318-321, 330, 332, 339, 341, **343-349**, 353, 358-361, 370, 375-387, 390-391, 395, 401, 411, 420, 425
government, 9, **103-119**, 128, **137-145**, 156, 174, 219, 255, 305, 382, 400, 409, 414, 423
grace, 56, 72, 77, 81, 92, 115, 166, 169-174, 192-193, 197, 201, 217, 223-226, 239-240, 244, 251, 256-259, 279, 284-286, 295-301, 306, 311-322, 344-354, 359-364, 380, 417
Grindal, Edmund, 210, 211, 241
heaven, 78, 80, 143, 183, 189, 198, 212, 213, 224, 237, 246, 250, 277, 278, 286, 289, 290, 321, 343, 345, 365, 406, 420
hell, 45, 165, 238, 342, 347, 377-378, 421
holiness, 57, 66, 115, 127, 166, 187, 190, 224, 225, 265, 295, 304, 351, 426, 446
Holy Spirit, 25, 40, 47, **53-94**, 105, 132, 134, 208, 224, 255, 257, 270, 280, 286, 298-303, 308, 311, 344, 352, 411, 414, 418, 421, 425
homilies, 128, 210
Hooker, Richard, 8, 155, 159, 404, 405
Horton, Thomas, 211, 212, 217, 268, 292
humility, 194, 287
impropriations, 6-8, 11-13, 16-17, 20-21, 26, 28, 30, 32, 34-36, 38, 40-41
institutions, 17, 109, 125, 127, 139, 142, 146, 259, 334, 402, 409, 411-413, 418, 424
judgment, 29, 117, 132, 136-137, 168, 187, 193, 274, 369, 383, 411, 420-421

justice, 108, 178, 198, 298, 360, 382, 425

Latimer, Hugh, 8

law, 6, 26, 30, 41, 68, 118-119, 139-142, **151-204**, 244, 250, 271-272, 334, 343, 351, 354, **359-360**, 375, 378, 380, **383-389**, 391, 403, 405, 409, 414-416, 420-423

laymen, 7, 12, 13, 16, 18, 21, 41, 43, 130, 138, 139, 177, 213, 215, 255, 256, 264, 309, 321, 383

leadership, 61, 104, 112, 125, 126, 128-130, 139, 140, 145, 159, 266, 293, 309, 314, 321, 322, 347, 372, 389, 390, 407, 416, 418

lecturer, 16, 32, 39, 150, 158, 384

letters, 71, 106-107, 118, 125, 151, 241, 244, 249, 305-306, 310-311, **312-314**, 318, **363**, 416

liturgy, 144, 145, 157, 264, 265, 314, 325, 365, 370, 372, 388

love, 66, 74, 76, 92, 102, 144,, 163, 166, 169, **174-175, 179-183, 186-192, 196-202**, 208, 225-226, 249, **275-276**, 279, 297, 301-311, **320**, 337, 358-359, 364-366, 371-374, 377, 394, 425

Luther, Martin, 59, 84, 129, 229, 267, 285, 335, 342, 344, 416, 422

marriage, 152, 184, 195, 293, 319, 320, 335, 402, 406-408, 411-414, 417, 419

meditation, 161, 186, 197, 233

meetings, 24, 54, 75, 82, 83, 119, 120, 157, 216, 245, 251, 299, 308-311, 314, 376, 384, 385-390

ministry, 5-22, 38-45, 51-60, 71, 78, 91, 99, 127, 130-138, 150-161, 207, 210, 221-235, 239-241, 244, 247, 251-253, 257, 265-273, 278, 285, 286, 290-296, 301-313, 321-322, 326, 348, 372-395

mission, 14, 16, 46, 369-370, 391-395, 420

morality, 65-91, 126-144, 186, 188, 202, 250-255, 298, 311, 318, 412-423

Newton, John, 18, 64, 66, 94, **293-323**, 342, 377, 378

non-conformity, 372, 399

obedience, 15, 76, 109, 129, 132, 150, 163-197, 223, 242, 265, 298, 330, 342, 363, 370, 378, 387, 388, 394, 400, 424

order, church 99, **105-120**, 133-141, 146, 198, 231, 265, 305, 309, 364, **369-395**, 406, 416, 421, 423

Owen, John, 15, 24, 26, 54, 62, 63, 65, 70, 95, 227, 301, 325, 328-340, 343-357, 362-365, 416

pastoral, 77, 95, 119, 126, 129, 130, 131, 135, 138, 144-146, **152-155**, 161, 206, 215, 217, 256, 258, 285, 292, 293, 301, 304, **309-313**, 340, 363, 374, 385

patronage, 7, 13, 16, 21, 22, 31, 38, 44, 372, 393

Perkins, William, 58, 76, 128, 159, 161, 185, 248, 267, 292

piety, 25, 257, 265, 290, 387

pilgrimage, 67, 193, 402

politics, 14, 283, 381, 400, 409, 424

power, 11, 15, 22, 26-27, 31-34, 53, 58, 63-69, 81-90, 113, 121, 126, 131-138, 163-164, 171-172, 178, 214-215, 221, 225-226, 230, 237-238, 244, 248, 250, 253-255, 257, 268, 279-283, 290, 297, 299, 303, 308, 326, 400-402, 406, 409, 413, 414, 425-426

prayer, 76, 117, 133, 137, 152, 157, 172-175, 208, 215, 217, 218, 221-224, 232, 245, 247, 249, 298-305, 308-314, 320-321, 330, 341, 386, 389-390, 420, 423

preaching, 8, 9, 13, 19, 20, 21, 26-27, 31, 36-38, 46, 51-52, 60-61, 75-78, 85, 101-102, 111, 137, 141, 152-155, 158, 161, 167, 168, 175, 176, 205, **207-259, 263-291**, 293, 295, **299-308**, 314, 327, 333, **370-394**, 411, 420

Presbyterian, 52, 77, 103, 111, 206, 214, 221, 236, 255-257, 295, 342-349, 366

providence, 76, 164, 170, 181, 187, 296, 300, 389

Quaker, 49, 53-55, 58-60, 63-68, 70-78, 81-83, 86-89, 91, 92, 94
rats, 38
reading, 56, 75, 80, 100, 143, 200, 208, 210, 215, 218, 221-226, 234, **241-245**, 290, 299, 301, 305, 308, 310, 350, 400
redemption, 58, 64, 191, 276, 353, 420
reform, 7-11, 14-18, 24, 34, 36, 41, 45, 47, 51, 52, 68, 74, 84, 88, 91, **97-115**, 119-121, 125-146, 157, 162, 173, 180, 185, 187, **195**, 207, 256, 258 **264-273**, 290, 301, 332, 336, 341, 344-346, 351, 404, 407-408, 421
reformation, 23, 47, 51-53, 62, 67, 68, 88, 102-104, 123-146, 234, 238, 258, 265, 267, 298, 371, 401-403
regeneration, renewal 126, 201, 241, 298, 325, 343, 345, 348-352, 359, 360
regulative principle, 180
religion, 67, 73, 86, 125, 149, 159, 160, 169, 178, 184, 197, 199, 211, 268, 273, 298, 311, 402, 410, 415
repentance, **132-137**, 141, 169-170, 223, 274, 298, 330, 331, 333, 357
sacraments, 52, 75, 76, 106, 111, 128, 131-133, 134, 136, 157, 210, 212, 215, 217, 218, 222-224, 226, 241, 249, 278, 279, 338
salvation, 14, 16, 46, 56, 57, 62-66, 68, 71, 73, 81-89, 94, 109, 136-138, 143, 169, 197, **210-213**, 221, 223-226, 230, 239, 241, 250-252, **271-273**, **276-278, 288-289**, 296, 309, 325, 329, 330, 336, 338, 341, **343-353**, 363, 377-378
Satan, 15, 133, 143, 177, 377
Scripture, *see also Bible* 8, 14-17, 26,35-36, 44, **55-95**, 109, 111, 121, 129, 135-138, 146-153, **162-168**, 176-178, 186-192, **207-259**, 266, **269-272**, **277-285**, 300-308, 313, 328-335, 340-342, 347-350, 379, 387, **405-406**, 417
secularism, 410-414, 421, 424
sex, 318, 335, 406, 413-419

Simeon, Charles, 44, 45, 156, 321, 323, 367-395
sin, 27, 54, 59, 65, 72-73, 132-133, 136-138, 141, 144, 165-171, 173-175, 181, 188-204, 224, 246, 252, 274-275, 279, 284, 298-299, 346-347, 352, 359, 364, 420
slavery, 16, 144, 293, 296, 316-319, 424
society, 25, 133, 136, 180, 186, 195, 198, 201, 242, 256, 2863, 286, 295, 335, 381, 385, 391-394, **399-424**
spirituality, 50, 76, 88, 174, 262, 371, 399
St Helen's, Bishopsgate, 26-27
suffering, affliction 76, 149, 165, 175, 178, 187, 270, 274, 423
teaching, 43, 51-52, 56, 60-63, 75-78, 87, 109, 114, **126-138**, 161-168, **176**, 201, **228-231, 246-247**, 281, 298, 305-311, 336, 340-341, 386, 389, 400, 402, 418, 421
theology, 14, 18, 46-50, **64-66**, 69, 84, **87, 90-95**, 99-102, 145, **163, 201-203, 207-257**, 264-274, 284-286, **300-302**, 313, 316, 321, 329-335, 338, 343-347, 356, 366, 375, 387, **399-409**, 422, 426
training, 24, 45, 77, 233, 254, 258, 268, 285, 303, 326, 340, 372, 394
Trent, Council of 6, 267
truth, 6, 33, 49, 53-54, 57-58, 73-74, **81-90**, 115, 153, 162, **168-169, 176**, 178, 185, 189-196, 208, 220-228, 238, 241, 247, 250, 256, 277, 284, 295, 304-307, 319, 329, 346, 353, 360-363, 401, 409, 422-423, 426
unity, 69, 127, 214, 228, 255, 271, 393, 409
Ussher, James 52, 53, 97-114, 155, 159, 212, 222, 265, 266
Vermigli, Peter Martyr 123, 124, 126, 133- 139, 142, 147
Walker, George, 27
women, 21-22, 52, 82, 290, 335, 399, 415, 417-420

Latimer Publications

LS 01	The Evangelical Anglican Identity Problem – Jim Packer	LS 17	Christianity and Judaism: New Understanding, New Relationship – James Atkinson
LS 02	The ASB Rite A Communion: A Way Forward – Roger Beckwith	LS 18	Sacraments and Ministry in Ecumenical Perspective – Gerald Bray
LS 03	The Doctrine of Justification in the Church of England – Robin Leaver	LS 19	The Functions of a National Church – Max Warren
LS 04	Justification Today: The Roman Catholic and Anglican Debate – R. G. England	LS 20/21	The Thirty-Nine Articles: Their Place and Use Today – Jim Packer, Roger Beckwith
LS 05/06	Homosexuals in the Christian Fellowship – David Atkinson	LS 20/21	Los Treinta Y Nueve Artículos: Su Lugar Y Uso Hoy
LS 07	Nationhood: A Christian Perspective – O. R. Johnston	LS 22	How We Got Our Prayer Book – T. W. Drury, Roger Beckwith
LS 08	Evangelical Anglican Identity: Problems and Prospects – Tom Wright	LS 23/24	Creation or Evolution: a False Antithesis? – Mike Poole, Gordon Wenham
LS 09	Confessing the Faith in the Church of England Today – Roger Beckwith	LS 25	Christianity and the Craft – Gerard Moate
LS 10	A Kind of Noah's Ark? The Anglican Commitment to Comprehensiveness – Jim Packer	LS 26	ARCIC II and Justification – Alister McGrath
LS 11	Sickness and Healing in the Church – Donald Allister	LS 27	The Challenge of the Housechurches – Tony Higton, Gilbert Kirby
LS 12	Rome and Reformation Today: How Luther Speaks to the New Situation – James Atkinson	LS 28	Communion for Children? The Current Debate – A. A. Langdon
LS 13	Music as Preaching: Bach, Passions and Music in Worship – Robin Leaver	LS 29/30	Theological Politics – Nigel Biggar
LS 14	Jesus Through Other Eyes: Christology in a Multi-faith Context – Christopher Lamb	LS 31	Eucharistic Consecration in the First Four Centuries and its Implications for Liturgical Reform – Nigel Scotland
LS 15	Church and State Under God – James Atkinson	LS 32	A Christian Theological Language – Gerald Bray
LS 16	Language and Liturgy – Gerald Bray, Steve Wilcockson, Robin Leaver	LS 33	Mission in Unity: The Bible and Missionary Structures – Duncan McMann
		LS 34	Stewards of Creation: Environmentalism in the Light of Biblical Teaching – Lawrence Osborn

LS 35/36	Mission and Evangelism in Recent Thinking: 1974–1986 – Robert Bashford	LS 59	The Parish System: The Same Yesterday, Today And For Ever? – Mark Burkill
LS 37	Future Patterns of Episcopacy: Reflections in Retirement – Stuart Blanch	LS 60	'I Absolve You': Private Confession and the Church of England – Andrew Atherstone
LS 38	Christian Character: Jeremy Taylor and Christian Ethics Today – David Scott	LS 61	The Water and the Wine: A Contribution to the Debate on Children and Holy Communion – Roger Beckwith, Andrew Daunton-Fear
LS 39	Islam: Towards a Christian Assessment – Hugh Goddard		
LS 40	Liberal Catholicism: Charles Gore and the Question of Authority – G. F. Grimes	LS 62	Must God Punish Sin? – Ben Cooper
		LS 63	Too Big For Words?: The Transcendence of God and Finite Human Speech – Mark D. Thompson
LS 41/42	The Christian Message in a Multi-faith Society – Colin Chapman		
LS 43	The Way of Holiness 1: Principles – D. A. Ousley	LS 64	A Step Too Far: An Evangelical Critique of Christian Mysticism – Marian Raikes
LS 44/45	The Lambeth Articles – V. C. Miller		
LS 46	The Way of Holiness 2: Issues – D. A. Ousley	LS 65	The New Testament and Slavery: Approaches and Implications – Mark Meynell
LS 47	Building Multi-Racial Churches – John Root		
LS 48	Episcopal Oversight: A Case for Reform – David Holloway	LS 66	The Tragedy of 1662: The Ejection and Persecution of the Puritans – Lee Gatiss
LS 49	Euthanasia: A Christian Evaluation – Henk Jochemsen	LS 67	Heresy, Schism & Apostasy – Gerald Bray
		LS 68	Paul in 3D: Preaching Paul as Pastor, Story-teller and Sage – Ben Cooper
LS 50/51	The Rough Places Plain: AEA 1995		
LS 52	A Critique of Spirituality – John Pearce	LS69	Christianity and the Tolerance of Liberalism: J.Gresham Machen and the Presbyterian Controversy of 1922-1937 – Lee Gatiss
LS 53/54	The Toronto Blessing – Martyn Percy		
LS 55	The Theology of Rowan Williams – Garry Williams		
LS 56/57	Reforming Forwards? The Process of Reception and the Consecration of Women as Bishops – Peter Toon	LS70	An Anglican Evangelical Identity Crisis: The Churchman – Anvil Affair of 1981-1984 – Andrew Atherstone
		LS71	Empty and Evil: The worship of other faiths in 1 Corinthians 8-10 and today – Rohintan Mody
LS 58	The Oath of Canonical Obedience – Gerald Bray		

LS72	To Plough or to Preach: Mission Strategies in New Zealand during the 1820s – Malcolm Falloon	LB09	Witnessing to Western Muslims: A Worldview Approach to Sharing Faith – Richard Shumack
LS73	Plastic People: How Queer Theory is Changing Us – Peter Sanlon	GGC	God, Gays and the Church: Human Sexuality and Experience in Christian Thinking – eds. Lisa Nolland, Chris Sugden, Sarah Finch
LS74	Deification and Union with Christ: A Reformed Perspective on Salvation in Orthodoxy – Slavko Eždenci		
LB01	The Church of England: What it is, and what it stands for – R. T. Beckwith	WTL	The Way, the Truth and the Life: Theological Resources for a Pilgrimage to a Global Anglican Future – eds. Vinay Samuel, Chris Sugden, Sarah Finch
LB02	Praying with Understanding: Explanations of Words and Passages in the Book of Common Prayer – R. T. Beckwith		
		AEID	Anglican Evangelical Identity – Yesterday and Today – J.I.Packer and N.T.Wright
LB03	The Failure of the Church of England? The Church, the Nation and the Anglican Communion – A. Pollard	IB	The Anglican Evangelical Doctrine of Infant Baptism – John Stott and J.Alec Motyer
LB04	Towards a Heritage Renewed – H.R.M. Craig	BF	Being Faithful: The Shape of Historic Anglicanism Today – Theological Resource Group of GAFCON
LB05	Christ's Gospel to the Nations: The Heart & Mind of Evangelicalism Past, Present & Future – Peter Jensen		
		FWC	The Faith We Confess: An exposition of the 39 Articles – Gerald Bray
LB06	Passion for the Gospel: Hugh Latimer (1485–1555) Then and Now. A commemorative lecture to mark the 450th anniversary of his martyrdom in Oxford – A. McGrath	TPG	The True Profession of the Gospel: Augustus Toplady and Reclaiming our Reformed Foundations – Lee Gatiss
		SG	Shadow Gospel: Rowan Williams and the Anglican Communion Crisis – Charles Raven
LB07	Truth and Unity in Christian Fellowship – Michael Nazir-Ali		
LB08	Unworthy Ministers: Donatism and Discipline Today – Mark Burkill	TTB	Translating the Bible: from William Tyndale to King James – Gerald Bray

www.ingramcontent.com/pod-product-compliance
Lightning Source LLC
Chambersburg PA
CBHW021955160426
43197CB00007B/139